Taxation

Incorporating the Finance Act 2011

30th edition 2011

Taxation

Incorporating the Finance Act 2011

Alan Combs BA, MSc, FCCA
Stephanie Dixon LLB, LLM, DipLP, ACA, CTA
Peter Rowes BSc(Econ), FCA, ATII

Taxation: incorporating the 2011 Finance Act – 30th Edition 2011/2012

For more information, contact Fiscal Publications, Unit 100, The Guildhall Edgbaston Park Road, Birmingham, B15 2TU, UK or visit: http://www.fiscalpublications.com

British Library Cataloguing-in-Publication Data
A catalogue record for this book is available from the British Library

Lecturer supplement and other materials are available from the Rowes 2011 website – see http://www.fiscalpublications.com/rowes/2011

ISBN 978-1906201159

Thirtieth edition 2011

Cover design by FD Design Ltd
Printed in Great Britain by Antony Rowe, Chippenham, Wiltshire

Typesetting and production by

 P. K. McBride, Southampton

Contents

Acknowledgements

The authors would like to express thanks to the following for giving permission to reproduce past examination questions and forms:

Association of Chartered Certified Accountants (ACCA)
Chartered Institute of Management Accountants (CIMA)
Chartered Institute of Taxation (CIOT)
Controller of Her Majesty's Stationery Office

Many of the questions and answers in the 30th edition are from a bank of materials compiled by Jill Webb of Leeds Metropolitan University and Dora Hancock of Birmingham City University. The use of these questions and answers is gratefully acknowledged. Richard Andrews of the University of Hull shared authorship of the 25th to 28th editions, and the authors gratefully acknowledge his contribution.

Preface

Aims of the book

1. The main aim of this book is to provide a thorough basic knowledge of taxation, covering Income Tax, Corporation Tax, Taxation of Chargeable Gains, Inheritance Tax, and Value Added Tax.

It has been written for students of the following:

Association of Chartered Certified Accountants
Paper F6 (UK) Taxation

Certified Accounting Technicians
Paper 9 Preparing Taxation Computations

Association of Accounting Technicians
Unit 18 Preparing Business Taxation Computations
Unit 19 Preparing Personal Taxation Computations

Association of Taxation Technicians
All papers (introductory text)

Association of International Accountants
Professional 2 Paper 16 Taxation and Tax Planning

Universities and colleges
Accounting and Business Studies Degrees – Taxation Modules

Approach

2. a) This book should provide the student with:

i) A knowledge of the basic relevant statutory law

ii) A knowledge of some of the case law developed to interpret statutory law.

It should enable the student to apply these legal principles to practical problems and prepare the necessary computations, and to understand the importance of tax planning.

b) Each of the areas of taxation is introduced by a general principles chapter which outlines the main features of each tax. Subsequent chapters develop the principles in detail with examples.

c) Illustrative examples form an important feature of this text. At the end of each chapter and each section (except the introductory text) there are questions with answers for student self-testing. Also provided are further questions, the answers to which are contained in a separate supplement which can be obtained direct from the publishers by lecturers recommending the manual as a course text.

3. Students should be aware the terminology being used in taxation examinations of professional bodies is changing. As a result what was previously called a balance sheet may be a statement of financial position, with fixed assets called non current assets; a profit and loss account may become a statement of income; stock, debtors and creditors may be inventory, receivables and payables.

This edition incorporates the provisions of the Finance Act 2011 in so far as they relate to the year 2011/12.

Alan Combs, Stephanie Dixon, Peter Rowes, 2011.

Abbreviations and statutes

Abbreviations

All.ER	All England Law Reports
BSI	Building society interest
CAA	Capital Allowances Act 2001
CFC	Controlled foreign company
CGT	Capital gains tax
CIHC	Close Investment Holding Company
CRC	Commissioners for Revenue and Customs
CT	Corporation tax
CTA2009	Corporation Tax Act 2009
CTA2010	Corporation Tax Act 2010
CTAP	Corporation tax accounting period
DTR	Double taxation relief
E U	European Union
GAAP	Generally Accepted Accounting Practice
FA 2011	Finance Act 2011
HMRC	HM Revenue and Customs
IAS	International Accounting Standards
IBA	Industrial buildings allowance
IHT	Inheritance tax
ITA	Income Tax Act 2007
ITEPA	Income tax (Earnings & Pensions) Act 2003
ITTOIA	Income Tax (Trading and Other Income) Act 2005
ORI	Official rate of interest
PAYE	Pay as you earn
PRT	Petroleum revenue tax
RPI	Retail prices index
Sch.	Schedule
STC	Simon's Tax cases
STI	Simon's Tax Intelligence
TA 1988	Income and Corporation Taxes Act 1988
TIOPA	Taxation (International and Other Provisions) Act 2010
TC	Tax Cases
TCGA 1992	Taxation of Chargeable Gains Act 1992
TMA 1970	Taxes Management Act 1970
VAT	Value added tax
VATA	Value Added Tax Act 199

Statutes

Income Tax	Income Tax Act 2007
Income Tax	Income Tax (Trading and Other Income) Act 2005
Income Tax	Income Tax (Earnings & Pensions) Act 2003
Income Tax	Finance Act 2011
Corporation Tax	Corporation Tax Act 2009, Corporation Tax Act 2010, Taxation (International and Other Provisions) Act 2010,
Corporation Tax	Finance Act 2011
Capital Gains Tax	Taxation of Chargeable Gains Act 1992
Inheritance Tax	Inheritance Tax Act 1984
Value Added Tax	Value Added Tax Act 1994
Capital Allowances	Capital Allowances Act 2001

Summary of main changes 2011/12

Part II. Income tax

1. Personal reliefs

	2011/12	2010/11
	£	£
a) Personal allowance	7,475	6,475
Abatement of allowance where income exceeds	100,000	100,000
Blind person's allowance	1,980	1,890
Allowances: Aged 65–74		
Personal allowance	9,940	9,490
Abatement of relief where income exceeds	24,000	22,900
Allowances: Aged 75+		
Personal allowance	10,090	9,640
Married couple's allowance	* 7,295	* 6,965
Minimum married couple's allowance	* 2,800	* 2,670
Abatement of relief where income exceeds	24,000	22,900

b) The allowances marked with an asterisk (*) allowed at the 10% rate are given as a deduction in computing the tax liability.

2. Income tax rates

	2011/12	2010/11
Starting rate - savings	10%	10%
- where savings income comprises taxable income up to	£2,560	£2,440
Remaining rates are unchanged i.e.		
Basic rate		
- savings income	20%	20%
- non-savings income	20%	20%
- dividends	10%	10%
Higher rate – savings and non-savings	40%	40%
- dividends	32.5%	32.5%
Additional rate – savings and non-savings	50%	50%
- dividends	42.5%	42.5%

3. Taxable bands

Taxable income	Band	2011/12 Rate	Tax payable on band
£	£	%	£
0 – 35,000	35,000	20	7,000
35,001 – 150,000	115,000	40	46,000
150,001+		50	

Taxable income	Band	2010/11 Rate	Tax payable on band
£	£	%	£
0 – 37,400	37,400	20	7,480
37,401 – 150,000	112,600	40	45,040
150,001+		50	

4.Class 4 National Insurance

	2011/12	2010/11
Taxable band (£)	7,225-42,475	5,715-43,875
Rate of tax	9%	8%
Taxable band (£)	above 42,475	above 43,875
Rate of tax	2%	1%

5. Class 2 National Insurance

Payment dates will be 31 January and 31 July from 2011/12 onwards.

6. Enterprise Investment Scheme

Legislation is introduced in the Finance Act 2011 to increase the rate of tax relief from 20% to 30%.

7. Company car benefit

Car benefit is based on a % of the list price of the car graduated according to CO_2 emissions. The percentage charge is 15% – 35% of the list price adjusted by certain criteria. For 2011/12 the 15% level of CO_2 emission is 125 grams. Cars with CO_2 emissions of up to 120 grams will be charged at 10%. Cars with CO_2 emissions of 75 grams or less will be charged at 5%. Diesel engines are subject to a 3% surcharge. Cars which cannot produce CO_2 emissions have a zero percentage and thus create no benefit. The upper limit on price to be used in the calculation has been removed for 2011/12 (£80,000 2010/11).

8. Car fuel benefit

	2011/12	2010/11
Car fuel petrol/diesel	CO_2 emissions % x £18,800	CO_2 emissions % x £18,000

9. Company van benefit £3,000.

10. Company van fuel benefit £500.

11. Authorised mileage rates

The statutory tax- and NIC-free mileage rates are:

	2011/12	2010/11
Car and Vans		
First 10,000 miles	45p per mile	40p per mile
Over 10,000 miles	25p per mile	25p per mile
Motorcycles	24p per mile	24p per mile
Bicycles	20p per mile	20p per mile
Additional passenger	5p per mile	5p per mile

12. Class 1 National Insurance Thresholds – contracted in

	2011/12	2010/11
Weekly pay	£	£
Upper earnings limit	817.00	844.00
Upper accruals limit	770.00	770.00
Earnings threshold (employee)	139.00	110.00
Earnings threshold (employer)	136.00	110.00
Lower earnings limit	102.00	97.00

13. Official rate of interest

4%

14. Capital allowances

a) Short life asset elections will be extended to allow plant or machinery to be depooled where it is expected to be sold or scrapped within an 8 year period; previously 4 years.

b) Industrial Buildings Allowance, Agricultural Buildings Allowance and Hotels Allowance are withdrawn completely from April 2011.

15. Pensions

Limits on tax-allowable contributions to pension schemes have been reduced. From 6 April 2011 there is a £50,000 annual allowance (2010/11 £255,000).

A lifetime limit of £1,800,000 for the value of pension savings will be reduced to £1,500,000 from 2012/13.

16. Furnished holiday lettings

From April 2011 loss relief may only be offset against income from the same furnished holiday lettings business.

Also, the minimum conditions for furnished holiday lettings status are changed, to increase the number of let weeks and available weeks required to qualify.

17. Individual Savings Accounts ISAs

a) The annual ISA allowance for 2011/12 is increased to £10,680, with a limit of £5,340 in the cash ISA element.

b) The government intends to introduce, in autumn 2011, a Junior ISA, for children not currently holding a Child Trust Fund.

c) Individuals aged 16 or 17 may take out a cash ISA (but not a shares ISA) in 2011/12 up to the cash ISA limit of £5,340.

Part III. Corporation tax

1. Rates

	FY 2011 - y/e 31.3.2012	FY 2010 - y/e 31.3.2011
Full rate	26%	28%
Small profits rate/ Small companies rate	20%	21%
Marginal profits band	£300,000 - £1,500,000	

2. Research and Development Tax Credit

SME rate will increase from 175% to 200% from April 2011.

Part IV. Capital gains tax

1. Annual exempt amount

Annual exemption will be £10,600 for 2011/12 (£10,100 2010/11)

2. Entrepreneurs' relief

The lifetime limit for entrepreneurs' relief increases from £5m to £10m from 6 April 2011 onwards.

Part V. Inheritance tax

Rates

For 2011/12 the IHT death rates are unchanged: for transfers

On or after 6th April 2011		On or after 6th April 2010	
£	%	**£**	%
0 - 325,000	0	0 – 325,000	0
325,001 -	40	325,001 –	40

Part VI. Value added tax

1. Registration

Registration levels applicable from 1 April 2011.

	£
Taxable turnover in previous 12 months	73,000
Taxable turnover in next 30 days	73,000

2. Deregistration

The annual limit for deregistration is £71,000 from 1 April 2011.

3. VAT fuel rates 2011/12

Scale charges for supply of private use fuel by a VAT-registered business to its proprietors or employees are calculated on the basis of CO_2 emissions. New rates are applicable from 1 May 2011.

2011/12	1 Month period		3 Month period	
CO_2 emissions	VAT inc. scale charge	VAT due per car	VAT inc. scale charge	VAT due per car
	£	£	£	£
120g/km or less	52	8.67	157	26.17
	increasing in bands of 5g/km to			
225g/km or more	183	33.50	551	91.83

2010/11	1 Month period		3 Month period	
CO_2 emissions	VAT inc. scale charge	VAT due per car	VAT inc. scale charge	VAT due per car
	£	£	£	£
120g/km or less	47	7.00	141	21.00
	increasing in bands of 5g/km to			
230g/km or more	165	24.57	496	73.87

See chapter 36, section 16 for the full 2011/12 table of fuel charges."

Part I

Introduction

1 Principles of taxation

'In this world nothing can be said to be certain, except death and taxes' Benjamin Franklin[1].

Definition of tax

1. Taxes are contributions levied on persons, property or business, for the support of national or local government[2].

Reasons for tax

2. Organised societies are said to exist because they provide greater benefits to members than living individually or in small groups[3]. Highly developed societies who use money for exchange fund the benefits by public expenditure. Some of the oldest records in history are of wealth used as a basis for raising the money for public expenditure by taxation.

3. Tax is justified by the benefits it provides. In a society that tolerates free speech public spending is subject to intense scrutiny. One reason for this may be that if benefits are not being provided to the members of society, the reason for collecting tax is lost. Adverse comments, and civil disobedience, can also result where taxation is seen as unfair.

A balanced budget

4. The amount of money raised by taxation and the amount of public expenditure will not necessarily equal each other in a particular year. A 'budget deficit' arises in a year where public expenditure is more than the amount raised by taxation. The government can fund the extra expenditure by inviting people to lend it money, in the form of government securities or investments in National Savings. Years of 'budget surplus' where taxation exceeds public expenditure would give the opportunity for government borrowings to be repaid.

Early in the history of modern Western economics 'classical' economists, such as Adam Smith, formed a view that market forces would produce the most efficient allocation of resources of labour and financial capital[4]. If there was unemployment, for example, market forces would cause wages to fall, until lower wages encouraged employers to take on more workers. It was believed the wages received by the newly employed workers would stimulate demand for more goods and services, and a virtuous circle of growth would continue until equilibrium was reached when everyone was employed. The belief in efficient markets implied it was best for governments to intervene as little as possible in the economic choices made by people and businesses. This 'fiscal neutrality' would include running a 'balanced budget' where necessary public expenditure was financed by an equal amount of taxation.

'Keynesian' economists formed the view that equilibrium in the economy could be reached at points below full employment[5]. In times when market demand was low it would be beneficial for the government to use reflationary policies to stimulate demand, and start the cycle of growth. These policies might include[6]:

- increasing government expenditure;
- cutting direct or indirect taxation to encourage spending;
- cutting interest rates to discourage saving and encourage spending;
- allowing money supply growth.

The first two techniques are 'fiscal' policies which directly affect public expenditure and tax revenue. Applying these policies could cause a budget deficit. Keynesian economics accepts a budget deficit in years when the market economy is in recession, providing it is matched by a budget surplus in years of high growth in the market economy. The deflationary policies available to achieve budget surpluses and restrain demand would be the opposite of the reflationary policies above. Budgets should still be balanced over the long term. Applying Keynesian economics to the government's budget would involve using changes in public expenditure and taxation to affect demand for goods and services[7], and so counteract the effects of the 'boom and bust' cycles in the market economy: 'counter-cyclical demand management policies'.

The UK Treasury predicts[8] total government receipts for 2011/2012 will be £589bn and total managed expenditure will be £710bn. This is a budget deficit of £121bn, with expenditure 20% more than receipts. In 2010/2011 the government planned for a budget deficit with an excess of 27% expenditure compared to receipts, and in 2009/10 35%.

For each of the 6 preceding years from 2003/04 onwards the budget deficit of excess of expenditure compared to receipts varied between 6.1% and 7.5%.

Desirable characteristics of taxation

5. Adam Smith[9] proposed 'Canons of Taxation' which listed desirable features for a system of taxation. These may be restated in contemporary terms as equity, certainty, convenience and efficiency.

Equity means taxes should be fair. Horizontal equity would require justice and equality of treatment, so taxpayers having similar circumstances would be treated in a similar way by the tax authorities and have similar tax liabilities. Vertical equity would mean the burden of tax fell fairly across taxpayers with different circumstances. This requires a subjective value judgement about what is fair. Adam Smith believed fairness would link tax liabilities with the taxpayer's ability to pay, so taxpayers with high income and wealth would pay more tax than those with low income and little wealth. Another possible approach to fairness would be linking the amount of a taxpayer's liability with the value of benefits from public expenditure they receive.

Certainty means taxpayers should be able to establish how taxes will result from their economic decisions such as whether to work in return for income, save or spend their wealth, or deal in assets. This would mean the tax law and regulations would need to be clearly written, and not applied retrospectively.

Convenience would minimise the taxpayer's costs in complying with tax laws and regulations. A tax requiring only simple calculations by a taxpayer would satisfy the 'Canons of taxation' better than a tax requiring complex calculations based on records kept over many years.

Efficiency has two elements:

Administrative efficiency means that the costs of collecting tax should be as low as possible in comparison with the revenue raised.

Economic efficiency means that tax does not distort taxpayers' economic decisions, such as whether to work or take leisure, and whether to save or spend their income and wealth.

In working through this book it will be seen there are limits to which taxes in the UK achieve the ideals set out as the Canons of Taxation. Indeed some features of UK taxes are intended to influence taxpayers and have distorting effects on economic decisions. There is a current theme of encouraging spending on assets which help minimise environmental damage, and discouraging spending on vehicles with high levels of carbon dioxide emissions. Taxes with an intentional distorting effect are called 'corrective'.

Tax bases

6. What to tax? The most basic form of tax is a poll tax, where every taxpayer has an equal liability. Such a tax is widely regarded as inequitable, because it is not related to ability to pay, or to benefits consumed. A form of poll tax was used for local taxation in the UK during the 1980s and 1990s. The tax was administratively inefficient because of widespread non-payment through lack of public acceptance and the impossibility of collecting tax from people without the ability to pay. The 'community charge' caused riots and the prime minister of the time was removed from office.

Major tax bases in modern economies are income, expenditure and wealth. Taxing income or expenditure recognises transactions are taking place, and so it has some relationship to ability to pay. Wealth may not be in the form of cash and so does not necessarily show an ability to pay. In the UK wealth taxes at the national level are linked to wealth being transferred by sale, gift or inheritance. The existence of a transaction increases the likelihood of cash being available to pay tax.

Direct and indirect taxes

7. Direct taxes are related to a taxpayer's circumstances, for example income or wealth. The taxpayer will in some cases be responsible for making payments of tax directly to the tax authorities. However, for some types of income, including bank and building society interest and earnings from employment, income tax is deducted by the savings institution or employer before the taxpayer receives the income. The institution or employer then pays the tax over to HM Revenue and Customs. This is still direct tax, as the tax is related to the taxpayer's personal circumstances.

8. Indirect taxes are charged to a taxpayer, but with the effect that the cost of the tax is suffered by another person or organisation. For example, retailers are responsible for paying Value Added Tax (VAT) to HM Revenue and Customs, but the tax is paid to the retailer by customers, who actually bear the cost of the tax.

Incidence of tax

9. The 'incidence' of tax may simply be described as the person or organisation obliged to pay the tax. Indirect taxes have a different 'formal incidence', the taxpayer legally responsible for making tax payments to the tax authorities, and 'effective incidence', the person or organisation whose wealth is actually reduced by the tax. Direct taxes are more likely to have the same formal and effective incidence.

Hypothecated taxes

10. Hypothecated taxes are collected to fund a particular service. Money collected from the television licence is used to pay for the television programmes of the BBC.

Excise duties

11. Excise duties are indirect expenditure taxes on goods such as alcohol, tobacco and fuel oil. They are unit taxes based on the quantity of the product. This distinguishes them from indirect taxes based on value, such as value added tax and insurance premium tax.

Withholding taxes

12. Withholding taxes are deducted from certain types of income before a taxpayer receives it. Withholding taxes are in general used as a safeguard against certain types of income escaping tax. In states with developed self-assessment tax systems, they survive mainly as deductions imposed on certain payments of "passive income" (i.e. interest, dividends, royalties and rents) which might otherwise escape tax, especially if paid to persons not resident in the state where the income source is located.

Another form of withholding tax is the UK income tax at basic rate deducted by banks and building societies paying interest to individuals on deposit and savings accounts. Also, currently UK individuals must deduct 20% tax at source from patent royalty payments made, and account for it to HMRC on behalf of the royalty recipient. This is a classic domestic (as opposed to cross-border) withholding tax. The person who deducted the tax pays it over to the tax authorities on behalf of the patent owner, who can later claim it back if they do not owe the tax (e.g. because they had tax losses to set off).

Double taxation

13. If a taxpayer receives interest, royalty, rent or dividend income from foreign individuals, firms or companies, withholding tax may have been deducted in the foreign country. If domestic tax is also charged in the taxpayer's home country the same income has been taxed twice. Double taxation treaties between countries will arrange for some relief to be available against double taxation.

There are various possibilities for the practical workings of double taxation relief:

- income taxed in one country may be exempted from tax in another;
- withholding tax deducted in a foreign country may be deducted from the taxpayer's liability in their home country;
- the proportion of the 'underlying tax' on a foreign company's profits that relates to dividend income distributed to the home country may be deducted from the taxpayer's liability in their home country;
- the net income, after foreign tax, may be taken as the amount of income to be taxed in the home country.

Imputation system of Corporation Tax

14. A problem of double taxation arises when a company distributes dividends to shareholders. The company will pay corporation tax on its profits and gains. When dividends are received by a shareholder the profits being distributed might be taxed a second time. In the UK this is avoided for companies by excluding dividends received from their total of taxable income. Individuals can claim a tax credit on the value of dividends received, as if some tax had already been paid on their dividend income. This is the tax the individual is 'imputed' to have paid as a result of the company having paid corporation tax on its profits. However, the imputation tax credit only covers the personal income tax liability on dividends at basic rate. For a non-taxpayer the tax credit on dividend income is not refundable.

Evasion and Avoidance

15. Tax evasion involves breaking the law to reduce tax paid. Examples could include failing to record income, falsifying accounting records, or failing to make any returns of income, gains, or taxes collected. Tax avoidance would involve a taxpayer arranging their affairs so as to minimise the tax they legally have to pay. It has been an established principle for many years that a taxpayer should not be expected to pay more tax than they legally must. Indeed some features of the tax system depend on a taxpayer making choices in order to reduce tax liabilities, for example encouraging taxpayers to buy a car with low levels of exhaust emissions. However, a view has started to be put forward from the Treasury and HM Revenue and Customs that tax avoidance can be either 'acceptable' or 'unacceptable'. Tax avoidance schemes which are considered unacceptable tend to be complex transactions which do not reflect the economic substance of the taxpayer's activities, but have a reduction in tax liability as a leading motive, or the main motive, for the transactions undertaken. In recent years the UK and other governments have legislated against such tax avoidance schemes, so that while the arrangements are still legally effective, they will not be effective in saving tax.

Tax gap

16. The 'tax gap' is a term used to describe the shortage of actual tax collected, compared to the total tax which should be collected if there was no non-payment through tax evasion.

'Stealth taxes'

17. Increases in taxation which are not the result of explicit changes in rates, allowances or methods of calculating tax, have come to be called 'stealth taxes' by the media.

As prices inflate the practice in recent years has been for the allowances for income which can be earned tax free, and the bands of income taxed at the various rates of income tax to rise in line with general price inflation. This means income tax remains at a similar proportion of most people's income, provided the inflation in their wages is at a similar level to general price inflation.

Some goods have increased at a much greater rate of inflation than general prices. This can unexpectedly increase the tax revenue generated by a transaction. In the UK increased tax revenue has been generated for value added tax (VAT) from increases in the cost of fuel, and for stamp duty land tax and inheritance tax from the increases in house prices. Until recently, the government would face a problem in reducing tax on transactions experiencing rapid inflation, as a reduction in tax could cause even more severe inflation in the prices of the goods. Recessionary price falls have allowed the UK government the opportunity of temporarily increasing exemptions from stamp duty land tax.

Some UK tax limits have not been linked to inflation and the result is that over the years their real value has diminished. Greater tax liabilities are incurred from benefits in kind received by employees earning more than £8,500 a year, than on benefits received by their 'lower paid' colleagues. This limit has remained unchanged over many years, to a point where all full-time employees earning the minimum wage for 18-year-olds are subject to the rules for those who were once called 'higher paid employees' (this official term was changed in 2005 to 'P11D employees').

Timing of tax changes may have the effect of increasing tax revenues generated for a year. For the Financial Year 2007 the rate of corporation tax paid by small companies was increased from 19% to 20%. The rate of corporation tax for large companies was reduced from 30% to 28%, but not until the Financial Year 2008.

Questions without answers

1. What "corrective" taxes, if any, might you introduce in the UK at present?

2. Discuss the extent to which taxes on income create disincentive effects.

3. What are the advantages of an indirect tax such as VAT compared with an income tax?

References

1 Franklin, Benjamin (1789). Letter to Jean-Baptiste le Roy 13 Nov 1789, in Cohen JM & MJ, New Penguin Dictionary of Quotations, Penguin, Harmondsworth, 1992.
2 Sykes, J.B. ed. Concise Oxford Dictionary of Current English, Oxford University Press, 1976.
3 Hobbes, Thomas (1651). Leviathan, Penguin, Harmondsworth, 1968.
4 http://www.bized.co.uk/virtual/economy/library/theory/classical
5 Keynes, John Maynard (1936). General Theory of Employment Interest and Money, Prometheus Books, Amherst, New York, 1997.
6 http://www.bized.co.uk/virtual/economy/library/theory/keynesian
7 Sheehan, Brendan. Understanding Keynes' General Theory, Palgrave Macmillan, Basingstoke, 2009.
8 http://budget.treasury.gov.uk
9 Smith, Adam (1776). The Wealth of Nations, Penguin, Harmondsworth, 1999.

Part II

Income Tax

2 General principles

Introduction

1. Income tax is a direct tax. Tax on some types of income is paid directly by the taxpayer to HM Revenue and Customs. For other types of income, including bank and building society interest and earnings from employment, income tax is deducted by the savings institution or employer before the taxpayer receives income. The institution or employer then pays the tax over to HMRC.

Income tax is the largest single source of tax revenue, planned to raise £158bn out of a total revenue of £589bn in 2011/12. In this chapter the main features of the income tax system are outlined, all of which are developed in detail in later chapters. It begins with some basic expressions. A summary of taxable income, its classification and basis of assessment is then provided. The remainder of the chapter deals with savings income, and non-taxable income. A summary of tax rates relating to 2011/12 is given at the end of the chapter, and also in the full reference tax tables at the end of the book.

The Income Tax (Employment and Pensions) Act 2003, Income Tax (Trading and Other Income) Act 2005 and Income Tax Act 2007 rewrote in "plain English" the previous technical language of UK income tax, some of which dated from the nineteenth century.

Basic expressions

2. Tax Year 2011/12

This runs from the 6th April 2011 to the 5th April 2012. The Income Tax Act 2007 uses the term "Tax Year" but the period from 6 to 5 April is also still referred to elsewhere as the "fiscal year". Personal Self-assessment Tax Returns are made by reference to tax years.

Tax rates Rates of income tax for a tax year are determined annually in the Finance Act.

Taxable persons Income tax is charged on the income of individuals and trusts resident in the UK. Non-residents deriving any income from a UK source are also in principle liable to UK income tax, though this liability may be varied or removed by the terms of a Double Tax Treaty.

Taxable income Income on which income tax is payable is known as taxable income. This consists of the sum of income from all taxable sources, as defined, less deductions for allowable payments, less personal allowances and reliefs (other than allowances and reliefs given "in terms of tax", that is as a deduction from tax liability rather than from income).

Order of taxing income The ITA 2007 requires income to be classified into three types: non-savings income (also called "other income"), savings income and dividend income.

Allowable deductions and personal reliefs and allowances reduce total income in the following order: non-savings income first, then savings income, finally dividend income. This order is prescribed because dividend income is treated as the highest part of total income and savings income as the next highest part (section 16, ITA 2007).

The order in which the various sources of income are combined and the reliefs and allowances against total income are deducted is shown in the following Summary of taxable income for 2011/12:

Summary of Taxable Income 2011/12

		£
Non-savings income:		
Income from employment	– salaries, wages, pensions etc	–
	– benefits in kind treated as earnings	–
Social security income	– retirement pensions etc.	–
Income from trade profits	– business income less capital allowances	–
Income from property		–
Foreign non–savings income		–
Miscellaneous income not savings or dividends in nature (e.g. patent income received by someone who was not the original inventor)		–
Savings income:	– UK bank/building society interest	–
	– interest on Government stocks	–
	– other UK savings income, eg gains on life assurance policies taxed as income	–
Foreign savings income		–
Dividend income:	– dividends from UK companies	–
	– dividends from foreign companies	–
Total income		–
LESS:		
Allowable payments		–
Loss Reliefs against total income		
Net income		–
LESS:		
Personal allowances		–
Taxable income		–

Note: Allowable payments, loss reliefs and personal allowances reduce total income in the following order: non-savings income, then savings income, then dividend income.

Tax calculation on taxable income

(see section 4 or the introductory Summary for the tax rate bands in 2011/12)	£
Starting rate – tax at 10% (applies to savings income only)	–
Basic rate – at 20% on non-savings and savings income (10% on dividends)	–
Higher rate – at 40% on non-savings and savings income (32.5% on dividends)	–
Additional rate – at 50% on non-savings and savings income (42.5% on dividends)	–
Subtotal - tax on taxable income at full rates	–
LESS: Allowances and reliefs given in terms of tax:	
Age-related Married Couple's Allowance – 10% relief	–
New Enterprise Investment Scheme investments – 30% relief	–
New Venture Capital Trust investments – 30% relief	–
Double tax relief on foreign income (limited to maximum of UK tax on same income)	–
UK Tax borne on taxable income	–
Add: UK tax retained on rent paid to overseas resident landlords and patent royalties	–
Tax liability 2011/12	–
Less :	
Tax suffered at source (PAYE and CIS deductions, tax on savings income, etc.)	–
Tax credits on dividend income	–
Tax payable by self-assessment	–

The following points should be noted at this stage:

a) The Married Couple's Allowance is only available where one or both spouses reached the age of 75 before 6th April 2010; relief is given at a 10% tax rate. See chapter 4.

b) The Personal Allowance is available to most UK taxpayers but there are exceptions, and for the tax year 2011/12 it is gradually withdrawn for incomes over £100,000. See chapter 4.

c) Income from employment is after the deduction of any expenses specifically allowable against employment income, and includes taxable benefits in kind from employment. See chapters 7 and 8.

d) Income from self-employment is the taxable profits of a trading business for the tax year, less capital allowances, and is measured using "basis period" rules which mean the profit measurement period does not always match the tax year. See chapters 10 to 15.

e) Savings income paid by banks and building societies to individuals is, in general, subject to deduction at source of income tax at the basic rate of 20%. Savings income derived by UK residents from UK Government sources is generally received gross. See chapter 6.

The nature of income

3. Income for a tax year is measured in accordance with the Income Tax (Earnings and Pensions) Act 2003 and the Income Tax (Trading and Other Income) Act 2005.

Nature of Income	Source
Employment income, pensions income, social security	ITEPA 2003
Income taxed as trade profits Savings income Dividend income Property business income (Income from UK land and Foreign income Miscellaneous income	ITTOIA 2005

Details of the rules for measuring each type of income are contained in later chapters.

Tax rate bands 2011/12

4. In 2011/12, taxable income is taxed at the basic rate up to £35,000. Up to this limit the rate of income tax is 20% for non-savings and savings income (subject to the lower starting rate for some savings income – see below), and 10% for dividend income.

The higher tax rate of 40% (32.5% for dividends) applies to taxable income in excess of £35,000 and up to £150,000.

The basic rate band limit of £35,000, and the higher rate band limit of £150,000, are extended on an individual basis to give relief at higher and additional rates of tax for any qualifying charitable donations or personal pension plan contributions. See chapters 5 and 16.

The additional rate of 50% (42.5% for dividends) applies to taxable income in excess of £150,000.

The initial savings rate of 10% instead of 20% applies to savings income falling within the first £2,560 of income falling to be taxed in the basic rate income band.

As already noted, ITA 2007 prescribes that dividend income is the highest "slice" of total income, and savings income is the next highest. It follows that if taxable non-savings income exceeds £2,560, there can be no benefit from the special savings rate of 10%, because the first £2,560 of taxable income is not seen as savings income.

If under the matching rules in ITA2007 the first £2,560 of taxable income includes dividend income, then the tax rate on this is only 10% anyway.

Basis of assessment and doctrine of the source

5. In order to ascertain an individual's taxable income for a tax year, it is necessary to identify all the sources of income that existed in that year, and then measure the income under the statutory rules (ITEPA 2003 or ITTOIA 2005) for that type of income.

Since the introduction of income tax self-assessment in 1997, all sources of income are measured on a current year basis for income tax purposes.

PAYE system

6. A substantial proportion of all income tax due on employment and pension income is collected under the Pay As You Earn (PAYE) system. The main features of this are covered in Chapter 8.

Due dates for payment – 2011/12 Tax Year

7. Under the system for self-assessment introduced in 1997, a taxpayer whose tax liability is not substantially collected at source is required to make two payments on account of income tax before the self-assessment return for the tax year is due, and then a third balancing payment to meet any remaining liability, by which time the completed self-assessment return should have been submitted. The dates of payment for 2011/12 income tax under the payments on account system are:

First payment on account	31 January 2012
Second payment on account	31 July 2012
Balancing payment	31 January 2013

Taxpayers whose income is largely or wholly received net of tax deducted at source do not have to make payments on account. The date for them to pay any balance of income tax payable for a year is 31 January following the tax year end (ie 31 January 2013 for tax year 2011/12). If they are employees taxed under PAYE then there is an optional alternative of having a remaining 2011/12 income tax liability of under £2,000 collected via the 2012/13 PAYE code.

Further details of the income tax payment system are in Chapter 3.

Non-taxable income

8. The following types of income are exempt from UK income tax:

a) Certain NSI (Government-backed) savings products: Index-Linked Savings Certificates, Fixed Interest Savings Certificates, and Children's Bonus Bonds.

b) Interest and bonuses on certified Save As You Earn (SAYE) contractual savings schemes.

c) NSI Premium Bond prizes.

d) Interest on certain UK government securities held by non-residents.

e) Ex gratia compensation for loss of office/employment, up to £30,000, so long as not paid for services, and not contractually promised (which is what "ex gratia" means). See chapter 7.

f) Redundancy payments, statutory or contractual, within the same £30,000 limit.

g) Job release allowances, if paid within one year of normal retirement age.

h) War widows' pensions.

i) Interest payable on damages for personal injury or death.

j) Gambling winnings (including the National Lottery) and competition prizes.

k) Scholarship awards and other educational grants.

l) Payments for service in the armed forces relating to:

   i) wound and disability pensions

   ii) service grants, bounties and gratuities

   iii) annuities and additional pensions paid to holders of the Victoria Cross, George Cross and other gallantry awards.

m) Long service awards to employees, subject to certain limitations. (See Chapter 7.)

n) Certain social security income: Child Benefit, Working Tax Credit, Child Tax Credit, Pension Credit, housing benefit, Maternity Allowance, attendance allowance, mobility allowance, disability living allowance, Guardian's Allowance, means-tested Employment Support Allowance, the first 28 weeks of Incapacity benefit, Industrial Injuries Benefit, Severe Disablement Allowance, winter fuel payment.

   Note that Job Seeker's Allowance, statutory sick pay, and contributions-based Employment Support Allowance are taxable. Incapacity Benefit becomes taxable after the first 28 weeks of payment.

o) Lump sum Bereavement Payment (currently £2,000) paid to the spouse of a deceased person who has paid NI contributions. Bereavement Allowance paid weekly thereafter (formerly called Widow's Pension) is taxed as pension income.

p) Free TV licence for the Over 75s

q) Up to £4,250 p.a. of gross rent received on furnished lettings in the taxpayer's only or main residence.

r) Outplacement counselling paid for by a third party or an employer.

9. Income Tax Personal allowances 2011/12 (for more details see Chapter 4)

	Deducted from net income	Relief at 10% rate
	£	
Personal allowance	7,475*	
Abatement income level*	100,000	
Blind person's allowance	1,980	
Allowances aged 65–74:		
Personal age allowance	9,940*	
Allowances aged 75–:		
Personal age allowance	10,090*	
Married couple's age allowance		7,295**
Abatement income level for ** above	24,000	
Minimum married couple's allowance		2,800

Note

Married couple's allowance is available where one or both spouses reached the age of 65 before 6th April 2000, so in 2011/12 this means one or both must have reached the age of 75 before 6th April 2010. It is also now available to civil partners, if the age condition is met – see Chapter 4.

Student self-testing questions

1. In 2011/12 Jules had the following income:

	£
Income from employment (salary) - amount before tax	35,100
Building society interest - net of 20% tax	7,200

Jules' personal allowance is £7,475 and there were no payments to be treated as allowable deductions from income.

Required: How much tax is due in total and, if £5,525 was deducted under PAYE, what is the tax remaining payable?

Solution:

			Non-savings	Savings	£
Income			£	£	
Salary/ bonus			35,100		35,100
Taxed interest B Soc. 7,200 x 100/80				9,000	9,000
Total income			35,100	9,000	44,100
Less Personal allowance			(7,475)		(7,475)
Taxable income			27,625	9,000	36,625
Tax on this income:		£		£	£
At starting rate		n/a	x 10%		0
At basic rate	- on non savings	27,625	x 20%		5,525
	- on savings	7,375	x 20%		1,475
Basic rate income limit		35,000			
At higher rate – on savings		1,625	x 40%		650
		36,625			
Income tax borne on taxable income					7,650
(= also Income tax liability)					
Less: PAYE already paid				5,525	
Tax already suffered on interest				1,800	
					(7,325)
Remaining income tax due 31.1.2013					325

Note: The 10% savings tax rate band is not available to Jules because the first £2,560 of taxable income is not classed as savings income.

2. During 2011/12 Jamie has income from employment of £86,000 gross, from which PAYE of £34,400 has been deducted. He also received Building Society interest of £11,200 net, and dividends from UK companies of £54,000.

Required: Show the income tax liability and tax remaining payable by Jamie in respect of 2011/12.

Solution

			Non-savings £	Savings £	Dividends £
Employment			86,000		
Interest	£11,200	x 100/80		14,000	
Dividends	£54,000	x 100/90			60,000
Total/net income		£160,000	86,000	14,000	60,000
Personal allowance	7,475				
Restricted for high income:					
(160,000 – 100,000) x 1/2					
	(30,000)		0		
Taxable income		£160,000	86,000	14,000	60,000

Tax:		£		£
Basic rate	Non-savings	35,000	@ 20%	7,000
Higher rate	Non-savings	51,000	@ 40%	20,400
		86,000		
	Savings	14,000	@ 40%	5,600
	Dividends	50,000	@32.5%	16,250
		150,000		
Additional rate	Dividends	10,000	@42.5%	4,250
		£160,000		
Tax borne/ liability				53,500
Less: Tax suffered			£	
	PAYE		34,400	
	Interest		2,800	
Tax credit	Dividends		6,000	(43,200)
Tax payable by self assessment				£10,300

3 The following concerns the tax payable by Adam:

	2010/11	2011/12
	£	£
Total income tax payable	20,000	24,000
Tax deducted under PAYE	12,000	13,000

The income tax payable has been computed by self-assessment and accepted by HMRC.

Requirement: Show how the tax for 2011/12, not deducted at source, is required to be paid.

Solution:

Tax paid under self-assessment 2010/11:

	£
Tax liability	20,000
Less PAYE	(12,000)
Payable under self-assessment for 2010/11	8,000

Tax payable by self-assessment for 2011/12:

	£
Tax liability	24,000
Less PAYE	(13,000)
Payable under self-assessment	11,000

Payments to be made under self-assessment for 2011/12:

	£	£
Total payable		11,000
Interim payments		
31 January 2012 : 8,000 x 1/2	4,000	
31 July 2012 : 8,000 x 1/2	4,000	
		(8,000)
Balancing payment 31 January 2013		3,000

3 Administration

1. This chapter outlines the administrative features of the income tax system.

2. Income tax is administered by the Commissioners for Revenue and Customs, who are responsible to HM Treasury and the Chancellor of the Exchequer, through the Financial Secretary to the Treasury.

HM Revenue and Customs is an executive agency of the UK Government and was formed by a merger on 18 April 2005 of the Inland Revenue and Her Majesty's Customs and Excise.

The merged HMRC operates through Revenue Officers (formerly called Inspectors of Taxes and Customs and Excise Officers).

HMRC Area and District offices are responsible for the issue and receipt of tax returns for all income tax payers whose affairs are handled in that office. However, as income tax returns are now increasingly submitted online, and enquiries handled by telephone call centres, for many people who complete tax returns the link to a particular district is no longer very significant.

HMRC Accounts Offices are concerned with the collection of the assessed (usually this means **self-**assessed) amounts of tax and matching these to the liabilities shown by the self-assessment returns.

HMRC Enquiry Centres give an initial point of contact for taxpayers with queries of any kind. It is possible for anyone to visit these Enquiry Centres in person, though an increasing number of enquiries are now handled by telephone and email.

HMRC also has dedicated telephone numbers and email addresses for the use of professional tax agents such as accountants and chartered tax advisers acting for their taxpaying clients.

HMRC Specialist Offices and Agencies exist to handle particular administrative areas. Examples of these in the income tax field are the Charities Office, three Enterprise Investment Scheme (EIS) offices, the Employee Shares and Securities Unit (ESSU), the Pension Schemes Office (PSO), and the Financial Intermediaries and Claims Office (FICO).

Legal appeals in all tax disputes are handled by a common tax tribunals system, which took over all new and existing cases on 1 April 2009 from the judicial bodies that formerly existed for different taxes (General Commissioners, Special Commissioners, VAT and Duties Tribunals).

Criminal prosecutions in income tax matters are handled by the Crown Prosecution Service in England, Wales and Northern Ireland, and by the Crown Office and Procurator Fiscal Service in Scotland. Previously (from 18 April 2005) all such prosecutions were handled by a separate Revenue and Customs Prosecution Office, and before April 2005 they were conducted by the Inland Revenue directly.

Tax returns

3. A paper Short Self-Assessment Tax Return was issued immediately after the end of the tax year 2010/11 to all taxpayers who either had submitted a paper return for 2009/10 or had since registered for self-assessment. The return issued in April 2011 covered the Tax Year 2010/11.

Taxpayers who filed their self-assessment return online for 2009/10 were not sent a paper self-assessment return for 2010/11 in the post in April 2011. They were instead simply sent a Notice to Complete a Tax Return (Form SA316). A paper return can still be requested by these taxpayers, or downloaded from HMRC's website, but the assumption made by HMRC is that these taxpayers will file online again for 2011/12.

Taxpayers receiving a paper return for 2010/11 were initially sent a tax return headed "Short Tax Return 2011 for the Tax Year 6 April 2010 to 5 April 2011", together with any extra pages that they were previously known to need. Further extra pages can be requested, or downloaded from HMRC's website as can the full Tax Return Guide and Helpsheets for 2010/11.

For taxpayers who did not have a registered tax agent, any paper return issued in April 2011 was accompanied by the Tax Return Guide 2010/11 and the Tax Calculation Guide 2010/11. For taxpayers whose tax agent filed a paper return for 2009/10, only the paper Tax Return itself was issued to the taxpayer in April 2011, as the tax agent was assumed to have the rest.

Self-assessment

4. The following is a summary of the main administrative features of self-assessment.

a) The Tax Return consists of one main return and supplementary pages.

b) The issued Tax Return is accompanied by a separate Tax Return Guide explaining how income for each page of the tax return, and capital gains where relevant, are to be computed, and by a Tax Calculation Guide for the self-calculation of the final tax due or repayable. Helpsheets are also available explaining how to deal with specific types of income and allowable deductions and reliefs including loss claims.

c) There are two key dates for the filing of tax returns.

   i) By the 31st October following the end of the tax year, for those taxpayers filing a paper return.

   ii) By the 31st January following the end of the tax year for taxpayers filing online.

d) Thus for 2011/12 the two filing dates are 31st October 2012 and 31st January 2013.

e) Failure to file a tax return in respect of 2011/12 on or before 31st January 2013 will incur an automatic fixed penalty of £100. If the return is filed 3 months late penalties of £10 per day up to a maximum of £900 will be charged. If the return is still outstanding 6 months after the filing date a further penalty applies of 5% of tax due, or £300, whichever is the greater. For returns filed 12 months late there are further penalties. However, these filing penalties are legally limited to a maximum of any tax still unpaid at the 31 January filing date. Therefore even if the return is late, these late filing penalties will be cancelled once the return has been received, if all tax due is shown to have been paid in time.

f) Under self-assessment, the obligation to pay tax is not linked to the issue of any assessments or demands by HMRC. Instead, the taxpayer is automatically required to make the necessary tax payments based on his or her self-assessment. The taxpayer is liable to interest, and eventually surcharges, on any part of the tax liability that is not paid on time.

g) For taxpayers whose tax is not mainly collected by deduction at source, two payments on account are required and a third balancing payment to meet any tax outstanding at 31 January following the tax year-end.

h) The expected payments on account are notified by HMRC in a Self-assessment Statement of Account, which shows the due dates for payment and contains a payslip.

i) If the expected payments on account for the current year are believed excessive (because total tax payable by self-assessment is reasonably expected to be lower for the current tax year than in the previous tax year), the taxpayer can make a formal application to reduce one or both payments on account. Interest will be charged from the original due dates if a reduction applied for in this way is later seen (when the complete self-assessment return is submitted) to have been excessive.

Rules for Self-assessment payments on account (POAs)

5. The following general points should be noted:

i) Taxpayers do not need to make POAs if:

   a) their income tax (and Class 4 national insurance contributions) liability for the preceding year – net of tax deducted at source and tax credits on dividends – is less than £1,000 in total; or

   b) more than 80% of their total income tax (and Class 4 NIC) liability for the preceding year was met by deduction of tax at source or by tax credits on dividends.

ii) The most common ways of paying tax by deduction at source are through Pay As You Earn (PAYE), the construction industry sub-contractors' (CIS) scheme, and the tax suffered on interest received from banks and building societies. Other income such as patent royalties may also be received net of basic rate tax.

iii) Income tax and Class 4 NIC liability (net of tax deducted at source and tax credits) for the preceding year will determine whether payments on account are needed. If they are due, they will normally be half the tax (and Class 4 NIC) payable for the preceding year, net of last year's tax deducted at source and dividend tax credits.

iv) Where payments on account do not meet the entire tax (and Class 4 NIC) liability – net of tax deducted at source and tax credits – for this tax year, a final payment will be due by 31st January after the end of the tax year. Where the payments on account are found to exceed the total tax payable, a repayment will arise.

Interim payments on account for 2011/12

6. To summarise the above, payments on account are due in the following circumstances:

Assessment to income tax	– Income tax deducted	=	"Relevant amount"
& Class 4 NIC 2010/11	at source 2010/11		for 2011/12

Relevant amount	≥ £1000	→ POA required 2011/12
Relevant amount	≥ 20% of tax liability 2010/11	→ POA required 2011/12

Notes

i) Income tax deducted at source includes tax credits on savings income such as dividends and building society interest, PAYE and CIS deductions.

ii) Capital gains tax is excluded from the assessment to income tax and is therefore only payable on the final tax payment date. No payments on account operate for CGT.

Example

For 2010/11 X's self-assessment return showed the following:

	£
Gross income tax liability	10,000
Class 4 NIC (see chapter 17 for more on this tax)	1,030
PAYE deducted at source (relating to 2010/11)	2,570
Tax deducted at source from bank interest	430

Calculate the interim payments to be made by X on account for the year 2011/12.

Solution

Relevant amount	Income tax liability 2010/11		10,000
Less income tax at source	PAYE	2,570	
	Tax on Interest	430	(3,000)
			7,000
Class 4 NIC			1,030
Paid by self assessment 2010/11			8,030
2011/12 Payments on Account	31st January 2012		4,015
	31st July 2012		4,015

Example

Mrs J has the following data shown on her self-assessment tax return for 2010/11

	£
Gross income tax liability	7,500
PAYE deducted at source	6,900
Tax suffered at source on savings income	150

Calculate the interim payments to be made on account of 2011/12.

Solution

Relevant amount	Income tax liability		7,500
Less	PAYE	6,900	
	Tax on savings	150	(7,050)
			450

As this is less than £1,000, no POA for 2011/12 is required.

Final payment (repayment) of tax

A final payment (or repayment) of income tax appears in the following circumstances:

2011/12 self-assessment tax return 2010/11 self-assessment tax return

Income tax liability
Class IV NIC
Capital gains tax liability } — POAs = Final payment or repayment

Example

P has the following income tax and capital gains tax liabilities for the year ended 5th April 2012 based on his self-assessment tax return.

	£
Trade profits & NIC	25,000
Capital gains tax	1,000

The relevant amount for 2010/11 was £18,000 all attributable to income tax on trade profits and NIC.

Show the payments to be made in respect of the tax year to 5th April 2012 and the due dates.

Solution: P's tax and Class 4 NIC liability for 2011/12

		£
31st January 2012	50% × Relevant amount 2010/11 = 50% × 18,000	9,000
31st July 2012	50% × Relevant amount 2010/11 = 50% × 18,000	9,000
31st January 2013	Balance of tax and NIC due	8,000
		26,000

Note

The total tax due for 2011/12 is

	Income tax and Class 4 NIC	25,000
	Capital gains tax	1,000
		26,000
Less Payment on account (2010/11 relevant amount)		18,000
	Balance due	8,000

Surcharges on income tax

7. In addition to any interest that may arise on any tax paid late there is a scheme of surcharges to encourage prompt payments.

Interest on under and overpayments

8. A charge to interest will automatically arise on any tax paid late whether in respect of income tax, NIC or capital gains tax in respect of:

i) any payment on account

ii) any balancing item

iii) any tax payable following an amendment to self-assessment whether made by the taxpayer or HM Revenue and Customs

iv) any tax payable in a discovery assessment by HM Revenue and Customs.

Interest will arise from the due dates for payment to the date on which payment is finally made for payments on account and balancing payments.

For amendments to self-assessments, the interest charge runs from the annual filing date for the income tax year, i.e. the 31st January following the end of the income tax year. Interest on any overpayments of tax will be paid automatically when the repayment is made.

HM Revenue and Customs enquiries

9. Revenue Officers may carry out an 'enquiry' into a taxpayer's self-assessment tax return. Such returns may be selected on a sample basis, or because the Officer has concerns about some of the information returned. The enquiry system includes both powers for the Revenue Officer and rights for the taxpayer. For example, the Officer may request a meeting with the taxpayer, but the taxpayer has a right to representation, and to decline to attend. The enquiry should be restricted to a specified area of investigation, and concluded within a regulated time limit.

The normal "enquiry window" period is twelve months from the date of submitting the return. (Originally, it was twelve months from the latest date for filing (31 January) regardless of the actual filing date, but this was altered to encourage early filing.)

The enquiry window is reopened if the taxpayer submits an amendment to a submitted return. This includes the lodging of a further claim or withdrawal of a claim made on the original return. HMRC has up to twelve months to enquire into the amendment or any related matter on the return.

After the enquiry window period has closed, HMRC can only reopen the return if there is a discovery of "incomplete disclosure". This means that HMRC finds out (sometimes by reviewing information from a third party) that something was omitted or concealed from the submitted return, causing a loss of tax to the Crown. A discovery assessment can only be made if HMRC could not reasonably have been able to tell the true tax liability from the self-assessment return and supporting information as originally submitted.

Incomplete disclosure that was not the result of fraudulent or negligent conduct by the taxpayer allows a discovery assessment by HMRC in the period up to five years after the original last filing date for the return (ie nearly five years and ten months after the end of the tax year to which the incomplete return relates).

Incomplete disclosure that was the result of fraudulent or negligent conduct by the taxpayer allows a discovery assessment at any time up to twenty years from the original last filing date. There are penalties for taxpayer fraud and negligence in addition to the additional tax due and interest on it at normal rates.

Challenging the decisions of HM Revenue and Customs

10. Letters informing taxpayers of HMRC decisions will include information on rights to appeal. Appeals should be sent to HMRC in writing, within 30 days of the disputed decision. Some appeals may be settled by agreement with HMRC.

When agreement is not reached, HMRC may offer an internal review of the decision by another officer. The taxpayers may ask for a review if HMRC do not offer one. Whether or not a review takes place, a taxpayer may then appeal to the Tribunal Service.

Tribunal service

11. The tax appeals system is a two-tier tribunal system:

Most cases are heard by the First Tier Tribunal (Tax Chamber);

The Upper Tribunal (Finance and Chancery Chamber) hears complex cases, and all appeals from the First Tier Tribunal. The Upper Tribunal is a court of record, whose decisions create binding precedents for the First Tier.

Appeals from the Upper Tribunal are to the Court of Appeal (Inner House in Scotland), and finally to the Supreme Court of the UK.

Penalties

12. Taxpayers are expected to take 'reasonable care' in making and keeping accurate records to enable them to provide a complete and accurate tax return. This principle applies to all income tax and national insurance contributions information in the self-assessment income tax return, along with return documents for other taxes (principally CGT for individuals).

Taxpayers can demonstrate they have taken reasonable care by: keeping accurate records, confirming the correct position when they do not understand tax issues, answering any enquiry questions raised by HMRC, and telling HMRC promptly about any errors discovered in tax returns after they have been sent.

Where taxpayers do not pay enough tax, and have not taken reasonable care, they may have to pay a penalty in addition to the tax due and any interest on late payment. The penalties can be reduced if the taxpayer makes an 'unprompted' disclosure of the underpayment, rather than one forced by the result of investigations by the tax authorities:

Taxpayer's approach to disclosure of underpayment	Minimum penalty	Maximum penalty
Reasonable care	No penalty	No penalty
Careless unprompted	0%	30%
Careless prompted	15%	30%
Deliberate unprompted	20%	70%
Deliberate prompted	35%	70%

Deliberate and concealed unprompted	30%	100%
Deliberate and concealed prompted	50%	100%

Error or mistake relief

13. The relief formerly called error or mistake relief under Taxes Management Act 1970 section 33 was replaced from 1 April 2010 by Overpayment Relief under new Schedule 1AB of the same Act.

The taxpayer can claim relief in writing against any over-payment of tax made due to an error or mistake (including an omission) in any return or statement. The relief must be claimed within 4 years of the end of the tax year.

The claim in writing must be separate from a submitted self-assessment return and must provide the following information (Source HMRC Brief 22 / 2010):

- State that the person is making a claim for overpayment relief under Schedule 1AB TMA 1970
- Identify the tax year for which the overpayment or excessive assessment has been made.
- State the grounds on which the person considers that the overpayment or excessive assessment has occurred.
- State whether the person has previously made an appeal in connection with the payment or the assessment.
- If the claim is for repayment of tax, include documentary proof of the tax deducted or the tax being suffered in some other way.
- Include a declaration signed by the claimant stating that the particulars given in the claim are correct and complete to the best of their knowledge and belief.

Student self-testing question

A has the following data relating to 2010/11 and 2011/12.

	2010/11	**2011/12**
Total income tax liability	18,500	22,000
Capital gains tax liability	1,500	3,000
Tax credit on dividend income	(1,000)	(1,500)
Total tax due by self -assessment	19,000	23,500

Calculate the tax payments in respect of 2011/12 and show the due dates for payments.

Solution:

	2011/12 Payments		
	Interim Payments		Final Payment
	31. 1. 12	**31. 7. 12**	**31. 1. 13**
1st Interim payment 50% × (18,500 – 1,000)	8,750		
2nd Interim payment 50% (18,500 – 1,000)		8,750	
Final payment (23,500 – 17,500)	———		6,000
	8,750	8,750	6,000

Notes

i) The interim payments are computed by reference to the tax liability for 2010/11, i.e. (18,500 – 1,000) = 17,500 excluding any capital gains tax.

ii) The final payment for 2011/12 includes the capital gains tax liability for that year, i.e. £3,000:

(22,000 + 3,000 – 1,500) = 23,500 – POA,

i.e. 23,500 – 17,500 = £6,000.

(For CGT generally see chapter 26 onwards.)

4 Personal allowances and reliefs

Introduction

1. This chapter is concerned with the main features of the system of taxation in relation to the personal allowances and reliefs for individuals, blind persons, and married couples.

List of topic headings

2.

Personal allowance

Personal age allowance

Husbands and wives /civil partners

Married couple's allowance

Blind person's allowance

Death of husband or wife

Year of permanent separation and divorce

Non-residents

Personal allowance (PA) 2011/12 £7,475 (2010/11 £6,475)

3. This allowance is given automatically to all individuals, male or female, single or married, except non-domiciled UK residents who choose to file on the remittance basis (who are in general outside the scope of this book). It is subject to withdrawal/restriction where the adjusted net income exceeds £100,000.

For 2011/12, it is reduced by £1 for every £2 excess of an individual's "adjusted net income" over £100,000. This means that it is removed completely once adjusted net income exceeds £114,950.

There are higher rates of personal allowance for people over the age of 65, discussed below in Section 5.

Where not withdrawn, the personal allowance is deducted from total income in arriving at the taxable income of an individual, and is thus given relief at the taxpayer's marginal rate of tax.

Net income is defined as total income less any trading losses (see chapter 14) and pension contributions paid gross (see chapter 16). "Adjusted net income" is the taxpayer's net income, less the gross amount of any Gift Aid donations (see chapter 5) or personal pension contributions (see chapter 16) which have received tax relief at source. Any relief given against employment income for subscriptions to trade unions or police organisations is added back in calculating adjusted net income.

The personal allowance is not transferable.

Example

A is single, has a salary income from employment for 2011/12 of £105,000 and no other income.

Compute his income tax liability for 2011/12

Solution: A's Income tax computation 2011/12

			£
Income from employment			105,000
Personal allowance		7,475	
Restricted (105,000 – 100,000) x ½		(2,500)	
			(4,975)
Taxable income			100,025
Tax liability	n/a @ 10%		0
	35,000 @ 20%		7,000
	65,025 @ 40%		26,010
	100,025		33,010

Note

With such high income from employment, most of the tax liability would have already been collected by way of the PAYE system which would reduce any final balance due accordingly. See Chapter 8.

The personal age allowance (PAA)

4. **2011/12**

Age 65–74	£9,940
Age 75–	£10,090

For taxpayers over the age of 65 at any time during the tax year, a higher personal allowance is available, and there is a further additional amount for those aged 75 and over. This increased level of allowances is available even if the taxpayer dies before the specified age, if he or she would have attained that age in the year of assessment.

The full amount of the PAA may be claimed where adjusted net income is not greater than £24,000.

Where adjusted net income is greater than £24,000 then the PAA is reduced by half the excess, until the basic personal allowance becomes more beneficial.

For a taxpayer aged over 65, unless adjusted net income exceeds £100,000, the personal allowance can never be reduced below the basic personal allowance for a person under 65, i.e. £7,475 for 2011/12.

The basic personal allowance is subject to the standard further restriction /withdrawal if a person over 65 has an adjusted net income that exceeds £100,000.

Income limits for Age Allowance	PAA starts being restricted at	Normal PA
	£	£
Age 65–74	24,001	28,930 – 100,000
Age 75–	24,001	29,230 – 100,000

Age 65–74 9,940 – 1/2 (28,930 – 24,000) = £7,475

Age 75 10,090 – 1/2 (29,230 – 24,000) = £7,475

Example

K, who is 66 and single, has income from employment in 2011/12 of £20,000 and a state retirement pension of £5,000.

Compute K's income tax liability for 2011/12.

Solution: K's Income tax computation 2011/12

			£	£
Income from employment				20,000
State Pension				5,000
Total income (all non-savings)25,000				
PAA			9,940	
Less abatement 1/2 (25,000–24,000)			500	(9,440)
Taxable income				15,560
Tax liability:				
	Non-savings	n/a @ 10%		0
	Basic Rate	15,560 @ 20%		3,112
		15,560		
Tax				3,112

Note: The restricted age allowance of £9,440 is greater than the personal allowance of £7,475.

Husbands and wives /civil partners

5. The main features of income tax for husbands and wives are as follows. Since the legalisation of same-sex civil partnerships in the UK from December 2005, all references to "spouses" in tax legislation apply equally to registered civil partners from the tax year 2005/06.

For income tax purposes, in order to count as "married" at a given date, a couple must be both legally married and living together, which means "not separated in circumstances where the separation is likely to be permanent". A mid-tax-year permanent separation terminates the marriage relationship for income tax.

(The position is not the same for capital gains tax or inheritance tax; see chapters 27 and 35).

a) Husband and wife / civil partners are treated as separate taxpayers, each completing their own tax returns and responsible for their own tax liabilities.

b) Each spouse/civil partner is entitled to the full basic rate band of income tax and the starting rate band where available.

c) Each spouse receives a personal allowance, which is non-transferable to the other spouse even if the first spouse has not enough net income to use it all. As noted above, the allowance is increased for persons over 65, and again for those over 75. As already noted, the personal allowance in tax year 2011/12 is withdrawn progressively for incomes over £100,000 and disappears at income of £114,950. These limits operate separately for married couples.

e) The married couple's allowance (MCA) was abolished from 6 April 2000 except where one spouse had reached the age of 65 before 6 April 2000. For persons married before 6 December 2005, the MCA is claimed by the husband, but is transferable to the wife if the parties elect. In effect therefore, it can be allocated between spouses/civil partners (though any abatement for higher incomes is made by reference to only the husband's income).

   For people who married or registered as civil partners on or after 6 December 2005, if one was born before 6 April 1935, then the MCA is given primarily for each tax year to the spouse or civil partner with the higher income (even if that is not the older partner) . However, it is transferable for tax calculation purposes to the other partner, if both elect. High-income abatement for income over £24,000 for partners married since 6 December 2005 is still calculated by reference to the spouse or partner with the higher income.

f) Each person entitled to the personal age allowance is subject to the annual income limit of £24,000 for 2011/12 above which the Age Allowance is abated. There is no sharing of this limit between spouses.

g) Joint property giving rise to income is assumed to be enjoyed by spouses in equal shares for income tax purposes, regardless of the true or beneficial ownership split. This would apply to rent from a let property, or to a joint bank deposit account or shares held jointly. The measurement of the income for income tax would be 50:50 between the spouses. It is possible for the spouses to elect for a different split of the income arising from joint property, but they must if doing so declare that the alternative proportions being specified reflect the true beneficial ownership of the underlying asset.

The married couple's age related allowance (MCA) – 10% rate relief

6.

	2011/12
Age 65–75	n/a
Age 76–	£7,295
Minimum amount	£2,800

a) The MCA is only available where one or both spouses has/have reached the age of 75 before the 6th April 2010. A claim for the higher level of married couple's allowance is made by the husband for marriages before 6 December 2005, and by the partner with the higher taxable income, for marriages since then. In the rest of this section, to save space, the husband is assumed the one claiming the allowance.

b) The full amount of both the age-related allowances (i.e. PAA and MCA) is reduced by 1/2 of the excess where the husband's income exceeds £24,000. Note that the wife's income never affects the level of the MCA. Where the husband's MCA is reduced because of his total income, it can never be reduced below the minimum notional (non-age-enhanced) MCA, which is £2,800.

   In applying the reduction in the MCA for higher income, the following rules should be used:

   i) First – reduce the PAA by £1 for every £2 of excess income, until it reaches the level of the PA for people under the age of 65.

   ii) Second – reduce the MCA by £1 for every £2 of excess income, until it reaches the level of the MCA for people under 65.

   The above has the effect of preserving as late as possible any MCA that can be transferred to the wife.

   If the husband cannot use all the MCA, the unused amount can be transferred to his wife.

c) The MCA is given relief at the 10% rate. So if the MCA due after partial abatement is £4,500, then this is relieved by £450 (10% of £4,500) being deducted from the tax liability of the taxpayer.

Example

Mr Z is aged 66 and his wife is aged 77. They have been married for 40 years. In the year 2011/12 Mr Z has employment and pension income of £25,000 and Mrs Z has employment and pension income of £26,000.

Compute the tax payable by Mr and Mrs Z for 2011/12.

Solution: Mr Z's Income tax computation 2011/12

	£	£
Employment and pension income		25,000
Reduction in total allowances		
1/2 (25,000 – 24,000) = 500		
PAA	9,940	
Less reduction	(500)	
PAA as abated (9,440)		
Taxable income (non-savings)		15,560
Tax liability:		
n/a @ 10%		0
15,560 @ 20%		3,112
15,560		
Less deduction for MCA 7,295 @ 10%		(730)
Tax payable		2,382

Mrs Z's income tax computation 2011/12

	£	£
Employment and pension income		26,000
PAA	10,090	
Less 1/2 (26,000 – 24,000)	(1,000)	
		(9,090)
Taxable income (non-savings)		16,910
Tax liability: n/a @ 10%		0
16,910 @ 20%		3,382
16,910		
Tax payable		3,382

Notes

i) The PAA of £10,090 for Mrs Z is reduced to £9,090.

ii) The level of Mrs Z's income has no effect on the MCAA claimed by her husband.

iii) The MCAA due to Mr Z is not abated because abatement for high incomes applies first to the PAA, and would only reduce the MCAA after the PAA had been reduced to the basic personal allowance.

Blind person's allowance 2011/12 £1,980

7. This allowance is available to any person who is on the local authority blind person's register. Where both husband and wife are blind then each can claim the allowance. If either the husband or the wife cannot fully use the amount of their blind allowance then the balance can be transferred to the other spouse. This rule applies whether or not the spouse receiving the transferred allowance is a registered blind person. A notice to transfer any unused allowance must be made in writing to HMRC within four years of the end of the year of assessment.

This allowance is deducted from total income to arrive at taxable income, and is thus given relief at the taxpayer's marginal rate of tax.

Example

K, who is a widow aged 55, is a registered blind person. K's income for the year 2011/12 consists of the following.

	£
Widow's pension	6,000
Wages for part-time employment (gross)	14,505
(PAYE deducted £1,406)	

Compute K's income tax liability for 2011/12.

Solution: K income tax computation 2011/12

		£	£
Income from employment			14,505
Widow's pension			6,000
			20,505
Personal allowance		7,475	
Blind person's allowance		1,980	(9,455)
Taxable income			11,050
Tax liability			
	n/a @ 10%		0
	11,050 @ 20%		2,210
	11,050		2,210
Less PAYE			(1,406)
Tax payable			804

Year of death of either spouse

8. The following points should be noted under this heading:

   Death of either spouse /civil partner

   a) A full personal allowance and full MCAA, if applicable, is available in the tax year of death.

   b) Total income up to the date of death, less allowances and reliefs for the whole year, is ascertained and any remaining income tax due is payable from the deceased's estate.

c) The balance of any age related MCAA not used against the husband's (or higher earning partner's, for marriages after 5.12.05) tax liability on income up to the date of death is available for set -off against the surviving partner's own tax liability for the whole year.

Personal allowances for Non-residents

9. A 'qualifying' non-resident can claim full personal allowances against his or her UK income to the extent that the income is within the charge to UK tax.

Qualifying non-residents means:

a) residents of the European Union or the European Economic Area;

b) residents of the UK Commonwealth;

c) residents of any other Taxing State where UK personal allowances are given on UK source income as part of double tax treaty arrangements.

Student self-testing question

B aged 68, a widower, looks after his mother aged 92. For the year to 5th April 2012 the following data applies:

Salary and pension income B	£27,000

Calculate the tax payable by B for 2011/12.

Solution: B income tax computation 2011/12

		£	£
Income from employment and pension			27,000
P.A.A.		9,940	
(less $\frac{1}{2}$) × (27,000 – 24,000)		(1,500)	8,440
Taxable income			18,560
Tax liability	n/a @ 10%		0
	18,560 @ 20%		3,712
	18,560		
Tax payable			3,712

Note. PAA is £8,440 which is greater than the basic PA of £7,475.

5 Allowable payments and Gift Aid

Introduction

1. Allowable payments reduce total income, but are not referable to any particular source of income – unlike for example the specific reliefs that are deductible only against income from employment (see Chapter 8).

Total income is reduced by allowable payments to give net income (see Chapter 2).

The concept of allowable payments remains that these costs have the character of "annual payments". Before the Income Tax Act 2007, 'charges on income' was the term used to describe all annual payments.

Until the Finance Act 2000, personal charitable donations (other than payroll giving) had to be over £250 if they were to obtain tax relief, and were deducted from total income as such. However since 2000, personal Gift Aid payments can be small payments, and under ITA 2007 they are not dealt with as allowable payments, but by the "extended basic rate band" method of tax relief.

Annual payments

2. These are payments which possess the quality of annual recurrence, are not voluntary transactions, and are usually supported by a legal obligation.

Annual payments are not allowable payments unless they fall within the following categories:

a) payments of interest;

b) payments of patent royalties;

c) other annual payments made for bone fide commercial reasons in connection with the payer's trade, profession or vocation.

Qualifying interest payments

3. Interest due in the UK on a loan used for any of the under-mentioned purposes is payable without deduction of income tax, and is an allowable payment against total income, and the higher rate of income tax.

a) To purchase plant or machinery for use in a partnership or employment.

b) To purchase an interest in or make a loan to a partnership, where the taxpayer is a partner, but not a limited partner.

c) Loans made in acquiring an interest in a co-operative enterprise as defined in section 2 of the Industrial Common Ownership Act 1976.

d) To pay inheritance tax. Relief is available for one year only.

e) To acquire ordinary shares or make loans to a close company, but not a close investment company. (See chapter 18 for what these are.) The borrower must, with his associates:

i) have a material interest in the company, i.e. more than 5% of the ordinary share capital or be entitled to more than 5% of the assets on a notional winding up; or

ii) if having less than a 5% interest, have worked for the greater part of his time in the management of the company.

Business loan interest

4. Interest paid on loans taken out for business purposes by traders is charged as an expense of trading, and not as a separate allowable payment. This applies to bank loan or overdraft interest, providing the loan is used wholly and exclusively for the purposes of trade. Similar interest on loans to buy property for letting is allowable as an expense of the letting and not as an allowable payment against total income.

Annual payments for business purposes – patent royalties

5. Payments made by an individual for bona fide commercial reasons in connection with his or her trade, profession or vocation are eligible to be treated as allowable payments. However, where an individual is trading, a patent (or copyright) royalty related to that trade may alternatively now be treated as a trading expense deducted in the business accounts, rather than deducted under the separate rules for allowable payments.

Whether treated as a trade expense or an allowable payment, patent royalty payments by an individual must be paid to the patent owner after deduction of basic rate income tax at source. The gross amount of the royalty is the deductible trading expense or allowable payment for the royalty payer. The tax withheld is added to the paying individual's own tax borne, to give a total liability for the tax year that in effect includes 20% basic rate tax paid over on behalf of the patent owner.

The Budget Announcements of 22 June 2010 included a commitment by the new Government to review this system of collecting UK tax on patent royalties which was stated to be little known, old fashioned and open to unintentional lawbreaking.

Copyright royalties

6. Copyright royalties differ from patent royalties because they may be paid gross without any deduction of tax. They are still trading expenses if related to trading income, and only have to be treated as an allowable payment if paid for some other purpose (e.g. in connection with an investment asset).

Present system of giving income tax relief for Gift Aid donations

7. As already stated Gift Aid donations to Charities or Community Amateur Sports Clubs (CASCs) are no longer classed as an allowable payment for income tax, though they were formerly dealt with as such.

The system works as follows:

a) The donor must give the charity a gift aid declaration either at the time of the donation, or beforehand (to cover future donations). This must include a statement that the donor pays tax for the year of at least as much as the tax withheld from the donation.

b) The declaration may be given in writing, over the phone or over the Internet, and the charity or CASC must keep a record of the date of the declaration and the donor's name and address.

c) The amount donated is treated for all tax purposes as paid net of 20% basic rate tax withheld by the donor.

d) Donors must pay an amount of income tax and /or capital gains tax, whether at the basic rate or some other rate, equal to the tax deducted from their donations.

e) Donors who pay tax at higher or additional rates may also claim higher or additional rate tax relief for the gross donation against income tax. This may be done on the self-assessment tax return or by letter.

f) Relief at the higher rate is given by extending the basic rate band by the gross amount of Gift Aid payment(s); and relief at the additional rate is given by extending the higher rate band limit by the same figure.

g) Gift Aid payments made after the end of a tax year but before submission of the self-assessment return may be related back to the tax year to which the return relates.

h) Charities claim back basic rate tax withheld on their total Gift Aid income from HMRC Charities using Form R68. The names of all Gift Aid donors must be stated on the form.

i) If a taxpayer does not pay enough income tax and capital gains tax for a tax year (including tax credits on dividend income) to cover the total tax reclaimed by charities on his gift aid donations, then he or she must pay HMRC the difference, under section 424 ITA 2007. This situation could arise where trading losses of a later year are carried back against total income so that an earlier tax liability is eliminated – see Chapter 14.

Computational rules for gift aid – extended basic rate band

a) **Higher rate taxpayer:** Gross the gift aid payment up by the basic rate of income tax and extend the basic rate band by that gross amount.

b) **Additional rate taxpayer:** Extend the basic rate band by the grossed up amount of the gift aid payment, and also extend the top limit of the higher rate band by the same amount. This ensures the higher rate band remains the same size.

c) **Basic rate taxpayer**: Ignore in the income tax computation, as full relief for the gross payment was given at source by the fact the payment was made net. The gross amount is however relevant for a basic rate taxpayer in computing adjusted net income for the purpose of Age Allowance income limits etc. (see chapter 4).

Example

T, who is married, has employment income of £49,000 for 2011/12. His wife has salary income of £15,000. T makes payments of £800 net (£1,000 gross) to a registered charity by way of Gift Aid.

Compute the income tax liability for 2011/12 for T and Mrs T who are both aged less than 65.

Solution: Income tax computation 2011/12

			T	Mrs T
			£	£
Income from employment			49,000	15,000
Personal allowance			(7,475)	(7,475)
Taxable income			41,525	7,525
Tax liability:			£	£
Income tax	n/a	@ 10%	0	0
BR	35,000 / 7,525	@ 20%	7,000	1,505
Extend band	1,000	@ 20%	200	0
	36,000			
HR	5,525 / 0	@ 40%	2,210	0
	41,525 7,525			

Note

The Gift Aid payment to the charity is grossed up and the basic rate is extended to arrive at the total tax payable

i.e. 35,000 + 1,000 = 36,000. £800 x 100/80 = £1,000.

If Mrs T had also made a Gift Aid payment of a similar amount to Mr T, only basic rate tax relief due would have been due and this has been received already so there is no need to deal with the Gift Aid in the tax computation. So her computation would look no different (as she does not have taxable income in excess of the basic rate band).

In Mr T's case he is due higher rate relief at (40-20)% on his Gift Aid donation and this is achieved by extending the amount of income on which he only pays basic rate tax by £1,000 or the gross amount of the donation.

The charity meanwhile receives £1000 in total, £800 from Mr T and the other £200 by application to HMRC as a Gift Aid tax reclaim.

Payroll giving scheme for charitable donations

8. Another way in which individual taxpayers can give to charity with tax relief for all donations is to make donations via a payroll deduction scheme. Relief is available without limit up to the total of the cash earnings from the employment. The employer is responsible for making the payments to the charity, and uses the 'net pay arrangements' in computing the employee's PAYE liability.

This relief has become less used since Gift Aid was extended in 2000 to single payments under £250 and since Gift Aid declarations were permitted by telephone and internet. See further on payroll giving in Chapter 8.

Student self-testing question

J and Mrs J, who are married, has the following data relating to 2011/12.

	£
Employment earnings J	48,000
Mrs J employment earnings	28,000

On 1st February 2012 J paid £960 (net) by way of a Gift Aid payment to a recognised charity.

Compute the income tax liability for 2011/12 of J and Mrs J, both aged 55.

Solution: Income tax computation 2011/12

		J	Mrs J
		£	£
Income from employment J		48,000	–
Income from employment Mrs J		–	28,000
		48,000	28,000
Personal allowance		7,475	7,475
Taxable income (non-savings)		40,525	20,525
Taxation liability			
n/a / n/a	@ 10%	0	0
36,200* / 20,525	@ 20%	7,240	4,105
4,325	@ 40%	1,730	
40,525 20,525			
Tax payable		8,970	4,105

Note *

As the gift aid payment by J is allowed at the higher rate, his basic rate income tax band is extended i.e. £35,000 + £1,200 = £36,200.

(gross up donation: £960 x 100/80 = £1,200)

6 Savings and investment income

Introduction

1. This chapter is concerned with the taxation of savings and investment income and with income tax relief for investment in EIS shares and Venture Capital Trusts (VCTs).

Savings income is often (but not always) received after deduction of tax at source. The tax treatment of dividend income and the associated dividend tax credit is dealt with in section 4.

Bank/building society interest etc – 20% rate deducted at source

2. a) The rate of 20% income tax deducted at source applies to the following savings income:

interest from banks and building societies

interest from some government securities (but see 3(i) below)

interest on corporate loan stocks and debentures

purchased life annuities (non-capital element)

interest distributions from authorised unit trusts.

b) Where the taxpayer is only taxable at the starting rate of 10% for savings income, or the basic rate of 20%, then there will be no further liability. The deduction at source is deemed to have satisfied the full charge. (A net repayment may be due if the rate applying is only 10 %.)

c) For higher or additional rate taxpayers the 40% or 50% rate applies to the gross income with due allowance for the basic rate deduction at source.

d) Non-taxpayers who receive taxed interest will be able to claim the 20% deduction by way of repayment.

e) Savings income (including dividends – see below) are to be treated as the top slice of an individual's taxable income.

f) In the case of bank and building society interest, an individual can register to receive interest gross without any tax deducted in appropriate circumstances, namely if their situation means they have no tax liability and would be claiming a full repayment of tax on savings income if it were deducted. Individuals cannot register to receive bank interest gross merely because they expect only to pay the 10% rate on savings income.

g) The 10% starting rate band applies to savings income.

h) In general, savings income of individuals arises on the date of the payment of the income (receipts basis).

Interest received gross

3. The following forms of investment pay interest gross:

a) certificates of deposit and sterling or foreign currency time deposits, provided that the loan is not less than £50,000 and is repayable within five years;

b) NSI interest is paid gross on the following taxable National Savings products: Easy Access Account, Investment Account, Pensioners Income Bonds, Fixed Rate Savings Bonds, Capital Bonds;

c) general client accounts with banks and building societies operated by solicitors or estate agents;

d) accounts held at overseas branches of United Kingdom banks and building societies;

e) bank and building society accounts where the owner is not ordinarily resident in the United Kingdom and has made a declaration to that effect;

f) bank and building society accounts in the names of companies, clubs, societies and charities;

g) loans from unincorporated borrowers;

h) all holdings of government securities acquired after 5th April 1998, and any other holdings before that date provided the holder has elected to receive the interest gross.

Example

A has the following income for the year ended 5th April 2012.

Income from property	£16,000
Building Society interest (net)	£8,000

Compute A's income tax liability for 2011/12, and the tax payable by self assessment.

Solution: A's income tax computation 2011/12

	£
Income from property	16,000
Building Society interest	10,000
	26,000
Less PA	(7,475)
Taxable income	18,525
Tax liability	
n/a @ 10%	0
18,525 @ 20%	3,705
Less deducted at source	(2,000)
Tax payable	1,705

Note

The savings income is taxed at the rate of 20% at source and no further liability on it arises as A is not a higher rate taxpayer. The tax payable by self assessment relates to the property income.

Example

B has the following income for the year ended 5th April 2012.

Income from property	£44,000
Building Society interest (net)	£ 8,000

Compute B's income tax liability for 2011/12.

Solution: B's income tax computation 2011/12

	£
Income from property	44,000
Building Society interest	10,000
	54,000
Less PA	(7,475)
Taxable income	46,525
Tax liability	
n/a @ 10%	0
35,000 @ 20%	7,000
35,000	7,000
11,525 @ 40%	4,610
46,525	11,610
Less income tax deducted at source	2,000
Tax payable	9,610

Note

Savings income is deemed to be the top slice of taxable income in this example.

Dividends received from UK and foreign companies

4. The main features are as follows:

a) There is a tax credit attached to each dividend received. In 2011/12, this includes dividends received by individuals from companies resident outside the UK.

b) The tax credit is one-ninth, which is equivalent to a tax credit rate of 10% of the sum of the distribution and the tax credit

e.g. Dividend payment	900	
Tax credit 10/90 × 900	100	(10% × 1,000)
Gross dividend	1,000	

c) Dividend income is taxed in the basic rate band at the "ordinary dividend rate" of 10%.

d) Where tax is payable on dividend income in the higher rate band, it is charged on the gross dividend at the "dividend upper rate", which is 32.5%, and within the additional rate band, dividends are taxed at 42.5%.

e) Dividend income is treated as the top slice of income when allocating rate bands.

f) Non-taxpayers do not have the right to repayment of the dividend tax credit of 10% in the event that this exceeds their final tax liability on the income.

Example

R, aged 50, has the following income for the year ended 5th April 2012.

Income from property	£24,000
Dividend income received	£1,800

Compute R's income tax liability for 2011/12.

Solution: R's income tax liability 2011/12

	£
Income from property	24,000
Dividends 1,800	
Tax credit 10/90 × 200	2,000
	26,000
PA	7,475
	18,525
Tax payable	
n/a @ 10%	0
16,525 @ 20% non savings	3,305
2,000 @ 10% dividends	200
18,525	3,505
Less tax credits on dividends	200
Tax payable by self assessment	3,305

Notes

i) Dividends have a tax credit of 10/90 attached to each payment.

ii) The basic rate of tax is deemed to be satisfied.

iii) Dividend income is treated as the top slice of taxable income and taxed at the Dividend rate of 10%.

iv) The tax credit is not repayable to non-taxpayers.

Example

A, aged 50, has the following income for the year ended 5th April 2012.

Income from property	£25,000
Dividend income received	£18,000

Compute A's income tax liability for 2011/12, and the tax payable by self assessment.

Solution: A 2011/12

	£
Income from property	25,000
Dividends 18,000 x 100/90	20,000
	45,000
PA	(7,475)
	37,525
Tax liability	
n/a @ 10%	0
17,525 @ 20%	3,505
17,475 @ 10%	1,747
35,000	5,252
2,525 @ 32.5%	820
37,525	6,072
less income tax on dividends	(2,000)
Tax payable by self assessment	4,072

Note

Dividend income is taxed partly at 10% (£17,475) and partly at 32.5% (£2,525).

Dividends from Real Estate Investment Trusts (REITs)

5. REITS are a special kind of investment vehicle, which invests in property for letting. They have existed in the UK since 2007. Individuals can buy shares in REITS and receive "dividends" on these. However, "dividends" from REITS have not been subjected to tax in the REIT before being distributed. They do not carry a dividend tax credit. They are not taxed on the individual as dividends, but as property rental income. (See chapter 9.)

Individual savings accounts (ISAs)

6. The main features are summarised as follows:

a) ISAs can only be held by UK resident individuals over the age of 16. All income received from an ISA, whether interest or dividends, is exempt from income tax. Trustees cannot hold ISAs for other people.

b) The capital must remain in an ISA for five years from the date of first investment but can then be withdrawn. Income can be withdrawn at any time.

c) ISAs are classified into two categories, 'cash' and 'stocks and shares'.

d) The annual subscription limit for 2011/12 is £10,640, of which not more than £5,320 may be in cash. (Up to the full amount can be invested in shares). From 6 April 2011 onwards individuals from the age of 16 can invest in a cash ISA, but not a shares ISA, so their limit is £5,320.

e) As ISAs have existed since 1999 with an annual subscription limit, some individuals could by 2011/12 have large holdings built up in ISAs and generating tax-free capital gains (for shares), interest or dividends. There is no overall lifetime limit but ISA status is lost on all investments if the individual ceases permanently to be UK resident.

f) ISA income does not have to be recorded in the self assessment tax return. It is not included as income for the purposes of the calculations causing restriction (abatement) of the Personal Age Allowance and the Married Couple's Allowance for higher incomes.

g) The 1/9 tax credit on dividends received in a stocks and shares ISA is not repayable to the investor, despite the "tax-free" description, but there is no further tax liability on ISA dividends. Thus they are exempt from the higher and additional rates.

h) The government intends to introduce in autumn 2011 a junior ISA for children not holding a child trust fund.

Other exempt savings income, apart from ISAs

7. Interest on some NSI savings products is exempt from tax: Index-Linked Savings Certificates, Fixed Interest Savings Certificates, Children's Bonus Bonds, and Premium Bond prizes.

Enterprise investment scheme (EIS) shareholdings

8. Investment in new EIS shares attracts income tax relief at 30% on the amount subscribed if qualifying conditions are met by the EIS company. Any income from EIS shares is taxable as dividend income. However if the shares are held for capital growth for long enough, the gains can be tax-free. (See Capital Gains Tax Chapters 26 to 33.)

The main features of the EIS that apply for income tax are as follow.

a) An individual can subscribe for up to £500,000 (minimum £500) of EIS company shares in 2011/12 and obtain tax relief at the 30% rate. The relief is given "in terms of tax", so 30% of the qualifying subscription cost is deducted from the tax liability of the individual. (The relief is not available to the extent the individual's tax liability was met by the tax credits on dividend income, as these are not repayable.) Legislation s included in the Finance Act 2011 to increase the rate of tax relief to 30% from 6 April 2011. The rate of relief was 20% in previous years.

b) To qualify for income tax relief

   i) the eligible shares must be held for at least three years from the date the trade started or the date of the share subscription, whichever is later.

   ii) the individual and his associates (this includes family, business partners etc) must not be connected with the company as an employee, lender or shareholder at any time in the two years before the subscription or the three years after it (except as a shareholder of no more than 30% of the share and loan capital combined).

   iii) In particular the individual must not be an employee of the company and must not receive any value from the company during the three years qualifying period.

c) The company must also retain EIS status throughout the qualifying 3-year period. An EIS company must be an unquoted trading company (or an unquoted company that is preparing to trade) and various other conditions apply as to its activities. EIS status is granted to the company by HMRC and notified to the investors by the company.

d) 50% of the amount invested by an individual in EIS shares between 6th April and 5th October in any year can be carried back to the previous tax year subject to a maximum of £25,000.

e) If EIS shares are sold at a loss, the taxpayer can elect to claim that loss against total income of that or the preceding tax year, instead of as a capital loss. If this is done they must deduct from the loss claim the value of EIS relief given against income tax.

f) For other EIS reliefs affecting investors' capital gains tax (one of them available even if the individual is connected with, works for or controls the company), see Chapter 32.

Venture capital trusts

9. The main features of this type of investment are as follow.

   a) The scheme is designed to stimulate individual investment in a spread of unquoted trading companies through the mechanism of quoted venture capital trusts.

b) Individuals can invest up to a maximum of £200,000 per tax year in VCT shares, attracting income tax relief at 30%, providing the shares are held for five years.

c) Dividends received are tax-free.

d) There are also capital gains tax reliefs (see chapter 32)

Miscellaneous income

10. a) **Patent royalties received.** These are normally received by individuals under deduction of basic rate income tax at source. The gross amount is treated as non-savings income under section 579 ITTOIA 2005. (Miscellaneous income for an investor, and trading income if the recipient is the original creator).

b) **Copyright royalties received**. These are paid to authors gross without deduction of income tax at source. Like patent royalties, they are taxable under section 579 as non-savings income (miscellaneous income for an investor in the copyright, and trading income if the recipient is the original creator).

Pre-owned assets

11. As a result of some inheritance tax anti-avoidance legislation , an income tax charge may arise in respect of any benefit people get by having free or low-cost enjoyment of assets they formerly owned but gave away, or provided the funds to purchase. The charge applies to both tangible and intangible assets but will not apply to the extent that:

i) The property in question ceased to be owned before 18 March 1986;

ii) property formerly owned by a taxpayer is currently owned by their spouse;

iii) the asset in question still counts as part of the taxpayer's estate for inheritance tax purposes under the existing 'gift with reservation' rules (see chapters 35-36);

iv) the property was sold by the taxpayer at an arm's length price, paid in cash: going further than the consultation document, this will not be restricted to sales between unconnected parties;

v) the taxpayer was formerly the owner of an asset only by virtue of a will or intestacy which has subsequently been varied by agreement between the beneficiaries; or

vi) any enjoyment of the property is no more than incidental, including cases where an out-and-out gift to a family member comes to benefit the donor following a change in their circumstances. This exception was introduced to cover the situation where an individual contributes to the price of a house for other family members, but later moves to live there as a result of age of age or infirmity. The exception would not apply if the donor expected to live in the house when the gift was made.

Student self-testing questions

1. The following information relates to the self-assessment tax return of A.

	Year ended 5th April 2012
	£
A salary (gross before PAYE deducted of £7,970)	46,000
Taxed dividends (net)	540
Bank interest (net)	400
Gift Aid to Oxfam (net)	1,600

Calculate the income tax liability and remaining tax payable by A for 2011/12.

Solution: Income tax computation 2011/12

	Non-savings income £	Savings income £	Dividend income £	Total £
Salary	46,000			46,000
Bank interest 400 x 100/80		500		500
Dividends 540 x 10/9			600	600
Total income				47,100
Personal allowance	(7,475)			(7,475)
Taxable income	38,525	500	600	39,625

Tax liability:

		n/a	@ 10%	0
On non-savings:	Basic rate	35,000	@ 20%	7,000
	Extend for gift aid	2,000	@ 20%	400
		37,000		
	Higher rate	1,525	@ 40%	610
		38,525		
On savings:	Higher rate	500	@ 40%	200
On dividends	Higher rate	600	@ 32.5%	195
		39,625		
Tax liability				8,405
Less tax paid under PAYE				(7,970)
Tax deducted on savings income				(100)
Tax credit on dividends				(60)
Tax still payable				275

Notes

i) Tax credit on dividends 10/90 × 540 = £60 + tax on bank interest 20/80 × 400 = £100.

ii) The basic rate is extended by (1,600 x 100/80) £2,000 to £37,000 to give relief for the Gift Aid at the higher rate.

2. Emma, a 25 year-old, has business trading profits of £22,500 for the year ended 5 April 2012. She also receives building society interest of £6,400 (net).

What is her income after tax for 2011/12, ignoring National Insurance?

Solution

	Non-savings £	Savings £	Total £
Income:			
Trading income	22,500		22,500
Taxed investment income BSI gross		8,000	8,000
Net Income	22,500	8,000	30,500
Personal allowance	(7,475)		(7,475)
Taxable income	15,025	8,000	23,025
Tax:			
At savings rate	n/a x 10%		0
At basic rate	23,025 x 20%		4,605
	23,025		
Income tax borne on taxable income			4,605
(= Income tax liability)			
Tax suffered on building society interest			(1,600)
Final income tax due 31.1.2013			3,005
Calculation of income after tax but before NIC:			
Profits of trading			22,500
Net Building society interest			6,400
			28,900
Balance of tax payable			3,005
Net income after tax			25,895

Note: for self-employed NIC see Chapter 17

3. Chris, aged 35, has the following income and outgoings for the year ended 5 April 2012

Business trading profits	7,840
Salary	22,975
Bank interest received net	416
Building society interest received net	712
Rent receivable from let property (not in Chris's own home)	1,890
Allowable expenses of employment	95

Requirement: Calculate Chris's tax liability for 2011/12

Solution

	Non savings	Savings	Total
	£	£	£
Income from employment			
(22,975 – 95)	22,880		22,880
Income from trading	7,840		7,840
Income from property	1,890		1,890
Bank & building society interest (712+416) x 100/80		1,410	1,410
Total income/ Net income	32,610	1,410	34,020
Personal allowance	(7,475)		(7,475)
Taxable income	25,135	1,410	26,545
Non savings			
n/a x 10%	0		
25,135 x 20%	5,027		
Savings			
1,410 x 20%	282		
Tax borne = Tax liability	5,309		

Note: The question asked for tax liability, not tax payable, so the calculation stops here.

4. Pat has the following income for 2011/12

	£
Income from his business	19,450
Dividends	1,944
Income from property	1,000

Pat claims the personal allowance of £7,475

Requirement:

(a) Calculate Pat's income tax payable by self assessment for 2011/12

(b) How would your answer differ if Pat had £144,450 income from his business?

Solution

Pat : Income tax computation for 2011/12

			Non-savings	Dividends	Total
Income			£	£	£
Income from property			1,000		1,000
Income from trading			19,450		19,450
Dividends gross (1944 x 10/9)				2,160	2,160
Net income			20,450	2,160	22,610
Less: personal allowances			(7,475)		(7,475)
Taxable income			12,975	2,160	15,135
Income tax					
	n/a	x 10%	0		
	12,975	x 20%	2,595		
	2,160	x 10%	216		
	15,135				
Tax borne			2,811		
Less: tax credits on dividends					
	2,160 x 10%		(216)		
Tax payable by self assessment			2,595		

Part b Income tax computation for 2011/12

Income	Non-savings	Dividends	
Income from property	1,000		1,000
Income from trading	144,450		144,450
Dividends gross (as before)		2,160	2,160
Net income	145,450	2,160	147,610

Personal allowance	7,475			
Restricted				
(147,610 – 100,000) x 1/2				
	(23,805)	0		0
Taxable income		145,450	2,160	147,610
Income tax				
n/a x 10%		0		
35,000 x 20%		7,000		
110,450 x 40%		44,180		
2,160 x 32.5%		702		
147,610				
Tax liability		51,882		
Less: tax credits on dividends				
2,160 x 10%		(216)		
Tax payable by self assessment		51,666		

Questions without answers

1. Jacqui, aged 35, has the following income for 2011/12

Salary (PAYE £5,200)	26,000
Building society interest (net)	4,800
Dividends (net)	11,700
Gift aid donation (net)	700

Requirement: Calculate Jacqui's income tax payable.

2. Jackie is aged 42.

Requirement: Calculate Jackie's tax position in 2011/12 if her income was:

a) trading profits of £148,500 and building society interest of £6,400 net.

b) trading profits of £2,500 and building society interest of £6,400 net.

7 Income from employment I – general aspects

Introduction

1. This chapter is concerned with the taxation of income from employment.

The major part deals with the taxation of earnings from employment and benefits treated as earnings. A summary of the benefits treated as earnings within the 'benefits code' is provided, showing the taxation effects on "Non P11D employees" (employees earning less than £8,500pa), and "P11D employees" (i.e. directors, and employees earning more than £8,500pa).

The legislative background is contained in the Income Tax (Earnings and Pensions) Act 2003.

Summary of taxable income

2. Tax under the ITEPA 2003 is charged in respect of the following income.

   Employment income.

   Pension income.

   Social security income.

Employment

3. a) Employment includes in particular:
   - i) any employment under a contract of service;
   - ii) any employment under a contract of apprenticeship;
   - iii) any employment in the service of the crown; and
   - iv) any office, which includes in particular any position which has an existence independent of the person who holds it and may be filled by successive holders.

   b) Employment is usually evidenced by a contract of employment or service. On the other hand, a contract for services rendered is normally associated with self-employment, the rewards of which are assessable as trading profits. See Hall v Lorimer 1992 CA STC 23.

   c) An office can be thought of as a position with duties attached to it which do not change with the holder. It is the income of the office that is taxable. Examples of office holders are: a judge; a trustee or executor; a town clerk; a company director or secretary.

Employment income

4. a) Earnings, in relation to employment, means:
   - i) any salary, wages or fee;

ii) any gratuity or other profit or incidental benefit of any kind obtained by the employee if it is money or money's worth; or

iii) anything else that constitutes either earnings or specific income of the employment.

(Before ITEPA 2003, the term "emoluments" covered the chargeable earnings of an employment. This word is still found in discussions of the leading cases, but no longer appears in the main statute.)

b) For the purposes of subsection (ii) money's worth means something that is:

i) of direct monetary value to the employee; or,

ii) capable of being converted into money or something of direct monetary value to the employee.

Receipt of money earnings

5. a) General earnings consisting of money are to be treated as received at the earliest of the following times:

Rule 1

The time when payment is made of or on account of the earnings.

Rule 2

The time when a person becomes entitled to payment of or on account of the earnings.

Rule 3

If the employee is a director of a company and the earnings are from employment with the company (whether or not as a director), whichever is the earliest:

i) the time when sums on account of the earnings are credited in the company's accounts or records (whether or not there is any restriction on the right to draw the sums);

ii) if the amount of the earnings for a period is determined by the end of the period, the time when the period ends, and

iii) if the amount of the earnings for a period is not determined until after the period has ended, the time when the amount is determined.

b) Rule 3 applies if the employee is a director of the company at any time in the tax year in which the time mentioned falls.

c) In this section director means:

i) in relation to a company whose affairs are managed by a board of directors or similar body, a member of that body;

ii) in relation to a company whose affairs are managed by a single director or similar person, that director or person, and

iii) in relation to a company whose affairs are managed by the members themselves, a member of the company, and includes any person in accordance with whose directions or instructions the directors of the company (as defined above) are accustomed to act.

d) For the purposes of subsection (c) a person is not to be regarded as a person in accordance with whose directions or instructions the directors of the company are accustomed to act merely because the directors act on advice given by that person in a professional capacity.

Gifts and voluntary payments

6. In principle, gifts and voluntary payments unconnected with an employment are not taxable, but there is an assumption that payments from an employer to an employee are in return for services, apart from the situations noted below.

a) Reasonable gifts made by an employer in connection with marriage or retirement are not taxable.

b) Long service awards in the form of gifts of objects or non cash vouchers are not taxed providing that: the award is in respect of not less than 20 years service; no similar payment has been made during the previous 10 years; and the cost to the employer does not exceed £50 (previously £20) for each year of service. A cash award would be taxable.

c) Benefit matches for sports personnel are not taxed providing that they are not a condition of their employment contract. However, transfer signing fees were held to be taxable earnings from employment.

d) An award of £130 to a bank clerk for passing his professional examinations was held to be a non-taxable gift. (However, if such an exam payment were set out as a conditional payment in the contract of employment, it would be taxable.)

e) £1,000 paid by the Football Association to each of the members of the 1966 England World Cup team was held to be a gift and not remuneration.

f) Tips of an employed taxi driver were held to be taxable in Calvert v Wainwright 1947 27 TC 475. ITEPA section 62 now confirms specifically that tips and gratuities received from customers by employed taxi drivers, postmen, hairdressers, waiters, etc, in respect of services provided, are in principle taxable as earnings.

g) The Easter offerings given to a vicar in response to an appeal made by his Bishop were held to be taxable.

h) Gifts from third parties made to an employee in the course of employment costing not more than £100 in any tax year are not taxable, by concession.

i) Payments to a footballer to join his new club were held to be taxable as emoluments (now called simply "earnings" since 2003), i.e. as a payment on retirement or removal from office. The inducement fee was also held to be taxable as emoluments from an employment.

Benefits treated as earnings – Benefits Code

7. As a general rule, all benefits provided by an employer are treated as earnings in accordance with the Benefits Code. However, some benefits are specifically exempted.

The Benefits Code is now found in ITEPA 2003, including general rules for taxing all benefits for which no special rules exist, and particular rules dealing with specific types of benefit, e.g.,

Cars, vans and related benefits	Loans
Living accommodation	Cash equivalent benefits

Lower-paid employment ("Non-P11D employment" - ITEPA 2003)

8. a) The Benefits Code does not apply to an employment in relation to a tax year if:

i) it is lower-paid employment in relation to that year, and

ii) condition A or B is met.

An employment is lower-paid employment in relation to a tax year if the earnings rate for the employment for the year is less than £8,500.

b) Condition A is that the employee is not employed as a director of a company.

c) Condition B is that the employee is employed as a director of a company but has no material interest (broadly defined as a 5% shareholding) in the company and either:

i) the employment is as a full-time working director, or

ii) the company is non-profit-making or is established for charitable purposes only.

Non-profit-making means that the company does not carry on a trade and its functions do not consist wholly or mainly in the holding of investments or other property.

The taxation of benefits as earnings

9. The taxation of benefits in kind as earnings depends upon placing a value on the goods and services that are provided at less than full cost, for an employee. This is achieved as follows.

a) In respect of non-P11D employees, unless provided otherwise by ITEPA, benefits are only taxable if they can be converted into money's worth, at their second-hand value.

Benefits which cannot be converted into money's worth are therefore in principle not taxable, e.g. interest free loans, or the private use of a company car.

b) For directors and employees earning £8,500 or more (called 'P11D employees' in ITEPA), benefits are taxable whether or not they can be converted into money's worth. The P11D employee rules state that benefits are to be valued at the cost to the employer, unless another prescribed method is laid down (eg. as it is for private cars).

c) Following the decision in Pepper v Hart HL 1992 STC 898 (which related to the taxable value of a private school place provided to the child of a school-teacher), benefits provided 'in-house' in the form of the employer's own goods or services are valued at 'cost to the employer' on the marginal cost basis, not on an average cost basis including a share of overheads.

   In Pepper v Hart it was held that as long as there were still places unfilled at the school, the taxable value of the benefit of a free school place for a teacher's child was only the incidental cost of books, meals and laundry, so far as not paid by the employee.

Directors and employees earning £8,500 or more p.a. (P11D Employees)

10. The rules of the benefit code apply to P11D employees. These are defined as:

a) Any employee whose total earnings, plus reimbursed expenses and benefits treated as earnings, are greater than £8,500 p.a. (this means 'at a rate of £8,500 pa', so if the employee was only employed for 3 months in a tax year the applicable limit is £2,125)

b) Any director who has a material interest in the company i.e. is either the owner of or able to control more than 5% of the ordinary share capital of the company.

c) A full-time working director with a material interest of 5% or less in the company, if his or her total earnings and benefits treated as earnings is greater than £8,500 p.a.

Employers must complete a return (form P11D) of all expenses reimbursed and all benefits in kind provided each year in respect of each P11D employee, unless a dispensation is obtained (see 11 below).

Any benefits provided for the members of the family or household of an employee are treated as if they were provided for the employee personally. The term family or household covers the employee's spouse, children and their spouses, his or her parents, servants, dependants and guests.

Dispensations

11. Where the company is able to explain to HMRC its arrangements for paying expenses and providing benefits, and satisfy HMRC that these would be fully matched by a 'necessary expenses of employment' in the personal tax computation of the employee, then it is possible for the employer to obtain a 'P11D dispensation' in respect of named types of expense reimbursements and benefits.

The nature of the expenses covered by a dispensation depends to some extent on the particular circumstances, but they can cover:

travelling and subsistence

cost of entertaining incurred wholly and exclusively for business

subscriptions to professional bodies related to employment

telephone rentals to employees on call outside normal hours.

overnight incidental cost allowances within the permitted tax-free limits

Benchmark rates for day subsistence

12. HMRC has introduced advisory benchmark scale rates for day subsistence, which will not give rise to taxable benefits. Employers may alternatively use dispensations agreed with HMRC. The benchmark rates are:

Five-hour rate – Up to £5 may be paid where the worker has been away from his or her home or normal place of work for at least five hours, and incurred cost on a meal.

Ten-hour rate - Up to £10 may be paid where the worker has been away from his or her home or normal place of work for at least ten hours, and incurred cost on a meal, or meals.

Breakfast rate (irregular early starters only) – Up to £5 may be paid where a worker leaves home earlier than usual and before 6.00 a.m. and incurs a cost on breakfast taken away from home.

Late evening meal rate (irregular late finishers only) – Up to £15 may be paid where the employee finishes work late after 8.00 p.m. and buys a meal which he or she would usually eat at home.

Summary of benefits treated as earnings 2011/12

13 The Benefit Code	**P11D employees**
Private use of employer's car	Car and fuel benefits (see below)
Private use of employer's van	Van and fuel benefits (see below)
Accommodation (see below).	Accommodation can be wholly or partly exempt, otherwise taxed on rent paid, or annual value if owned, plus expenses paid, plus an additional charge for accommodation costing more than £75,000. (see below)
Board and lodging	Taxed on cost to the employer
Suits and clothing	Taxed on cost to employer
Medical insurance	Premiums paid by employer taxable
Beneficial loans (see below)	Generally taxable at the deemed interest saving, with some exceptions
Cash vouchers, saving certificates	Full value taxable (even if employer pays less)

Assets loaned	20% of market value when first provided is taxable for each complete tax year
Assets transferred	Taxed on increase in value enjoyed (see section 24 below for details)
Season tickets and transport vouchers.	Taxed on cost to the employer
Private sick pay	Taxed on amount received
Scholarships provided by reason of employment	Taxed on cost to employer
Employer-subsidised nursery facilities	Taxed on cost to employer (unless the nursery is at the workplace, in which case it is a tax-free benefit)
Loan written off	Taxed on full value

14. Benefits with exemptions from Income Tax	**All Employees**
"Green commuting" benefits, including: loan of cycling equipment, works buses, subsidised fares on public buses.	Tax-free
Mobile telephones with private use	One phone provided to employee personally is exempt; any further phones are taxed at cost to the employer
Job related accommodation (see below).	Accommodation can be wholly or partly exempt, otherwise taxed on rental cost or annual value, plus expenses paid (see below)
Industrial clothing	Tax-free
New share option schemes	Grant of option and any discount on exercise is not subject to income tax, CGT on final disposal
Savings related approved share options	Not subject to income tax, CGT applies on final disposal
Free or subsidised meals in staff canteen	Tax-free if generally available to all employees

In-house sports facilities	Not taxable, if not available to the public
Overnight expenses	Up to £5 per night UK, and £10 overseas, exempt
Workplace nurseries	Not taxable
Child care vouchers	Up to £55 per week exempt. Limited, for new joiners of a scheme in 2011/12 or later, to basic rate tax relief only.

Private use of employer-provided motor cars 2011/12 – benefit valuation rules

15.

	£	£
The benefit is calculated as follows:		
List price of car and optional accessories when first provided	X	
Less capital contribution (if any) by employee	(X)	
= **Net Value**		X
Value of benefit = Percentage of net value based on		
CO_2 emissions (per table)		X
Less reduction for unavailability		(X)
Less payment by employee (if any) for private use		(X)
Car **Benefit treated as earnings**		X

Notes

i) The percentage of the net value of car is determined from the CO_2 emission table reproduced below.

ii) List price is the published price when first registered plus the list price of any optional accessories. If the car has no published price a 'notional value' will be used.

iii) Where the car is more than 15 years old at the end of the income tax year of assessment then its value, if more than £15,000, is taken to be £15,000.

iv) There is no maximum for the list price taken into account for any car in applying the rules. In 2010/11 the price was limited to £80,000, but this upper limit was removed for 2011/12.

v) The benefit before private use is reduced proportionally if the car is not available for any period of 30 days or more in the year. Periods of less than 30 days of unavailability are ignored.

vi) Where the employee makes a capital contribution to the cost of the car, then, subject to a maximum of £5,000, the amount is deducted from the list price.

vii) Where an employee is required to make a revenue contribution to the employer for private use of the car, then this is deducted in arriving at the assessable benefit.

16. CO_2 emission table

CO_2 emissions in grams per kilometre	% of list price
2011/12	**Petrol cars**
75 or less	5%
80-120	10%
125	15%
130	16%
135	17%
140	18%
145	19%
150	20%
155	21%
160	22%
165	23%
170	24%
175	25%
180	26%
185	27%
190	28%
195	29%
200	30%
205	31%
210	32%
215	33%
220	34%
225	35%

Notes

i) The exact CO_2 figure is always rounded down to the nearest 5 grams per kilometre (g/km). For example, CO_2 emissions of 188g/km are treated as 185g/km.

ii) The maximum charge is 35% of the list price.

iii) The rates in the above table are increased for cars using diesel fuel by 3% (but not so as to increase the maximum percentage above 35%):

iv) For cars with no approved CO_2 emissions figure, the percentage of the car's list price to be taxed is determined using the car's engine size. One scale is for all cars registered before 1998; and another for the small number of cars registered from 1998 onwards without approved CO_2 emissions.

Engine size (cc)	Pre 1998 car	1998 or later car
0 – 1,400	15%	15%
1,401 – 2,000	22%	25%
2,001 and over	32%	35%

Example

A has a Ford petrol company car for 2011/12 with a list price of £16,000. CO_2 emissions are 187g/km.

Compute the assessable car benefit for 2011/12.

Solution: Cash equivalent benefit 2011/12

List price × 27% = 16,000 × 27%	4,320

Notes

i) CO_2 emissions of 187g/km rounded down to 185g/km.

ii) Percentage for 2011/12 per table for 185g/km is 27%;

iii) Alternatively the percentage may be calculated:

185g – 125g = 60g

60g/5g = 12 graduations of 5g at 1% each, above the 15% base level for 125g/km emissions

15% + 12% = 27%.

Private motor cars 2011/12 £18,800 – fuel benefit CO_2%

17. Fuel scale charges for employees receiving free fuel for private mileage in company cars are based on the same percentage as was calculated for the car benefit (linked with the car's CO_2 emissions) which is applied to a scale charge of £18,800 (2010/11 £18,000).

The same percentage is used for valuing the car and fuel benefits for Class 1A National Insurance contributions (see Chapter 17).

The fuel benefit charge is proportionally reduced where an employee stops receiving free fuel part way through the tax year. However, opting back into free fuel in the same year will result in a full year's charge becoming payable.

Notes

i) The fuel benefit is reduced to nil where all private fuel is paid for by the employee/director.

ii) The charge is not reduced pound for pound to the extent that the employee/director reimburses only a partial amount of private fuel provided

iii) Employers (not employees) are required to pay NIC at the main rate of 13.8% on cars and fuel provided for private use of employees earning more than £8,500 p.a. This liability is assessed on an annual basis using the car scale and fuel rates quoted above, and collected in July following the previous tax year.

iv) Where one car is used jointly by two or more employees a separate liability can arise in respect of each user.

Example

A is employed by Beta Ltd and is provided with a car (CO_2 emissions 240g/km) which cost £22,000 on 1st January 2005. A used the car during 2011/12 and Beta Ltd paid for all fuel, business and private. A pays £300 to the company each year for the use of the car.

Calculate the value of any car benefit for 2011/12.

Solution: A – Value of motor car benefits 2011/12

	£
Motor car benefit 35% × £22,000	7,700
Less contribution	300
	7,400
Motor fuel benefit	6,580
Total	13,980

Notes: i) The CO_2 emission percentage for 240g/km is 35% for 2011/12.

ii) The fuel benefit is 35% × £18,800 i.e. 6,300

Vans - private use of vans 2011/12

18. Private use of a van with a vehicle weight up to 3,500kg is taxed at a fixed benefit value of £3,000 for a full tax year (proportionately reduced for part-year use only).

There is no taxable benefit where the employee is required to take the van home overnight for security or efficiency, so long as there is no other personal use.

Vans - fuel benefit 2011/12

19. Where the employer provides fuel for unrestricted private use in a company van, there is a flat rate fuel benefit of £500.

Authorised mileage allowance payments

20. Where an employee uses his or her own vehicle to complete business journeys, mileage allowances are allowed by HMRC to be paid tax-free up to rates deemed not to involve a profit element for the employee. There are separate rates for cars and vans, motorbikes, bicycles and for carrying passengers.

An authorised mileage allowance payment must be:-

a) paid to the employee, not to someone else for the employee's advantage

b) specifically for business mileage

The rates are as follows:	2011/12	2010/11
Cars and vans		
- First 10,000 miles	45p per mile	40p per mile
- Over 10,000 miles	25p per mile	25p per mile
Motorcycles	24p per mile	24p per mile
Bicycles	20p per mile	20p per mile
Carrying a passenger	5p per passenger	5p per passenger

Where employers pay less than the statutory rate, employees can claim tax relief on the difference. Payments made in excess of the statutory rates will be liable to tax and NICs.

Living accommodation

21. Cash-equivalent value of benefits (directors and all employees)

Where any individual (i.e. earnings could be above or below the £8,500 threshold) is provided with living accommodation by an employer, then subject to certain exemptions noted below, he or she is liable to tax on the cash equivalent value of the benefit. This is defined as

Annual value + Cost of ancillary services – Employee's contribution – business use.

Annual value is the gross rating value of the property whether rented or owned by the employer. (Gross rateable values can still be obtained from Government sources although domestic rates are no longer collected based on them, having been replaced by council tax.).

For a property rented by the employer, the annual value benefit is the greater of the annual value or the actual rent paid by the employer.

Cost of ancillary services is the total of any expenses incurred in providing services such as heating, lighting, rates, domestic services or gardening, and the provision of furniture.

Employee's contribution means any rent paid by an employee. Any payment by the employee towards expenses may also be deducted from the value of the taxable benefit.

Business use means the proportion of any benefit attributable to business use.

Total exemption from annual value

An individual is not taxed on the annual value of the accommodation providing it is:

a) necessary for the proper performance of his or her duties, or

b) customary for the better performance of his or her duties, and in general provided for others in the same employment, or

c) required for security reasons.

A full time working director with less than 5% interest in a company is eligible for the exemption under (a) and (b) but not under (c). All other directors are ineligible for any exemption.

Partial exemption from ancillary costs benefit

If an individual is exempted under any of the categories noted above, then the taxable value of all ancillary services is limited to a maximum of 10% of net assessable earnings for the year, i.e. remuneration benefits etc. (excluding ancillary benefits) less any amount paid by the employee for use of the services.

Net earnings (ignoring the benefit in question) are after deducting allowable expenses, superannuation and approved pension scheme payments and capital allowances.

Example

Q is an employee of T plc occupying a house with an annual value of £1,000, which is exempt accommodation. The employer pays the following expenses:

	£
Heating and lighting	1,200
Gardening	800
Domestic servant's wages	500
Furniture costing	10,000

Q's salary for the year 2011/12 is £40,000 and he pays the company £300 for the use of the services.

Calculate the value of the benefit for 2011/12.

Solution: Cash equivalent value accommodation benefit 2011/12

i)	Annual value of property exempted		–
	Ancillary services:		
	Heating and lighting	1,200	
	Domestic service	500	
	Gardening	800	2,500
	Use of furniture 20% × 10,000		2,000
			4,500
less employee contribution			(300)
			4,200
ii)	Q – Emoluments £40,000 × 10%		4,000
	Less contribution paid by Q		(300)
	Cash equivalent benefit		3,700

Notes

i) The furniture is valued as an asset loaned to an employee, at 20% of its market value when first provided, i.e. £10,000.

ii) If Q's occupation was non-exempted, the value of his benefit would be the gross value plus expenses i.e. £1,000 plus £4,500 less contribution of £300 i.e. £5,200. The emolument restriction applies in this case.

Living accommodation costing more than £75,000

22. An extra taxable benefit arises where the employer owns accommodation if:

a) The cost of providing accommodation is greater than £75,000, and

b) The living accommodation is provided for a person by reason of his office or employment, and

c) The occupier is liable to a taxable benefit in respect of the living accommodation, as outlined in the previous section. If the employee is exempt from the 'annual value' charge noted above he or she is also exempted under this heading.

d) The additional value is determined from:

ORI % × [cost or deemed cost – £75,000] – "contribution" by taxpayer

ORI % = the official rate of interest in force on the 6th April of the year of assessment. For 2011/12 it is 4%.

Cost = cost of acquisition + cost of improvements carried out before year of assessment.

"Contribution" = the amount by which any rent paid by tenant is greater than the annual value of the accommodation.

The £75,000 disregard has not been increased since this legislation was introduced in the late 1980s. Its purpose was to deal with the situation where residential annual values were vastly less than market rents, especially in London. Without this deemed loan benefit an employer could reduce the taxable benefit by buying property rather than renting it.

Example

J plc acquired a property in October 2008 for £265,000 which had an annual rateable value of £10,000. In May 2012 improvements costing £25,000 were incurred. On 7th April 2011, Z, the marketing director, occupied the property paying a rent of £5,000 p.a. He paid £15,000 towards the original cost.

Calculate the value of the taxable benefits in kind for 2011/12.

Solution: Cash equivalent value of benefit 2011/12

	£	£
2011/12 value of accommodation benefit:		
Annual value of property	10,000	
Less rent paid by director	(5,000)	5,000
Additional value of accommodation:		
Cost of accommodation	265,000	
Part of cost paid by director	(15,000)	
Benefit loaned to director	250,000	
Less exempt amount	(75,000)	

	175,000	
Less "contribution"	0	
	175,000	
4% × 175,000 =		7,000
		12,000

Notes

i) The £12,000 would be benefit earnings of Z for 2011/12 chargeable to income tax.

ii) The improvement expenditure of £25,000 will fall into the computation of the additional value for 2012/13.

iii) As the rent paid by Z is less than the gross value there is no further deduction for this rent in the computation of the additional value.

iv) The official rate of interest for 2011/12 is 4%.

v) Where the property is not occupied throughout the year the charge is pro-rated.

vi) Additional value is [175,000] × 4% = £7,000.

Assets other than cars – private use

23. Where assets are made available for use by P11D employees, then the annual benefit is calculated as follows.

a) Land and property (other than accommodation) is valued at a market rent.

b) Other assets e.g. a company motor cycle, are valued at 20% of the original market value when provided, or if higher, the rental paid by the employer.

Assets transferred to an employee

24. If an asset made available on loan to a P11D employee is subsequently acquired by that person, then the assessable benefit on the acquisition is the greater of:

a) the excess of the current market price over the price paid by the employee and,

b) the excess of the market value when first provided for use by the employee, less any amounts assessed as annual benefits (at 20%) over the price paid by the employee.

When an employee buys, from his or her employer, a previously loaned computer or bicycle for its full market value, no tax charge arises on the transfer of ownership.

Beneficial loans

25. Where an individual is provided with an interest-free or cheap loan, in principle the financial benefit derived from such an arrangement is taxable. There is an exemption for a loan that at no time in the tax year exceeded £5,000.

This allows employers to offer season ticket loans to employees without tax consequences.

Employees earning less than £8,500 p.a. are not assessable on loan benefits, since the benefit is not convertible into cash. The following are the benefit valuation rules for everyone else:

a) The loan giving rise to the benefit to an employee or his or her relative must be obtained due to an employment.

b) The assessable amount is calculated by two methods, (see below) using the **official rate of interest** less any interest actually paid by the employee.

(ORI 2011/12 = 4%)

c) No benefit arises where the interest on such a loan would normally qualify for tax relief such as a loan for the purchase of plant or machinery for use in employment.

d) If the value of all the loans outstanding during the year does not exceed £5,000, there will be no charge.

Methods of calculation

26. I. **Average method**

a) This method averages the loan over the tax year by reference to the opening and closing balances at the beginning and end of the year (or date of creation and discharge) and applies the official rate to this amount.

b) Interest paid if any on the loan is deducted from the amount computed in (a) above to determine the amount chargeable to tax.

c) This method is applied automatically unless an election is made, by either the taxpayer or HMRC, to apply the second method.

Example

Z Ltd makes an interest free loan to R, one of its higher paid employees on the 1st October 2011 of £24,000, repayable by eight quarterly instalments of £3,000, payable on the 1st January, April, July and October. The first payment is made on the 1st January 2012. Calculate the assessable benefit for 2011/12. The official rate is 4%.

Solution: Computation of interest benefit 2011/12

		£
1.10.2011	Loan granted	24,000
5.4.2012	Balance of loan outstanding	
	24,000 – 6,000	18,000
		42,000
	Average loan outstanding	
	$\frac{42,000}{2}$	21,000

Period of loan

1.10.2011–5.4.2012 = 6 months. (i.e. completed tax months)

$$\text{Interest } 4\% \times \frac{6}{12} \times 21{,}000 = \qquad \underline{420}$$

Assessable benefit 2011/12 420

27. II. **Alternative method**

a) Under this method, the interest is calculated on the balance outstanding on a day-to-day basis, using the official rate of interest.

b) Any interest paid is deducted from the amount calculated in (a) above.

Example

Using the data relating to Z Ltd in the previous example, calculate the assessable benefit under the alternative method.

Solution: Computation of interest benefit – 2011/12

		£	£	£
1.10.2011	Loan granted	24,000		
1.1.2012	Loan repayment	3,000		
		21,000		
	Number of days from 1.10.2011 to 1.1.2012 = 92			
	Interest 92/365 × 4% × 24,000			242
1.1.2012	Balance outstanding		21,000	
1.4.2012	Loan repayment		3,000	
5.4.2012	Balance outstanding		18,000	
No. of days from	1.1.2012 to 1.4.2012 = 90			
do.	1.4.2012 to 5.4.2012 = 5			
Interest	90/365 ×4% × 21,000			207
	5/365 × 4% × 18,000			10
Assessable benefit 2011/12				217

Deductions from earnings

28. The following may be deducted in arriving at taxable earnings under the ITEPA.

a) Expenses falling within the general rule of Section 336. This states that a deduction from earnings is allowed for an amount if

  i) the employee is obliged to incur and pay it as holder of the employment and

  ii) the amount is incurred wholly and exclusively and necessary for the performance of the duties of the office or employment; for example, industrial clothing; tools of trade. Travelling expenses from home to place of employer's business are not permitted deductions, see Ricketts v Colquhoun 1926 10 TC 118.

b) Travel and subsistence costs incurred on employer's business. Further rules on travel and subsistence costs are as follows:

   i) site-based employees receive tax relief for travel and subsistence costs from home to the site.

   ii) employees who have a normal place of work may receive tax relief for the cost of business journeys which start from home if these are no longer than the equivalent journey starting from work.

   iii) employees who are seconded by their employer to a temporary place of work receive tax relief for subsistence and travel to the temporary workplace, providing there is the intention to return to the normal place of work within two years.

c) Those deductions permitted specifically by ITEPA e.g. fees and subscriptions to professional bodies, and contributions to exempt approved pension schemes.

d) Capital allowances on plant or machinery necessarily provided by the employee in order to perform his duties may be deducted, e.g. office equipment, but not a private car.

e) Payroll giving to an approved charity or charitable agency (see section 33 below).

None of the above deductions can be claimed against total income as allowable payments. They can only be deducted from employment earnings.

Employee liabilities and indemnity insurance

29. Income tax relief is available to employees and directors for payments they make to secure indemnity insurance against liability claims arising from their job or to meet uninsured work-related liabilities. Relief is also extended to situations where the employer or a third party pays the insurance which would otherwise give rise to a benefit in kind. The cost of the insurance is deducted as an expense from the earnings in the year in which the payment is made.

Relief is extended to payments made by ex-employees for periods of up to six years after the year in which employment ceases.

Employees' incidental expenses paid by employer

30. Payments by employers of certain miscellaneous personal expenses incurred by employees are exempt from income tax and NIC.

The exemption covers incidental expenses such as newspapers, telephone calls home and laundry bills incurred by employees when they stay away from home overnight on business.

Payments of up to £5.00 a night in the UK (£10.00 outside the UK) are tax free. However, if the employer pays sums greater than these limits, the whole amount becomes taxable.

Removal expenses and benefits

31. The amount that can be paid tax-free to an employee as qualifying removal expenses has been greatly restricted since the 1990s and now stands at £8,000. This figure has not been increased for many years. The low limit means that in 2011/12 relocating employees who are at all adequately reimbursed for genuine removal costs will find that part of the payment is liable to tax and NIC.

Within this limit, any of the following removal expenses may be paid tax-free in connection with moving his or her home (for work reasons).

a) sums paid to an employee, or to a third party on behalf of an employee in respect of quantifying removal expenses, and

b) any qualifying removal benefit provided for the employee or to members of his or her family or household (including sons and daughters in law, servants, dependants and guests).

I) Qualifying removal expenses comprise the following.

1) Expenses of disposal, i.e. legal expenses, loan redemption penalties, estate agents' or auctioneers' fees, advertising costs, disconnection charges, and rent and maintenance, etc. costs during an unoccupied period in the employee's former residence.

2) Expenses of acquisition i.e. legal expenses, procurement fees, survey fees, etc. relating to the acquisition by the employee of an interest in his or her new residence.

3) Expenses of abortive acquisition.

4) Expenses of transporting belongings, i.e. expenses, including insurance, temporary storage and disconnection and reconnection of appliances, connected with transporting domestic belongings of the employee and of members of his or her family or household from the former to the new residence.

5) Travelling and subsistence expenses (subsistence meaning food, drink and temporary accommodation).

6) Bridging loan expenses, i.e. interest payable by the employee on loan raised at least partly because there is a gap between the incurring of expenditure in acquiring the new residence and the receipt of the proceeds of the disposal of the former residence.

7) Duplicate expenses, i.e. net expenses incurred as a result of the change in the replacement of domestic goods used at the former residence but unsuitable for use at the new residence.

II) Qualifying removal benefits consist of benefits or services corresponding to the seven headings noted above, with the restriction that the provision of a car or van for general private use is excluded from category 5 above.

Payroll giving to charities

32. An employee can obtain income tax relief on donations to a charity to any value. The main features of the scheme are as follows:

a) Schemes are operated through charity agencies that must be approved by HMRC.

b) Employers are legally bound to pay the donation over to the agency charity and they may not be refunded to the employee.

c) The employer will make the deduction of the donation before PAYE is applied, in the same way that pension contributions are dealt with. This is called the 'net pay' arrangements.

d) National Insurance contributions are due on the gross pay amount, before payroll giving.

e) Pensioners can be incorporated into the scheme if they are subject to PAYE.

Gift aid

33. Gift Aid has no special connection with employment income, but is included here for comparison, because it has taken over from payroll giving as the main way in which individuals in the UK make tax allowable charitable donations.

An individual can make a single gift of any amount to a qualifying charity.

The gift is treated as if the donor had made a payment to a charity equal to the grossed up amount of the gift.

A payment of £800.00 to a charity is treated as a gross gift of

800 x 100/(100-20) = 800 x 100/80 = £1,000.

The charity can recover tax from HMRC. Higher and additional rate taxpayers can obtain relief at the higher or additional rate on the gross amount (see Chapter 5).

Termination of employment

34. The provisions concerned with the taxation of payments for loss of office or employment are in Part 6 Chapter 3 of the ITEPA, and these include the following:

a) First £30,000 exempt, if "ex gratia" or redundancy compensation;

Excess over £30,000 taxed in full as employment earnings.

b) Complete or partial exemption is available for termination payments which relate to foreign service, ie employment duties performed wholly outside the UK.

c) A general exemption applies to payments made:

i) on the death or permanent disability of an employee

    ii) to benefits provided under a pension scheme
    iii) to terminal payments made to members of the armed forces.

d) Termination payments and benefits are taxed as income in the year in which they are actually received rather than the year of termination.

e) A loss-of-office payment made to an employee who is at or nearing retirement age may be rejected by HMRC as not genuinely paid to compensate for the pain and distress of being dismissed , unemployed : HMRC have been known to argue that such payment is in reality a unapproved lump-sum pension payment.

Example

N is dismissed as a director of T Limited on the 1st October 2011 and receives the sum of £35,000 by way of compensation. N has no service agreement with the company.

N's other income for 2011/12 is a salary of £38,000, and bank interest of £3,200 (net).

Calculate the taxable income.

Solution: N's taxable income 2011/12

	£	£
Income from employment		38,000
Bank interest gross 3,200 x 100/80		4,000
Terminal payment	35,000	
Less exempt amount	(30,000)	5,000
Taxable income (£4000 savings, rest non-savings)		47,000
Personal allowance		(7,475)
Taxable income		39,525

Outplacement counselling

35. This involves the provision of services normally paid for by the employer, for employees who are or become redundant, to help them find new work. Expenditure will be exempt from tax whether or not it exceeds the £30,000 limit for redundancy payments.

Pension income

36. Any pension paid to a former employee is taxable as earned income on the recipient. This includes payments from company operated schemes, from schemes operated by assurance companies, and voluntary payments where there is no formal pension scheme.

If the scheme is approved by and registered with HMRC then any contributions made by the employee into the pension scheme are deductible from taxable earnings. The company's contributions are also allowed as an expense in computing taxable profits.

Pensions paid by the state are taxable as social security income of the recipient and these include: retirement pensions, widows' pensions and service pensions.

Social security pensions

37. The following social security pensions are taxed as earned income of the recipient.

State pension	Graduated retirement pension
State Second Pension	Widowed Parent's Allowance

Social security benefits

38. The following benefits are taxable under this heading.

Job seeker's allowance

Carer's allowance

Statutory maternity pay/paternity pay

Bereavement allowance; but not the bereavement lump sum payment of £2,000

Statutory sick pay

Incapacity benefit

Company share options schemes (CSOP)

39. The UK government's policy is to encourage limited participation by employees as shareholders in the employing group or company. To obtain HMRC approval a CSOP must be open to all permanent employees on similar terms.

Under these schemes an employee is given the option to buy shares at a fixed price in future. Any discount on current market value reflected in the option exercise price will not be subject to income tax as a benefit in kind if the shares are retained for a minimum (usually either 3 or 5 years) period. The main features of these schemes are as follows.

a) The exercise price of the share option is fixed at not less than the market value, at the time the employee gets his or her option.

b) The share option must relate to part of the ordinary share capital of the company.

c) Employee participants in the scheme must work at least 20 hours a week for the company, and full-time working directors must work at least 25 hours a week.

d) Options are limited in value to £30,000, being the value of the shares under option at the date of grant.

e) There is normally no income tax liability on the grant of the option or on any increase in the value of the shares providing that the option is used at least three years and no more than ten years after the employee exercised the option.

f) On an eventual disposal of the shares by the employee the normal rules of capital gains tax apply, and the cost for CGT is the exercise price of the options.

g) A savings-related share option scheme is also available with similar rules to those noted above.

h) Approved schemes are not limited to quoted shares but include shares in a company which is not controlled by other companies.

Enterprise management incentive schemes (EMI)

40. The main features of these schemes are:

a) unlike CSOPs they can be restricted to key employees and still get approval;

b) employees can receive options with an annual value of up to £120,000;

c) to be eligible employees must work for the employing company for at least 25 hours per week or, if less, for 75% of their working time;

d) trading companies with gross assets equal to or less than £30m can participate in the scheme;

e) there is no income tax liability on the grant of the option or on any increase in the value of the shares between grant and exercise, providing that the option is only exercisable, and actually exercised, at least three years and no more than ten years after the grant;

e) on the eventual disposal of the shares then the normal rules of capital gains tax apply.

Share incentive plans (SIP)

41. The rules for these Plans enable a company to give an employee free shares worth up to £3,000 per tax year (for which performance targets may be set) and also enable an employee to buy shares worth up to £1,500 per tax year (called 'partnership shares') by deductions from salary. The company may also give the employee up to two free shares for each share he or she purchases. All shares have to be held in the Plan for specified periods to remain free of tax and national insurance. The amount of dividends on Plan shares that can be reinvested in the plan tax-free on a participant's behalf are £1,500 per year.

8 Income from employment: II – PAYE

Introduction

1. The Pay As You Earn system of deducting income tax at source applies to monetary employment income (see Chapter 7) from offices or employments such as wages, salaries, bonuses, taxable expenses and pensions. The system is operated by employers who collect the income tax on behalf of HMRC.

National Insurance contributions payable be employees on money earnings (see Chapter 17) are also collected under the PAYE system.

The PAYE system does not apply to self-employed individuals. However there is a system of deducting tax from payments to subcontractors in the construction industry, known as CIS (the Construction Industry Scheme), which for the principal contractor has some similarities to PAYE including the payment dates for the tax.

Taxable pay

2. For the purposes of tax deduction pay includes the following:

a) salaries, wages, fees, bonuses, overtime, commissions, pensions, honoraria, etc. whether paid weekly or monthly

b) holiday pay

c) Christmas boxes in cash

d) terminal payments (see Chapter 7)

e) statutory sick pay (see Chapter 17).

The tax on benefits in kind, other than cash benefits is, as far as practicable, taken into account by adjustment of the employees' PAYE coding notice (see below) rather than by being treated as pay, see 7 below.

Net pay arrangements

3. In calculating taxable pay, the employer must deduct any contribution to a pension scheme on which the employee is entitled to relief from tax as an expense. The agreement applies only to schemes which have been approved by the HMRC Pension Schemes Office. The net pay scheme also applies to the payroll deduction scheme for gifts to charities.

Code numbers

4. a) All employees, including Directors and some pensioners, are allocated a code number which is based on the personal allowances, reliefs and charges on income available to individuals, as evidenced by the information contained in their Tax Return. In appropriate cases the code number also takes into consideration other factors such as untaxed interest and tax underpaid or overpaid in previous years.

The PAYE code number is equal to the sum of all allowances and reliefs, less the last digit, rounded down.

Other income such as casual profits, property income, interest and state pensions may be recognised in the main tax code number. The tax code then tells the employer the amount of tax-free employment income an employee may earn, and the level of income at which tax must start to be deducted.

b) Some of the letters used at present after a code number are as follows:

- L Basic personal allowance
- P Personal allowance for those aged 65 – 74
- V Personal allowance for those aged 65 – 74 plus the MCAA
- Y Personal allowance for those aged 75 or over
- K An amount to be added to pay
- T This is for cases in which the taxpayer notifies the tax office that he or she does not wish to use one of the other letters.

c) The following special codes are also used:

- BR This means that income tax is to be deducted from all pay at the basic rate. It is also called the "emergency code", because employers use it temporarily while waiting for evidence of the correct code to be received from the employee or HMRC.
- F This code, followed by a number, means that the tax due on a social security benefit, e.g. retirement pension, or widow's pension or allowance, is to be collected from the taxpayer's earnings from an employment.
- NT This means that no tax is to be deducted.
- D This code followed by a number means that the pension/benefit is more than the allowances.
- OT This code means that no allowances have been given against the earnings from the employment

Deductions from allowances in code numbers

5. The following items may be deducted in arriving at the code number:

a) State benefits or pension

b) Income from property

c) Unemployment benefit

d) Untaxed interest

e) Taxable expense allowances and benefits in kind

f) "Excessive basic rate" adjustment where too much tax is paid at the basic rate and not enough at the higher rate

g) Savings or dividend income taxed at the higher rate

h) Allowance restriction. This is to compensate for allowances and reliefs that are due in terms of tax, at a lower rate than the marginal rate, e.g. MCA.

i) Tax underpaid in earlier years: under self-assessment the balancing amount due for last year by a PAYE taxpayer may be 'coded out' up to £2,000. (See chapter 3)

K Codes

6. 'K' codes arise where there is a negative coding allowance, which usually occurs where the non-PAYE income, e.g. accommodation benefits in kind, are greater than the total allowances due.

The excess number shown is added to the taxable pay and taxed accordingly.

Statutory sick pay

7. Where any amount of sick pay, whether private or statutory sick pay, is paid to an employee then this is treated as gross pay for the purposes of both deduction of income tax and National Insurance contributions. 100% of the gross amount of any SSP entered on the deduction working sheet, together with an extra amount to compensate for the employer's NIC paid on the SSP called 'NIC compensation on SSP' is deductible from the total NIC due for the period if the employer's SSP payments for an income tax month exceed 13% of their Class 1 contributions for that month. See Chapter 17 for National Insurance.

Forms for use with PAYE

8.	P2	Notice of coding – tells employee their code, showing how it is calculated
	P9 various	Coding Notice to employer (does not show how the code is calculated)
	P9D	Return of expenses payments, fees, bonuses etc. for an employee to whom form P11D is not applicable (a "non-P11D employee").
	P11D	Return for the tax year of reimbursed expense payments, and the value of all benefits provided, to or for each "P11D employee". An exact copy of the form P11D must be given to the employee also, for information.
	P11D (b)	Employer's form sent to HMRC showing the Class IA National Insurance due on P11D non-cash benefits to employees (see chapter 17)
	P14	End of year return of pay, tax and National Insurance contributions for each employee.
	P35	Employer's annual statement, declaration and certificate of the total of P14

P45	Particulars on leaving an employment: current PAYE tax code of the employee, cumulative pay and tax and NIC deducted so far this tax year. Part 1. Front page - sent to HMRC by old employer. Part 2. Copy retained by old employer. Part 3. Copy given by employee to new employer, who sends it to HMRC Part 4. Copy retained by employee.
P46	Notice to HMRC of details regarding a new employee without a P45.
P46 (expat)	Notice to HMRC of a new employee who is on secondment from abroad
P60	Employer's certificate of total pay and tax deducted, given to employee at the end of the year.

Payment of tax

9. Income tax and National Insurance contributions (employer's and employee's) are due for payment not later than the 19th day of each month. Thus the tax and NIC due for period 8, 2011, which covers the period from 6th November to 5th December, is payable on or before the 19th December 2011.

The National Insurance payable to HMRC by employers may be reduced by statutory sick pay paid.

Employers whose average monthly payments of PAYE and NIC are less than £1,500 in total are allowed to pay quarterly. Payments are due on the following dates: 19th July, 19th October, 19th January and 19th April. Similar arrangements apply to contractors in the construction industry.

Interest on late payment of tax

10. Late payments of PAYE (income tax, Class 1 and 1A NIC contributions) are charged interest at the prescribed rate.

Bonus and commission payments

11. As a general principle, taxable pay is assessed in the year in which it is paid under the rules of the ITEPA as outlined in Chapter 7.

Thus, for example, where J has a salary of £20,000 for 2010/11 and earns a commission of an additional £5,000 for that year which is only ascertained and paid in July 2011, then the commission is assessable in the tax year 2011/12.

Directors' remuneration

12. The rules of taxation under ITEPA apply to directors and all other employees or office-holders. (See Chapter 7)

PAYE regulations

13. Regulations for the operation of PAYE are provided under Part II of the ITEPA and embodied in The Income Tax (PAYE) Regulations 2003 (S.1 2003/2682). Where failure to operate PAYE takes place it is the employer who is primarily responsible for making good any deficit and an assessment subject to appeal may be issued for recovery. If the determined amount is not paid within 90 days then the tax may be recovered from an employee/director. This can arise where the employee/director received his or her emoluments knowing that the employer has wilfully failed to deduct tax. In general wilful means 'with intention or deliberate' – see R v IRC Chisholm 1981 STC 253.

In R v CIR ex parte Keys and Cook 1987 QB. DT. 25.5.87 the controlling directors of a company which failed to deduct income tax under the PAYE system from their remuneration were held to be liable for that tax.

PAYE investigations

14. The main regulations enabling HMRC to undertake a PAYE audit are contained in The Income Tax (PAYE) Regulations 2003.

These provide that, wherever called upon to do so by any authorised officer of HMRC, the employer must produce at his or her premises to that officer, for inspection, all wages sheets, deduction working sheets and other documents and records whatsoever, relating to the calculation or payment of PAYE income of his employees, or to the deduction of tax from such income, or to the amount of earnings-related NI contributions payable.

End of year returns

15. At the end of the tax year the employer must complete and return to the tax office the following forms:

Form P35 (P35SC for sub-contractors within the CIS)

Form P14.

The P35 is the employer's Annual Statement, Declaration and Certificate, which is signed by the employer and returned to the tax office by 19th May following the end of the income tax year.

The back of Form P35 contains a summary of the deduction card totals for the year, while the front contains a list of questions concerning payments for casual employment, expenses and Forms P11D etc.

Form P14 is an end of year summary made out in respect of each employee for whom a tax deduction card (P11) has been used.

The P14 is in effect a summary of all the P60 information for all employees on the staff at the end of the year, plus all P45 information for those who have left during the year.

An automatic penalty will arise if end of year returns are late. The statutory deadline for the P14 and P35 is the 19th May. There is a penalty of £100 per month (or part) per unit of 50 employees. Employees must be given their individual P60 information by 1st June.

Where forms P11D are required then these must be returned to the tax office before 6th July following the end of the tax year, with an initial penalty of up to £300 per 50 employees.

Online PAYE filing

Online filing increases the efficiency of the PAYE system.

Student self-testing question

T's P60 for the year 2011/12 shows total gross pay of £31,500. He is employed as a sales manager with a salary of £22,000 p.a. for 2011/12. In addition, he receives commission paid by reference to the profits shown by the company's accounts amounting to:

Year ended 31st December 2010 £9,500 – confirmed and paid June 2011

Year ended 31st December 2011 £13,000 – confirmed and paid June 2012

Tax deducted under PAYE for the year 2011/12, according to the P60, amounted to £4,600. T has no other income.

Compute the Income Tax liability for 2011/12.

Solution: Income tax computation 2011/12

		£
Income from employment	- salary	22,000
	- commission paid June 2011	9,500
		31,500
Personal allowance		(7,475)
		24,025
	n/a @ 10%	0
	24,025 @ 20%	4,805
Tax liability	24,025	4,805
Less deducted by PAYE		(4,600)
Amount due		205

Note: It is likely this liability will be "coded out" in future PAYE coding provided HMRC knows about it in time.

9 Income from UK land and property

Introduction

1. This chapter deals with the rules applicable to UK Property income, together with computational examples.

Basis of charge

2. a) The definition of "property business income" is: "the annual profits or gains arising from any business carried on for the exploitation, as a source of rents or other receipts, of any estate interest, or rights in or over land in the UK".

Receipts in relation to land include:

i) any payment in respect of any licence to occupy or otherwise use any land, or in respect of the exercise of any further right over land.

ii) rent charges, ground annuals and any other annual payments derived from land.

b) The following are not taxed as property income, but as trade profits.

i) Profits or gains from the occupation of any woodland managed on a commercial basis.

ii) Farming and agriculture.

iii) Mines, quarries and similar concerns.

c) The letting of furnished accommodation is taxed as property income, with no separate assessment for the furniture element; but there are special rules for furnished holiday lettings, which can be treated as a kind of trade for limited purposes (see section 11).

d) The letting of caravans on fixed sites and houseboats on fixed moorings is chargeable as property income, while the hire or leasing of mobile caravans and boats is a trade.

Basis of assessment

3 The basis of assessment is the annual profits or gains arising in the income tax year. It is not possible to use an 'accounts basis' of taxation for property income tax. Therefore, the income tax basis period runs from 6 April to 5 April even if the letting business draws up its balance sheet at some other date for business reasons.

Computation of taxable profits of a 'property business'

4. a) All profits or gains are computed in accordance with the rules applicable to a trading business (i.e. normal commercial accounting principles).

b) All property situated in the UK is to be treated as one letting business regardless of the type of lease or whether or not it is furnished accommodation.

c) Any business expenditure incurred in earning the profits from letting is to be deducted from the total pooled income, and is subject to the same rules for allowable expenditure as apply to trading income.

d) Capital allowances available are given as an expense chargeable against property income so that the adjusted taxable profits are after capital allowances.

e) Capital allowances are not generally available for plant and machinery (e.g. furniture) located in a let dwelling house. Therefore, the renewals basis or the wear and tear allowance for furnished lettings (currently 10% of annual rents less council tax) applies for furniture and moveable items included in the lease. Capital allowances are available for plant and machinery used for estate management or property maintenance (e.g. office equipment, or garden lawnmowers). Landlords can claim a deduction up to a maximum of £1,500 when they install loft or cavity wall insulation.

f) Interest payable in respect of a loan to acquire assets for a property business is allowed as a deduction in calculating the profits of the business, under the same rules as apply to other expenses incurred for the purposes of the business. This would allow interest on a 'buy to let' mortgage to be set against rents.

Rental business losses must in general be carried forward and set against future profits from the same rental business. Where there are capital allowances due in respect of the rental business, that part of the loss attributable to capital allowances may be set against total income of the year as an allowable payment. The rest of the loss, if any, must still be carried forward.

Expenses of properties which are let on uncommercial terms (for example, at a nominal rent to a relative) can only be deducted up to the amount of the rent or other receipts generated by the uncommercially let property. The excess of the expenses over the receipts from the uncommercially let property cannot be deducted in the rental business and therefore cannot create a loss. These expenses can, however, be set against future rentals from the same tenant, should the lease be renegotiated.

Example

Z purchased a freehold factory site on the 6th April 2011 which he lets for an annual rental of £15,000 payable quarterly in advance. First payment due 6th April 2011 covered the period to 5th July 2011. Property expenses paid by Z for the year to 5th April 2012 amounted to £2,500 and interest paid on a loan to purchase the factory was £3,500.

Landlord's capital allowances for the 12 months to 5th April 2012 have been agreed at £2,000.

Compute Z's property business income for 2011/12.

Solution: Z's property business income 2011/12

		£	£
Rents receivable	- let 12 months for £15,000		15,000
Less expenses:-			
	Property expenses	2,500	
	Loan interest	3,500	6,000
Adjusted profit			9,000
Less capital allowances			(2,000)
Taxable profits			7,000

Notes

i) The rents received are computed on an accruals basis.

ii) Property business income is not 'trading income'.

Lease premiums

5. One way of looking at lease premiums is to regard them as a capitalised part of future rental income which would otherwise have been received by way of annual rent. They include any sum whether payable to the immediate or a superior landlord, arising in connection with the granting of a lease, but not arising from an assignment, of an existing lease.

Under an assignment, the new tenant takes the position of the original tenant, with the same terms and conditions.

Where a lease is granted (but not assigned) at a premium, for a period not exceeding 50 years, then the landlord is deemed to be in receipt of a rental income equal to the premium, less an allowance of 2% of the premium for each complete year of the lease remaining, excluding the first 12 month period. This deduction recognises what tax law treats as the 'capital element' of the premium.

Example

B granted a lease for 24 years of his warehouse to a trader on the following terms:

> A lease premium of £12,000 to be paid on 1 May 2011 and an annual rent of £7,200 payable monthly in advance from 1 May 2011.

B's allowable letting expenditure for the year 2011/12 was £5,800.

Solution: B Property business income 2011/12

	£
Lease premium received	12,000
Less 2% × 12,000 × (24 – 1)	
i.e. 1/50 × 12,000 × 23	(5,520)
	6,480
Annual rent 7,200 × 11/12	6,600
	13,080
Less allowable expenses	(5,800)
Taxable profits	7,280

In effect the lease premium is discounted by reference to its duration, and the longer the unexpired portion, the greater the discount. Thus if a lease had 49 years to run, the discount would be:

(49 – 1) × 2% i.e. 96%.

A premium on a lease for a period greater than 51 years would not be taxed as property income. If the lease premium is paid by instalments, the full amount, less the discount, is taxable in the usual way. However, if hardship can be proved the landlord's tax on a premium may be paid over a period not exceeding 8 years.

Sub-leases and assignments

6. The creation of a sub-lease out of the main or head lease for a premium could give rise to an income tax liability for the intermediate lessee; but assignment of that lease by the tenant could not, as it is a potentially chargeable disposal under the CGT rules. Where a charge to income tax arises from the granting of a lease at a premium, and this is followed by the lessee granting a sub-lease at a premium, then any liability arising on the second occasion is reduced, as shown in the example below.

Example

J grants a lease for 20 years to M for a premium of £10,000. After occupying the premises for five years, M grants a sub-lease to another person for a period of 10 years at a premium of £6,000.

Show the computation of J's and M's liability to income tax.

Solution: Computation of J's liability

	£
Lease premium (20 year lease)	10,000
Less 2% × 10,000 × (20 – 1) i.e. 38% × 10,000	(3,800)
	6,200

Computation of M's liability

	£
Lease premium (10 year lease)	6,000
Less 2% × 6,000 × (10 – 1) i.e. 18% × 6,000	(1,080)
	4,920

$$4,920 - \frac{\text{Duration of sub lease}}{\text{Duration of head lease}} \times \text{(Income on main lease premium of J, i.e. 6,200)}$$

4,920 – [10/20 × 6,200] i.e. 1,820

The amount of the lease premium assessed on M is therefore £1,820.

Lease premiums and the lessee

7. Where the lessee pays a lease premium on the granting of a lease, then a proportion of that premium may be set against the following:

a) any trading income, providing the premises are used for business purposes.

In effect, the amount of the premium assessed as income of the lessor can be claimed as a deemed rental expense of trading by the lessee, the taxable portion being spread over the remaining life of the lease.

b) any rental income or lease premium received from any sub lease granted by the lessee, as illustrated above in section 6 (a).

Example

S is granted a lease of premises to be used for trading purposes, for a period of 20 years at an annual rent of £600 p.a. and an initial lease premium of £32,000.

	£
Lease premium	32,000
Less capital element 2% × 32,000 × (20 – 1) i.e. 38% × 32,000	(12,160)
Lease premium charged on lessor as income	19,840

Deemed rental relief available to S is $\frac{19840}{20}$ i.e. £992 p.a.

Furnished accommodation

8. Rents from furnished accommodation are assessed as property income.

Relief for depreciation of furniture and fittings is not given, but relief for gradual replacement of furniture and kitchen equipment etc. may be given either on the 'renewals method', or as an agreed 10% deduction from "net rent", known as the wear and tear allowance.

Net rent is gross rent receivable less charges and services normally borne by a tenant, but in fact under some inclusive leases borne by the landlord, such as council tax, water and sewerage rates.

Rent a room

9. For 2011/12 householders can let rooms in their own home for £4,250 p.a. tax free provided it is furnished accommodation with the following effects.

a) Gross rents up to £4,250 p.a. are exempt.

b) Gross rents greater than £4,250 are taxable as follows:

i) pay tax on excess rent i.e. (rent – £4,250); or

ii) pay tax on gross rents less expenses including capital allowances.

A claim must be made for the exemption not to be applied in writing within one year of the tax year to which it is to apply. If joint householders let a room or rooms in the same home the exemption is split between them.

It is possible for the income to be taxed as trade profits where the taxpayer is deemed to be carrying on a trade, and provides substantial services in connection with the letting e.g. meals, cleaning, laundry, and goods and services of a similar nature.

10. Real Estate Investment Trusts (REITS)

As already noted in chapter 6 (section 5), dividends from REITS are treated on the self-assessment return and in the tax computation as property rental income of the period in which they are received.

11. Furnished Holiday Lettings

The property income from a special class of letting called "furnished holiday letting" is subject to additional rules giving more generous offset of losses and certain other "trading" treatments such as the ability to treat FHL property as a business asset for capital taxes purposes (see Parts IV and V), and FHL income as net relevant earnings for pension contributions (see Chapter 16).

The FHL rules were originally due to be repealed with effect from tax year 2010/11, but this was repealed after the General Election of June 2010. Full details of the qualifying conditions for FHL treatment in 2011/12 are at:

http://www.hmrc.gov.uk/manuals/pimmanual/PIM4105.htm

Student self-testing questions

1. (a) Geta rents out a room in her house. In 2011/12 she received rent of £4,900 and paid expenses of £2,000.

Requirement: Calculate the amount of Geta's assessable income from property for 2011/12 assuming any necessary election is made. (2 marks)

1. (b) Raj owns three flats which he lets out.

Flat 1. The flat was purchased on 6 September 2011 and let unfurnished from 29 September 2011. The new seven-year lease was at an annual rental of £3,500 payable on the usual quarter days. The incoming tenant was required to pay a premium of £5,000.

Flat 2. The flat was let unfurnished at an annual rental of £4,000 on a lease which expired on 23 June 2011, the rent having been paid on the usual quarter days. The property was re-let on 30 September 2011 on the same conditions at an annual rent of £6,000.

Flat 3. The flat was let furnished for the full year on a weekly rental of £120.

The usual quarter days are 25 March, 24 June, 29 September and 25 December.

Details of expenditure in the year ended 5 April 2012 were:

	Flat 1	Flat 2	Flat 3
	£	£	£
Insurance	400	200	600
Repairs	4,500	600	350
Water rates	-	-	400
Council tax	-	-	800

Notes

1. The amount of £400 was an annual premium

2. £4,000 was spent on UPVC double glazing on 10 September 2011 replacing leaking wooden window frames. To replace with wooden frames would have cost £1,200. The windows needed to be repaired to make Flat 1 habitable.

Requirement: Calculate Raj's profit from property for 2011/12. (8 marks)

NB Calculations may be made to the nearest month.

(c) State how loss relief is given where the loss is in respect of property let unfurnished. (1 mark)

(Total: 11 marks)

Solutions

(a) Geta

		£
(i)	Ordinary basis	£
	Rent	4,900
	Expenses	2,000
		2,900
(ii)	Alternative basis	£
	Rent	4,900
	'Rent a room' limit	4,250
		650

Assessment of income from property (lower figure) £650

(b) Raj: Income from property 2011-12

		£	£
Rent receivable	- Flat 1		1,750 (W1)
	- Flat 2		4,000 (W2)
	- Flat 3		6,240
Premium on lease	- Flat 1		4,400 (W3)
			16,390
Insurance	- Flat 1	233 (W4)	
	- Flats 2&3	800	
Repairs	- Flat 1	500 (W5)	
	- Flats 2&3	950	
Wear and Tear			
Allowance	- Flat 3	504 (W6)	
Water rates and council tax	- Flat 3	1,200	4,187
Property business income			12,203

Working 1

6/12 x £3,500	£1,750

Working 2

3/12 x £4,000	£1,000
6/12 x £6,000	£3,000
	£4,000

Working 3

Premium	£5,000
less (7-1) x 2%	600
	£4,400

Working 4

7/12 x £400	£233

Working 5

As the replacement of the window frames was necessary before the flat could be let, the expenditure is deemed to be capital expenditure and not, therefore, allowable.

Working 6

The 'wear and tear' allowance is 10% of the rent less the items which are the tenant's responsibility, ie, water rates and council tax.

£6,240 – (400 + 800) = £5,040; 10% - £504

If the expenses of letting property in a tax year exceed the income from property, the excess is carried forward to be set against the first available income from property in the future.

Question without answer

1. Arthur has two shops for unfurnished letting.

Shop 1. The annual rent was £3,000 on a lease which expired on 30 June 2011. Arthur took advantage of the shop being empty to carry out repairs and decorating. The shop was let to another tenant on a five-year lease at £4,000 per annum from 1 October 2011.

Shop 2. The shop was purchased on 10 April 2011 and required treatment to wood damaged by dry-rot before it could be let out. Arthur also undertook some normal re-decorating work before the shop was let on 1 October 2011 on a seven-year lease at an annual rental of £6,000. A premium of £2,000 was received from the incoming tenant upon signing the lease 1 October 2011.

The rent for both shops was due in advance on the usual calendar quarter days (25 March, 24 June, 29 September and 25 December).

The following expenditure was incurred for 2011/12:

	Shop 1	Shop 2
	£	£
Insurance	190	300
Ground rent	10	40
Repairs and decorating	3,900 (1)	5,000 (2)
Accountancy	250	250
Advertising for tenant	100	100

Notes:

(1) Includes £2,500 for re-roofing the shop following gale damage in February 2012. Because the roof had been badly maintained the insurance company refused to pay for the repair work.

(2) Includes £3,000 for remedial treatment to dry-rot damaged wood flooring discovered when the shop was bought. The floor needed to be repaired before the shop could be let out.

Requirement: Calculate the income assessable on Arthur for 2011/12 from the shops, and show how any losses would be dealt with.

(ACCA Tax Framework Pilot paper updated)

10 Income taxed as trade profits: I - general principles

Introduction

1. In this chapter the determination of business income for taxation purposes is examined. A summary of the order in which the topic is considered is given first. This is followed by an analysis of the main principles within each topic heading. Questions and answers illustrating the adjustment of profit for tax purposes appear at the end of the chapter.

The "basis period "rules for matching trade profits to tax years are dealt with in the next two chapters. These basis period rules only apply for unincorporated traders as companies have their own tax periods (see part III).

However most of the principles discussed in this chapter on determining trade profits, apply equally to unincorporated and incorporated traders. If a rule differs when the trader is a company, it will be briefly noted in this chapter. In other cases, the trade profits rules may be assumed to be the same for companies. This chapter is therefore also relevant to answering questions on computing the trade profits of companies (see Part III for corporation tax).

List of topic headings

2. Charge to tax on trade profits

The concept of trading

Capital receipts

General rules restricting deductions

Allowable expenditure

Non-allowable expenditure

Asset values for tax purposes

Other adjustment of profits

Charge to tax on trade profits

3. Income derived from a trade in the form of profits is chargeable to income tax where the trade is conducted by an individual, either as a sole trader or in partnership with someone else. Where the trade is undertaken by an incorporated person, typically a company, trade profits from part of the total taxable profit charged to corporation tax, not income tax.

> **Tax** under this heading is charged on the full amount of the profits or gains arising or accruing to any person residing in the UK from any trade, profession or vocation, whether carried on in the UK or elsewhere.

Trade is defined to include any 'manufacture, adventure, or concern in the nature of trade'. All farming and market gardening in the UK are treated as carrying on a trade.

The concept of trading

4. As Lord Wilberforce pointed out in the case of Ransome v Higgs 1974 STC 539 'everyone is supposed to know what trade means so Parliament, which wrote this into the law in 1799, has wisely abstained from defining it'.

The Royal Commission on the Taxation of Profits and Income in 1955 looked at all the case law up to that time and listed 'six badges of trade' which are still used by the courts in determining what is a trade or an adventure in the nature of trade. These are:

a) the subject matter of the realisation

b) the length of the period of ownership

c) the frequency or number of similar transactions by the same person

d) supplementary work on or in connection with the property realised

e) the circumstances that were responsible for the realisation

f) motive.

5. The present day meaning of "trade" must therefore be deduced from a mixture of previous and subsequent legal decisions, accepted practice and the 'badges of trade'. The following is a summary of some general points.

a) Betting and gambling are not regarded as trading unless carried on by an authorised bookmaker. This is in HMRC's interest as statistically more losses than profits are made by gamblers.

b) The fact that a trade is illegal does not mean that it is not taxable.

c) Even where transactions are concluded within a year they may nevertheless be regarded as 'annual profits or gains'. See Martin v Lowry 1926 11 TC 297.

d) Isolated transactions can amount to trading if they are of a commercial nature. See Wisdom v Chamberlain 1968 45 TC 92. Rutledge v CIR 1929 14 TC 490.

e) All farming and market gardening carried on in the UK are treated as carrying on a trade.

f) Changes in the activities of a trade may amount to the establishment of a separate and different trade for tax purposes.

Capital receipts

6. Profits arising from 'capital transactions' are not treated as income for the purposes of trade profits, although they may be taxable under some other tax, such as capital gains tax. Any profit on the disposal of a fixed asset would not therefore be subject to income tax, and conversely, any loss arising would not be allowed as a business expense. There is an exception for companies disposing of bonds or intangible assets at a profit, which can be income under the corporation tax legislation.

Where a person receives a sum of money which is paid under a legal obligation in return for goods or services provided in the normal course of trade, then this is clearly a trading transaction. However, where the receipt does not arise from any contractual obligation, and the person has given nothing in return, then it may be accepted as a non-taxable receipt. Some types of such transaction are considered below.

Exchange profit and loss

For individuals exchange profits and losses arising from trading transactions are potentially chargeable to taxation whereas those relating to capital or non-trading transactions will not be chargeable.

For companies all exchange gains and losses fall under the corporation tax loan relationships rules and are thus part of the companies' total taxable profits for corporation tax. However, it is a trading loan relationship if the foreign currency was held for trading, and a non-trade loan relationship gain or deficit if the foreign currency was held for investment.

Insurance claims

Insurance compensation received in connection with damage or loss to a fixed asset is not taxable as a trading receipt; it may be subject to CGT treatment instead. Claims for loss of profits under personal accident insurance, and claims relating to any loss on a current asset, are generally taxable as trading receipts.

Damage compensation and voluntary payments

If these transactions arise in the ordinary course of a trade then they are taxable on the recipient. If they are voluntary ex gratia payments, arising outside the domain of trading, then they are generally not taxable for the recipient or deductible by the payer.

General rules restricting deductions in computing profits

7. a) In calculating the profits of a trade no deduction is allowed for items of a capital nature.

b) 1) In calculating the profits of a trade no deduction is allowed for –

a) expenses not incurred wholly and exclusively for the purposes of the trade, or

b) losses not connected with or arising out of the trade.

2) If an expense is incurred for more than one purpose, subsection (1) does not prohibit a deduction for the identifiable part or proportion of the expense which is incurred wholly and exclusively for the purposes of trade.

The concept of materiality applied by accounting standards is not formally incorporated into tax law and this causes differences in particular when the question arises of whether to capitalise or expense certain regular purchases which may individually last the business for more than one year.

While an acceptable division between capital and revenue can normally be drawn on sound accounting principles, it does not follow that the accounting treatment is conclusive as to what is definitely "capital" and what is not for tax purposes. Case law has supplied most of the guidance on this matter, and the words of Viscount Cave in Atherton v British Insulated and Helsby Cables Ltd 1925 10 TC 155, are the most frequently quoted:

> 'when an expenditure is made not only once and for all but with a view to bringing into existence an asset, or an advantage for the enduring benefit of a trade, I think that there is a very good reason for treating such expenditure as properly attributable not to revenue, but to capital'.

The following Court decisions provide some idea of the importance and range of these two sections.

1. Associated Portland Cement Mfs Ltd v Kerr 1946 27 TC 103. Payments to retiring directors in consideration of covenants not to carry on similar business in competition with the company were held to be capital.
2. The Law Shipping Co. Ltd v IRC 1924 12 TC 103. Repair expenditure at the time of purchase of a ship, necessary to enable it to be used as a profit-earning asset, was held to be capital.
3. Odeon Associated Theatres Ltd v Jones 1972 48 TC 257. Repair expenditure incurred some time after the purchase of the cinema, not necessary to make the asset commercially viable in the meantime, was held to be revenue. A significant point was that the cinema had been used in a state of disrepair during wartime conditions.
4. Strong & Romsey Ltd v Woodfield 1906 5 TC 215. Damages and costs of injuries to a guest, caused by a falling chimney were held to be non revenue expenditure. This case would be unlikely to be decided in the same way today due to occupiers liability laws.
5. Morgan v Tate & Lyle Ltd 1954 35 TC 367. Expenses incurred to prevent the nationalisation of their industry were held to be allowable deductions. This case is the exception to the rule that donations to a political campaign are generally not accepted as trade related.
6. Copeman v Flood (William) & Sons Ltd 1941 24 TC 53. Sums paid as director's remuneration are not necessarily expended wholly and exclusively for the purposes of trade.
7. ECC Quarries Ltd v Watkins 1975 STC 578. Abortive expenditure on planning permission was held to be capital expenditure.

8. Tucker v Granada Motorway Services Ltd 1979 STC 393. A sum paid to secure a change, favourable to the lessee, in the formula for determining variable rents for the lease of a service station was held to be capital, because it affected many future years of the business, and the lease was viewed by the court as a capital interest in the property.
9. C.S. Robinson v Scott Bader Co. Ltd 1980 STC 241. The salary, expenses and social costs of an employee, seconded to a foreign subsidiary, were held to be allowable expenses of the parent company.
10. Dollar v Lyons 1981 STC 333. Payments made to the farmer's children for work on a farm were held to be pocket money and not a trading expense. It was significant that the children were too young to be legal employees of the farm.

Allowable expenditure – a summary

8. Subject to the general principles noted above, the following is a list of the most common items of expenditure which are allowed as an expense in computing taxable trading income. Except where noted otherwise, accruals accounting under UK or International GAAP applies. Some of these items are open, in the case of an individual trader or partnership, to proportionate disallowance for 'private use' under the 'wholly and exclusively' rule.

1. Cost of materials, components and goods purchased for resale.
2. Gross wages and salaries, and employer's NIC.
3. Redundancy payments.
4. Ex gratia payments and compensation for loss of office.
5. Pension scheme contributions to approved schemes – not deductible on an accounts basis, but on the basis of what was actually paid in the year.
6. Rent business rates and telecommunication expenses.
7. Fuel and power.
8. Printing and stationery.
9. Vehicle and aircraft running and maintenance expenses.
10. Repairs and renewals, see below.
11. Bad and doubtful debts expenses, see below.
12. Travelling and accommodation expenses for business purposes, e.g. sales representatives, trade fairs and conferences.
13. Advertising and promotional expenditure.
14. Bank/loan interest, so long as the loan is wholly for trading purposes.
15. Leasing payments (except leasing high emissions cars, see Chapter 13 section 20).
16. Hire purchase interest.
17. Patent renewal fees and expenses, see below.

18. Insurance of assets, employees, goods etc.
19. Legal expenses arising from trading, such as debt collection, see below.
20. Professional charges such as audit fees and consultancy charges, but not those ancilliary to the acquisition of a non-current (fixed) asset.
21. Training expenditure incurred by an employer for staff. Where the trader is self employed and incur training expenditure for themselves, further questions must be asked about duality of purpose.
22. Welfare expenditure for employees.
23. Subscriptions and donations, see below.
24. Losses and defalcations of employees, see below.
25. Penalty payments for late delivery of goods.
26. Pre-trading expenditure of a revenue nature, incurred up to seven years before trading.
27. Incidental costs of obtaining loan finance, see below.
28. Expenditure on waste disposal.
29. Gifts to educational establishments.
30. Interest on late paid tax and VAT is deductible for companies, but not for sole traders or pertnerships.
31. R&D expenditure (companies only) small or medium sized companies 200% of qualifying costs (175% in 2010/11); - large companies 130% of qualifying costs.

Non-allowable expenditure – a summary

9. The following is a list of the most common items of expenditure which are not generally allowed as an expense in computing trading income.

1. Depreciation of fixed assets, and losses on disposals of fixed assets. (Companies may deduct amortisation of some post-2002 intangible fixed assets, see Chapter 19).
2. Professional charges concerned with a taxation appeal.
3. General provisions against future expenditure such as those for doubtful debts, pension schemes, furnace relining, or for preventive maintenance. These costs are however potentially allowable once actually paid, i.e. when the provision set up in the accounts is applied.
4. Legal expenses on the acquisition of a capital asset.
5. Entertainment, except staff functions.
6. Losses and defalcations by directors.
7. Repairs which involve any improvement, or amount to a complete or substantial renewal.

8. Fines for illegal acts, (except parking fines of employees in junior positions).
9. Political donations, (see exception in Tate and Lyle case section 7).
10. Non-trading losses.
11. Tax penalties for any tax default (distinguish this from interest on late tax which is allowable for companies), and surcharges arising from VAT late payments or returns.
12. Unpaid remuneration more than 9 months after an accounting date may only be deducted once actually paid.
13. Council tax of proprietors or partners and other personal expenses of the same.
14. Crime-related payments – blackmail or extortion.
15. Criminal bribes made in the UK or overseas.

Rent paid to non-resident

10. Where net rental profits are paid to a non-resident landlord then basic rate income tax must be deducted at source from these payments and accounted for to HMRC, unless a registered UK letting agent handles the collection.

Business entertainment and gifts

11. Entertaining expenses are not allowed unless they are incurred for the entertainment of one's own staff, and this must be the main purpose of the function and not merely incidental to the provision of hospitality to others (e.g. clients). Where an employer bears the cost of an annual Christmas party, or similar function such as a staff dinner and dance, which is open to the staff generally, then HMRC will not tax the staff on the benefit in kind, until it exceeds £150 per annum for each employee. Entertaining within this permitted limit need not be included on the employee's form P11D (see chapter 8). In theory there is no limit to the amount of staff entertaining allowed to the employer as a business expense, but it will be taxed on the staff as earnings if exceeding the annual limit.

Gifts of any kind given by way of entertainment are also disallowed, except small business gifts which:

a) carry a prominent advertisement;
b) are not food, drink or tobacco;
c) do not amount in value to more than £50 per person per year.

Modest donations or gifts to local charities or recreational associations are allowed, if they are incurred 'wholly and exclusively for the purposes of trade'. This suggests that they must not be anonymous but must promote the business name or product.

Repairs and renewals

12. Improvements to premises are not allowed, but repairs occasioned by normal wear and tear would be deductible. Repair is not defined but has been held to amount to 'restoration or replacement of subsidiary parts', whereas a renewal is the reconstruction of the entirety, meaning not the whole but substantially the whole. A renewal would therefore be regarded as capital expenditure and not allowed as a trading expense. As noted in the Odeon Theatre case above, repairs to newly acquired premises, necessary to make them usable, would also be disallowed.

Patent fees and expenses

13. Deduction as an expense is allowed for any fees paid or expense incurred in obtaining for the purposes of a trade:

a) the grant of a patent or extension of a patent period

b) the registration of a design or trade mark.

Expenditure on any abandoned or rejected application for a patent is also allowable.

Bad and doubtful debts

14. Bad debts proved to be such are allowed as a deduction, and doubtful debts are also allowed in so far as they are respectively estimated to be bad. Thus a provision for specific bad debts is allowable, but not a general provision based on some overall percentage of outstanding debtors.

Where a debt is incurred outside the trading activities of the business, e.g. loans to employees written off, then any loss arising will not be allowable. This would also apply to any bad debts arising from the sale of any fixed assets.

Any bad debts recovered are treated as trading receipts in the period when received.

Pension scheme contributions

15. Sums paid to an exempt approved retirement benefits scheme are allowed as a deduction. Approved in this sense means by the HMRC Savings, Pensions, Share Schemes Group which deals with the approval of all schemes. The sums must be actually paid and not just provided for, to make good any deficit in the pension scheme.

Redundancy payments/outplacement counselling

16. Payments made to employees under the Employment Rights Act 1996 are permitted deductions, and any rebates received are taxable as trading income. Payments made outside the provisions of the Act are also in general, allowed.

Training costs

17. Expenditure by employers on training for new work or skills undertaken by employees about to leave or those who have already left is allowed as a trading expense if not already so treated. (This complements the outplacement counselling allowance.)

Employees must undertake a qualifying course of training which lasts at least one year.

Legal expenses

18. Legal charges incurred in maintaining existing trading rights are allowable, and this would include costs of debt recovery, settling disputes, preparation of service agreements, defence of title to business property, and damages and costs arising from the normal course of trade.

As already noted, legal costs incurred in contesting an income tax appeal were held to be not allowable. However, accounting and legal expenses incurred in seeking taxation advice on matters relating to trading activities would normally be allowed.

Expenses concerned with the acquisition of an asset would not be allowed, but those arising in connection with the renewal (not acquisition) of a short lease (i.e. less than 50 years) are permitted.

The legal and professional costs of raising or altering any share capital of a company are disallowed, but costs relating to issuing loan capital are permitted as "incidental costs of obtaining loan finance".

Losses and defalcations

19. Any loss not arising from the trade, or not incurred wholly and exclusively for the purposes of trade, will not be allowable as a deduction in computing taxable profits. Two categories give substance to this principle and indicate types of loss which are not deductible:

a) Any loss not connected with or arising out of the trade, profession or vocation.

b) Any sum recoverable under an insurance or contract of indemnity.

With regard to losses arising from the sorts of risks that are usually insured against such as fire, burglary, accident or loss of profits, then the loss sustained is allowable if arising from the trade, e.g. loss of stocks, and any compensation received must be treated as a trading receipt.

Where assets are involved then any loss arising would be of a capital nature and not allowable as a deductible expense.

Losses arising from defalcations or embezzlement by an employee would normally be allowable, but defalcations by a person having control over the business would not. See Curtis v Oldfield J & G Ltd 1925 9 TC 319.

Post-cessation expenditure

20. For payments made in connection with a trade that has been permanently discontinued, relief is available for payments made wholly and exclusively

a) in remedying defective work done, goods supplied or services rendered

b) in meeting legal and professional charges.

The relief is available within seven years of the discontinuance for self-employed individuals.

Relief is given primarily against an individual's total income for the year but where this is insufficient it may be set against any chargeable gains for that year.

Miscellaneous items

21. Unpaid remuneration

In calculating the profits of a trade, no deduction is allowed for employees' remuneration paid more than 9 months after the end of the period of account. A deduction is given instead in the period when the remuneration is paid.

Apart from this, all bona fide salaries to employees and directors, including commissions and bonuses, and including amounts paid after the period-end but accrued for at the period-end, are allowable if they are incurred for the purposes of trade. See Copeman v Flood 1941 24 TC 53.

However, pension schemes contributions by employers are not allowed against trade profits as a deduction on an accruals basis. These may only be claimed as an expense once the cash has actually been paid to the scheme. There is a logical reason for this rule: the technicalities of accounting for employers pension contributions may be seen from a tax point of view as akin to "general provisions"; also, the funds once paid to an approved pension scheme are in a tax free growth vehicle , so HMRC will not give tax relief on the outgoing until the funds have been transferred.

Subscriptions and donations

Subscriptions to trade associations or other bodies for the purposes of trade are allowable, but not those unconnected with trade, or involving entertainment of a non-deductible nature.

Where the payment is for the benefit or welfare of employees it will usually be allowed, e.g. a donation to a hospital or convalescent home which is used by employees of the firm. Gifts to registered charities are allowed if made for the purposes of trade.

Where a donation is a Gift Aid payment then it is not recognised as a business expense in calculating taxable trading profit, and the taxpayer receives relief through another method (see Chapter 5 sections 3 and 4, and Chapter 21 section 4).

Employees seconded to charities

When an employer seconds an employee temporarily to a charity, then any expenditure attributable to that employment by the employer is deductible as a business expense.

Costs of loan finance

Incidental costs of obtaining loan finance (including convertible loan stock) are allowed as a deduction in computing trading income, and this includes: fees, commissions, advertising, printing and stationery, but not stamp duty. This is a statutory deduction. It should be noted, however, that incidental costs of raising new equity finance are generally disallowable as capital.

Pre-trading expenses

Expenses incurred within seven years prior to the actual commencement of trading is allowed if the expenditure would have been allowed as a trading expense had trading taken place during that period. See Chapter 14.

Gifts to educational establishments

Where a person carrying on a trade, profession or vocation makes a gift of plant and machinery to an educational establishment, then the proceeds of sale can be treated as zero.

Capital allowances

Capital allowances are deducted from the adjusted profits for the purposes of computing income taxed as trade profits. See Chapter 13.

Mileage rates – self-employed

Self-employed persons can use the authorised mileage rates applicable to employees (see Chapter 7) instead of claiming actual motor expenses and capital allowances. To be eligible the taxpayer's turnover must not exceed the current VAT registration threshold (£73,000 in 2011/12).

Urban regeneration companies

Contribution to the running cost of an URC are deductible expenses in computing taxable profits.

Asset values for tax purposes

22. Tangible fixed assets

Fixed assets such as land and buildings or plant and machinery, fixtures and fittings etc., do not usually affect the determination of taxable trading income, except where the cost of an asset is charged against income, or in so far as there is a charge for depreciation. In the former case, the cost would be disallowed as capital, whether or not capital allowances are available. With regard to the charge for depreciation, then this is not allowed as a business expense, however computed.

Where a short lease of property is acquired by the taxpayer on payment of a premium, and the property is used for purposes of the trade, then an extra allowance based on the notional rental element of the premium is available, but must be spread over the lease term. See Chapter 8.

Intangible fixed assets

Under this heading are included goodwill, patents and trade marks, licences of intellectual property, copyrights and know how. In the hands of an unincorporated trader these are viewed as capital assets, and may give rise to a claim for capital allowances, see Chapter 13.

Different rules for the tax treatment of Intangible Fixed Assets (other than leases of premises) apply to companies, as explained in Chapter 19. Amortisation of patents, licences, purchased goodwill etc. may be deductible for a company on certain conditions.

Long-term investments

Long-term investments held as a fixed asset do not give rise to any particular problems as they are normally non-trading assets, and any surpluses or deficits arising from annual revaluations are not brought into the computation of taxable income. Realisations would require capital gains tax consideration, however. For companies the "loan relationships" regime, and not the chargeable gains regime applies to any fixed or current assets defined as a loan relationship. See Chapter 19.

Where the investments are trading assets then they will be valued on the same basis as other current assets.

Current assets

Current assets held by a business for the purposes of its trade would normally be valued for accounts purposes at the lower of cost or net realisable value. The same principles are applied for taxation purposes, but there are some special factors relating to stock and work in progress.

Stock and work in progress

The following is a summary of the position with regard to the valuation of stock and WIP.

1. In the absence of statutory authority stocks should be valued at the lower of cost or market value. Market value means selling price less selling expenses, and not replacement value. See CIR v Cock Russell & Co. Ltd 1949 29 TC 287: BSC Footwear Ltd v Ridgway 1971 47 TC 495.

   Under the International Accounting Standard 2 (IAS 2) mandatory for listed companies from 1 January 2005, inventory value needs to be shown in accounts at the lower of cost and net realisable value (NRV).

2. Consistency of method of valuation does not of itself guarantee that a correct method of valuation has been used. See BSC Footwear v Ridgway case noted above.
3. Overhead expenditure does not have to be included in the valuation of work in progress or finished stocks, however desirable this may be for accounting purposes. See Duple Motor Bodies v Ostime 1961 39 TC 537.
4. Standard cost values may be used but due allowance for variances from standard must be made where they are material.
5. In general neither the base stock method nor the LIFO method of stock valuation is an acceptable method of valuation for taxation purposes. See Patrick v Broadstone Mills Ltd 1953 35 TC 44; Minister of National Revenue v Anaconda American Brass Ltd 1956 AC.

   From 1st January 2005 the LIFO method of valuation is not permitted for accounts of listed companies under IAS 2.
6. Where there is a change in the method of valuation from one valid basis to another, then the opening and closing stocks in the current period must be valued on the same basis. A valid basis of valuation is one which does not violate the tax statutes as interpreted by the Courts, and which is recognised by the accounting profession.

   If the charge is from one valid basis to another then the opening stock of the current period must be equal to the closing stock of the previous period. Thus if the new valuation gives rise to a surplus in that period it will be taxable, and if a deficit, a repayment can be claimed.
7. Where a trade is discontinued, then, stock must be valued at an open market price, or if sold to another trader, at realised selling price.

   Where the trade is discontinued the stock must be valued on an 'arms length basis' if the purchaser and the vendor are connected persons.
8. Professional work in progress (e.g. solicitors' and accountants' work already completed but unbilled) must be valued at selling price unless the realisation is uncertain at the year end. This recognises profit in the year activity takes place, applying the accruals principle.

Trading stock appropriated by traders

Where a trader takes goods from the trading stock for personal consumption or consumption by his or her household, then it must be valued at its open market realistic value.

Tax and accounting principles

23. United Kingdom tax law requires that tax computations are prepared in accordance with generally accepted accounting practice subject to any adjustment required by law. Generally accepted accounting practice is defined as being the accounting practice that is used in preparing accounts which are intended to give a 'true and fair' view. The various financial reporting standards issued by the

United Kingdom Accounting Standards Board generally require that the relevant Financial Reporting Standard needs to be applied to all transactions of a reporting entity whose financial statements are intended to give a true and fair view. Since 1 January 2005 listed companies apply International Financial Reporting Standards, and these are acceptable for tax purposes under CTA 2009 subject to the adjustments required by corporation tax law..

Student self-testing questions

1. Hilary has been in business many years as a tile maker. Her profit and loss account for the year ended 31 March was as follows:

	Notes	£	£
Sales			900,000
Cost of sales			(553,795)
Gross profit			346,205
Less: Expenses			
Salaries and wages	1	55,000	
Rent & rates		8,500	
Motor expenses	2	12,000	
Legal expenses	3	13,000	
Advertising		5,500	
Loss on sale of fixed asset		150	
Depreciation		9,095	
Donation to Oxfam made with Gift Aid declaration (net amount paid)		50	
Employees' Christmas party		1,450	
			(104,745)
Net profit			241,460

1. Salaries and wages include Hilary's drawings of "salary" of £12,000.
2. Motor expenses include Hilary's private use of the car amounting to 25%.
3. Legal expenses comprise the following:

Costs associated with a tax appeal	3,000
Costs associated with the renewal of a short term lease	5,000
Defending a litigation case with a customer	5,000

Requirement: Calculate Hilary's income from trading for the year.

Solution: Adjusted trading profits calculation

	£	£
Profit per financial statements		241,460
Add: disallowable expenditure:		
Hilary salary	12,000	
Hilary motor expenses	3,000	
Legal costs : tax appeal	3,000	
Loss on sale of fixed asset	150	
Depreciation	9,095	
Donation to Oxfam - Gift Aid scheme applies	50	
		27,295
Income from trading		268,755

2. Mr S Eason

Mr Eason has the following business accounting results:

	£	
Profit and Loss Account for the year to 31st Dec 2011		
Gross operating profit		171,000
Taxed interest received		900
		171,900
Wages and salaries	48,000	
Rent & rates	2,500	
Depreciation	1800	
Bad debts written off	120	
Provision* for future building repair costs	5500	
Entertainment expenses	800	
Patent royalties	1250	
Bank interest	350	
Legal expenses on acquisition of factory	300	
		(60,620)
Net profit		£111,280

Notes:

(i) Salaries include £22,000 paid to Mrs R Eason who worked as an employee in the business

(ii) No staff were entertained

(iii) The provision * is charged because of an anticipated expense for future building repair costs

(iv) Patent royalties were paid net, as required by law, but are shown gross

Requirement:

Compute the assessable profit from trading for the year to 31 December 2011.

Solution

Profit per accounts		111,280
Add		
Depreciation	1,800	
Provision for future building repair costs (not GAAP)	5,500	
Entertainment expenses	800	
Legal expenses (relating to non current asset)	300	
		8,400
		119,680
less interest received (non trading savings income)		(900)
Adjusted trading profit		118,780

Notes:

(i) Patent royalties are allowable as an expense in calculating income from trading, if wholly and exclusively for business purposes; otherwise treat as an allowable payment deducted from total income in the main income tax computation.

(ii) The adjustment for interest received is based on the figure actually included in the business P&L. However, Mr Eason's self assessment tax return should include the gross amount of interest as savings income in the tax year it is received.

11 Income taxed as trade profits: II - basis periods

Introduction

1. This chapter deals with the basis of assessment of income arising from any trade, profession or vocation carried on by an individual. The rules applicable to a partnership are discussed in Chapter 15. These are contained in ITTOAI 2005.

Part I Trade profit assessments

Part II Averaging of profits for farmers, market gardeners, authors and artists.

PART I – Trade profit assessments

2. This topic is covered under the following headings:

General rule

Commencement provisions

Cessation provisions

General rule

3. The general rule is that the basis period for a tax year is the period of 12 months ending with the accounting date in that tax year. The basis period is the period used for measuring assessable trade profit for the tax year. The accounting date means a date, normally annually, on which a balance sheet is drawn up on generally accepted accounting principles.

Commencement provisions

4. Where an individual starts trading the following rules apply for determining the basis of assessment.

a) Profits of the first year are the "actual" profits from the date of commencement to the 5th April. Where the accounting date is not 5 April (or 31 March), time apportionment is used to estimate profit earned to the end of the first tax year.

b) Profits of the second year are normally either:

   i) profits for the 12 months ending with the accounting date in that year or

   ii) profits of the 12 months from the date of commencement.

   Where the first accounting period ends in the third year of assessment then the second year will be assessed on an actual tax year basis, using time apportionment.

c) For subsequent years the profits are for the 12 months ending with the accounting date in the tax year.

Example

T commenced trading on the 1st June 2008 with the following tax adjusted profits for the first 3 periods of account:

	£
1.6.2008 – 31.5.2009	6,000
1.6.2009 – 31.5.2010	10,000
1.6.2010 – 31.5.2011	12,000

Compute the taxable profits for relevant tax years.

Solution

Tax year	Basis period	Assessed amount
2008/09	1.6.08 – 5.4.09 (10/12 × 6,000)	5,000
2009/10	1.6.08 – 31.5.09 (12 months to 31.5.09)	6,000
2010/11	1.6.08 – 31.5.10 (12 months to 31.5.10)	10,000
2011/12	1.6.10 – 31.5.11 (12 months to 31.5.11)	12,000

Notes

i) The second year is assessed on the profit of the 12 month accounting period ending in the second year i.e. 12 months to 30th May 2009.

ii) The second tax year contains an 'overlap period' where profits are measured for a second time. This is the period 1 June 2008 to 5 April 2009 with overlap profit of 10/12 x 6,000 = 5,000.

iii) The amount of overlap profits is recovered on the earlier of the following:

a) a change of accounting date that results in a period of account more than 12 months or

b) the cessation of trading.

iv) Calculation should strictly be made in days and not months, although for the examinations of professional accounting bodies the latter will be accepted. HMRC have stated that an accounting date of 31 March may be treated as 5 April, so long as the rule is consistently applied for all tax years.

v) The assessed profits less the overlap profits to be recovered are therefore equal to the actual profits (33,000 – 5,000) = 28,000.

Example

A commenced trading on the 1st July 2008 and has the following tax adjusted results for the first 3 periods of account:

	£
1.7.2008 – 31.12.2009	24,000
1.1.2010 – 31.12.2010	30,000
1.1.2011 – 31.12.2011	40,000

Compute the taxable profits for all relevant tax years.

Solution

Tax year	Basis period	Assessed amount
2008/09	1.5.08 – 5.4.09 (9/18 × 24,000)	12,000
2009/10	1.1.09 – 31.12.09 (12/18 × 24,000)	16,000
2010/11	1.1.10 – 31.12.10 (12 months to 31.12.10)	30,000
2011/12	1.1.11 – 31.12.11 (12 months to 31.12.11)	40,000

Notes

i) The second year is assessed on the profits of the 12 months ending 31st December 2009.

ii) The overlap period is from 1 January 2009 to 5 April 2009, with profits of 3/18 × 24,000 = 4,000.

iii) Assessed profits less the overlap profits to be recovered are thus equal to the actual profits.

(12,000 + 16,000 + 30,000 + 40,000) – 4,000 = 94,000

Example

T started business on the 1st January 2009 with first accounts for the 16 months to 30th April 2010 and thereafter:

	£
1.1.2009 – 30.4.2010	32,000
1.5.2010 – 30.4.2011	28,000

Compute the taxable profits for relevant tax years.

Solution

Tax year	Basis period	Assessed amount
2008/09	1.1.09 – 5.4.09 (3/16 × 32,000)	6,000
2009/10	6.4.09 – 5.4.10 (12/16 × 32,000)	24,000
2010/11	1.5.09 – 30.4.10 (12/16 × 32,000)	24,000
2011/12	1.5.10 – 30.4.11 (12 months to 30.4.11)	28,000

Notes

i) There is no period of account ending in the second year 2009/10 therefore the actual basis applies.

ii) The overlap period is 1 May 2009 – 5 April 2010 i.e. 11 months

11/16 × 32,000 = 22,000

iii) Assessed profits less the overlap profits are thus equal to the actual profits

(6,000 + 24,000 + 24,000 + 28,000) – 22,000 = 60,000

Cessation provisions

5. The profits of the tax year in which cessation takes place are measured as follows.

i) The final tax year has a basis period from the end of the previous basis period to the date of cessation.

ii) Any profits from the overlap period on commencement not previously recouped are deducted from the profits of the final basis period.

iii) The effect of the above is that over the life of a business only its actual taxable profits will be assessed.

Example

Q commenced trading on the 1st June 2006 and sold the business on the 30th April 2011 with the following tax adjusted results.

	£
1.6.2006 – 31.5.2007	6,000
1.6.2007 – 31.5.2008	10,000
1.6.2008 – 31.5.2009	12,000
1.6.2009 – 31.5.2010	16,000
1.6.2010 – 30.4.2011	8,000

Compute the assessable trading income for all tax years of the trade.

Solution

Year of assessment	Basis period	Assessed amount
2006/07	1.6.06 – 5.4.07 (10/12 × 6,000)	5,000
2007/08	1.6.06 – 31.5.07	6,000
2008/09	1.6.07 – 31.5.08	10,000
2009/10	1.6.08 – 31.5.09	12,000
2010/11	1.6.09 – 31.5.10	16,000
2011/12	1.6.10–30.4.11 (8,000–5,000 overlap)	3,000

Notes:

i) The overlap period is 1 June 2006 – 5 April 2007 i.e. 10 months.

Overlap profit = 10/12 × 6,000 = 5,000

ii) The final period of profits is from 1 June 2010 to 30 April 2011 assessed in 2011/2012 i.e. £8,000. Overlap profits of £5,000 are deducted leaving a net assessment of £3,000.

iii) Total profits over the life of the business are £52,000 which is equal to the taxable profits assessed.

PART II – Averaging of profits – farmers and creative artists

6. Farmers market gardeners and creative artists (not companies) can claim to have their adjusted profits averaged for any two years of assessment. The main provisions are:

a) Profits of the first or last year of trading cannot be included in any claim.

b) Profits are adjusted profits after capital allowances and before loss relief.

c) Once averaged the profits become fixed for all future averaging.

d) Averaging is only available where the difference between the assessable profits of two successive years is 30% or more of the higher of the two years' profits.

Example

T, who commenced farming on the 1st January 2006, has the following adjusted profits after capital allowances:

	£
Year ended 31st December 2009	56,000
Year ended 31st December 2010	35,000
Year ended 31st December 2011	10,000

Compute the assessable profits for 2009/10 and 2010/11 if an averaging claim is made.

Solution: Computation of averaged profits

		£
2009/10	basis period y/e 31.12.09	56,000
2010/11	basis period y/e 31.12.10	35,000

As the difference (56,000 – 35,000) = 21,000 is more than 30% of the higher year (30% × 56,000 = 16,800) full averaging for both years is possible.

2009/10 $\frac{91,000}{2} =$ 45,500

2010/11 $\frac{91,000}{2} =$ 45,500

e) Trading losses are to be taken as nil in making the average computation. Normal claims for loss relief are not affected by the averaging process, thus a claim under Section 64 could be made after the averaging computation.

Example with loss relief

V who has been in business for many years has the following tax adjusted results:

		£
12 months to 31st March	2007	25,000
12 months to 31st March	2008	15,000
12 months to 31st March	2009	(10,000) loss
12 months to 31st March	2010	30,000
12 months to 31st March	2011	50,000

Compute the assessments for relevant tax years, with and without averaging.

Solution: Assessments without averaging

		£
2006/07	12 months to 31.3.07	25,000
2007/08	12 months to 31.3.08	15,000
2008/09	12 months to 31.3.09	–
2009/10	12 months to 31.3.10	30,000
2010/11	12 months to 31.3.11	50,000
		120,000

Calculation of averaged profits

		Adjusted profit	**Increase (decrease)**	**Averaged profits**
2006/07 Year to 31.3.2007		25,000	(5,000)	20,000
2007/08 Year to 31.3.2008		15,000	5,000	20,000
		20,000		
Averaged profits	$\frac{40000}{2}$	20,000		
2007/08	As averaged	20,000	–	20,000
2008/09		–	–	–
		20,000		
Averaged profits	$\frac{20000}{2}$	10,000		
2008/09	As averaged	10,000	–	–
2009/10	Year to 31.3.2010	30,000	(10,000)	20,000
		40,000		
Averaged profits	$\frac{40000}{2}$	20,000		

			Adjusted profit	Increase (decrease)	Averaged profits
2008/09	As averaged		10,000	–	–
2009/10	Year to 31.3.2010		30,000	(10,000)	20,000
			40,000		
Averaged profits		$\frac{40000}{2}$	20,000		
2009/10	As averaged		20,000	15,000	35,000
2010/11	Year to 31.3.2010		50,000	(15,000)	35,000
			70,000		
Averaged profits		$\frac{70000}{2}$	35,000		
2010/11	As averaged		35,000		

	Averaged assessments	Assessments without averaging
2006/07	20,000	25,000
2007/08	20,000	15,000
2008/09	10,000	–
2009/10	35,000	30,000
2010/11	35,000	50,000
	120,000	120,000

Note

The total amount of profits is the same under both methods but the averaging has smoothed out the annual figures.

7. A form of marginal averaging can be claimed where the difference between the two years' profits is between 25% and 30% of the highest year. This is affected by increasing the lower profit and reducing the higher profit by an amount equal to: 3 (higher profit – lower profit) – (75% × higher profit)

Student self-testing questions

1.

(i) Hilary commenced business on 1 August 2007 and made up her first accounts for the twelve months to 31 July 2008. Her profits adjusted for tax purposes were:

12 months ended 31 July	Adjusted profit
	£
2008	24,000
2009	40,000
2010	32,000
2011	36,000

(ii) Julia commenced business on 1 January 2009, making up her first accounts to 31 October 2009, then annually to that date. Her profits as adjusted for tax purposes were:

	£
10 months ended 31 October 2009	42,000
Year ended 31 October 2010	52,000
Year ended 31 October 2011	65,000

(iii) James began business on 1 September 2008 and made up his first accounts to 31 January 2009. His profits adjusted for tax purposes were:

	£
5 months ended 31 January 2009	24,000
Year ended 31 January 2010	60,000
Year ended 31 January 2011	72,000

(iv) Jeremy began business on the 1 February 2008 and made up his first accounts to 31 July 2009, eighteen months later. His profits adjusted for tax purposes were:

	£
Eighteen months ended 31 July 2009	56,000
Year ended 31 July 2010	40,000
Year ended 31 July 2011	45,000

Requirement: In each case calculate the measured assessable trade profits in the first, second and third tax years and any overlap profits arising. You may make calculations in whole months.

Solution

1) Hilary

1st year	07/08	1 August '07 - 5 April '08 = 8 months 8/12 x 24,000	16,000
2nd year	08/09	Is there an accounting date ending in 08/09? Yes 31/7/08 The accounting period is greater than or equal to 1 year and therefore the basis of assessment is 12 months to the accounting date in the 2nd tax year. Year ended 31/7/08	24,000
3rd year	09/10	As there was an accounting date ending in the 2nd tax year the basis of assessment is the year ended 31/7/09	40,000
Overlap profit		1/8/07 - 5/4/08 = 8 months (8/12 x 24,000)	16,000

2) Julia

1st year	08/09	1 Jan '09 - 5 April '09 = 3 months 3/10 x 42,000	12,600
2nd year	09/10	Is there an accounting date ending in 09/10? Yes 31/10/09 The accounting date is less than 1 year therefore the basis of assessment is the first 12 months of trading 10 months ended 31/10/09 plus Nov & Dec '09 Assessment is therefore: 10 months ended 31/10/09 + 2/12 x 52,000	42,000 8,667 50,667
3rd year	10/11	As there was an accounting date ending in the 2nd tax year the basis of assessment is the year ended 31/10/10	52,000
Overlap profits		1/1/09 - 5/4/09	12,600
		1/11/09 - 31/12/09 (2/12 x £52,000)	8,667
			21,267

3) James

1st year	08/09	1 September 2008 - 5 April 2009 = 7 months (£24,000 + (2/12 x £60,000)	34,000
2nd year	09/10	Is there an accounting date ending in 09/10? Yes, year ended 31/1/10 The accounting date is greater than or equal to 1 year after commencement therefore the basis of assessment is the year to the new accounting date Year ended 31/1/10	60,000
3rd year	10/11	As there was an accounting date ending in the 2nd tax year the basis of assessment is the year ended 31/1/11	72,000
Overlap profits		1/2/09 - 5/4/09 (2/12 x 60,000)	10,000

4) Jeremy

1st year	07/08	1 February 2008 - 5 April 2008 2/18 x 56,000	6,222
2nd year	08/09	Is there an accounting date ending in 08/09? No. Therefore the basis of assessment is profits from 6/4/08 - 5/4/09 12/18 x £56,000	37,333
3rd year	09/10	Basis of assessment for the 3rd tax year is 12 months to the accounting date in the 3rd tax year i.e. 31 July 2009 12/18 x £56,000	37,333
	Overlap	The profits from 1 August 2008 to 5 April 2009 have been measured in both 08/09 and 09/10. Overlap profits are therefore £24,889 (8/18 x 56,000).	24,889

2. Mr E

In the spring of 2012, Mr E was considering starting a new business and had prepared a business plan. This showed that the business would commence trading on 1 July 2012, and that the pattern of profits would be:

Period to 31 December 2012	£600 per month
Twelve months to 31 December 2013	£1,200 per month
Thereafter	£2,400 per month

Mr E is considering two alternative dates on which to make up accounts each year, 31 March or 30 April.

(Note that he is not considering any other date and will not be making up accounts to 31 December.)

Required:

a) Compute the amounts which will be assessable as income from trading for each of the first three tax years under each of the two above alternative accounting dates. 10 marks

b) Indicate the main advantages and disadvantages of each alternative. 5 marks

CIMA May 1998 (updated)

Solution

Accounting profits arising under the 2 proposed dates

		£
31 March accounting reference		
1 July 2012 - 31 March 2013	(6 x £600) + (3 x £1,200)	7,200
Year ended 31 March 2014	(9 x £1,200) + (3 x £2,400)	18,000
Year ended 31 March 2015	(12 x £2,400)	28,800
30 April accounting date		
10 months to 30 April 2013	(6 x £600) + (4 x £1,200)	8,400
Year ended 30 April 2014	(8 x £1,200) + (4 x £2,400)	19,200
Year ended 30 April 2015	(12 x £2,400)	28,800

Based on the accounting profits, the tax year measures of trading income will be as follows:

31 March accounting date:

	Basis period	Assessable profits £
2012/2013	1 July 2012 - 5 April 2013	7,200
2013/2014	12 months to 31 March 2014	18,000
2014/2015	12 months to 31 March 2015	28,800
		54,000

30 April accounting date:

	Basis period	Calculation	Assessable profit £
2012/2013	1 July 2012 - 5 April 2013	9/10 x 8,400	7,560
2013/2014	1 July 2012 - 30 June 2013	8,400 + (2/12 x 19,200)	11,600
2014/2015	Year ended 30 April 2014		19,200
			38,360

(b)

30 April

The 30 April reference date gives a lower amount of total assessable profits for the first three years of assessment. There is a greater interval between earning profits and paying taxes. (The difference in tax liability occurs because the business's profits are rising. If there were the same profit every month exactly, it would make little difference which accounting reference date was chosen.)

With the 30 April reference date, profits in the periods 1 July 2012 to 5 April 2013 (£7,560) and 1 May 2013 to 30 June 2013 (£3,200) are counted twice in the first three tax years – creating 'overlap profits' of (7,560+3,200) = £10,760.

Relief for overlap profits is either on cessation or on a change of accounting date.

31 March

The 31 March reference date gives no 'overlap' profits

It has higher total assessable profits in early years giving rise to earlier tax liabilities on profits earned.

Hence there is a cash flow disadvantage compared to a 30 April reference date.

Questions without answers

1. Chatru commenced trading on 1 November 2007. His first accounts were made up to 30 April 2009 and thereafter to 30 April annually. He ceased trading on 31 March 2012.

   His trading results, adjusted for income tax purposes were:

	£
1.11.07-30.4.09	40,500
Year ended 30.4.10	12,000
Year ended 30.4.11	24,000
Period to 31.3.12	46,000

Requirements:

Calculate the assessable income for all years in question

Calculate whether there would have been an income tax benefit in Chatru continuing to trade one extra month and making up final accounts to his normal accounting date, on the assumption that his tax-adjusted profit for April 2012 was £4,200.

11 marks

ACCA June 1995 (updated)

2. Nan Pearson died on 30 June 2011 aged 58. She had been employed as a design engineer by Map plc, a company which specialises in the construction of motor bikes.

The following is supplied:

(1) Nan's salary, paid on the last day of each month, was £35,000 pa from which 5% was paid to an approved staff pension fund. The company's contribution was 8%. PAYE of £1,800 was deducted from the salary during 2011/12.

(2) Her other income comprised the following.

	Year ended 5 April 2011	6 April 2011 to 30 June 2011
	£	£
Net interest received from a building society on a deposit account	1,264	1,440
Dividends received from UK companies net received excluding the tax credit	3,888	4,248

Arthur Pearson, Nan's husband, had been employed until his retirement in March 2007 at age 55. Since that date he undertook some self-employed bookkeeping activities and recent tax adjusted profits of this business are as follows:

	£
Year to 30 April 2008	5,000
Year to 30 April 2009	4,100
Year to 30 April 2010	5,900
Year to 30 April 2011	6,700

No tax has yet been paid on Arthur's income from trading for 2011/12

(3) Arthur received gross interest from an NS&I Investment Account of £154 in 2010/11 and £130 in 2011/12. Interest was credited annually on 30 June.

The following events took place after Nan's death.

(1) A payment of £140,000, being the sum assured on Nan's life under the Map plc's pension scheme, was paid to Arthur.

(2) A pension of £22,980 (gross) per annum, payable on the first day of each month, was paid to Arthur by Map plc. The first payment was made on 1 July 2011 and a BR code was used by the company for PAYE purposes (i.e. basic rate tax was deducted from the pension by Map plc).

Arthur used the £140,000 assurance policy receipt to acquire and furnish a small studio apartment on 1 February 2012. He let this apartment under a ten year lease from 1 March 2012, the incoming tenant paying a premium of £4,000. The rent of £5,500 a year is payable quarterly in advance and was received when due. Arthur incurred the following expenses in connection with the letting.

	£
Interior decorating prior to letting	790
Year's insurance of premises and contents - 1 March 2012	384
Managing agent's fee (for tenancy agreement and March 2012 management)	250

Requirement:

Prepare income tax computations for 2011/12 for

(a) Nan Pearson, showing income tax payable or refundable (10 marks)

(b) Arthur Pearson, showing the final income tax position and indicating any final amounts of tax to be paid or repaid. (6 marks)

(Total: 16 marks)

12 Income taxed as trade profits: III - change of accounting date

Introduction

1. This chapter is concerned with the effects of a change of accounting date on the income taxed as trade profits for a tax year, under the basis period rules already described.

Detailed rules

2. An outline of the rules in respect of a change of accounting date follows:

a) HMRC will ignore any change of accounting date and require separate balance sheets as before for the original annual basis periods unless all of the three undermentioned circumstances apply.

   i) The first period of account (i.e. period for which business accounts are made up) ending with the new date does not exceed 18 months.

   ii) Notice of the change is given to an officer of HMRC in a personal tax return on or before the day on which that return is required to be delivered.

   Either

   1) no accounting change resulting in a change of basis period has been made in any of the previous five tax years;

   or

   2) the change is made for bona fide commercial reasons. In this case notice in (ii) above must set out the reasons for the change and HMRC do not, within 60 days, give notice to the trader that they are not satisfied that the change is made for bona fide commercial reasons.

b) There is a right of appeal against HMRC's decision not to accept a second change in five years as being for commercial reasons.

c) Obtaining a tax advantage by an accounting date change is not accepted as a valid commercial reason for a change.

d) Where all the conditions are satisfied, or the accounting change is made in the second or third tax year of the business, the basis period for the tax year of the change is as follows.

   i) If the year is the second tax year of the business, the basis period is the twelve months ending with the new accounting date falling in that tax year (unless the period from commencement of the business to the new date in the second year is less than twelve months, in which case the basis is the first twelve months of the business).

Overlap relief will arise to the extent that profits are brought into charge twice as a result of this rule.

ii) If the 'relevant period' is a period of less than twelve months, the basis period is the twelve months ending with the new date in the tax year. Further overlap profits will arise to the extent that profits are brought into charge twice as a result of this rule. These overlap profits will be added to any previous overlap profits

iii) If the 'relevant period' is a period of more than twelve months, the basis period consists of the relevant period, less any overlap relief available to deduct.

The 'relevant period' is the period beginning immediately after the end of the basis period for the preceding year and ending with the new date in the year.

In summary, when the accounting date change involves a move of the accounting date later in the tax year, previous overlap is released, and when it involves a move of the accounting date to earlier in the year, new overlap is created.

	Difference between end of preceding basis period and new accounting date	**Basis period**
1st year	< 12 months	12 months to new A/C date
1st year	> 12 months	Period to new A/C date
2nd year	—	12 months to new A/C date

Profits for the period of overlap will need to be computed when a change of accounting date takes place.

Example

A starts in business on 1st July 2007 and produces accounts to 5th April until 2010 when a new date of 30th June 2010 is the accounting date.

		£
Accounts	1.7.07 – 5.4.08	10,000
	6.4.08 – 5.4.09	12,000
	6.4.09 – 5.4.10	15,000
	6.4.10 – 30.6.10	2,000
	1.7.10 – 30.6.11	6,000

Compute the assessments.

Solution

			£
2007/08	1.7.07 – 5.4.08		10,000
2008/09	12 months to 5.4.09		12,000
2009/10	12 months to 5.4.10		15,000
2010/11	12 months to 30.6.10		
	1.7.09 – 5.4.10 = 9 months		
	9/12 × 15,000 =	11,250	
	6.4.10 – 30.6.10 =	2,000	13,250
2011/12	1.7.10 – 30.6.11 =		6,000

Notes

i) Overlap Memo

There was no overlap profit arising on the commencement of the business, as a 5 April accounting date was adopted.

Overlap relief on change of accounting date:

Overlap period 1.7.2009 – 5.4.2010

= 9/12 × 15,000 = 11,250

Amount carried forward as overlap profits 11,250

ii) Total profit assessed less overlap relief

= £45,000 : (10,000 + 12,000 + 15,000 + 13,250 + 6,000) – 11,250.

Example

V started business on the 1st January 2007 with the following results.

6 months to 30.6.2007	20,000
12 months to 30.6.2008	40,000
12 months to 30.6.2009	50,000
18 months to 31.12.2010	75,000
12 months to 31.12.2011	60,000

Compute the assessable trading profits for all tax years and the overlap relief.

Solution

Years	Period		£
2006/2007	1.1.07 – 5.4.07		
	3/6 × 20,000 =		10,000
2007/2008	First 12 months trading		
	20,000 + ((6/12) × 40,000)		
	20,000 + 20,000		40,000
2008/09	CY 30.6.2008		40,000
2009/10	CY 30.6.2009		50,000
2010/11	1.7.2009 – 31.12.2010		
	total for period	75,000	
	less overlap released	20,00055,000	
2011/12	CY 31.12.2011		60,000

Notes

i) Overlap Memo

Original overlap profits (1.1.07–5.4.07)+(1.7.07–31.12.07) = 9 months

= 10,000 + 20,000 =	30,000
2010/11 overlap released 1.7.09 – 31.12.10 = 549 days	
18 – 12 = 6 months	
6/9 × 30,000 =	(20,000)
Reduced overlap carried forward at 2011/12	10,000

ii) Total profit assessed less overlap relief

= £245,000 : (10,000 + 40,000 + 40,000 + 50,000 + 55,000 + 60,000) – 10,000

Example

B has been in business for many years with the following results.

12 months to 31.12.2007	10,000
12 months to 31.12.2008	30,000
12 months to 31.12.2009	20,000
6 months to 30.6.2010	12,000
12 months to 30.6.2011	36,000

Compute the assessable trading profits for all tax years and the overlap relief arising on the change of accounting date and carried forward by the taxpayer.

Solution

Years	Period	£
2007/08	12 months to 31.12.2007	10,000
2008/09	12 months to 31.12.2008	30,000
2009/10	12 months to 31.12.2009	20,000
2010/11	12 months to 30.6.2010:	
	12,000 + ((6/12) × 20,000)	
	12,000 + 10,000	22,082
2011/12	30.6.2010	36,000

Overlap relief 1.7.09 – 31.12.09

6/12 × 20,000 = 10,000

Total assessed profits less overlap relief = (10,000 + 30,000 + 20,000 + 22,082 + 36,000) – 10,000 = £108,000.

Student self-testing question

A starts in business on 1st May 2006 making accounts up to 5th April each year until 2010 when a new date of 30th November 2010 is chosen as the accounting date.

Business periods of account	Adjusted profits (£)
1.5.06 – 5.4.07	10,000
6.4.07 – 5.4.08	12,000
6.4.08 – 5.4.09	14,000
6.4.09 – 5.4.10	16,000
6.4.10 – 30.11.10	8,000
1.12.10 – 30.11.11	20,000

Compute the measured assessable trading profits for all tax years.

Solution

			£
2006/07	1.5.06 – 5.4.07		10,000
2007/08	12 months to 5.4.08		12,000
2008/09	12 months to 5.4.09		14,000
2009/10	12 months to 5.4.10		16,000
2010/11	12 months to 30.11.10		
	6.4.10– 30.11.10	8,000	
	1.12.08 – 5.4.09 = 4 months		
	4/12 x 16,000 =	5,333	13,333
2011/12	1.12.10 – 30.11.11 =		20,000
Overlap relief 1.12.10 – 30.11.11			5,333
Carried forward			5,333
Total profits = 85,333 – 5,333 = £80,000			

Question without answer

1. X starts trading on 1st December 2007 with the following results:

	£
Period to 5th April 2008	7,000
Year to 5th April 2009	10,000
Year to 5th April 2010	15,000
6 months to 30th September 2010	8,000
Year to 30th September 2011	20,000

Compute the measured assessable trading profits for all tax years.

13 Capital allowances

Introduction

1. The chapter is about the allowances available to a taxpayer in respect of capital expenditure on fixed assets. These allowances, which are called capital allowances, consist of a mixture of annual and other allowances which are available in respect of qualifying expenditure incurred under the following headings.

Plant and machinery	Patent rights (not available to companies)
Conversion of certain premises into flats	Know-how (not available to companies)
Scientific Research Assets	

The main statute is the Capital Allowances Act 2001 as amended by subsequent Finance Acts. The UK government has a tendency to alter capital allowances rules for reasons of economic policy. It is an area of domestic law which is not currently subject to EU scrutiny to the same extent as other economic incentives which the government can propose.

The chapter is divided into the following sections:

Part I	–	Plant and machinery
Part II	–	Other assets

Examples in this chapter which cover a number of periods of account may be projected into the future. This is to avoid confusion that could result from including obsolete allowances, or transitional rules of no future significance, in workings shown for earlier tax years.

Nearly all of the rules on tangible assets described in this chapter apply in the same way for corporate taxpayers (See Chapter 18 on company capital allowances). Where there are differences, the difference is noted.

PART I – Plant and machinery – general conditions

2. a) Allowances are available under this heading if a person carries on a qualifying activity and incurs qualifying expenditure.

b) "Qualifying activity" has the following meaning

i) a trade, profession or vocation,

ii) an ordinary property business,

iii) a furnished holiday lettings business,

iv) an overseas property business,

v) the management of an investment company,

vi) special leasing of plant or machinery,

vii) an employment or office.

c) Expenditure is qualifying expenditure if –

i) it is capital expenditure on the provision of plant or machinery wholly or partly for the purposes of the qualifying activity carried on by the person incurring the expenditure, and

ii) the person incurring the expenditure owns the plant or machinery as a result of incurring it.

Qualifying expenditure

3. a) Plant and machinery is not conclusively defined in tax statute though Schedule AAI to the CAA 2001 attempted to codify existing case law. The definition most frequently referred to is that contained in a non revenue case, Yarmouth v France 1887 QBD. The case was brought under the Employers Liability Act 1880, and consideration given as to whether or not a horse was plant and machinery. In the course of his judgement, Lindley LJ made the following statement:

> '... in its ordinary sense it includes whatever apparatus is used by a business man for carrying on his business, not his stock in trade which he buys or makes for sale, but all goods and chattels, fixed or moveable, live or dead, which he keeps for permanent employment in his business.'

b) In another important case it was stated that "plant" excludes buildings and parts of buildings to the extent they are the "setting" of the trade, rather than the "apparatus" of the trade.

c) Capital expenditure on alterations to an existing building, incidental to the installation of plant, may be treated as plant and machinery, where a qualifying activity is carried on.

d) Expenditure on the thermal insulation of an industrial building.

e) Fire safety expenditure.

f) Personal security expenditure.

g) Buildings and structures – see below.

Features integral to a building – the special rate pool

4. Since 2008 certain features integral to a building, thermal insulation and long-life assets (see section 14) are placed for capital allowances purposes in a separate 'special rate pool'.

The writing down allowance is at a lower rate for this pool, compared to other items of plant and machinery.

The special rate pool also includes cars with carbon dioxide emissions exceeding 160g/km, acquired for business use after 31 March 2009 (5 April 2009 for sole traders/partnerships).

Features integral to a building are defined as: electrical systems; cold water systems; heating, ventilation, air cooling or purification systems including related floors and ceilings; lifts, escalators and moving walkways; external solar shading; active facades.

Allowances are available for both initial expenditure and replacement expenditure on integral features. "Replacement" is expenditure on replacing or renewing over 50% of the asset within a 12 month period. Where capital allowances apply under this rule, a normal repairs deduction is not available as a deductible expense against profits.

Plant and machinery – buildings (to 5 April 2008 Income Tax and 31 March 2008 Corporation Tax)

5. Prior to the rules on 'features integral to a building' the following rules applied:

Plant and machinery did not include:

a) buildings – List A (references to Sch AAI CAA 2001)

b) fixed structures – List B

c) interests in land.

Note The items included in list C of each table could be claimed as plant and machinery of a trade, subject to the case-law criteria.

List A: Buildings

1. Walls, floors, ceilings, doors, gates, shutters, windows and stairs
2. Main services, and systems, of water, electricity and gas
3. Waste disposal systems
4. Sewerage and drainage systems
5. Shafts or other structures in which lifts, hoists, escalators and moving walkways are installed
6. Fire safety systems

List B: Structures

1. Any tunnel, bridge, viaduct, aqueduct, embankment or cutting
2. Any way or hard standing, such as a pavement, road, railway or tramway, a park for vehicles or containers, or an airstrip or runway
3. Any inland navigation, including a canal or basin or a navigable river
4. Any dam, reservoir or barrage (including any sluices, gates, generators and other equipment associated with it)
5. Any dock
6. Any dike, sea wall, weir or drainage ditch
7. Any structure not within any other item in this column

List C: Assets which can be included in buildings, but expenditure on which is unaffected by the buildings rules i.e. These items could still be claimed as plant and machinery, subject to established case law principles.

1. Electrical, cold water, gas and sewerage systems –
   a) provided mainly to meet the particular requirements of the trade, or
   b) provided mainly to serve particular machinery or plant used for the purposes of trade
2. Space or water heating systems; powered systems of ventilation; air cooling or air purification; and any ceiling or floor comprised in such systems
3. Manufacturing or processing equipment; storage equipment, including cold rooms; display equipment; and counters, checkouts and similar equipment
4. Cookers, washing machines, dishwashers, refrigerators and similar; washbasins, sinks, baths, showers, sanitary ware and similar equipment; furniture and furnishings
5. Lifts, hoists, escalators and moving stairways
6. Sound insulation provided mainly to meet the particular requirements of the trade
7. Computer, telecommunications and surveillance systems (including wiring or other links)
8. Refrigeration or cooling equipment
9. Sprinkler and other equipment for extinguishing or containing fire; fire alarm systems
10. Burglar alarm systems
11. Any machinery (including devices for providing motive power) not within any other item in this column
12. Strong rooms in bank or building society premises; safes
13. Partition walls, where moveable and intended to be moved in the course of the trade
14. Decorative assets provided for the enjoyment of the public in the hotel, restaurant or similar trades
15. Advertising hoardings; signs, displays and similar assets
16. Alteration of land for the purpose only of installing machinery or plant
17. Provision of dry docks
18. Provision of any jetty or similar structure provided mainly to carry machinery or plant
19. Provision of pipelines
20. Provision of towers used to support floodlights
21. Provision of any reservoir incorporated into a water treatment works
22. Provision of silos used for temporary storage or on the provision of storage tanks

23. Provision of slurry pits or silage clamps
24. Provision of swimming pools, including diving boards, slides and any structure supporting them
25. Provision of fish tanks or fish ponds
26. Provision of rails, sleepers and ballast for a railway or tramway
27. Swimming pools
28. Cold stores
29. Any glass house with integral environment controls
30. Movable buildings intended to be moved in the course of the qualifying activity

Cases on plant and machinery

6. The following is a summary of some of the cases concerned with the definition of plant and machinery. Cases prior to 2001 were influential in the drawing up of lists A B and C above :

1. Jarrold v John Good & Sons Ltd 1962 CA 40 TC 681. In this case movable metal partitioning used to divide office accommodation was held to be plant.
2. CIR v Barclay Curle & Co. Ltd 1969 H.L. 45 TC 221. The company constructed a dry dock, the whole cost of which, including excavation, was held to be plant.
3. Cooke v Beach Station Caravans Ltd 1974 CD 49 TC 524. The company constructed a swimming pool with an elaborate system of filtration, as one of the amenities at a caravan park. The cost, which included excavation, was held to be plant of the leisure business.
4. St Johns School v Ward 1974 CA 49 TC 524. A special purpose prefabricated structure, for use as a laboratory and gymnasium in a school, was held not to be plant.
5. Schofield v R & H Hall Ltd 1974 NI 49 TC 538. A grain importer built a concrete silo with gantries, conveyors and chutes, which was held to be plant.
6. Benson v The Yard Arm Club Ltd 1978 CD STC 408. The purchase and conversion of an old ferry boat into a floating restaurant was held not to be plant, but the setting of the business.
7. Dixon v Fitch's Garage Ltd 1975 CD STC 480. A metal canopy covering the service area of a petrol filling station was held to be a shelter, and not plant.
8. Munby v Furlong 1977 CA STC 232. Books purchased by a barrister to create a library in his practice were held to be plant.
9. Leeds Permanent Building Society 1982 CD Decorative screens incorporating the society's name were held to be plant.

10. Wimpey International Ltd v Warland 1988 CA Expenditure on items of decoration installed in the company's restaurants was held not to be plant or machinery. However, item 14 in List C now effectively allows such items as plant.
11. Hunt v Henry Quick Ltd: King v Bridisco Ltd CHD. 1992 STC 633. The construction of mezzanine platforms in a warehouse was held to be plant and machinery, as they had a trade function.
12. Gray v Seymour's Garden Centre C.H.D. 1993. The construction of a special horticultural greenhouse was held not to be plant and machinery.
13. Attwood v Anduff C.A. 1997. The expenditure on a purpose built car wash site was held not to be plant and machinery. However, while structural expenditure on the site was not accepted as plant, car wash machinery clearly would be plant.
14. Shove v Lingfield Park C.D. 2003. An artificial all weather track at a racecourse was held to be part of the premises and not plant.

When capital expenditure is incurred

7. The expenditure is normally treated as incurred on the date on which the obligation to pay becomes unconditional. However, if payment in whole or in part is not required until more than four months after the date on which the obligation to pay becomes unconditional, then so much of the amount as can be deferred is taken to be incurred on that later date when the obligation to pay becomes unconditional. This is to prevent artificial acceleration of "purchase dates" beyond a normal credit period, to obtain allowances in an earlier period.

Example

K orders an item of plant from X plc on the following terms:

31.12.2011	plant delivered and invoiced on same date to K.
21.1.2012	due date for payment by K, being the end of the month following date of delivery.
3.2.2012	K makes payment.

The expenditure is deemed to have been incurred by K on 31.12.2011.

Example

L orders an item of plant from T plc costing £50,000 as follows:

31.12.2011	plant delivered and invoiced on same date.
31.1.2012	90% of invoice amount due for payment.
30.6.2012	balance of 10% due for payment.

L is deemed to have incurred the expenditure as follows:

31.12.2011	90% × £50,000 i.e. £45,000
30.6.2012	10% × £50,000 i.e. £5,000

Allowances available

8. The types of allowances which can be claimed in respect of expenditure on plant or machinery are:

annual investment allowance (AIA)

enhanced capital allowances (ECA) – also called 100% First Year Allowance (FYA) in the case of low emission cars

writing down allowance (WDA)

balancing allowance (BA)

sometimes the above are offset by a 'negative allowance' – a balancing charge (BC).

Annual investment allowance (£100,000)

9. Annual investment allowance of 100% of expenditure up to £100,000 a year will be available on any category of plant and machinery other than cars, for all categories of business. The limit was £50,000 per year up to 5 April 2010 for unincorporated taxpayers and 31 March 2010 for companies.

Notice has been given by the government that Annual Investment Allowance will fall to £25,000 a year on 6 April 2012 for income tax, and 1 April 2012 for corporation tax.

Annual Investment Allowance can be allocated to eligible assets in any order of the taxpayer's choice. The most efficient order of allocation is to the special rate pool first, then to the general pool, then short life assets and finally private use assets.

Enhanced capital allowances – 100% First Year Allowance for Energy/water saving plant

10. Enhanced capital allowances (ECAs) are designed to encourage the use of energy efficient equipment by giving a 100% allowance on purchase. Only products included on the UK Energy Technology Lists approved by the Department of Environment Transport and the Regions (DETR) will qualify. These lists are available at www.eca.gov.uk .

The allowance, which is available to all businesses, is also extended to qualifying energy saving assets purchased for leasing or hire to others.

Enhanced capital allowances – 100% FYA for Low-emission cars

11. a) A 100% FYA is available on the purchase of a new car if:

i) it is a low-emission car i.e. emits not more than 110g/km of carbon dioxide, or

ii) it is electrically propelled.

b) The 100% FYA is also available for plant and machinery to refuel vehicles with natural gas or hydrogen fuel, e.g. storage tanks, pumps, etc.

c) The allowance is extended to assets acquired to be leased, let or hired.

General pool plant and machinery writing down allowance – rate 20%

12. a) A writing down allowance is available in respect of expenditure incurred in the capital allowances basis period (the accounting period for companies), other than assets attracting ECA or FYA in that year.

b) The allowance is available whether the plant or machinery is brought into use for the trade by the end of the basis period, so long as it was acquired for the trade.

c) WDA is given on a reducing balance basis on the unrelieved general pool of plant expenditure, after adjusting for in year additions and disposals other than additions qualifying for FYA / ECA, as shown in the specimen computation below (section 18).

d) Before computing WDA the pool is reduced by reference to the Total Disposal Receipts (TDR) (limited to the original cost) from any of the following events at any time during the chargeable period.

- i) The plant or machinery ceases to belong to the taxpayer.
- ii) The taxpayer loses possession of the plant or machinery in circumstances where it is reasonable to assume that the loss is permanent.
- iii) The plant or machinery ceases to exist as a result of destruction, etc.
- iv) The plant or machinery begins to be used wholly or partly for purposes other than those of the trade.
- v) The trade is permanently discontinued.

e) The balance remaining on the pool after deducting any proceeds of disposals is written down in the normal way. If the pool balance after deducting sale proceeds, and bringing in qualifying additions, is negative there is a balancing charge calculated to bring the balance on the pool to nil.

f) The taxpayer can claim any proportion of the allowances available, but must accept the full balancing charge arising on a disposal.

g) If a plant asset has any private use, the asset must be kept outside the pool. The 20% allowance is calculated in the normal way and deducted from the cost or written down value of the asset; the amount given as the full writing down allowance is then reduced accordingly for the private use element. A separate (single-asset) pool is required for each asset with a private use element so that private use can be accurately adjusted for.

h) Companies do not have "private use assets" as a company has no private identity. Assets used privately by directors or staff are in business use by the company and the private use is dealt with by the income tax Benefits Code (see chapter 7).

i) A writing down allowance is not available in the year of cessation of trading.

j) If the balance on the general pool before WDA in any year is less than £1,000 the taxpayer may take the whole amount remaining as WDA of that period, writing the pool down to nil.

k) A writing down allowance is not available in the same period as first year allowance on assets which have received first year allowance; but WDA is available in the same year as additional investment allowance, to the extent the expenditure is not fully covered by the AIA allocated.

l) Cars with CO_2 emissions of 160 g/km or less qualify for the 20% writing down allowance and are added to the general pool, but do not qualify for AIA.

The government gave notice in the June 2010 Budget that the general pool WDA rate will fall to 18% from April 2012. However, as the legislation has not yet been enacted the examples which follow apply the current rates of allowance.

Special rate pool - 10% WDA

Assets in the special rate pool attract a writing down allowance of 10%. They are:

13. Features integral to a building;

14. Thermal insulation in a building;

15. Cars with CO_2 emissions of more than 160 g/km;

16. Machinery and plant which has an expected working life when new of 25 years or more, described as "long-life assets". (This special rate pool category is unlikely to affect income tax payers because of the minimum value rules set out below)

a) Expenditure on long life assets which does not exceed a minimum limit is excluded from the long life asset rules.

For companies, the minimum limit is £100,000 a year divided by one plus the number of associated companies.

The minimum of £100,000 a year also applies to individuals and to partnerships made up of individuals.

b) The exclusion for expenditure below the minimum limit does not apply to shared contributions to expenditure on machinery or plant, nor to expenditure on a share in machinery or plant, on machinery or plant for leasing, or on machinery and plant on which allowances have been given to a previous owner at the long-life asset rate.

c) If a long life asset is sold for less than its tax written down value in order to accelerate allowances, it is treated as sold for that tax written down value.

The government gave notice in the June 2010 Budget that the special rate pool WDA rate will fall to 8% from April 2012. However, as the legislation has not yet been enacted the examples which follow apply the current rates of allowance.

Separate pooling rules

17. A separate expenditure pool must be kept for each of the following classes of assets:

- i) general pool of plant and machinery (as detailed above);
- ii) special rate pool (as detailed above);
- iii) assets with any private use (one pool per asset);
- iv) short life assets where a de-pooling election is made (one pool per asset, or per class of identical assets).
- v) cars (except low-emission cars) costing more than £12,000 acquired before 1/6 April 2009 are subject to transitional rules from FA 2008 and must remain in single-asset pools until April 2014 or until earlier disposal.

Specimen computation layout

18.

		General pool	Special rate pool
Unrelieved qualifying expenditure (WDV) b/fwd		-	-
Qualifying expenditure not eligible for AIA (=cars) (not eligible for AIA)		-	-
Qualifying expenditure eligible for AIA (not eligible for 100% FYA)	-		
Less: Annual Investment Allowance (maximum £100k per year)	(-)		
Excess of expenditure over AIA taken to pool or special rate pool depending on asset type		-	
Available qualifying expenditure for WDA (before disposals)		-	-
Less: Total disposal receipts (limited to cost)		(-)	(-)
		-	-
Less: Writing down allowances 20% or 10%		(-)	(-)
Qualifying expenditure for 100% ECA /FYA	-		
Less: First year allowance 100%	(-)	0	
Unrelieved qualifying expenditure (WDV) c/fwd		-	-

Capital allowances and accounts

19. For all businesses the following provisions apply.

1) Capital allowances are given for a 'chargeable period' based on the period of account for individuals, and on the corporation tax accounting period for companies.

2) Capital allowances are treated as a trading expense of the business in the chargeable period and any balancing charge is treated as a trading receipt. This means that the trade profit for tax purposes is after the deduction of capital allowances. However, the taxpayer is not obliged to claim the maximum allowances available. If lower capital allowances are claimed than are available, the unrelieved expenditure (written down values) carried forward to the next period will be correspondingly higher.

3) Where the period of account for income tax purposes is not a 12 month period, the writing down allowance and the annual investment allowance are contracted or expanded on a pro-rata basis. e.g.

Period of account 8 months – writing down allowance	8/12 × 20%
Maximum AIA (from April 2010 to March 2012)	8/12 x £100,000
Period of account 15 months – writing down allowance	15/12 × 20%
Maximum AIA (from April 2010 to March 2012)	15/12 x £100,000

4) The prorating rules above also apply to companies where the accounting period is shorter than 12 months. If a company has a period of account longer than 12 months then this is split into one corporation tax accounting period of 12 months and one short period covering the rest of the period of account. Therefore companies can never have WDAs and AIAs prorated upwards for long periods, but only downwards for short periods.

5) ECAs, FYAs, balancing allowances or charges are not adjusted for long or short periods.

6) On the commencement of a new unincorporated business, or on a change of accounting date, in order to deal with the taxable profits of the first and second years of assessment it will be necessary first to compute and deduct the capital allowances for the period(s) of account.

Example

P started trading on the 1st May 2010 with the following results:

Adjusted profits 1.5.10 – 30.4.2011	162,000
Adjusted profits 1.5.11 – 30.4.2012	156,000
General plant and machinery purchased 10.04.2011	110,000

Compute the capital allowances available assuming current rules continue to apply in future years, and show the assessable trading profits for the years 2010/11 to 2012/13.

Solution

Capital allowances period 1.5.10 – 30.4.11		**General plant and machinery pool**
Opening WDV		0
10.04.2011 additions	110,000	
Less: Annual investment allowance – maximum	(100,000)	
		10,000
		10,000
30.4.11 writing down allowance 20%		(2,000)
WDV 30.04.2011		8,000
Capital allowances period 1.5.11 – 30.4.12		
30.4.2012 writing down allowance 20%		(1,600)
WDV 30.04.2012		6,400

Period of Account	**Adjusted Profits**	**Capital Allowances**	**Taxable Profit**
1.5.10 – 30.4.11	162,000	102,000	60,000
1.5.11 – 30.4.12	156,000	1,600	154,400

Assessments

2010/11 (1.5.10 – 5.4.11) 11/12 × 60,000	55,000
2011/12 (1.5.10 – 30.4.11)	60,000
2012/13 (1.5.11 – 30.4.12)	154,400

Notes

i) The overlap period is from 1.5.10 – 5.4.11, i.e. 11 months, or profits of £55,000. When the business ceases trading an adjustment in respect of this amount will be made in the final self-assessment of trading profits.

ii) The assumption current rates continue to apply means the UK government proposals to reduce AIA and WDA are not reflected in the solution, as the legislation has not yet been enacted.

Example

Q started trading on 1 October 2010 with first accounts for the 15 months to 31 December 2011. Capital expenditure of £100,000 on general plant and machinery was incurred on 1 October 2010. Capital expenditure of £64,000 was incurred on features integral to a building on 1 November 2010. Adjusted profits, before capital allowances, for the 15 months amounted to £209,500.

			General pool	Special rate pool
Period of account				
Capital expenditure	1.10.2010	100,000		
	1.11.2010	64,000		
Annual investment allowance	100,000 x 15/12	(125,000)		
Transfer unrelieved cost to pool			39,000	0
Writing down allowance	20% x 15/12		(9,750)	
Written down value carried forward			29,250	0

Assessments

	Adjusted profits 1.10.10 – 31.12.11	209,500
	Capital allowances (125,000 + 9,750)	134,750
		74,750
2010/11	1.10.10 – 5.4.11	
	74,750 x 6/15	29,900
2011/12	1.1.11 – 31.12.11	
	74,750 x 12/15	59,800

Notes

i) The capital allowances are computed for the period of account of 15 months.

ii) Capital allowances are deducted from the profits of the period of account before computing the assessments for tax years using the basis period rules.

iii) Overlap profits are January to March 2011: 74,750 x 3/15 = £14,950.

iv) If the first period of account had been less than 12 months' duration the writing down allowance and annual investment allowance would have been pro-rated down.

v) First year allowances are not scaled up or down for the length of a period of account.

Restriction on leasing costs for cars with high emissions

20. This is not a capital allowances rule, but was introduced as a result of the capital allowances rules for cars. The legislators considered that, given the slower rate of writing down allowances for cars with emissions over 160g, businesses would seek to lease these cars instead of buying them outright (obtaining a revenue deduction for the lease costs).

To discourage this, if a private car is leased or hired for trading purposes which emits more than 160 g/km of CO_2, then the hiring or leasing charge allowed as a business expense is restricted by 15%. This rule applies equally to incorporated and unincorporated businesses.

Example

C hires a car for £3,200 p.a. which emits 190 g/km CO_2. C uses the car 30% for private use.

Total of hire charge	3,200
Restriction for high emissions 15%	(480)
	2,720
Restriction for private use 30%	(816)
Allowable expense	£1,904

Plant purchased by hire purchase

21. With this method of purchase the interest element is allowed as an expense of trading. With regard to the capital element, capital allowances can be claimed:

a) Before the plant is brought in to use, for any instalment due.

b) When the plant is brought in to use, for all instalments outstanding, as if the whole of the balance of capital expenditure had been paid on at that date.

c) Where an HP agreement is not eventually completed after the plant has been brought into use, then an adjustment is made which claims back part of the allowance granted.

Leased plant and machinery

22. In general a lessor of plant and machinery is entitled to the full amount of capital allowances on eligible expenditure, and the rental payments of the lessee are an allowable business expense on an accruals basis (except for some cars, as noted in section 21 above).

Separate pooling arrangements apply to assets leased outside the UK, other than ships, aircraft and containers leased in the course of a UK trade.

Balancing charges and allowances: general rules

23. A balancing charge arises when the total disposal receipts (TDR) (limited to the original cost) of any pooled or non-pooled asset is greater than the amount of pool written down value existing for offset in the period of the sale.

Disposal value is the amount of the proceeds of sale, or where the asset is lost or destroyed, any insurance or compensation moneys received. In other circumstances, e.g. if plant is given away, the market price is used.

Where plant or machinery is demolished giving rise to a disposal treatment, the net cost of demolition can be added to the amount of unallowed expenditure at the time of the demolition.

A balancing allowance arises when the amount of pool written down value is greater than the total disposal receipts (TDR), but only in the following circumstances:

a) in the terminal period when trading permanently ceases
b) when there is, or is deemed to be, a cessation of trade, see below
c) when the asset has been de-pooled by election, or by reason of private use. (However, a balancing allowance is not given on a private use asset if it is sold to a connected person for less than its tax written down value.)
d) if a car which cost over £12,000 is in a single-asset pool dating from before April 2009, under the transitional rules for cars acquired before April 2009.

No balancing allowance is given on the sale of all remaining assets in the general or special rate pool unless the trade also ceases.

Deemed cessation

24. For capital allowance technical purposes the triggering of balancing adjustments is done by deeming the assets in "special pools" as forming a separate notional trade to that of any actual trade undertaken, so that on a disposal the notional trade is deemed to have ceased. This applies to the following categories:

a) private use assets
b) short life assets
c) ships
d) each letting of machinery otherwise than in the course of a trade of letting

Where capital allowances are computed on the basis of a deemed trade, this is assumed to be discontinued when a disposal has to be brought into account in respect of a single item or the last item in a pool of assets.

Example

B, who has been trading for many years, has the following data relating to his year ended 31st March 2012.

		£
a)	Additions to general plant – 31.12.11	12,000
	Proceeds of sale of plant (original cost £1,500)	2,500
	Purchase of Renault car for sales manager purchased 31.1.2012	14,000
	CO_2 emissions of Renault car 180 g/km	
	Sale of Peugeot car used by sales staff (original cost £9,000)	4,500
	CO_2 emissions of Peugeot car 140 g/km	

b) At the 1st April 2011 the tax written down value of assets was:

	£
Plant and machinery	15,000
Citroen car for B, purchased since May 2009 (private use 30%)	7,400
CO_2 emissions of Citroen car 150 g/km	

Compute the capital allowances claimable for the AP to 31st March 2012.

Solution

		general pool	**motor car (p.u.30%)**	**special rate pool**
		£	£	£
Written down value b/f 31.3.11		15,000	7,400	
Addition not qualifying AIA (staff car)		–	–	14,000
		15,000	7,400	14,000
Proceeds of asset sales (1,500 + 4,500)		(6,000)	–	–
		9,000	7,400	14,000
Addition AIA	12,000			
AIA 100% (under £100k)	(12,000)	0		
		9,000		
WDA 31.03.12		(1,800)	(1,480)	(1,400)
WDV c/f 31.3.12		7,200	5,550	12,600

Notes

i) The proceeds of sale of the plant are limited to the original cost of £1,500.

ii) The total allowances available to B for 2011/12 are:

	£
Plant pool AIA 12,000 + WDA 1,800	13,800
Car with private use 30%	1,036
Special rate pool	1,400
	16,236

iii) Plant purchased is eligible for AIA up to £100,000 of expenditure.

iv) Notice that the car with private use forms a separate pool and the WDA is first computed at the 20% rate and deducted in full within that pool, then restricted as regards the actual allowance given. This method allows for varying proportions of private use over the life of the asset.

v) A car with CO_2 emissions of more than 160 g/km is entitled to WDA of only 10%.

vi) Private use of cars by employees is irrelevant to the capital allowances position.

Plant and machinery – short-life assets

25. Short-life assets, other than cars, may be removed from the general pool ("de-pooled") at the option of the taxpayer. As a general rule, an election to de-pool will only be advantageous if the proceeds of sale are expected to be less than the written down value at the date of future disposal, so that the de-pooled treatment will give the chance of an immediate balancing allowance in the future chargeable period. De-pooling can last for a maximum of nine accounting (or basis) periods, but sometimes for only eight, depending on how dates interact.

The provisions on short life assets are as follows.

a) The rules apply in respect of plant and machinery from the general pool, but do not apply to motor cars, ships or assets leased to non-traders, or assets already required to be pooled separately.

b) Where the taxpayer expects to dispose of an item of plant or machinery at less than its tax written down value, within eight years of the end of the period of acquisition, then they can elect to have the item extracted from the general plant pool, and a separate pool created. The plant is treated as being in use for a separate notional trade.

c) The election to de-pool a short life asset or class of assets must be made within two years of the end of the period of acquisition.

d) Any balancing adjustment arising on the disposal is calculated separately.

e) If the item of plant or machinery has not been sold or scrapped by the end of eight years from the end of the year of acquisition (increased from four years with effect from 6 April 2011 for income tax and 1 April 2011 for corporation tax), then its tax written down value is transferred back to the general plant pool on the day after the 8th anniversary.

Example

T, who has traded for many years, has an accounting year end of 31 March. On the 1 May 2007 he purchases equipment for £9,375, electing for de-pooling.

Show the computations in the following circumstances:

a) The plant is sold in the year to 31 March 2012 for £2,000.

b) The plant is sold in the year to 31 March 2012 for £5,000.

c) The equipment is not sold by the 31 March 2012.

Solution: Capital allowances computation

		£
2007/08	Basis period to 31.3.2008: cost	9,375
	Writing down allowance 25% (pre-2008 rules)	(2,344)
WDV 1.4.08		7,031
2008/09	BP to 31.3.09: Writing down allowance 20%	(1,406)
WDV 1.4.09		5,625
2009/10	BP to 31.3.10: Writing down allowance 20%	(1,125)
WDV 1.4.10		4,500
2010/11	BP to 31.3.11: Writing down allowance 20%	900
WDV 1.4.11		3,600

a) 2011/12 year to 31.3.2012.

Disposal proceeds	(2,000)
Written down value b/f 1.4.11	3,600
Balancing allowance	1,600

b) 2011/12 year to 31.3.2012.

Disposal proceeds	(5,000)
Written down value b/f 1.4.11	3,600
Balancing charge	(1,400)

c) As the item of plant has not been sold by 31.3.12, WDA of (20% x 3600) = £720 applies for the year to 31.3.12. If the plant is not sold within eight years of the end of the year of acquisition, the written down value must then be transferred at the end of that period to the general plant pool.

Notes

i) Where short life assets of a similar nature are acquired in fairly large numbers e.g. small tools or returnable containers, then the cost of the assets may be aggregated and treated as one sum.

ii) Where assets used in a trade are stocked in large numbers and individual identification is possible but not readily practicable, then the computation can be based on the number of each class of asset retained. Assets falling under this heading could be calculators, amusement machines and scientific instruments, and videos.

The renewals basis

26. This is really a non-statutory method of obtaining relief on expenditure on plant and machinery, quite distinct from the capital allowance system outlined above. In fact where the renewals basis is adopted then the capital allowance system does not apply. The main points arising are:

a) The initial cost of any item of plant or machinery does not give rise to any allowances whatsoever, and no writing down allowance is available with this basis.

b) When an item is replaced then the cost of the new item, less anything received for the old one, is allowed as a deduction in computing trade profit. Any element of improvement or addition is excluded, and can only be claimed when it is replaced. Subsequent replacements are dealt with on a similar basis.

c) A change from the renewals basis to the normal capital allowance system can be made at any time, but the decision must apply to all items of plant in that class. In the year of the change, capital allowances can be claimed, irrespective of whether the expenditure is on a replacement or not.

The renewals basis effectively gives 100% relief in the year of expenditure on the replacement of an asset, but no relief at all for the first investment in an asset.

PART II –Other assets

Capital allowance for conversion of parts of business premises into flats

27. Rates of allowance

Initial allowance	100% of expenditure (less may be claimed)
Writing down allowance	25% (to extent unrelieved cost remains)

For expenditure incurred on the renovation or conversion of vacant or underused space above shops and commercial properties in traditional shopping areas to provide flats for rent.

The allowances are available where:

a) the property was built before 1980, has not more than five floors (excluding basements), and was originally constructed so that the upper floors were primarily for residential use;

b) most of the ground floor falls within certain rating categories at the time the conversion work starts (broadly retail shops, certain offices including those used for financial and professional services, and premises used for medical and health services or for providing food and drink);

c) the upper floors have either been unoccupied, or used only for storage, for at least one year before the conversion work starts;

d) apart from any extension required to provide access to the flats, the conversion takes place within the existing boundaries of the building; and

e) each new flat is self-contained, with its own external access, and has no more than four rooms (excluding the kitchen and bathroom and other small areas).

f) The rules governing the IBAs allowance code apply , with certain modifications and simplifications: there will be no balancing charge if a balancing event (e.g. a sale of the property, the flat ceasing to be let, or the grant of a long lease of the flat) occurs more than seven years from the time the flat or flats are completed, and the allowance is not transferable to a purchaser.

Renovation of business premises – disadvantaged areas

28. Initial Business Properties Renovation Allowance (BPRA) is given for 100% of qualifying expenditure incurred on or after 11 April 2007. The scheme allows people or companies, who own or lease property that has been vacant for a year or more in one of the designated disadvantaged areas of the UK, to claim immediate, full tax relief on their capital spending on the conversion or renovation of the property, in order to bring it back into business use.

Scientific research capital allowances

29. Allowances for capital expenditure on scientific research and development related to a trade carried on by a taxpayer are given against trading profits at 100% in the year the expenditure is incurred. The rules are as follows:

a) 'Research and development' means activities that fall to be treated as research and development in accordance with normal accounting practice.

b) Expenditure on research and development includes all expenditure incurred for:

   i) carrying out research and development, or

   ii) providing facilities for carrying out research and development.

   But it does not include expenditure incurred in the acquisition of rights in research and development, or rights arising out of research and development.

c) 'Normal accounting practice' means normal accounting practice in relation to the accounts of companies incorporated in a part of the United Kingdom.

d) Capital expenditure under this heading would include buildings and plant and machinery, but not land.

e) The amount of the allowance is 100% of capital expenditure.

Balancing adjustments can arise when assets representing research and development expenditure cease to be used for such purposes and either they are sold or destroyed.

Note Companies, but not income tax payers, can also get special allowances on research and development expenses that are revenue in character, equal to more than the total cost of that research and development expenditure. See Chapter 19.

Student self-testing questions

Note: These questions all relate to unincorporated taxpayers' capital allowances. Questions involving capital allowances for companies will be found in and after part III.

1. Ryan incurred the following expenditure on plant and machinery in the year ended 31 December 2011:

		£
6 January 2011	New plant	126,000
11 February 2011	Second hand lorry	25,000
14 February 2011	Burglar alarm system	1,500
17 July 2011	Ryan's car (30% private use)	13,000
14 August 2011	Car fleet for sales team (6 cars)	60,000

CO_2 emissions of all cars were 180 g/km.

Requirement: Calculate the capital allowances available to Ryan for the year ended 31 December 2011.

Solution

Year to 31 December 2011		General pool	Special rate pool	Car,30% private, 180g emissions
Qualifying expenditure incurred (not eligible for AIA) - cars			60,000	13,000
Qualifying expenditure (eligible for AIA but not 100% FYA)	152,500			
Less: Annual Investment Allowance (maximum)	(100,000)			
Excess of expenditure over £100,000		52,500		
			-	-
Less: Writing down allowance 20% or 10%		(10,500)	(6,000)	(1,300) 70% business
(WDV) carried forward		42,000	54,000	11,700

Allowances:	Annual investment allowance	100,000
	Writing down allowance 20%	10,500
	Writing down allowance 10%	6,000
	WDA 13,000 @ 10% = 1,300 x 70% business	910
		117,410

2. Tom commenced trading on 1 July 2010 and produced his first set of accounts to the period ended 30 September 2011. He purchased the following assets during this 15 month period:

		£
10 July 2010	Plant	147,500
18 July 2010	Car (private use 25%)	16,000
20 July 2010	Van	18,000
30 July 2010	Office furniture	2,000
1 August 2011	Computer equipment	5,400

CO_2 emissions of the cars were 180 g/km.

Requirement: Calculate the capital allowances available to Tom for the period of account.

Solution

15 month period of account 1 July 2010 to 30 September 2011		General pool	Car 25% private
Qualifying expenditure incurred (car) (not eligible for AIA)		-	16,000
Qualifying expenditure - AIA (not eligible for 100% FYA)	172,900		
Less: Annual Investment Allowance – maximum (£100,000 x 15/12)	(125,000)		
Excess of expenditure over £100,000		47,900	
Less: Writing down allowances 15/12 x 20% or 10% [= 25% and 12.5%]		(11,975)	(2,000) 75% business
Written down value (WDV) carried forward		35,925	14,000

Allowances	Annual investment allowance	125,000
	Writing down allowance 20% x 47,900 x 15/12	11,975
	WDA 10% x 16,000 x 15/12 x 75%	1,500
		138,475

Questions without answers

1. Wilton starts a trade on 1 March 2011 and has the following results before capital allowances

Period of account	Profits
1/3/11 - 31/7/12	189,167
1/8/12 - 31/7/13	173,600
1/8/13 - 31/7/14	164,000

General plant is bought as follows:-

Date	Cost
1/5/11	110,000
30/6/11	14,000
1/12/11	77,248
1/10/12	162,000
1/2/14	4,000

On 1 May 2013 plant which cost £14,000 was sold for £8,000

Requirement: Calculate assessments on profits from trading for the first five tax years. Assume no changes in future years to the plant and machinery capital allowance rules applying in 2011/12.

2. Homer started a business on 1 February 2011 and prepared accounts for the 18-month period to 31 July 2012 and then to 31 July each year. Between 1/2/11 and 31/7/13 he had the following capital expenditure and disposals.

Additions			**Disposals**		
1/5/11	2nd hand plant	179,882			
1/5/11	Ford car	11,000			
13/6/11	lorry	9,000			
1/10/11	photocopier	7,000			
10/11/12	Office equipment	5,000	30/11/12	Photocopier (bought 1/10/11)	9,000
15/6/13	machinery	11,000			
20/6/13	VW car	16,000			
30/6/13	new lorry	19,000	30/6/13	Lorry (bought 13/6/11)	7,500

The private use of Homer's Ford and VW cars is 40%.

CO_2 emissions of the Ford car purchased on 1/5/11 were 190 g/km.

CO_2 emissions of the VW car purchased on 20/6/13 are 150 g/km.

Requirement: Calculate the maximum capital allowances available to Homer for the periods ending 31/7/12 and 31/7/13. Assume no future changes in plant and machinery capital allowance rules applying in 2011/12.

14 Relief for trading and capital losses

Introduction

1. This chapter is concerned with the tax reliefs available to an income tax-payer who incurs a trading loss and also certain 'capital losses' that may be claimed against income. Losses by companies are covered separately in Chapter 22.

List of loss reliefs

2.

Set against total income of the same or prior tax year.	Section 64 ITA 2007
Carried forward and set against future trading income from the same trade.	Section 83 ITA 2007
Losses incurred in each of the first four years of trading can be set against total income of the three preceding tax years.	Section 72 ITA 2007
Terminal loss relief for losses of the last 12 months of a trade.	Section 89 ITA 2007
Relief for losses where a business is transferred to a limited company.	Section 86 ITA 2007
Relief for capital losses.	Section 131 ITA 2007
Relief for pre-trading expenditure.	
Trading loss set against capital gains.	
Property rental business losses.	

Set against 'other income' Sec 64 ITA 2007

3. The following points should be noted:

i) Capital allowances are deducted in computing adjusted taxable profits.

ii) Profits and losses are calculated by reference to periods of account, except the terminal loss computation for Section 89.

iii) The basis period rules apply to allocate losses to tax years, but there can be no "overlap" so losses are only measured once.

iv) Any loss which would otherwise count in two basis periods can only count in the earlier period.

v) Relief against total income can be claimed in the year of the loss or the preceding year.

vi) Where Section 64 total income claims are made in respect of both years the taxpayer can choose which claim should be taken in priority. Partial claims are not permitted.

vii) Any unused loss is carried forward under Section 83.

Example

A, who has been in business for many years, has an adjusted loss from trading for the year ended 31st December 2011 of £12,000. Under the basis period rules this is a trade loss of tax year 2011/12.

For tax year 2010/11, A's self-assessed taxable income, before any loss claims, was as follows:

	£
Trade profits year to 31.12.2010	10,000
Property business profit	30,000

Compute A's income tax liability for 2010/11 on the assumption that he claims relief for the trading loss of 2011/12 in the previous tax year, under s64 ITA 2007.

Solution:

Income tax computation 2010/11	**£**
Trade profits	10,000
Property income	30,000
Total income	40,000
Section 64 loss relief from 2011/12	(12,000)
Net income	28,000
Personal allowance	(7,475)
Taxable income (non-savings)	20,525
Income tax liability:20,525 @ 20%	4,105

Notes

i) Personal allowances are claimed after relief for a loss, so that there may be wasted personal allowances if a large trade loss is carried back.

ii) The whole of the loss to 31st December 2011 has been used against total income of the year preceding the loss, i.e. 2010/11.

Capital allowances

4. Capital allowances are deducted in computing trade profits, but the taxpayer does not have to claim the full allowances available in computing his or her taxable profits. Unusable losses can therefore sometimes be avoided by forgoing capital allowances in a period.

Example

T, who started in business in January 2006, has an adjusted trading profit for the 12 months to 31st December 2011 of £795, and capital allowances available of £4,000. T has property income for 2011/12 of £8,600 and no other income.

Compute T's optimal loss claim and income tax liability for 2011/12.

Solution: Income tax computation 2011/12

	£
Property income	8,600
Trading profit after capital allowances (see working)	nil
Total income	8,600
Less Section 64 relief – claimed current year (see working)	(525)
Net income	7,475
Personal allowance	(7,475)
Taxable income	NIL

Trading loss. Claimed Section 64 (795 profit – 1,320 capital allowances) = 525

Assessable trading profit	NIL

Note

T has claimed only £1,320 of his maximum capital allowances so that he does not waste his personal allowance in 2011/12.

The balance of the capital allowance unclaimed of (£4,000 – £1,320), increases the pool WDV carried forward at 1 January 2012, on which WDA may be given for y/e 31 December 2012.

Tax planning considerations in making a Section 64 claim

5. The following points should be taken into consideration in deciding whether to make a claim for loss relief against total income under Section 64 for the current or prior year, or both, and in what order. .

a) *Loss of personal allowance*: Cannot be carried forward, or back.

b) *Transfer of married couple's allowance, spouses aged 65 at 5.4.2000:* Can all be transferred to the spouse, on a joint election, although only obtaining relief at the 10% rate.

c) *Loss of personal pension plan relief (see Chapter 16)*: Net relevant UK earnings are after deduction of loss relief.

d) *Saving tax at higher rates*: A claim can be made for the tax year of the loss or the preceding year, or both in either order. The top tax rate of the taxpayer in these years may not be the same.

e) *Reduction in Class 4 NIC*: Profits for Class 4 National Insurance purposes (see chapter 17) are after deduction of loss reliefs set against trade income (s83), but are not reduced by loss reliefs set against total income (s64).

Carried forward – Section 83 ITA 2007

6. To the extent that a trading loss has not been relieved by claims under section 64 or 72, which take priority, it may be carried forward and set against the first available profits of the same trade.

Any loss brought forward must be set off as soon as possible against trade profits, even where this causes a loss of personal allowances.

Example

Mr R has tax adjusted profits for the year to 31st December 2011 of £26,000, and no capital allowances. Trade losses brought forward under Section 83 amount to £3,105. R started in business on 1.7.2007, and has no other income.

Compute the income tax liability for 2011/12 of Mr R.

Solution: Income tax computation 2011/12

(basis period year to 31.12.11)			£	£
Trade profits			26,000	
Section 83 losses b/f			(3,105)	22,895
Personal allowance				(7,475)
Taxable income				15,420
Tax Liability	n/a	@ 10%		0
	15,420	@ 20%		3,084

Relief for losses in first four years of trading – Section 72 ITA 2007

7. The relief which is available under this section is in addition to that under Sec 64 or 83, but is only available in the first four tax years of a new trade. The relief is as follows.

a) Trading losses incurred in the first four tax years may be carried back and set against the total income of the taxpayer, in the previous three tax years in each case.

b) The set-off under section 72 is against income of an earlier year before a later year, i.e. on a FIFO basis.

c) The trade loss is calculated on the normal basis period rules for losses.

d) Each loss is set against income of the first available year in the following order: non savings income, savings income, and dividend income of the claimant.

e) A claim must be made by the filing date for the tax year after the loss is incurred.

f) Each claim is a separate claim for a separate tax year loss. It is not necessary to make the section 72 claim for all tax years if losses are incurred in all the first four years.

g) Where a claim is made for relief under Sec 64 and under Sec 72, then the loss cannot be apportioned between them. Butt v Haxby 1983 STC 239.

Example

P left his employment on the 31st December 2008 and commenced trading on the 1st January 2009 with the following results for tax purposes:

	£ (Loss)
12 months to 31.12.2009	(3,000)
12 months to 31.12.2010	(2,000)
12 months to 31.12.2011	(5,000)

Compute the losses available for set-off under section 72 and show the tax years in which they can be utilised.

Solution

2008/09	1.1.09 – 5.4.09 3/12 × 3,000 =		(750)
2009/10	Year ended 31.12.09	(3,000)	
	Less allocated to 2008/09	750	(2,250)
2010/11	Year ended 31.12.10		(2,000)
2011/12	Year ended 31.12.11		(5,000)

Loss relief available is as follows:

	2008/09	2009/10	2010/11	2011/12
	750	2,250	2,000	5,000
Set against total income				
2005/06	750	–	—	
2006/07	–	2,250	—	
2007/08	–	–	2,000	
2008/09	–	–	–	5,000

Notes

i) If the losses cannot be fully used by a section 72 claim then the balance can be carried forward in the usual way under Section 83.

Terminal loss relief – Section 89 ITA 2007

8. Under this section relief is available where a cessation of trading takes place, and a loss arises attributable to all or part of the last 12 months of trading. The rules for computing the loss are designed to be fair to all traders, regardless of what point in the final tax year they cease trading.

A terminal loss may optionally be carried back and set against the trading profits (less capital allowances) of the three tax years prior to the tax year in which the trade ceases. The terminal loss is made up of 3 elements:

(a) The loss from 6 April to the date of cessation in the final tax year; plus

(b) The loss for the other part of the final twelve months of trading; plus

(c) Overlap profits.

Where part (b) of the calculation shows a profit it is ignored in calculating the terminal loss.

Example

S has overlap profits brought forward of £1,000, and ceased trading on 30th June 2011 with the following results:

Adjusted profits	**£**
9 months to 30.6.11	(1,500)
12 months to 30.9.10	1,200
12 months to 30.9.09	1,600

Compute the terminal loss available for relief.

Solution: Calculation of terminal loss – 12 months to 30.6.2011

	£	£
2011/12 (6.4.2011 – 30.6.2011)		
3/9 × (1,500)	(500)	(500)
2010/11 (1.7.2010 – 5.4.2011)		
1.10.2010 – 5.4.2011 6/9 × (1,500)	(1,000)	
1.7.2010 – 1.10.2010 3/12 × 1,200	300	(700)
Overlap profits		(1,000)
Terminal loss		(2,200)

9. Some further points on terminal losses.

a) Capital allowances claimed are deducted before terminal loss relief is applied.

b) Terminal loss is computed after deducting capital allowances.

Transfer of a business to a limited company – Section 86 ITA 2007

10. If a sole trader or partnership transfers its business to a limited company, there is a cessation of trade. Accordingly, trading losses at the date of transfer are not available for set-off against any future corporation tax profits of the new company.

However, Section 86 provides some relief where the following conditions are met.

a) The consideration for the business consists wholly or mainly in allotted shares of the company. In this case 80% is often taken to satisfy 'mainly'.

b) The shares are beneficially held by the transferor throughout the period of any tax year for which a claim under Section 86 is made.

c) The company carries on the same business throughout any tax year for which a claim is made.

Relief is available in respect of trading losses from a former business which can be carried forward and they can be set against income received by the transferor from the company. The losses must be set against earned income first, e.g. directors' fees or remuneration, and then investment income, e.g. dividends.

Example

D transfers his business to a limited company on the 1st August 2011 wholly for shares.

At that date the business has trading losses of £10,000. In the year 2011/12 D receives director's remuneration of £8,000 and a net dividend of £900 from the company.

Income tax computation 2011/12

	£
Income from employment	8,000
Less Section 86 loss	8,000
Dividend income (£900 x 100/90)	1,000
Less Section 86 loss	1,000

Notes

i) With this example there would be trade losses to carry forward to 2012/2013 of £1,000 providing the conditions noted above are satisfied.

ii) In claiming the Section 86 relief for 2011/12 D has lost his personal allowances which cannot be carried forward.

Relief against total income for capital losses on unquoted trading companies – Section 131 ITA 2007

11. Under this section a loss made by an individual on the disposal of any unquoted shares can be set against his income for income tax purposes. The loss must arise from a number of shares originally subscribed for on the formation of the company, and not from an inheritance or subsequent acquisition.

The claim is similar to a claim under Section 64 ITA 2007, but takes precedence over relief under that section. The company must be a UK trading company at the date of the disposal. A qualifying loss can only be claimed in the following circumstances:

a) on a disposal for full market value, or

b) on a winding up, or

c) on a claim that the shares have become of negligible value.

The loss is deducted from the taxpayer's income in the year in which the disposal takes place or in the preceding year.

Example

Z and his wife have the following data relating to 2011/12.	£
Z Income from employment	45,000
Mrs Z Income from employment	7,600
Z Building society interest (net)	8,000
Z allowable loss under Sec 131 ITA 2007 arising from shares in A Ltd	3,000

Compute the income tax liability for 2011/12 of Z and his wife.

Solution: Income tax computation 2011/12

	Z	Mrs Z
	£	£
Non savings income		
Income from employment Z	45,000	–
Income from employment Mrs Z	–	7,600
	45,000	7,600
Savings income		
Building society interest (gross)	10,000	–
	55,000	7,600
Less capital loss relief Sec 131	3,000	–
	52,000	7,600
Personal allowance	7,475	7,475
Taxable income	44,525	125

Tax liability			
n/a / n/a	@ 10 %	0	0
35,000 / 125	@ 20%	7,000	25
9,525 / –	@ 40%	3,810	–
44,525 125		10,810	25

Notes

i) The relief for the capital loss is deducted from the earned income of Z in the computation. If this is insufficient it is set against his unearned income.

ii) As Z is paying tax at the 40% rate it would be tax efficient to transfer some of his investments to Mrs Z, to generate additional income in her own right.

Pre-trading expenditure

12. Relief is available for expenditure incurred by a person in the seven years before he or she commences to carry on a trade.

a) The expenditure must be allowable trading expenditure which would have been deducted in computing trading profits if incurred after the commencement of trading.

b) Pre-trading expenditure is treated as an expense of the trade.

c) The relief does not apply to pre-trading purchases of stock.

d) A trading loss in the first tax year caused by pre-trading expenditure relief may be relieved under Section 64, 83 and 72 ITA 2007 in the normal way.

Restrictions on claiming loss reliefs

13. a) A claim under Section 64 is only available to trades which were carried on with a view to profit, and on a commercial basis, in the tax year of the loss.

b) Farmers and market gardeners cannot obtain relief under Section 64 if in the previous five years their business has incurred successive trade losses, unless it can be shown that the trade is being carried on with a view to profit, and there is a reasonable expectation of profits in the future.

c) Loss relief under Section 83 is available in the earliest possible years only against the profits from the same trade, and not against total income or profits from any other trade.

d) From 2008/09 Income Tax loss relief against total income under section 64 is restricted to a maximum of £25,000 offset in a tax year, if an individual does not spend more than 10 hours per week on average working in the trade which incurred the loss. (This change was made to prevent 'hobby' traders getting unlimited reliefs for trading losses against other taxable income.)

Trading losses set against capital gains

14. Where a trading loss is incurred in a tax year, then to the extent that it has not been fully relieved by a total income claim under Section 64 ITA 2007, a claim for relief against net chargeable gains of the same year can be made. The amount set against capital gains cannot exceed the chargeable gains for the year, before deducting the CGT exemption amount of £10,600, for 2011/12.

Example

N has the following data relating to the year 2011/12:

	£
Trade loss for year to 31.3.12	(17,000)
Chargeable gains before exemption.	12,000

In the year to 5th April 2012 N has other taxable income totalling £16,000.

Compute the income tax liability for 2011/12, assuming N makes all possible current year loss claims.

Solution: Income tax computation 2011/12

	£
Total income	16,000
Less Section 64 claim	(16,000)
	–

CGT computation 2011/12

Chargeable gains	12,000
Less trading losses extended to gains (s280)	(1,000)
	11,000
Less annual exemption	(10,600)
Taxable chargeable gains	400

Notes

i) N's personal allowance of £7,475 for 2011/12 would be wasted.

ii) The trading loss of £17,000 has been dealt with as follows:

		£
Section 64	2011/12	16,000
Capital gains	2011/12	1,000

iii) The CGT on the remaining £400 is taxable at the 18% rate. For details of CGT see Chapter 30.

Property business losses

15. 1) Any rental business loss of an individual is automatically carried forward and set against rental business profits of the next year. It cannot be carried back, or set against other income of the year.

2) Property business losses can only be set off against profits from property business (apart from (4) below).

3) From April 2011 furnished holiday lettings losses may only be set against income from the same furnished holiday letting business. Previously they could be treated as trade losses and added to a s64 claim.

4) Where a rental business loss is attributable to capital allowances then all or part of that attributable loss can be set against total income as relief for non-trade capital allowances against total income.

Example

K has a property business loss of £3,500 for the year 2011/12 after claiming landlord's capital allowances of £1,500.

	£
Loss relief available against total income	1,500

Notes

i) The £1,500 loss can be set against total income of 2011/12. The balance of £2,000 must be carried forward against future property business profits.

ii) Loss relief is limited to the smaller of the total property business loss and the capital allowances included in computing it.

Student self-testing questions

1. James receives £3,000 per year income from property. He makes up business accounts for trading annually to 31 December. His recent tax adjusted results from trading have been:

Year to 31 December 2009	Profit	£42,000
Year to 31 December 2010	Profit	£48,000
Year to 31 December 2011	Loss	(£100,000)
Year to 31 December 2012	Profit	£5,000

Requirement: Show the net income before personal allowances in each of the years after making a tax effective claim for loss relief.

Solution

Tax year	2009/10	2010/11	2011/12	2012/13
Period of a/c	31.12.2009	31.12.2010	31.12.2011	31.12.2012
Income from trading	42,000	48,000	Loss	5,000
S83				(5,000)
				0
Income from property	3,000	3,000	3,000	3,000
	45,000	51,000	3,000	3,000
S64		(51,000)		
Net income	45,000	0	3,000	3,000

Loss Memorandum:-

		£
2011	Loss arising	100,000
2010	S64 carry back against total income	(51,000)
2012	S83 carry forward against trade profit	(5,000)
c/fwd		44,000

Note: A s64 claim against total income of the current year would not be tax effective, as the total income of 2011/12 is covered by the personal allowance.

2. Nathaniel started trading on 1 October 2009 and prepared accounts to 31 December of each year from 2010.

His results for the first two accounting periods were: -

15 months to 31 December 2010	Loss 23,700
Year to 31 December 2011	Loss 19,320

Prior to becoming self -employed he had the following other income:-

2006/2007	12,200
2007/2008	12,500
2008/2009	12,800
6/4/2009 to 30/9/2009	6,900

Requirement: Calculate Nathaniel's net income for 2006/2007 to 2009/2010 using all available s72 claims.

Solution

Losses eligible for s72 Relief

Year	Basis period	Workings	Loss	Years for s72 claim
2009/10	1.10.09- 5.4.10	23,700 x 6/15	9,480	06/07 – 08/09
2010/11	1.1.10-31.12.10	23,700 x 12/15 - 23700 x 3/15	14,220	07/08 – 09/10
2011/12	y/e 31.12.11		19,320	08/09 - 10/11

Using all possible s72 claims, total income is

		2006/07	2007/08	2008/09	2009/10
Income from trade					0
Other income		12,200	12,500	12,800	6,900
s 72 relief	2009/10 loss	(9,480)			
	2010/11 loss		(12,500)	(1,720)	
	2011/12 loss			(11,080)	(6,900)
Total income		2,720	0	0	0

c/fwd loss of 1,340 for year 2011/12

Questions without answers

1. Jensen started to trade on 6/4/2010. Projected results are:

Year to 5 April		
2011	Profit	24,000
2012 (projected)	Profit	32,000
2013 (projected)	Profit	36,000
2014 (projected)	Profit	30,000
2015 (projected)	Loss	(56,000)

Business is expected to be profitable thereafter

Jensen also has rental income of £12,000 per annum. Using the 2011/12 loss relief rules:

a) **Outline how Jensen could get relief for the loss in 2014/15;**

b) **Calculate the quickest way of relieving the loss.**

c) **How would the situation change if Jensen ceased trading on 5/4/2015?**

2. Mister Y was employed as an auditor until 1/1/2011 and on that date started in business as a commodity dealer making up accounts to 30 June each year:

Income as auditor		Results as dealer (loss)	
2007/2008	20,000	1/1/11 to 30/6/11	(6,000)
2008/2009	22,000	Year to 30/6/12	(3,000)
2009/2010	24,000	Year to 30/6/13	(2,400)
2010/2011	22,000	Year to 30/6/14	nil

Requirement: Show the revised net income for all tax years if Mr Y claims loss relief as soon as possible.

3. A business ceased on 30 September 2012. Results were

Year to 31/12/2009	4,000
Year to 31/12/2010	800
Year to 31/12/2011	600
9 months to 30/9/2012	(3,900)
Overlap profits on commencement (unrelieved)	900

Requirement: Calculate the terminal loss and show how it is relieved against earlier profits.

15 Partnership taxation

Introduction

1. A partnership exists where two or more persons join together for business purposes forming an association which is not a separate legal entity for taxation purposes.

A trading or professional partnership is taxed as a collection of sole traders.

The main special features of partnership taxation relate to

a) the allocation of profits for tax purposes,
b) the effect of changes in partnerships' members or profit-sharing arrangements, and
c) some loss restrictions for limited liability partnerships.

General provisions

2. The following provisions apply to any new partnership that has a trade or profession.

(The partnership trade tax rules in this chapter do not apply to partners in investment activities , including letting of property, who are simply treated as joint owners of an investment asset and taxed on their respective shares of the income less expenses for each tax year.)

a) For income tax purposes a partnership of two or more individuals is not treated as a separate legal entity distinct from the partners. The effect of this is that each partner is assessed individually.

b) A partnership tax return must be completed for HMRC by the representative partner. This return shows the adjustment of the firm's accounting profits for tax purposes and the allocation of those profits to each partner, before and after capital allowances . The profits and capital allowances figures are repeated on the individual partners' self assessment tax returns.

c) Taxable profits of the partnership are calculated in the same way as for a sole trader so that all partnership expenses and capital allowances will be given against the profits before allocation to the partners.

d) Profits are assessed on a current year basis with the normal basis being the period of account for twelve months ending in the year of assessment. The rules for determination of assessable profits of each partner in the first two or three and last year that he or she is a member of the partnership are the same as the opening and closing year basis period rules for a sole trader (see Chapter 11).

e) Partnership profits are allocated by reference to the partnership profit sharing agreement rules applicable in the period of account and not the related tax year.

f) Where there is a change in the members of a partnership, so long as there is at least one partner carrying on the business both before and after the change, the change does not constitute a cessation of the partnership's trade for tax purposes.

Adjustment and allocation of profits

3. The following points arise under this heading.

a) Partnership profits are adjusted for income tax purposes using the same principles as for a sole trader. See Chapter 10. Partners' "salaries" and interest on capital are treated as part of their share of the trading profits for tax purposes. If partners' salaries and or interest are payable then the amounts due will be allocated to each partner individually and the balance of profit then divided in profit-sharing ratios.

b) The adjusted partnership profit is reduced by any capital allowances on partnership assets, before any allocation is made to the partners.

Example

A and B formed a partnership in June 2006, sharing profits equally after charging interest of 5% p.a. on their fixed capital accounts of £160,000 and £100,000 respectively, and a salary for A of £50,000. Taxable profits for the year ended 31st December 2010 were £150,000.

Show the allocation of profits for 2011/12.

Solution: Partnership computation 2011/12

Adjusted profits after capital allowances year to 31st December 2011 – £150,000

Allocation of profit 2011/12

	Total	A	B
	£	£	£
Interest on capital: 10%	13,000	8,000	5,000
Salary – A	50,000	50,000	–
	63,000	58,000	5,000
Balance shared equally	87,000	43,500	43,500
	150,000	101,500	48,500

Notes

i) Each partner includes his share of profit, i.e. A. £101,500 , B. £48,500, in his personal self assessment tax return, being trading profits measured for 2011/12 based on the year to 31.12.11.

ii) All amounts shown in the partnership accounts for the year to 31st December 2010, for partners' salaries, share of profits or interest on capital, will have been added back as proprietors' drawings in arriving at the taxable profit of £150,000 as shown in the partnership tax return.

Example

A and B entered into partnership on the 1st June 2007 with the following results:

	£	£
	Adjusted profits	Capital allowances
1.6.2007 – 31.5.2008	20,000	2,000
1.6.2008 – 31.5.2009	30,000	5,000
1.6.2009 – 31.5.2010	40,000	15,000
1.6.2010 – 31.5.2011	50,000	10,000

The partners have agreed to share profits equally.

Show the individual partners' assessable trading profits for the relevant tax years

Solution

	Partnership A and B	Assessments	A	B
2007/08	Period of account 1.6.07 – 5.4.08 10/12 × (20,000 – 2,000)	15,000	7,500	7,500
2008/09	Period of account 1.6.07 - 31.5.08 (20,000 – 2,000)	18,000	9,000	9,000
2009/10	Period of account 1.6.08 - 31.5.09 (30,000 – 5,000)	25,000	12,500	12,500
2010/11	Period of account 1.6.09 - 31.5.10 (40,000 – 15,000)	25,000	12,500	12,500
2011/12	Period of account 1.6.10– 31.5.11 (50,000 – 10,000)	40,000	20,000	20,000

Notes

i) The overlap period is 1.6.07 to 5.4.08 with overlap profits of £7,500 carried forward by each partner (this is counting in whole months: the figure is £7,595 each if we count exact days). When the partnership ceases, or a partner leaves and is replaced by another, then the individual's final profits assessment from the partnership as a source of trading income will be reduced by his overlap relief.

ii) Paying income tax liability is the responsibility of the individuals in the partnership and not the partnership itself although a partnership return must be completed.

iii) Total profits assessed = £123,000

less overlap profits carried forward £15,000

= £108,000 actual profits after capital allowances.

Changes in partnership

4. The basis period rules apply separately for each new partner and each retiring (ceasing) partner. The trade is a source of income which is starting or ceasing for the individual, but the other partners are unaffected by a partner joining or leaving the partnership, so long as they themselves continue trading.

If there is a change in profit share ratio during a period of account, for study purposes it may be assumed that profits of a period of account accrue evenly.

In practice, the final information about the allocated profit shares of partners, for a period of account when there is a change in either the partners or the profit shares, or both, will be as reported to HMRC on the partnership tax return.

Example

X and Y started in partnership on 1st July 2004 sharing profits equally. Their accounts are made up to 31st December each year. On 1st January 2007 Z was admitted as an equal partner, the profit ratio then becoming one third each.

Tax-adjusted profits for the years to 31st December 2007 were as follows:

	£
1.7.2004– 31.12.2004	20,000
12 months to 31.12.05	40,000
12 months to 31.12.06	50,000
12 months to 31.12.07	60,000

Show the assessable trading profit of each partner for tax years 2004/05 to 2007/08. Calculations may be made to the nearest month.

Solution

Tax Year	**Basis period**		**Total £**	**X £**	**Y £**	**Z £**
2004/05	(1.7.04 – 31.12.04)	20,000				
	1.1.05 – 5.4.05 (3/12 × 40,000)	10,000	30,000	15,000	15,000	–
2005/06	12 months to 31.12.05		40,000	20,000	20,000	–
2006/07	X: 12 months to 31.12.06		50,000	25,000	25,000	–
	Y: ditto					
	Z: opening year rules					
	1.1.07 – 5.4.07 $3/12 \times 60{,}000 \times \frac{1}{3}$		5,000	–	–	5,000
			55,000	25,000	25,000	5,000
2007/08	12 months to 31.12.07		60,000	20,000	20,000	20,000

Notes

i) When Z is admitted on 1st January 2007, there is continuation of the trade for the others.

ii) The partners are assessed individually in respect of their shares of the profits.

iii) Z is deemed to have started in self-employment on 1st January 2007 and his individual overlap profit must be computed based on that date. This is as follows:

1.1.07 – 5.4.07 = 95 days (say 3 months)

3/12 × 60,000 (i.e. profits to 31.12.2007) × $\frac{1}{3}$ (Z's share) = 5,000

iv) When a partner leaves, his or her overlap profits are adjusted in his or her final assessment.

v) Overlap X and Y = 10,000 : Z 5,000

Basis periods

	X + Y	Z
2004/05	1.7.04 – 5.4.05	–
2005/06	1.1.05 – 31.12.05	–
2006/07	1.1.06 – 31.12.06	1.1.07 – 5.4.07
2007/08	1.1.07 – 31.12.07	1.1.07 – 31.12.07

Example

Using the data for X, Y and Z in the above example with the following further tax-adjusted results:

	£
12 months to 31.12.08	80,000
12 months to 31.12.09	90,000
12 months to 31.12.10	100,000
12 months to 31.12.11	140,000

Z leaves the partnership on the 30th September 2010.

Show the assessable trade profits of the partners for all tax years.

Solution

		Total	X	Y	Z
2008/09 to 31.12.08		80,000	26,667	26,667	26,666
2009/10 to 31.12.09		90,000	30,000	30,000	30,000
2010/11: ratio changes when Z leaves					
	1.1.09 – 30.9.10				
	9/12 × 100,000 1:1:1	75,000	25,000	25,000	25,000
	Less overlap relief Z				
	Z assessable profit	2010/11			
	1.10.10 – 31.12.10(only 2 partners)				
	3/12 × 100,000 1:1	25,000	12,500	12,500	–
	X and Y assessable profit		37,500	37,500	
		100,000			
2011/12	to 31.12.11	140,000	70,000	70,000	–

Notes

i) Z's assessment for the year 2010/11 comprises:

Proportion of profits from 1st Jan 2009 – 30th Sept 2010 =	25,000
Less overlap relief (see previous example)	(5,000)
	20,000

ii) There will be an automatic continuation for X and Y on the retirement of Z.

iii) **Basis periods**

	X + Y + Z	**X + Y**	**Z**
2008/09	1.1.08 – 31.12.08		
2009/10	1.1.09 – 31.12.09		
2010/11		1.1.10 – 31.12.10	1.1.10 – 30.09.10
2011/12		1.1.11 – 31.12.11	

Partnership taxed and untaxed income – notional business

5. a) Any other taxed or untaxed income of the partnership, after duly being allocated to individual partners, is treated as coming from a 'second notional business'. This second notional business commences when an individual becomes a partner and is treated as permanently discontinued only when the individual ceases to be a partner. It is taxed by applying the same basis period rules – including the possibility of 'overlap' profits – as apply to the principal partnership trade profits.

b) Where a partnership receives rents from subletting business accommodation, these rents can be treated as income of the primary trade (instead of forming income of a second deemed trade) in the following circumstances:

i) the accommodation must be temporarily surplus to current business requirements;

ii) the premises must be used partly for the business and partly let, in other words, rents from a separate property which is wholly surplus must be dealt with as property income;

iii) the rental income must be comparatively small;

iv) the rents must be in respect of the letting of surplus business accommodation only and not of land.

Partnership losses

6. a) Partnership losses as computed for tax purposes are apportioned between the partners in the same proportion as they share profits.

b) Where the business as a whole makes a profit as computed for tax purposes but after allocation of prior shares (e.g. salaries) an individual partner makes a loss then this cannot be used for normal loss claim relief.

c) For tax purposes the allocation of profit (or losses) between partners must result in a straight apportionment of the actual total profits (or losses) made by the partnership. If the initial allocation using the commercial profit sharing arrangement for all the partners produces a mixture of notional profits and losses, the actual partnership profit (or loss) must be re-allocated between the profit making (or loss making) partners alone. This re-allocation is made in proportion to the notional profit (or loss) initially allocated to those partners.

d) The trade loss of each partner may be dealt with as follows:

i) Set off against total income. Section 64.

ii) Carried forward against share of future partnership profits. Section 83.

iii) Used in a terminal loss claim. Section 89.

iv) Used in an opening years Section 72 claim

v) Used in connection with the transfer of the partnership to a limited company. Section 86.

Example

X, Y and Z have been in partnership for many years with an accounting period to 31st December.

Profits are shared equally after the provision of salaries to X and Y of £50,000.

Adjusted profits for the year ended 31st December 2011 before salaries amounted to £70,000.

Show the allocation of profits for 2011/12.

Solution: X,Y,Z partnership allocation 2011/12

	Total	**X**	**Y**	**Z**
Salaries	100,000	50,000	50,000	–
Balance of profit				
(70,000 – 100,000)	(30,000)	(10,000)	(10,000)	(10,000)
Net allocation	70,000	40,000	40,000	(10,000)

However as Z has a notional loss the actual partnership profits must be re-allocated between the profit making partners

i.e. 40,000 / 80,000 or $\times \frac{1}{2}$ each.

In effect, Z's notional loss is allocated to X and Y proportionately, i.e. £5,000 each

	Total	**X**	**Y**	**Z**
Partnership allocation as above	70,000	40,000	40,000	(10,000)
Re-allocation	–	(5,000)	(5,000)	10,000
Net allocation	70,000	35,000	35,000	–

Student self-testing question

Mars and Venus commenced in partnership on 1 July 2009 and decided to produce their accounts to 30 June annually. On 1 January 2011, Pluto joined the partnership.

The partnership's accounts show the following adjusted profits:

	£
Year ended 30 June 2010	100,000
Year ended 30 June 2011	135,000
Year ended 30 June 2012	180,000

Requirement: Show the trading income assessable on the individual partners for all the tax years affected by the above information, assuming that profits are shared equally. (11 marks)

Solution

		Mars	Venus	Pluto	TOTAL
		£	£	£	£
A/c to 30 June 2010		50,000	50,000	-	100,000
A/c to 30 June 2011	6/12	33,750	33,750	-	67,500
	6/12	22,500	22,500	22,500	67,500
		56,250	56,250	22,500	135,000
A/c to 30 June 2012		60,000	60,000	60,000	180,000

Mars and Venus will both be assessed as follows:

2009/10	£50,000 x 9/12	£37,500
2010/11	A/c to 30 June 2010	£50,000
2011/12	A/c to 30 June 2011	£56,250
2012/13	A/c to 30 June 2012	£60,000

Overlap profits carried forward are £37,500 for each of Mars and Venus.

Pluto will be assessed as follows:

2010/11	£22,500 x 3/6		£11,250
2011/12		£22,500	
	£60,000 x 6/12	£30,000	£52,500
2012/13	A/c to 30 June 2012		£60,000
Overlap relief on:	£11,250		
	£30,000		
	£41,250		

Question without answer

Vera and Jack commenced in business on 1 October 2007 as hotel proprietors, sharing profits equally. On 1 October 2008 their son Terry joined the partnership and from that date each of the partners was entitled to one-third of the profits. The profits of the partnership adjusted for income tax, are:

Period ended	30 June 2008	£30,000
Year ended	30 June 2009	£45,000
Year ended	30 June 2010	£50,000
Year ended	30 June 2011	£60,000

Requirement

Calculate the assessable profits for each of the partners for all relevant tax years from 2007/2008 to 2011/12 **(7 marks)**

Calculate the overlap profits for each of the partners. **(4 marks)**

16 Personal investment – pensions

Introduction

1. This chapter is concerned with the income tax aspects of a UK person's saving towards a retirement pension. Contributions to pension saving are encouraged by the tax system so tax relief is given on contributions up to generous limits. Approved schemes where an underlying fund exists (see below) also have a further investment advantage that no income tax or capital gains tax is paid on investments held within the pension fund.

It is important to understand the difference between:

- occupational pension schemes, for individuals in employment; and /or
- personal or stakeholder pension schemes, for those in employment, self-employment or no employment.

Up to £2,880 a year (net) - £3,600 a year (gross) - may be saved in a personal (stakeholder) pension scheme by someone who has no "relevant earnings" - they do not even need to be a taxpayer to benefit from the £720 "tax relief top-up" that is given by the Government on a net contribution of £2,880 to a stakeholder pension scheme.

To be approved for tax relief, a pension scheme must meet many conditions which are considered socially desirable and fair, with regard to the pensions it offers and the way in which entitlements accrue – in particular there must be a high minimum age at which a pension can be paid, or any other value returned to the member.

This chapter is not concerned with the taxation of pensions in payment to pensioners. Income from pension schemes is generally treated like employment income (see chapter 7 and 8) and may be subject to PAYE.

Background - UK tax-approved pension schemes from 1 April 2004

2. The tax system for pension savings in the UK was considerably simplified in 2004. Apart from arrangements that are still running from before 2004 (not covered further here), there are two basic kinds of current HMRC approved pension scheme to which taxpayers can contribute pension savings and get income tax relief on what they put in. These two types are:

a) Registered occupational schemes: these are linked to particular employers or groups of employers and only open to qualifying employees. Contributions to these are paid gross. The employee's own contributions are deducted from pay before it is received by the employee. If only the employer pays into the scheme, it is called "non-contributory" (because the employee does not have to pay anything), and there is no need to consider the pension contribution by the employer in the employee's total income computation.

In funded occupational schemes (where there is an underlying fund of investments being managed to pay future pensions), the pension fund's investments are normally pooled for all members. Therefore often no specific part of the total fund is allocated to an individual contributing member until his or her pension rights vest (i.e. pension becomes payable). In unfunded occupational schemes (eg some civil service and teachers' pension schemes) there is no underlying pool of investment. The future pension promise in an unfunded public sector scheme is effectively made by the Government, to be paid out of future State income.

Income tax relief is still given on an employee's contributions to unfunded public sector occupational schemes, even though these "pension contributions" are not being "invested" but are merely going back to the Government, and being spent on current outgoings.

b) Registered stakeholder schemes and other Personal Pension Plans . These are schemes where a specific fund is kept for each contributing member. They are available to anyone and not attached to a particular employer (though employers may make contributions to them on behalf of their employees, in addition to the contributions made by the employees themselves). All contributions to these funds are treated as paid to the scheme trustees net of basic rate tax. There are no exceptions. (Even employer's contributions are treated as paid net because they are paid on behalf of the employee.) The scheme provider adds to the fund for each contributing member an amount of 20/80 relating to all contributions, which it reclaims from the Government, in respect of the basic rate income tax relief on those contributions.

It is possible to set up group personal pension plans (GPPPs) for groups of members, which saves on administration costs .

Employers may offer GPPPs for their staff as an alternative to an occupational scheme: if so the employee's basic GPPP contributions are deducted from pay by the employer, but as a contribution net of basic rate tax, unlike occupational pension contributions.

An employee can make further net-of-tax payments into a GPPP directly, provided that the total contributed does not exceed the annual or lifetime limits.

A Self Invested Personal Pension (SIPP) is a normal personal pension plan (so the member's contributions are paid in net of basic rate tax) but the member can direct the fund manager where to invest his or her fund (subject to rules about suitable investments for pension funds).

Contribution rules

3. The maximum allowable contribution payable by an individual contributing member of a pension scheme of either kind for each tax year is the greater of:

£3,600 gross; or

100 percent of 'relevant UK earnings'.

'Relevant UK earnings' are defined as:

income from employment;

income chargeable derived from the carrying on or exercise of a trade, profession or vocation (whether individually or as a partner acting personally in a partnership);

earnings of overseas Crown employees subject to UK tax;

income from furnished holiday lettings;

patent or copyright income of the original artist, author or inventor.

There is no limit to the contributions that can be paid by an employer on behalf of a scheme member who is an employee, provided they meet the general rules on allowable deductions (eg trade expenses) and the annual allowance provisions (below). Employer contributions are only allowed for relief in the employer's accounting period in which they are actually paid.

Annual allowance – all individuals

4. The maximum amount of contribution relievable for tax purposes has been fixed for the year 2011/12 at £50,000 (2010/11 £255,000). The annual allowance includes both employee and employer contributions.

Employees can contribute up to 100% of their pay towards a pension scheme within this annual allowance, and obtain full tax relief.

Contributions in excess of the annual allowance are taxed on the employee as income at the 40% rate in the year of the excess.

Lifetime allowance

5. The lifetime allowance during the year 2011–2012 is £1.8m, but this is planned to be reduced to £1.5m in 2012/13.

This is the amount against which the value of an individual's prospective pension benefits must be tested each year prior to the date when pension payments begin.

Exceeding allowances

6. Employer's contributions to a defined contribution scheme in excess of the annual allowance are taxed as income of the employee at 40%.

Employer's contributions to a defined benefit scheme in a year which increase the actuarial value of current benefits to more than the lifetime allowance are also taxed as income of the employee at 40%, in the year of the contribution being paid.

Unapproved pension schemes

7. Unapproved schemes have no UK tax benefits. Therefore

i) the employer's contributions to an unapproved pension savings scheme will not receive tax relief until benefits are paid to the employee;

ii) investment income and capital gains made within an unapproved pension scheme fund are taxable at the rate applicable to trusts, ie 40% on income (32.5% on dividends) and 28% on capital gains in 2011/12;

iii) payments out of such schemes will be taxed as trust income at the individual's marginal rate.

However, contributions to unapproved schemes do not count towards the annual allowance, nor will the fund accrued count towards the lifetime allowance.

Stakeholder pensions

8. These schemes were originally announced in 2000 as intended for "workers on modest incomes" who did not have access to an occupational or private pension scheme. However, since the 2004 simplification, the term "stakeholder pensions" (whether or not used in practice) effectively describes almost all money-purchase personal pension plans, except SIPPS (see above).

All but the smallest employers must offer staff access to a stakeholder pension from October 2001, unless they offer an occupational scheme. Unlike occupational pension schemes, the employer has no choice about whether to provide a minimum stakeholder scheme.

Stakeholder pension contributions attract a similar tax relief to occupational pension scheme contributions, though the administration is different. All contributions are paid in net of tax which the scheme recovers directly from HMRC. This means that contributions are deducted from net pay rather than gross pay, as is the case for occupational pension scheme contributions.

An employer of at least five employees must offer a stakeholder pension scheme to employees. However, an employer does not have to offer the scheme to an employee who:

- is under 18 years old
- is within five years of retirement age
- is not resident in the UK
- earns less than the lower earnings limit for National Insurance (NI) purposes
- has less than three months' service.

Employees must be offered the chance to join a stakeholder pension scheme within three months of starting work. They cannot be compelled to join nor can they be a member of a salary-related occupational pension scheme and a stakeholder pension scheme at the same time. However, an employee may be a member of a stakeholder pension scheme at the same time as having a personal pension or being a member of a money purchase occupational pension scheme.

An employee in a stakeholder scheme must be allowed to:

- choose his or her own level of contributions
- vary those contributions at will
- make one-off payments of £10 or more
- stop and start making contributions at will, without penalty.

The contribution must always be at least £10.

A stakeholder pension scheme member may contribute up to £3,600 gross into a scheme, regardless of his or her earnings. This allows those with low incomes or high unearned income to benefit from some element of pensions tax relief.

(It also allows family members, if they wish, to pay into a personal/stakeholder pension for a child and get a 20% subsidy from the state via the tax repayment. However it should be borne in mind that approval rules about minimum retirement ages for members of stakeholder schemes mean that it is likely that a fund started for a child will not become accessible for a very long time after the first contributions were made.)

Unlike with Gift Aid, there is no requirement that a person who has made a personal pension plan contribution net of basic rate tax withheld actually hands that tax over to the tax authorities. The fund is still reimbursed the notional basic rate tax deducted, even if the contributing member has paid no income or capital gains tax for the year when the £3,600 gross contribution (£2,880 net contribution) was paid to the fund.

Personal Pension Plans

9. Since 2004 any PPP effectively works the same way as personal pensions that are specifically labelled stakeholder pension schemes.

As with stakeholder pensions (in fact all personal pension plans from 1 April 2004), the administrator of an HMRC approved personal pension plan can **only** accept pension contributions **net** of basic rate tax relief. The contributing member therefore receives the basic rate tax relief at source.

Where higher rate relief is due (ie the taxpayer has taxable income falling in the higher or additional rate band, before taking account of the personal pension contributions) then the basic rate band is extended in a similar way to obtaining higher and additional rate relief for Gift Aid donations (see Chapter 5).

Contributions to Occupational Pension Schemes

10. Contributions to occupational schemes are deducted gross from pay.

On the personal tax computation they should be shown as a specific deduction against earnings of the employment. This effectively gives income tax relief at the highest marginal rate, as the contributions expense is deducted in computing total income.

Pension contributions (whether occupations or PPPs) are not a deductible expense from gross pay/ profits for the purposes of National Insurance.

Student self-testing questions

1. Christa is sole proprietor of a beauty salon. Her tax adjusted trading profits for the year to 5 April 2012 are £180,000, and she has no other income. Christa makes net contributions of £14,400 to a personal pension during the year.

Required: Calculate Christa's income tax liability for 2011/12.

Solution

			£
Income from trading			180,000
Personal allowance			0
Taxable income			180,000

Income Tax

		35,000	@ 20%	7,000
Extend basic rate band £14,400 x 100/80		18,000	@ 20%	3,600
		53,000		
		115,000	@ 40%	46,000
Extend higher rate band	150,000			
£14,400 x 100/80	18,000			
		168,000		
		12,000	@ 50%	6,000
		180,000		
				£62,600

2. Olivia is an employee whose only income during 2011/12 is a salary of £180,000. She contributes 10% of her gross salary to an approved occupational pension scheme.

Required: Calculate Olivia's income tax liability for 2011/12.

Solution

		£
Salary	180,000	
Less; pension contributions	18,000	
Income from employment		162,000
Personal allowance		0
Taxable income		162,000

Income Tax

35,000	@ 20%	7,000
115,000	@ 40%	46,000
150,000		
12,000	@ 50%	6,000
168,000		
		£59,000

17 National Insurance contributions and social security

Introduction

1. National Insurance is planned to contribute £101bn out of a total UK tax revenue of £589bn for 2011/12. All National Insurance rates were increased by 1% for the tax year 2011/12 as compared to 2010/11. National Insurance is now generally regarded as a tax on earnings, although in original concept it was a contribution towards state benefits, principally the state old age pension. This chapter is concerned with National Insurance and some aspects of the Social Security system under the following main headings:

Classes of contribution	Statutory sick pay	Taxable state income
Gross pay	Statutory maternity pay	Non taxable state income
Directors	Tax Credits	Class 4 contributions
Class 1 A NIC – benefits, cars and fuel		

Note The Contributions Agency which deals with National Insurance is a branch of HMRC .

Classes of contribution

2. The classes of contribution payable to the Contributions Agency are as follows:

Class 1 All employed earners and their employers

Class 1A Employers' contributions on benefits in kind

Class 1B PAYE settlement agreements

Class 2 Self-employed persons

Class 3 Non-employed persons

Class 4 Self-employed persons, additional contribution based on 'profits'.

All employed persons and their employers must pay Class 1 contributions.

The weekly earnings thresholds and rates which apply for Class 1 NIC liability from 6th April 2011 are given below. Equivalent monthly thresholds apply to employees paid monthly, and annual thresholds apply to company directors (see section 5).

For simplicity, the accounting professional bodies allow thresholds for Class 1 to be applied on an annual basis in all cases in tax examinations.

An employed person is someone gainfully employed either under a contract of service, or as the holder of an office as defined for income tax purposes, e.g. a company director.

A self-employed person is liable for Class 2 and Class 4 contributions. The Class 2 contribution is a flat rate per week, payable 6 monthly; although before 2011/12 it was paid monthly or quarterly. The Class 4 contribution is payable as percentage of the annual 'profits' as determined for income tax purposes.

Class 3 contributions are voluntary contributions payable at a weekly flat rate, to preserve entitlement to some social security benefits. They may be paid up to 6 years after the relevant year.

Employees must be aged 16 or over before any liability to National Insurance arises.

For persons over the pensionable age of 65 years the position is as follows:

i) Primary contributions (employees' NIC) are not due on earnings paid after 65th birthday;

ii) Secondary contributions (employers' NICS) continue as before regardless of whether the state retirement age is reached.

Employer's Class 1A contributions apply to all taxable benefits in kind except:

i) where Class 1 National Insurance contributions are due (e.g. on cash vouchers)

ii) those covered by a dispensation

iii) those included in a PAYE settlement

iv) those provided for employees earning less than £8,500 p.a.

v) those otherwise not required to be reported through the P11D return arrangements.

Gross pay

3. Gross pay for Class 1 National Insurance purposes includes:

Wages/salaries

Bonus payments

Fees

Overtime pay

Sick pay and maternity pay

Petrol allowances unless charged to a company account

Cash allowances generally

Cash vouchers

Anything else readily convertible to money, e.g. quoted shares or commodities that can be sold on a readily-traded market

As noted in the previous section, non-cash benefits are not part of Gross Pay for National Insurance, and are liable not to Class 1 but to class 1A National Insurance. This is paid by the employer (at the end of the tax year) but not the employee.

National Insurance contributions – gross pay

4. Class 1 Employed earners from 6th April 2011

£ per week earnings	Not contracted-out	Contracted-out COSR	Contracted-out COMP
Employee			
Up to £139 a week – primary earnings threshold	Nil	Nil	Nil
Between £139 and £817 a week	12.0%	10.4%	10.4%
Over £817 a week	2.0%	2.0%	2.0%
Employer			
Up to £136 a week – secondary earnings threshold	Nil	Nil	Nil
Between £136 and £817 a week	13.8%	10.1%	12.4%
Over £817 a week	13.8%	13.8%	13.8%
Rebate on earnings between £102 and £136 a week	Nil	3.7%	1.4%

Notes

i) The employee's contributions are known as Primary Class 1 contributions.

The employer's contributions are known as Secondary Class 1 contributions.

Separate rates apply to employers who have contracted out of the state second pension (S2P), formerly called the State Earnings Related Pension scheme (SERPS).

COSR – "contracted out" salary related scheme.

COMP – "contracted out" money purchase scheme.

LEL – employees Lower Earnings Limit, p.a. £5,305.

Pay over the lower earnings limit must be recorded for the employees even when no national insurance contributions are due in order to protect entitlement to benefits such as Statutory Sick Pay and Maternity Pay.

ET – Employees' Earnings Threshold, p.a. £7,225. (2010/11 £5,715)

Upper earnings limit p.a. £42,475 (2010/11 £43,875)

The contracted out rates apply to employers who are members of approved occupational pension schemes where the benefits will match or exceed those offered by the state second pension and so the scheme members have elected to be excluded (contracted out) from the state second pension scheme.

Class 1A 13.8% (2010/11 12.8%)

Class 2 Weekly rate £2.50 (2010/11 £2.40). Collected 6 monthly on 31 July and 31 January in the tax year. No liability if earnings are below £5,315 for the tax year, and a certificate of exception is obtained.

Class 3 Weekly rate £12.60.

Class 4 See below.

Directors

5. The earnings period for employees is normally the interval at which regular payments are made e.g. weekly or monthly. For directors their earnings period is annual whether they are paid weekly, monthly or at other intervals.

The following rules should be noted.

i) For directors the earnings period runs from 6th April to the following 5th April.

ii) Directors appointed before 6th April have an annual earnings period even if they cease to be directors in the course of the year.

iii) Where a director is appointed after 6th April then the earnings period is pro-rated using a 52 week period for the whole tax year.

Example

A is a Director of K Ltd and receives a salary of £50,000 in 2011/12. Compute the primary and secondary NICs payable. The company has contracted out of the state earnings related pension scheme, and operates a salary-related scheme, i.e. COSR.

Solution: A National Insurance contribution 2011/12 COSR scheme

Primary contributions – employee

			£
ET	7,225	@ 0%	–
	35,250	@ 10.4%	3,666
	42,475		
	7,525	@ 2.0%	150
	50,000		3,816

Secondary contributions – employer

		£
7,075	@ 0%	–
35,400	@ 10.1%	3,575
42,475		3,575
7,525	@ 13.8%	1,038
50,000		4,613

Note

As the earnings have already exceeded the upper earnings level there will be a further primary contribution payable for the year of 1.0% on the excess.

Class 4 contributions

6. The following are the main features of this class of contribution.

a) Contributions are calculated by the tax payer on the self assessment tax return and collected by HMRC together with all other self assessed income tax.

b) Where a partnership exists then each partner's liability is calculated separately and paid separately, as for income tax.

c) The contributions are based on the trade profits as determined in accordance with chapter 11, with the following deductions:

i) Capital allowances (balancing charges are added)

ii) Loss relief under Sections 83 and 89, ITA 2007.

d) Personal allowances and pension payments of any kind are not deductible.

e) The rate of contribution is 9.0% of profits in between £7,225 and £42,475 for 2011/12, plus 1% on profits above £42,475.

f) Where the profits of farmers are averaged the revised amounts are used for Class 4 purposes.

g) Interest on late payment of Class 4 NICs is charged at the prevailing rate of interest for late paid income tax.

Where an individual is both employed and self-employed then Class 1 contributions will be paid on the employment earnings and Class 2 and Class 4 (if above the minimum level) on the self-employed earnings. If the self employment earnings would give rise to a total payment in excess of the maximum of (42,475 – 7,225) @ 12%, then NIC is only payable at 1% on the self employed earnings. It is possible to apply for a 'deferment' of the remaining Class 2 and 4, which in practice means a permanent reduction.

Example

X has been trading for many years with an accounting year end to the 30th June. He has the following data relating to the income tax year 2011/12:

	£
Trade profits to 30.6.2011	40,000
Capital allowances	2,965
Building society interest (net)	800

Calculate the income tax and Class 2 and 4 NI payable by self assessment for 2011/12.

Solution: X income tax, class 2 and 4 NI computation 2011/12

		£	
Income taxed as trade profits		40,000	
Less capital allowances		2,965	37,035
Building society interest (gross)			1,000
			38,035
Personal allowance			7,475
Taxable income			30,560
Tax liability	n/a @ 10%		0
	29,560 @ 20%		5,912
	1,000 @ 20%		200
	30,560		6,112
Less income tax deducted from Building society interest			200
Tax Payable			£5,912
Class 4 NIC contributions payable			
Trade profits			40,000
Less capital allowances			2,965
			37,035
(£37,035 – 7,225) = 29,810 @ 9.0%			2,683
Class 2 NIC 52 @ £2.50			130
National Insurance Payable			£2,813

Class 1A NIC cars and fuel

7. a) Employers are liable to pay Class 1A National Insurance contributions in respect of:

i) any car provided for a director or P11D employee (those employees who earn over £8,500 p.a. including benefits and expenses) where it is available for private use

ii) fuel provided for private use.

iii) and all other benefits liable to income tax (see Chapter 7).

b) The rate at which Class 1A NICs are calculated is the highest secondary Class 1 NIC applicable to the year in which the benefit is charged.

For 2011/12 this is 13.8%

Payment of the Class 1A NICs is due on or before the 19th of June following the end of the income tax year to which they relate. If a quarterly basis for paying PAYE has been claimed the Class 1A NICs are due on or before the 19th July of the following income tax year.

Directors liable for company's contributions

8. Where a company has failed to pay NICs on time and the failure appears to be attributable to fraud or neglect by one or more individuals who were officers of the company (culpable officers), the outstanding NICs may be sought from the culpable officers.

Statutory sick pay

9. Employers are responsible for paying statutory sick pay (SSP), statutory maternity, paternity, and adoption pay to their employees. In general the amounts paid are subsequently recouped from National Insurance contributions paid in respect of all employees.

A brief summary of the SSP scheme, is as follows:

a) SSP is payable for up to 28 weeks of sickness at the rates of £81.60.

b) The gross amount of sick pay paid is subject to income tax under the PAYE system and to National Insurance contributions.

c) Employers can claim full reimbursement if and to the extent that their SSP payments for an income tax month exceed 13% of their gross Class 1 contribution liability for that month.

Both employers' and employees' contributions count but not the Class 1A.

d) Where the SSP recoverable is greater than the NI contributions due for the income tax month, the balance may be dealt with as follows:

   i) Deducted from PAYE

   ii) Carried forward to the next payment period

   iii) Reclaimed from the collector of taxes by formal application.

e) Earnings for SSP purposes are the same as those used for National Insurance purposes.

f) To be eligible for SSP an employee must be incapable of work for at least four calendar days in a row, including Saturdays, Sundays and Bank Holidays.

g) Any two periods of incapacity for work (PIWs) which are separated by a period of eight weeks (56 calendar days) or less are linked together for SSP purposes.

Statutory maternity pay (SMP)

10. 1) A woman who has been continuously employed for at least 26 weeks continuing into the 15th qualifying week (QW) before the week when the birth is due is entitled to SMP.

2) The SMP rates are as follows:

Employment ≥ 26 weeks before QW

– 6 weeks at 90% of average weekly earnings, followed by

– £128.73 per week or 90% of average weekly earnings, which ever is the lesser,

up to a total of 39 weeks paid maternity leave. A mother may then take further weeks unpaid leave, giving one year in total.

3) SMP is subject to National Insurance contributions and income tax in the same way as wages and salaries.

4) Small employers can recover the gross amount of SMP, plus 5%, i.e. 105% as compensation for the employers' NIC, other employers can recover 92%.

5) Recovery of SMP is made by reduction from monthly income tax and National Insurance payable.

i) 'Small employer' is one whose gross Class 1 NIC for the preceding year did not exceed £45,000.

ii) To qualify for SMP women must be earning at least the lower earnings limit of £102 per week for 2011/12.

Statutory paternity pay

A father may take 2 weeks paid paternity leave at the lower of 90% of average weekly earnings and £128.73 per week.

Child benefit

11. Child benefit is a social security benefit paid to the person primarily responsible for caring for a child. The 2011/12 rate is £20.30 a week for the eldest child and £13.40 a week for each subsequent child. Child benefit is not affected by the income of the carer, and is not taxable.

Child tax credit

12. Child tax credit is a separate social security benefit, based on income. But it does not have an effect on tax liabilities.

Working tax credit

13. Working tax credit is for people with low incomes from employment or self employment. Again this does not have an effect on tax liabilities.

Student self testing questions

1. William Wong is the finance director of Glossy Ltd. The company runs a publishing business. The following information is available for the tax year 2011–12:

(1) William is paid director's remuneration of £2,400 per month by Glossy Ltd.

(2) In addition to his director's remuneration, William received two bonus payments from Glossy Ltd during the tax year 2011–12. The first bonus of £22,000 was paid on 30 June 2010 and was in respect of the year ended 31 December 2010.

William became entitled to this bonus on 15 March 2011. The second bonus of £37,000 was paid on 31 March 2012 and was in respect of the year ended 31 December 2011. William became entitled to this second bonus on 15 March 2012.

(3) From 6 April 2011 until 31 December 2011 William used his private motor car for business purposes. During this period William drove 12,000 miles in the performance of his duties for Glossy Ltd, for which the company paid an allowance of 30 pence per mile. The relevant HMRC authorised mileage rates to be used as a basis of an expense claim are 45 pence per mile for the first 10,000 miles, and 25 pence per mile thereafter.

(4) From 1 January 2012 to 5 April 2012 Glossy Ltd provided William with a diesel powered company motor car with a list price of £46,000. The motor car cost Glossy Ltd £44,500, and it has an official CO_2 emission rate of 234 g/km. Glossy Ltd also provided William with fuel for his private journeys.

(5) William was unable to drive his motor car for two weeks during February 2012 because of an accident, so Glossy Ltd provided him with a chauffeur at a total cost of £1,800.

(6) Throughout the tax year 2011–12 Glossy Ltd provided William with a television for his personal use that had originally cost £3,825.

(7) Glossy Ltd has provided William with living accommodation since 1 January 2010. The property was purchased in 1998 for £90,000, and was valued at £210,000 on 1 January 2010. It has an annual value of £10,400.

(8) Glossy Ltd pays an annual insurance premium of £680 to cover William against any liabilities that might arise in relation to his directorship.

(9) During May 2011 William spent ten nights overseas on company business. Glossy Ltd paid him a daily allowance of £10 to cover the cost of personal expenses such as telephone calls to William's family.

(10) William pays an annual professional subscription of £450 to the Institute of Finance Directors, an Inland Revenue approved professional body, and a membership fee of £800 to a golf club. He uses the golf club to entertain clients of Glossy Ltd.

(11) William has not 'contracted out' of the state earnings related pension scheme.

Required:

(a) State the rules that determine when a bonus paid to a director is treated as being received for tax purposes. (3 marks)

(b) Calculate William's taxable income for the tax year 2011–12. (15 marks)

(c) Calculate the total amount of both Class 1 and Class 1A national insurance contributions that will have been paid by William and Glossy Ltd in respect of William's earnings and benefits for the tax year 2011–12. (5 marks)

(d) Advise William of the forms that Glossy Ltd must provide to him following the end of the tax year 2011–12 in respect of his earnings and benefits for that year, and state the dates by which these forms have to be provided to him. (2 marks)

(25 marks)

ACCA December 2005 (updated)

Solution

(a) The earliest of:

(1) The date that the bonus is paid.

(2) The date that entitlement to the bonus arises.

(3) The date when the bonus is credited in the company's accounts

(4) The end of the period of account if the bonus relates to that period, and has been determined before the end of the period.

(5) The date that the bonus is determined if the period of account it relates to has already ended.

(b) William – Taxable income computation 2011–12

Director's remuneration	(2,400 x 12)		28,800
Bonus			37,000
			65,800
Benefits			
Car benefit		4,025	
Chauffeur		1,800	
Fuel benefit		1,645	
Television	(3,825 at 20%)	765	
Living accommodation			
– Annual value		10,400	
– Additional benefit		5,400	24,035
			89,835

Expenses		
Mileage allowance	1,400	
Professional subscription	450	1,850
		87,985
		7,475
		£80,510

(1) The first bonus of £22,000 will have been treated as being received during 2010–11.

(2) The relevant percentage for the car benefit is restricted to the maximum of 35%.

(3) The motor car was only available for three months of 2011–12 so the benefit is £4,025 (46,000 x 35% x 3/12). The list price must be used even though a lesser amount was actually paid.

(4) The car benefit does not cover the cost of a chauffeur, so this is an additional benefit.

(5) The fuel benefit is £1,645 (18,800 x 35% x 3/12).

(6) The living accommodation cost in excess of £75,000 so there will be an additional benefit.

(7) Since the property was purchased more than six years before first being provided to William, the benefit is based on the market value of £210,000.

(8) The additional benefit is therefore £5,400 (210,000 – 75,000) = 135,000 at 4%.

(9) The provision of liability insurance does not give rise to a taxable benefit, nor does the payment of the overseas allowance since it is not above the de minimis limit of £10 per night.

(10) The mileage allowance received will be tax-free, and William can make the following expense claim:

10,000 miles at 45p	4,500
2,000 miles at 25p	500
	5,000
Mileage allowance	
12,000 at 30p	3,600
	£1,400

(11) The golf club membership is not an allowable deduction despite being used to entertain customers.

(c) NIC

Employee Class 1	(42,475 – 7,225) =	35,250 @ 12%	£4,230
	(65,800 – 42,475)=	23,325 @ 1%	£466
Employer Class 1	(65,800 – 7,075) =	58,725 @ 13.8%	£8,104
Employer Class 1A		24,035 @ 13.8%	£3,316

(d) (1) Form P60 employee's certificate of pay, income tax and NIC must be given to William by 31 May 2012.

(2) A copy of form P11D detailing expense payments and benefits in kind must be given to William by 6 July 2012.

2. (a) Cecile Grand has been a self-employed antiques dealer since 1993. Her income for the last completed tax year (2010/2011) was as follows:

	£
Income from trading	42,400
Dividends (net)	4,860
Income from property	800

The income from property is for the period 6 April 2010 to 30 June 2010.

During 2010/2011 Cecile paid a personal pension contribution of £2,800 (net amount paid to pension company). Cecile's husband died on 15 June 2009 and she has not remarried. Her forecast income for 2011/12 is as follows:

	£
Adjusted profit from trading	22,750
Dividends (net)	4,320

Due to the fall in profits, Cecile will not pay a personal pension contribution during 2011/12.

Requirement:

(i) Calculate Cecile's payments on account and balancing payment or repayment for 2011/12. You should assume that Cecile does not make a claim to reduce her payments on account. (10 marks)

(ii) Based on the above figures, advise Cecile of the amount of the maximum claim that she could make to reduce her payments on account for 2011/12 (2 marks)

(b) Cecile's adjusted trading profit for 2011/12 is an estimated figure based on her provisional accounts for the year ended 31 March 2012. The actual figures will not be available until 31 August 2012 because of the difficulty that Cecile has in separating antiques acquired for business purposes from those acquired for private purposes.

Requirement:

(i) Assuming that Cecile makes the maximum claim to reduce the payments on account for 2011/12, explain the tax implications if her actual taxable income for 2011/12 is higher than the estimated figure.

(ii) Advise Cecile of the powers that HM Revenue and Customs have with regard to enquiring into her tax return for 2011/12 (2 marks)

(iii) Briefly advise Cecile of the tax implications if HMRC enquire into her tax return for 2011/12, and decide that the income from trading for the year ended 31 March 2012 is understated. (2 marks)

(Total 18 marks)

Solution

(a) (i) Cecile's payments on account for 2011/12 will be based on her final income tax and Class 4 NIC for 2010/11 as follows:

	£
Income from trading	42,400
Income from property	800
Dividends (4,860 × 100/90)	5,400
	48,600
Personal allowance	(6,475)
Taxable income	42,125
36,725 @ 20% non savings	7,345
675 @ 10% dividends	67
37,400	
3,500 extend basic rate band for pension contributions @ 10% divs	350
1,225 @ 32.5% divs	398
42,125	8,160
Tax suffered at source - Dividends (5,400 at 10%)	540
	7,620
Class 4 NIC (42,400 – 5,715) at 8%	2,934
	£10,554
Payments on account due 31.1.2012 - 50%	5,277
Payments on account due 31.7.2012 - 50%	5,277

Cecile's actual **tax liability for 2011/12** is as follows:

	£	£
Income from trading		22,750
Dividends (4,320 × 100/90)		4,800
		27,550
Personal allowance		7,475
Taxable income		20,075
Income tax:		
n/a @ 10%		0
15,275 @ 20% non savings		3,055

4,800 @ 10% dividends	480
20,075	3,535
Less: Tax credit - Dividends (4,800 at 10%)	480
	3,055
Add: Class 4 NIC (22,750 – 7,225) at 9%	1,397
	4,452
Paid on account	10,554
Balancing refund due 31.1.13	£6,102

(ii) If Cecile has enough information available before 31 January 2012 to make a reliable estimate of her 2011/12 income and income tax liability, she could claim to reduce her payments on account by £6,102 (10,554 – 4,452) so that £2,226 will be due on 31 January 2012, and on 31 July 2012.

It would be more likely, in many taxpayers' cases, to make the first payment on account of £5,277 in full, and then claim to reduce the second payment of account on 31 July 2012, when more information about the estimated business results for the year to 31 March 2012 might be known.

(b) (i) If Cecile's payments on account are too low, then she will be charged interest. This will run from the due dates of 31 January 2012 and 31 July 2012, up to the date of payment, which will presumably be 31 January 2013. A penalty will be charged if a claim to reduce payments on account is made fraudulently or negligently.

(ii) HMRC has the right to enquire into any tax return, provided they give written notice. Enquiries may be made by reference to information in the tax return, but they may also be made on a random basis. The time limit for giving notice of an enquiry for 2011/12 returns is 31 January 2014. An enquiry after that date can normally only be made where the taxpayer has been fraudulent or negligent.

(iii) Following the completion of an enquiry, the tax return would normally be amended by the taxpayer. The additional tax liability will be due 30 days from the date of the notice of amendment Interest will be charged on the additional tax liability from 31 January 2013 (the due date for the tax return) up to the date of payment. No surcharge will be due provided that the additional tax liability is paid within 28 days of the due date. A penalty will only be charged where a tax return is filed incorrectly due to fraud or negligence.

Questions without answers

1. You should assume that today's date is 15 March 2011.

Ali Patel has been employed by Box plc since 1 January 2008, and is currently paid an annual salary of £36,000. On 6 April 2011 Ali is to be temporarily relocated for a period of twelve months from Box plc's head office to one of its branch offices. He has been offered two alternative remuneration packages:

First remuneration package

(1) Ali will continue to live near Box plc's head office, and will commute on a daily basis to the branch office using his private motor car.

(2) He will be paid additional salary of £500 per month.

(3) Box plc will pay Ali an allowance of 38 pence per mile for the 1,600 miles that Ali will drive each month commuting to the branch office.

HMRC authorised mileage rates are 45 pence per mile for the first 10,000 business miles driven each year, and 25 pence per mile thereafter. Ali's additional cost of commuting for 2011–12 will be £1,800.

Second remuneration package

(1) Box plc will provide Ali with rent-free living accommodation near the branch office.

(2) The property will be rented by Box plc at a cost of £800 per month. The annual value of the property is £4,600.

(3) Ali will rent out his main residence near Box plc's head office, and this will result in income from property of £6,000 for 2011–12.

Required:

(a) **Calculate Ali's income tax liability and Class 1 national insurance contributions for 2011–12, if he:**

(i) Accepts the first remuneration package offered by Box plc; **(6 marks)**

(ii) Accepts the second remuneration package offered by Box plc. **(5 marks)**

(b) **Advise Ali as to which remuneration package is the most beneficial from a financial perspective. Your answer should be supported by a calculation of the amount of income, net of income tax and employees Class 1 national insurance contributions, which he would receive for 2011–12 under each alternative.** **(4 marks)**

(15 marks)

ACCA December 2004 (updated)

End of section questions without answers

1. Evaluate the advantages, disadvantages and feasibility of replacing the taxation of income by the following: a direct expenditure tax; an annual wealth tax.

2. For the purposes of this question you should assume that today's date is 15 March 2011.

Carol Courier is employed by Quick-Speed plc as a delivery driver, and is paid a salary of £26,000. She contributes 5% of gross salary into Quick-Speed plc's HMRC approved "contracted out" occupational pension scheme.

As an alternative to being employed, Quick-Speed plc have offered Carol the opportunity to work for the company on a self-employed basis. The details of the proposed arrangement for the year ended 5 April 2012 are as follows:

(1) Carol will commence being self-employed on 6 April 2011.

(2) Her income from Quick-Speed plc is expected to be £38,000.

(3) When not working for Quick-Speed plc, Carol will be allowed to work for other clients. Her income from this work is expected to be £4,500.

(4) Carol will lease a delivery van from Quick-Speed plc, and 100% of the mileage will be for business purposes. The cost of leasing and running the delivery van will be £4,400.

(5) When she is unavailable Carol will have to provide a replacement driver to deliver for Quick-Speed plc. This will cost her £2,800.

(6) Carol will contribute the equivalent of £2,000 gross into a personal pension scheme during 2011-12. This will provide her with the same benefits as the occupational pension scheme provided by Quick-Speed plc.

Required:

(a) Assuming that Carol does not accept the offer from Quick-Speed plc and continues to be employed by the company, calculate her income tax and Class 1 NIC liability for 2011-12. (5 marks)

(b) Assuming that Carol accepts the offer to work for Quick-Speed on a self-employed basis from 6 April 2011 onwards, calculate her income tax, Class 2 NIC and Class 4 NIC liability for 2011-12. (6 marks)

(c) Advise Carol as to whether it will be beneficial to accept the offer to work for Quick-Speed plc on a self-employed basis. Your answer should be supported by a calculation of the amount by which Carol's income for 2011-12 (net of outgoings, income tax and NIC) will increase or decrease if she accepts the offer. (4 marks)

(d) Critically comment on whether Carol would be considered an employee or self-employed under current HMRC policy.(5 marks)

(20 marks)

ACCA December 2002 (updated)

3. On 31 December 2011 Foo Dee resigned as an employee of Gastronomic-Food plc. The company had employed her as a chef since 2000. On 1 January 2012 Foo commenced self-employment running her own restaurant, preparing accounts to 30 September. The following information is available for 2011–12:

Employment

(1) During the period 6 April 2011 to 31 December 2011 Foo's total gross salary from her employment with Gastronomic-Food plc was £38,000. Income tax of £7,707 was deducted from this figure under PAYE.

(2) Foo used her private motor car for both business and private purposes during the period from 6 April 2011 to 31 December 2011. She received no reimbursement from Gastronomic-Food plc for any of the expenditure incurred. Foo's total mileage during this period was 15,000 miles, made up as follows:

Normal daily travel between home and permanent workplace	4,650
Travel between home and permanent workplace in order to turn off a fire alarm	120
Travel between permanent workplace and Gastronomic-Food plc's suppliers	750
Travel between home and a temporary workplace for a period of two months	3,800
Private travel	5,680
	15,000

The relevant HM Revenue & Customs authorised mileage rates to be used as the basis of any expense claim are 45 pence per mile for the first 10,000 miles, and 25 pence per mile thereafter.

(3) On 1 October 2011 Gastronomic-Food plc paid £12,900 towards Foo's removal expenses when she was permanently relocated to a different restaurant owned by the company. The £12,900 covered the cost of disposing of Foo's old property and of acquiring her new property.

(4) Foo contributed 6% of her gross salary of £38,000 into Gastronomic-Food plc's HM Revenue & Customs' approved occupational pension scheme.

Self-employment

(1) Foo's profit and loss account for her restaurant business for the nine-month period ended 30 September 2012 is as follows:

Gross profit		128,200
Depreciation	3,500	
Motor expenses (note 2)	4,200	
Property expenses (note 3)	12,800	
Other expenses (all allowable)	50,700	71,200
Net profit		£57,000

(2) During the period 1 January 2012 to 30 September 2012 Foo drove a total of 6,000 miles, of which 2,000 were for private journeys.

(3) Foo purchased her restaurant on 1 January 2012. She lives in a flat that is situated above the restaurant, and one-quarter of the total property expenses of £12,800 relate to this flat.

(4) On 1 January 2012 Foo purchased a motor car with CO_2 emissions of 140 g/km for £15,000 (see note 2 above) and equipment for £3,600.

Other income

(1) During the tax year 2011–12 Foo received building society interest of £640 and dividends of £360. These were the actual cash amounts received.

Other information

(1) Foo contributed £1,600 (net) into a personal pension scheme during the period 1 January 2012 to 5 April 2012.

(2) She did not make any payments on account of income tax in respect of the tax year 2011–12.

Required:

(a) **Calculate Foo's tax adjusted trading profit for the nine-month period ended 30 September 2012. (6 marks)**

(b) (i) **Calculate the income tax payable by Foo for the tax year 2011–12. (13 marks)**

(ii) **Calculate Foo's balancing payment for the tax year 2011–12 and her payments on account for the tax year 2012–13, stating the relevant due dates.** (Ignore national insurance contributions.) **(3 marks)**

(c) **Advise Foo of the consequences of not making the balancing payment for the tax year 2011–12 until 31 May 2013.**(Assume the HMRC interest rate on late paid income tax is 3.0%) **(3 marks)**

(25 marks)

ACCA December 2006 (updated)

4. Sue Macker was made redundant from her employment on 15 March 2011. She is a vintage motor car enthusiast, and so decided to take this opportunity to indulge her hobby.

On 6 April 2011 Sue took out a bank loan of £75,000 at an annual interest rate of 10%, rented a workshop for twelve months at a rent of £400 per month, and purchased equipment at a cost of £13,500.

On 10 April 2011 Sue purchased four dilapidated vintage motor cars for £8,000 each. The restoration of the four motor cars was completed on 10 March 2012 at a cost of £12,000 per motor car. Sue immediately sold all of the motor cars for a total of £200,000.

Sue was then offered employment elsewhere in the country commencing on 6 April 2012. She therefore sold the equipment for £5,800 on 20 March 2012, and repaid the bank loan on 5 April 2012.

Because she has just been indulging her hobby, Sue believes that the disposal of the vintage motor cars during the tax year 2011–12 should be exempt from tax. She has done some research on the Internet and has discovered that whether or not she is treated as carrying on a trade will be determined according to the six following 'badges of trade':

(1) The subject matter of the transaction.

(2) The length of ownership.

(3) Frequency of similar transactions.

(4) Work done on the property.

(5) Circumstances responsible for the realisation.

(6) Motive.

Sue had no other income during the tax year 2011–12 except as indicated above.

Required:

(a) Briefly explain the meaning of each of the six 'badges of trade' listed above. (You are not expected to quote from decided cases.) **(3 marks)**

(b) Briefly explain why Sue is likely to be treated as carrying on a trade in respect of her vintage motor car activities. (3 marks)

(c) Calculate Sue's income tax liability and her Class 2 and Class 4 national insurance contributions for the tax year 2011–12, if she is treated as carrying on a trade in respect of her vintage motor car activities. (Ignore VAT.) **(7 marks)**

(d) Explain why it would be beneficial if Sue were instead treated as not carrying on a trade in respect of her vintage motor car activities. (2 marks)

(15 marks)

ACCA December 2005 (updated)

5. Tony Note

Tony Note is self-employed running a music shop. His profit and loss account for the year ended 5 April 2012 is as follows:

	£	£
Gross profit		198,000
Expenses		
Depreciation	2,640	
Motor expenses (note 1)	9,800	

Professional fees (note 2)	4,680	
Repairs and renewals (note 3)	670	
Travelling and entertaining (note 4)	4,630	
Wages and salaries (note 5)	77,200	
Other expenses (note 6)	78,780	
		178,400
Net profit		19,600

Note 1 – Motor expenses
During the year ended 5 April 2012 Tony drove a total of 20,000 miles, of which 2,500 were driven when he went on holiday to Europe. The balance of the mileage is 20% for private journeys and 80% for business journeys.

Note 2 – Professional fees
The figure for professional fees consists of £920 for accountancy, £620 for personal financial planning advice, £540 for debt collection, and £2,600 for fees in connection with an unsuccessful application for planning permission to enlarge Tony's freehold music shop.

Note 3 – Repairs and renewals
The figure for repairs and renewals consists of £270 for a replacement hard drive for the shop's computer, and £400 for a new printer for this computer.

Note 4 – Travelling and entertaining
The figure for travelling and entertaining consists of £3,680 for Tony's business travelling expenses, £480 for entertaining suppliers, and £470 for entertaining employees.

Note 5 – Wages and salaries
The figure for wages and salaries includes a salary of £22,000 paid to Tony's wife. She works in the music shop as a sales assistant. The other sales assistants doing the same job are paid a salary of £18,000 p.a.

Note 6 – Other expenses
The figure for other expenses includes £75 in respect of a wedding present to an employee, £710 for Tony's health club subscription, £60 for a donation to a political party, and £180 for a trade subscription to the Guild of Musical Instrument Retailers.

Note 7 – Use of office
Tony uses one of the six rooms in his private house as an office for when he works at home. The total running costs of the house for the year ended 5 April 2012 were £4,320.

Note 8 – Private telephone
Tony uses his private telephone to make business telephone calls. The total cost of the private telephone for the year ended 5 April 2012 was £680, and 25% of this

related to business telephone calls. The cost of the private telephone is not included in the profit and loss account expenses of £178,400.

Note 9 – Goods for own use
During the year ended 5 April 2012 Tony took goods out of the music shop for his personal use without paying for them, and no entry has been made in the accounts to record this. The goods cost £600, and had a selling price of £950.

Note 10 – Plant and machinery
The tax written down values for capital allowances purposes at 6 April 2011 were as follows:

	£	
General pool	9,250	
Renault motor car	15,000	CO_2 emissions 150 g/km

The Renault car is used by Tony.

Required:

(a) Calculate Tony's tax adjusted trading profit for the year ended 5 April 2012. **(16 marks)**

(b) Calculate Tony's income tax liability for the tax year 2011/12.

(2 marks)

(18 marks)

ACCA June 2006 (updated)

Part III

Corporation Tax

18 General principles

Introduction

1. Corporation Tax is a direct tax on the income and capital gains of companies and other corporate bodies. It is planned to raise £48bn out of total UK tax revenues of £589bn in 2011/12. In this chapter the main elements of the corporation tax system are outlined. It begins with some basic expressions, then forms of organisation liable and exempt from corporation tax are examined, followed by corporation tax self-assessment. The remainder of the chapter deals with the corporation tax accounting periods, and the rates of tax. A summary of corporation tax rates and a specimen computation are provided at the end.

2. Corporation tax as a separate form of business taxation was introduced by the FA 1965. However, an entirely new set of rules for the determination of business income was not provided, and the substance of the income tax system was preserved, especially in the original rules for measuring companies' taxable income, and recognition of interest paid and received.

From the late 1990s, certain areas of company tax were reformed, so that the rules for certain types of transaction (such as borrowing for trade purposes) no longer match the income tax rules for the same type of transaction carried out by an individual or a trust. These corporate tax changes were influenced by several developments: partly by improvements in accounting standards, meaning that company directors had less choice about when to account for a company's revenue and costs; partly by the UK's move to corporation tax self-assessment; and partly by the Government's wish to counter tax planning structures which exploited timing and measurement differences which existed under the older systems for taxing economic profits and recognising costs.

Company tax on corporate finance, leasing and debt arrangements, including gains and losses on financial derivatives and foreign currency holdings, was reformed from 1999 onwards. The new system includes a "loan relationships tax regime" and a "leasing tax regime" for companies. These cover many types of financing transaction, other than those involving equity shares, and in general require companies to follow their financial accounting treatment when taxing profits and allowing expenses. Further reforms are still made periodically to the loan relationship and leasing tax regimes, if specific tax avoidance tactics are identified by HMRC.

Also, from 1 April 2002 Companies are subject to a different tax regime from unincorporated businesses in regard to tax relief for the costs of, and tax on the profits of, intangible non-current assets that are "intellectual property", such as goodwill, patents, and knowhow.

UK companies also qualify for extra tax reliefs for revenue expenditure on Research and Development (R&D) compared to unincorporated businesses (see chapter 19).

The Corporation Tax Acts 2009 and 2010 changed some of the main terminology of corporation tax without actually changing the rules, and represent the first time in UK tax law that the corporation tax rules have been placed in separate statutes on their own. (However, the term "the Corporation Tax Acts" is defined, by CTA2010, as also covering Income Tax statutes so far as these contain rules that also apply to companies.)

However, rules for computing (though not for taxing) corporate capital gains are still contained in the Taxation of Chargeable Gains Act 1992, as amended by subsequent Finance Acts, a statute which does still cover both individuals and companies.

The UK Government in November 2010 issued an important consultative policy document called "Corporate Tax Reform: Delivering a More Competitive System" which sets out further major reforms planned for the UK's corporate tax system during the expected life of the current Government (i.e. by FY 2015). The full document is available online from http://www.hm-treasury.gov.uk. Specific proposals (apart from a brief note on foreign branches tax reform) are not covered further in this book, as they have not yet been included in legislation.

Basic expressions in corporation tax law

3. Financial year

A financial year runs from the 1st April to the following 31st March, and each year is known by reference to the calendar year in which the 1st April occurs. Thus the financial year 2011 covers the period from the 1st April 2011 to the 31st March 2012. Corporation tax rates are fixed by reference to financial years.

Accounting period

Companies do not pay CT for financial years but by reference to corporation tax accounting periods, which are linked to their financial reporting periods. A CT accounting period can never exceed 12 months in length, but can be shorter.

Close company

This is a company which is owned or controlled by a small number of persons (called participators) and their close family members. Private family companies often fall into this category. The corporation tax consequences of a company being close are now quite limited, but special income tax and capital gains tax rules (and occasionally reliefs) can apply to transactions between a close company and its participators, especially if the participator is not also an employee or officer of the company.

Close investment holding company (CIHC for short)

This means a close company, other than one whose business consists substantially of trading activities (for this purpose "trading" includes acquiring and letting land or property to unconnected persons), or other than a company which is the managing or parent company of a group whose other companies all have a trade. CIHCs are excluded from the small profits rate.

Further key definitions

4. Total Profits

Paraphrasing slightly, the Corporation Tax Act 2010 defines "total profits" as:

i) all of a company's income from any source that is within the charge to CT, after giving effect to specific expense reliefs available against particular sources of income, plus
ii) all of a company's chargeable gains that fall within the charge to CT, after giving effect to any specific deductions and tax reliefs available against chargeable gains.

Taxable Total Profit (formerly "Profits Chargeable to Corporation Tax", "PCTCT")

This is a new term introduced by the CTA2010, and used in CT accounting periods ending after 31 March 2010. It is defined as:

i) Total profits, less
ii) Amounts which can be relieved against total profits.

(The term at (ii) covers certain loss reliefs, other special deductions, and qualifying charitable donations (see specimen computation at the end of this chapter). Where more than one such deduction is claimed, the order of set-off is usually fixed.)

Group relief

This is the term used to describe the voluntary set-off of a trade loss, excess management expenses, excess charitable donations, a net non-trade loan relationship deficit, or certain other net costs, of one member of a group of companies ("group" as specifically defined for group relief) against the profits of another member of the same group. See chapter 24 for details.

Franked investment income (FII)

When a UK resident company receives a qualifying distribution (broadly, an income dividend) from another company, the amount of the payment is notionally increased by the UK dividend tax credit (currently 1/9). The result of this calculation is known as "franked investment income" (FII).

FII is not liable to corporation tax in the hands of a UK resident company, but may affect the corporation tax rate paid on all other taxable profits. See Chapter 19.

Under Finance Act 2009, foreign dividends are FII from 1 July 2009 (23 November 2008 for dividends from non-UK companies resident in the European Union). Foreign dividends are therefore now grossed by 1/9 to convert them to FII for CT purposes, just like UK dividends.

Group FII

This is FII from a company (UK or foreign resident) in which the recipient company has a direct or indirect **controlling** holding ($\geq$ 50%). It is disregarded in computing Augmented Profits.

Augmented Profits

This is the term used to determine whether a company pays corporation tax at the main rate, or a lower rate. It is equal to:

Taxable Total Profits, plus FII, but excluding Group FII.

Associated companies

For corporation tax purposes, these are defined as companies under the same ultimate control as the company in question. More detail is in chapter 23.

Main rate of corporation tax

This is set in the Finance Act each year. For Financial Year 2011 (FY2011) it is 26%, reduced from 28% in FY2010. It is applied to taxable total profits to find the CT liability for an accounting period.

Small profits rate of corporation tax (formerly "Small companies rate")

This is a lower rate of CT payable by companies with "augmented profits" falling under certain levels. It is set in the Finance Act each year. For Financial Year 2011 it is 20%, reduced from 21% in FY2010t.

Further details on applying CT rates are in sections 15 to 17 below. Full rules about the small profits rate, and the rate relief for companies with profits in the marginal relief band, are in chapter 23.

Organisations liable to corporation tax (CTA 2009)

5. a) Companies resident in the UK are chargeable to CT on their taxable total profits (as defined for CT purposes), wherever in the world the profits arise. A company is resident in the UK if it is incorporated here. It is also UK resident if it is incorporated elsewhere, but has its place of "central management and control" in the UK.

At time of writing, the Finance Bill 2011 (expected to become law in July 2011) contains a new, irrevocable, opt-out election by which a UK resident company can choose to exclude the profits of an overseas branch or permanent establishment from inclusion in the UK company's worldwide profits charged to UK CT. The downside of this election is that net expenses /losses of the overseas branch cease to be allowed against UK profits, and UK capital allowances (see chapter 20) are no longer available on plant and machinery of the overseas branch. If this legislation is enacted, it will substantially change the options for UK tax on foreign branches of UK companies, with effect from 1 April 2011. See chapter 25 for more on taxation of foreign branches.

b) Companies not resident in the UK are chargeable to corporation tax on the profits of any UK permanent establishment of that company which carries on a trade in the UK. See also paragraph 6 below.

c) "Unincorporated associations" are liable to corporation tax. This term excludes partnerships and local authority associations but includes any form of club or society, including voluntary associations, if there is a trading or profit intention. If the club or society is non-profit making or charitable, tax exemption may apply (see paragraph 7).

d) Building societies, provident societies, and insurance companies. Special rules apply to these organisations.

e) Corporate members of partnerships: If a company enters into a trading partnership, it is charged to corporation tax in respect of its share of the partnership profits, but partners who are individuals pay income tax or capital gains tax on their profit shares. See chapter 15 for taxation of partnerships in general.

Non-resident companies

6. a) A company not resident in the United Kingdom is within the charge to corporation tax if, and only if, it carries on a trade in the United Kingdom through a permanent establishment in the United Kingdom.

b) If it does so, it is chargeable to corporation tax, subject to any exceptions provided for by the Corporation Tax Acts, on all profits, wherever arising, which are attributable to the UK permanent establishment. These profits are the company's 'total profits' for the purposes of corporation tax.

c) CTA2009 provides that the UK permanent establishment's profits reported on its CT self assessment must be computed on the "separate enterprise principle". This means that all transactions between a UK branch operation and its foreign headquarters or parent group must be priced "on arm's length terms", that is at the same transfer prices as would have been agreed between unconnected parties.

d) If a foreign resident company has investment or property income derived from UK assets, but no UK trade through a permanent establishment, then it is liable only to basic rate income tax, not corporation tax, on its UK income (subject to any Double Tax Treaty which may exempt the income from UK tax).

e) For the purposes of the Corporation Tax Acts a company has a permanent establishment in a territory if, and only if –

   i) it has a fixed place of business there through which the business of the company is wholly or partly carried on, or

   ii) an agent acting on behalf of the company has and habitually exercises there authority to do business on behalf of the company.

f) A fixed place of business includes:

   a place of management;

   a branch;

   an office;

   a factory;

   a workshop;

an installation or structure for the exploration of natural resources;

a mine, an oil or gas well, a quarry or any other place of extraction of natural resources;

a building site or construction or installation project.

Organisations exempt from corporation tax

7. a) Partnerships.

b) Local authorities.

c) Approved pension schemes.

d) Charities. A charity, which is defined as 'any body of persons or trust established for charitable purposes' is exempt from corporation tax in so far as its income is applied to charitable purposes only. If a charity carries on a trade then any profits arising will be exempt providing that:

i) they are applied solely for the purposes of the charity, and

ii) either the trade is exercised out of a primary purpose of the charity, or the work is mainly carried out by the beneficiaries of the charity.

e) Agricultural and scientific societies.

f) The Crown.

Notice of chargeability to corporation tax

8. A company must give notice to HMRC of the beginning of its first AP which brings it into the charge to corporation tax. The notice which must be in writing must be given within three months of the beginning of the AP. For a new company, the information is given on form CT41G which is sent by HMRC to all newly-incorporated UK companies.

Self assessment – CT return (Form CT600)

9. The main features of the corporation tax self assessment (CTSA) system are as follows:

a) The payment of CT and the filing of the company's tax return are separate activities. For required tax payment dates, see paragraph 10 onwards.

b) Between 3 and 7 weeks after the end of a company's accounting period (or what HMRC think is the end of an accounting period), HMRC issues a notice (form CT603) requiring the company to deliver a tax return for the specified period.

For periods ending after 31 March 211, the filing of the CTSA return (Form CT600) and accompanying financial statements and computations must be done entirely online, using HMRC-approved software. The accompanying financial statements must be filed in iXBRL format. This is a tagged electronic format readable by both humans and computers, and allows automated software to check key figures in the financial statements to the company tax computations and self-assessment return.

CT returns for accounting periods ending before 1 April 2010 are overdue if not submitted by 31 March 2011 (see latest filing dates in (d) below), but should still be filed as paper returns (subject to late filing penalties) after 1 April 2011. Online CT filing does not apply for periods ending before 31 March 2010.

c) Whether filed in paper form or online, the CTSA return must include:

   i) a self-assessment of CT payable for the accounting period

   ii) formal claims for allowances and reliefs

   iii) supplementary pages, if applicable, in respect of:

      loans to participators by close companies CT600A

      controlled foreign companies CT600B

      group and consortium relief CT600C

      insurance companies CT600D

      additional details where the company is a charity CT600E

For limited companies, the financial statements must also be sent (in iXBRL form if filing online for periods ending after 31 March 2010), together with any computations required to show how the financial statements link to the figures entered in the CT return.

Bodies that are liable to CT, but are not limited companies, should send whatever form of accounts they are required to prepare. Any additional computations necessary to link those accounts to the CTSA return figures should also be provided.

d) The latest filing date for a CTSA return is 12 months from the end of the accounting period, or in the case of a period of account that covers more than one accounting period, twelve months from the end of the period of account. The directors are at liberty to file the CTSA return earlier than the latest filing date.

e) The company can amend its submitted CTSA return by giving a notice of amendment, within 12 months after the filing date. An amendment may include additional claims for relief, or the withdrawal of previously submitted claims.

f) HMRC can amend the submitted tax return to correct obvious errors or omissions, without launching a formal enquiry. This cannot be done more than nine months after the actual filing date, and the company may, if it wishes, appeal.

g) HMRC has up to twelve months from the actual filing date to raise an aspect enquiry (limited in scope), or a full enquiry, into a submitted CT return and to propose its own amendments as a result of an enquiry. HMRC also has up to twelve months from the date of a submitted amendment to a return, to enquire into the amendment.

h) Penalties are automatically due if the corporation tax return is filed late. There are flat-rate and tax-related penalties depending on the extent of the delay in filing the corporation tax return:

Period of delay (months)	**Penalties**
1 – 3	£100
3 – 6	£200
6 – 9	£200 + 10% of tax unpaid
9 –	£200 + 20% of tax unpaid

For 3 or more late returns in a row, the flat rate penalties are increased from £100 and £200 to £500 and £1,000.

Penalties are also charged for an incorrect return, under the regime introduced in the Finance Act 2007, explained in Chapter 3, Section 12.

Payments on account of corporation tax

10. a) "Large" companies are required to make quarterly instalment payments of their corporation tax liability.

b) A company is "large" for a corporation tax accounting period (CTAP) if its corporation tax augmented profits are more than £1.5m (pro-rated for short accounting periods).

c) If there are associated companies, then the £1.5m limit for augmented profits is divided by the number of associated companies plus one. Thus a parent company with 4 active subsidiaries has an upper relevant limit of $\frac{1,500,000}{5}$ i.e. £300,000. See chapter 23 for more on dividing the "large profits" limits where there are associated companies, or a short accounting period.

d) A company that becomes "large" during a CTAP does not have to make CT instalment payments for that period, provided:

i) it was not a large company in the previous CTAP, and

ii) Taxable total profits for that CTAP do not exceed £10million (this limit is divided where appropriate by the number of associated companies in the group, and apportioned for a short CTAP).

e) No company is required to make instalment payments if its CT liability for the CTAP is less than £10,000.

f) Subject to the exceptions above, CT is payable by "large" companies in four quarterly instalments, based on anticipated current year's taxable total profits, as follows:

Instalment	Due date
1st	6 months + 14 days after start of CTAP
2nd	9 months + 14 days after start of CTAP
3rd	14 days after end of CTAP
4th	3 months + 14 days after end of CTAP

Thus a company with a 31st March year end pays CT instalments on 14th October, 14th January, 14th April and 14th July following the year end.

g) If management CT estimates are accurate then 100% of the CT liability is paid by four instalments of 25% each.

h) If management estimates are inaccurate, over and underpayments are liable to interest at different rates (currently 4% per year for underpayments, and 0.5% per year for overpayments).

i) Interest received/paid on over- or under-payments of CT is taxable/tax-deductible for the company as a non-trading loan relationship surplus/deficit for CT purposes.

j) Groups of companies are able to arrange to pay single instalments on behalf of the whole group, without having to specify exactly which companies' final liability each instalment relates to. The allocation of the group's instalment payments to individual companies can be settled when the companies' individual CT returns are finalised.

k) Companies which are not "large" pay corporation tax by nine months and one day after the end of the CT accounting period. (See more details in chapter 23.)

Notes

i) Instalments are based on the expected corporation tax liability for the current accounting period.

ii) The final payment of 25%, due 3 months and 14 days after the end of the AP, would ideally meet the balance of CT due for the AP.

Repayment supplement (interest on overpaid tax)

11. Where a repayment of corporation tax or income tax of £100 or more is made more than 12 months after the "material date", the repayment is increased by a supplement at the appropriate rate of interest for each complete tax month from the 'relevant date' to the end of the tax month in which the repayment is made.

The material date is the normal due date for payment of corporation tax i.e. nine months after the year end.

The relevant date is:

a) if the repayment is of corporation tax paid on or after the first anniversary of the material date – the anniversary of the material date that follows the date that tax was paid.

b) in any other case – the first anniversary of the material date.

c) The repayment supplement rate is 0.5% per year from 29th September 2009.

Financial years and accounting periods

12. As already noted, CT is charged on the profits of companies for financial years, running from 1 April and a financial year is known by the calendar year in which it begins, e.g.:

Financial year	Period
2011	1st April 2011 – 31st March 2012
2010	1st April 2010 – 31st March 2011

The corporation tax rates and the marginal relief fraction for a financial year are enacted in the Finance Act for that financial year.

Corporation tax accounting periods

13. a) A corporation tax accounting period (CTAP) is the period for which CT liability is computed, and can never exceed 12 months in length.

b) A CTAP begins in the following circumstances:

i) When a company comes within the scope of UK CT – for example, by starting a UK trade, acquiring its first source of taxable income (if incorporated in the UK), or becoming resident in the UK (if not previously so resident);

ii) immediately after the end of the last accounting period, provided the company remains within the scope of UK CT.

c) A CTAP ends when the earliest of the following events occurs.

i) The company reaches its reporting year end (i.e. its accounting reference date).

ii) The anniversary of the end of the last CTAP before the current one.

iii) The company starts or stops trading (a CTAP ends, and a new one begins, when all trade starts or stops, even if other business activities continue).

iv) The company ceases to be within the scope of CT (for example, by selling its trade and all its income-producing assets, or in the case of non-resident companies, by ceasing to trade in the UK or to carry on exploration or exploitation activities in the UK sector of the North Sea).

v) The company goes into liquidation (once a company is in liquidation, its CTAPs run for consecutive periods of 12 months until the completion of the winding-up).

vi) The company starts or stops being resident in the UK.

Periods of account longer than 12 months

14. If a company's period of account covers two or more CTAPs, the various types of taxable profits, gains, losses and reliefs must be allocated correctly to the CTAPs. The following rules apply to allocate income, capital gains, FII and reliefs to CTAPS:

i) Assessable (taxable) trading income/profit is first computed by adjusting accounting profits for the whole period of account, **before** deducting capital allowances (or adding balancing charges – see chapter 20). Taxable trading income is then allocated to APs by a straight time-apportionment regardless of actual fluctuations in sales or profitability.

ii). Capital allowances and balancing charges are calculated separately for each AP, and the trading profits are adjusted accordingly.

iii) Income from land and buildings (property business income) is computed for each AP on a business accounting (accruals) basis, applied for that period.

iv) Chargeable gains are assessable, and capital losses arise, in the accounting period in which the disposal contract was made.

v) Qualifying charitable donations are deducted from the total profits of the accounting period in which they are paid.

vi) Surpluses and deficits on non-trade loan relationships (See chapter 19 paragraph 8) are allocated to accounting periods on the same basis that they would be recognised in the company's financial accounts if they were drawn up for that same period.

Where a period of account exceeds twelve months, say 15 months, it is by law split into two accounting periods, the first of 12 months and one of three months.

Example

K Ltd has regularly prepared accounts to the 31st December. On 1st January 2011 the directors decide that the year end shall be 31st March, and the next set of accounts covers the period of fifteen months to the 31st March 2012.

Corporation tax accounting periods	**Periods of account**
12 months to 31st December 2010	12 months to 31st December 2010
12 months to 31st December 2011	} 15 months to 31st March 2012
3 months to 31st March 2012	
12 months to 31st March 2013	12 months to 31st March 2013

Note

There will be two CT return periods in the 15-month period of account:
12 months to 31.12.2011; and 3 months to 31.3.2012.

Corporation Tax rates

15. There are two rates of corporation tax, the small profits rate ("Small Companies Rate" until 31 March 2010) and the full or main rate. The level of augmented profits determines which rate applies, and there is marginal relief to smooth the average rate of CT between small profits rate and main rate where profits fall in the intermediate zone.

This method is a form of progressive taxation varying the average rate of CT according to how profitable the company is (including FII). The average rate of CT rises smoothly as taxable profits plus FII increase. Once the upper relevant profits amount is reached, the rate cannot go up any more.

Recent CT rates and profits limits/ marginal relief fractions:

Financial years	FY07	FY08	FY09	FY10	FY11
Year to 31st March	2008	2009	2010	2011	2012
Full rate	30%	28%	28%	28%	26%
Small profits rate	20%	21%	21%	21%	20%
Marginal relief fraction	1/40	7/400	7/400	7/400	3/200
Lower relevant amount	300,000	300,000	300,000	300,000	300,000
Upper relevant amount	1,500,000	1,500,000	1,500,000	1,500,000	1,500,000

Marginal relief formula: tax the company's profits at main rate first, then deduct:

$$(U - A) \times {}^{N}/_{A} \times \text{ the marginal relief fraction}$$

where N = Taxable total profit, U = upper relevant amount, A = Augmented profits

Several worked examples of CT calculations with marginal relief are in Chapter 23.

Effective marginal CT rates for FY 2010:

0 – 300,000	21%
300,001 – 1,500,000	29.75%
1,500,001 –	28%

Effective marginal CT rates for FY 2011:

0 – 300,000	20%
300,001 – 1,500,000	27.5%
1,500,001 –	26%

Change in the rate of CT part way through a CTAP

16. If a company's CT accounting period does not coincide with the financial year, and there is a change in the rate or rates of CT, the taxable total profits for the CTAP must be apportioned between the two financial years on a time basis, before adding on FII, and then tax is computed at different rates for each fraction of a financial year.

The CT rates changed on 1 April 2011, so CTAPs that straddle the date 1 April 2011 are taxed by apportioning the taxable total profit between the two financial years, applying the correct rates of tax, and treating the total as the single CT liability for the AP.

Example

D Ltd, a trading company, whose 12 month accounting period ended on the 30th June 2011, has taxable total profits for that period of £200,000 and no associated companies. As the CT small profits rate is 21% for FY2010 and 20% for FY2011, D's CT liability computation is as follows:

	£	£
Taxable total profits		
1.7.2010 to 31.3.2011 274/365 × 200,000	150,137	
1.4.2011 to 30.6.2011 91/365 × 200,000	49,863	200,000
Corporation tax payable		
Financial year 2010 to 31.3.2011 150,137 @ 21%		31,528
Financial year 2011 to 31.3.2012 49,863 @ 20%		9,972
Total CT liability		41,500

The small profits rate applies in this case, and it changed on 1st April 2011.

Although it is correct to apportion taxable profits of an AP to FYs using exact days, the calculation may be done in months for the tax exams of most UK professional accounting bodies.

17. Specimen corporation tax computation (based on CT600 form)

INCOME AND GAINS	£	£
Tax-adjusted trading profits	–	
Less capital allowances	–	
Less Trade losses brought forward against trading profits	–	
Subtotal: Net trading profits		–
ADD: Net non-trade loan relationship surplus *		
(typically interest receivable and similar income)		–
ADD: Overseas income	–	
ADD: Miscellaneous Income	–	
ADD: Income from which income tax has been deducted	–	

	£	£
ADD: Non-trading gains on intangible fixed assets	–	
ADD: Income from UK land and buildings	–	
ADD: Chargeable gains, net of allowable capital losses	–	
SUBTOTAL – NON-TRADE PROFITS	–	
DEDUCTIONS SPECIFICALLY FROM NON-TRADE PROFITS:		
Non-trade loan relationship deficit *	–	
Non-trade capital allowances	–	
		–
TOTAL PROFITS		–
LESS: DEDUCTIONS AND RELIEFS FROM TOTAL PROFITS:		
Losses on unquoted shares		–
Trading losses set against total profits		–
Excess management expenses		–
Profit before qualifying charitable donations and group relief		–
LESS: Qualifying charitable donations paid		–
LESS: Group relief claimed		–
= TAXABLE TOTAL PROFITS		–
CORPORATION TAX :		
Financial year 2010 @ 28% (21% if SPR applies)		–
2011 @ 26% (20% if SPR applies)		–
Total corporation tax before reliefs and set-offs in terms of tax		–
LESS: Marginal small profits relief		–
LESS: Double taxation relief		–
NET CORPORATION TAX LIABILITY		–
Add Tax due on profits of CFCs (see Chapter 25)		–
Less: relief for Income Tax suffered by deduction from income		–
= CORPORATION TAX DUE		–

Note: * non-trade loan deficits suffered are firstly netted against non-trade loan relationships income, and any negative balance is then taken to the non-trade loan deficit line.

Student self-testing questions

1. Tina Limited has TTP of £2,000,000 for the year ended 30 September 2011.

Requirement

Calculate the corporation tax liability for year ended 30 September 2011.

Answer

		£
FY 2010	2,000,000 x 6/12 x 28% =	280,000
FY 2011	2,000,000 x 6/12 x 26% =	260,000
		£540,000

2. Pirate Limited, a large company, has an estimated corporation tax liability of £700,000 for the year ended 31 March 2012. The company pays instalments in line with this estimate. The final assessment to corporation tax is £1,000,000 and the balancing payment was made on the final due date.

Requirement

Calculate each of the company's corporation tax instalments and state when they will be payable. Calculate each balance upon which interest on overdue tax will be calculated and state the periods over which this interest will be charged. Calculate the total interest charge.

Answer

	Paid	Correct payment	Balance on which interest due	Period over which interest charged
	£	£	£	£
14 October 2011	175,000	250,000	75,000	14/10/11 - 14/12/12
14 January 2012	175,000	250,000	75,000	14/1/12 - 14/12/12
14 April 2012	175,000	250,000	75,000	14/4/12 - 14/12/12
14 July 2012	175,000	250,000	75,000	14/7/12 - 14/12/12
1 January 2013	300,000	0		

Total interest charge = (14 /12 x £75,000 x 4%) + (11/12 x £75,000 x 4%) + (8/12 x £75,000 x 4%) + (/12 x £75,000 x 4%) = **£9,000.**

19 The charge to corporation tax

Introduction

1. This chapter is concerned with the determination of CT total profits before deductions and reliefs, which is an important stage in the determination of taxable total profit.

The chapter examines the most important components in the CT total profits computation as demonstrated in the specimen CT computation at the end of chapter 18. The chapter concludes with a comprehensive example of the adjustment of accounting profits to trading profits for corporation tax purposes.

Generally accepted accounting practice

2. United Kingdom tax law requires that tax computations are prepared in accordance with generally accepted accounting practice. Generally accepted accounting practice is defined as being the accounting practice that is used in preparing accounts which are intended to give a 'true and fair' view (section 836A, Taxes Act 1988). The various financial reporting standards issued by the United Kingdom/International accounting bodies generally require that the relevant financial reporting standard needs to be applied to all transactions of a reporting entity whose financial statements are intended to give a true and fair view.

Sources of income

3. Income is brought into Total Profits under the following headings;

Trading profits

Profits and gains from non-trading loan relationships

Overseas non-trading income (under CTA2009 overseas trading income is included with UK trading profits)

Other/ Miscellaneous Income

Income from which income tax has been deducted

Non-trading gains on intangible fixed assets

Income from land and buildings

Chargeable gains, net of allowable capital losses

Trading Profits

4. The following points should be noted under this heading.

a) The general principles of what is tax-deductible trading expenditure for sole traders (see Chapter 10) also apply to companies; except where a specifically different rule exists for corporation tax. Profits and losses arising from trade loan relationships form part of trading profits. Companies do not have a private or personal existence and therefore there is not usually scope for expenses to be apportioned between private and business use. Expenses of providing private benefits or assets for loan to staff or directors are allowable for the company as trade or management expenses, being part of remuneration costs.

b) Petroleum revenue tax is a deductible expense for corporation tax purposes.

c) Incidental costs of obtaining loan finance, including costs in connection with the issue of convertible loan stock, are allowed as a deduction in computing trading income. This applies even to long-term non-trading loan finance and would include such costs as professional fees, accountants' reports, commissions, advertising and communication costs related to bond or debenture issues, or any other borrowings, secured or not.

d) Pre-incorporation expenses incurred up to seven years prior to the actual commencement of trading can be treated as being incurred on the first day of trading. Eligible expenditure includes all expenses which, had the company already been trading, would have been allowed as a trading expense, such as rent, rates, staff wages and salaries, but not company formation expenses, stamp duties, or capital expenditure.

e) Unpaid remuneration:

   i) A deduction for employees' or directors' remuneration is not allowed in the computation of trading profits if the remuneration was paid more than nine months after the end of the period of account. Instead a deduction is allowed in the period of account when paid.

   ii) "Payment" in this case is based on the same rules used to determine when remuneration is received by the director or employee for the purpose of taxes on earnings (and PAYE). See Chapter 7 on this.

   iii) Where the corporation tax return is submitted before the end of the nine month period, any remuneration unpaid at that time should be added back in calculating the taxable profits. If the remuneration is subsequently paid before the end of the nine month period, an adjustment can be made to the submitted return within two years of the end of the period of account.

f) Just as for income tax (see chapter 10), there is an even stricter rule regarding deductions claimed for pension contributions paid to a separate pension plan or fund on behalf of employees or directors. The payment is only deducted once it has actually been made: no accruals basis may be applied for this type of cost.

g) A company's taxable profits are computed without any adjustment in respect of dividends paid or other distributions made by the company out of its profits.

h) For allowable amortisation of intangible fixed assets, see 9 below.

Research and development reliefs and credits – 200% for SMEs/130% for large companies

5. Relief is available for qualifying research and development expenditure (of a revenue nature) by UK companies, in an amount that is greater than the cost actually incurred. The rate is 200% for Small or medium sized companies and 130% for large companies. These terms are define as for company law reporting purposes, and have nothing to do with the "large profits" company as defined for CT rates.

The following is an outline of the rules on R&D tax credits:

a) Rates of R&D tax credits:

   i) 200% of qualifying R&D expenditure (175% before1 April 2011) for small or medium sized companies

   ii) 130% of qualifying R&D expenditure for large companies

b) Minimum threshold level of expenditure to qualify in any year – £10,000.

c) A company's qualifying R&D expenditure is deductible in an accounting period if it relates to an actual trade or a future or potential trade. That is, either:

   i) it is allowable as a deduction in computing for tax purposes the profits for that period of a trade carried on by the company, or

   ii) it would have been allowable as such a deduction, had the company, at the time the expenditure was incurred, been carrying on a trade consisting of the activities in respect of which it was incurred.

d) 'Qualifying R&D expenditure' of company means expenditure that meets the following conditions:

   i) it is not of a capital nature.

   ii) it is attributable to relevant research and development directly undertaken by the company, or on its behalf.

   iii) it is incurred on staffing costs, or on consumable stores (including power, fuel, water, and software or is qualifying expenditure on sub-contracted research and development.

   iv) any intellectual property created as a result of the research and development to which the expenditure is attributable is, or will be, vested in the company (whether alone or with other persons). It has been announced that this condition was removed for SME companies' R&D relief with effect from FY 2010.

   v) the expenditure is not incurred by the company in carrying on activities the carrying on of which is contracted out to the company by any person.

   vi) the expenditure is not subsidised.

e) Where:

   i) A company is entitled to R&D tax relief for an accounting period,

   ii) it is carrying on a trade in that period, and

   iii) it has qualifying R&D expenditure that is allowable as a deduction in computing for tax purposes the profits of the trade for that period, it may (on making a claim) treat that qualifying R&D expenditure as if it were an amount equal to 200%/130% of the actual amount.

The effect of making an R&D claim, if the company is profitable, is that tax is saved equal to between 20% and 26% of the qualifying R&D expenditure for an SME, and at 3/10 of these rates if the company is a large company.

If the company making the claim is an SME and is not profitable, so R&D tax credits simply increase trade losses, then the Board may elect to receive immediate payment from the government for the tax value of the excess R&D credits, instead of allowing them to be carried forward or back as part of a trade .

Surplus on non-trading loan relationships

6. The income taxable under this heading is as follows.

a) Interest Income. Bank and building society interest, normally paid gross to a corporate account-holder, are taxed under this heading. If a company does receive interest net, i.e. with 20% deducted at source, the gross amount is still chargeable to corporation tax.

b) Other finance income from non-trade loan relationships. Measurement is based on the amount treated under GAAP (either International or UK GAAP is acceptable) as the finance receivable for the accounting period (e.g. the unwinding profit on an investment bond purchased at a discount or redeemable at a premium, under IAS39). So there is no need to adjust interest totals in the income statement for opening and closing accruals and prepayments.

   Upward revaluations of debt instruments recognised through profit and loss account are also taxable as surplus on loan relationships.

   Loan relationships of companies are never chargeable assets for the calculation of chargeable gains for Corporation Tax. Thus for example the write-off or waiver of a non- trade loan to another company is a deficit on a non trade loan relationship, not a capital loss.

Where income is received after deduction of income tax at source, since the gross amount is chargeable to corporation tax, the income tax deducted at source is recoverable as follows:

a) It can be set against any income tax payable in respect of payments made by the company under deduction of basic rate tax at source – e.g. payment of patent royalties to a non-incorporated royalty recipient.

b) If relief is not fully available under (a) then any excess may be deducted from the main corporation tax liability, or if this is exceeded, a cash repayment may be obtained.

Taxed investment income of companies is accounted for under what is known as the 'quarterly return system' outlined in Chapter 21.

Loan relationships

7. a) In general a loan relationship exists whenever there is a creditor or debtor for a debt which is regarded as a loan under general law. Thus the issue of a loan or debenture would fall within this definition, as well as other financial securities.

b) The definition in (a) above encompasses practically all Government gilt-edged securities, building society PIBS (permanent interest-bearing shares), and corporate bonds and corporate debts. Bank interest receivable by a trading company is taxed as a non-trading credit.

c) To give effect to the loan relationship tax rules there are two methods of accounting which companies are authorised to use, mirroring current accounting standards on financial instruments.

   i) an accruals basis;

   ii) a market-to-market basis - by which a loan relationship is accounted for in each accounting period at a fair value in the balance sheet and any movement is taken to profit and loss account.

   As a general rule, companies follow their accounts treatment for taxation purposes.

d) Where companies enter into a loan relationship for the purposes of a trade, then all profits, losses and costs relating to the loan relationship are treated as receipts or expenses of that trade and therefore included in the calculation of trade profits or losses.

e) Where a company enters into a loan relationship which is of a non-trade nature, i.e. it is not a loan relationship in the course of activities forming an integral part of the trade, then any net income is taxed as interest income and any net loss is dealt with as below:

   i) by offset against the company's other income and gains chargeable to corporation tax for that accounting period; or

   ii) by surrender as group relief to other United Kingdom group companies (see Chapter 24); or

   iii) by carry back on a last in first out basis against the company's previous three years' net profits arising from its loan relationship, to the extent that such profits arise on a company's non-trading foreign exchange and financial instrument transactions; or

   iv) by carry-forward against its future non-trading profits (including capital gains). This treatment is also extended to losses arising from non-trading foreign exchange and financial instrument transactions.

f) The loan relationships rules apply to all UK companies in the charge to corporation tax, including UK branches of overseas companies.

g) A company issuing corporate debt is able to obtain tax relief for interest on an accruals basis, provided the interest is paid within 12 months of the accounting year end.

Intangible fixed assets

8. a) Companies (but not unincorporated businesses) are able to obtain tax relief for the cost of intangible assets/ intellectual property, in most cases based on the amortisation or impairment charged in the accounts.

Intangible assets include:

i) patents, trade marks, registered designs, copyright or design rights;

ii) database rights, computers and software licences, know how;

iii) goodwill, excluding that arising on consolidation after purchase of shares.

Intangible assets for this purpose do not include leases of property or land

a) Expenditure on intellectual property is any expenditure incurred on the acquisition, creation, maintenance, preservation or enhancement of that property. It includes abortive expenditure and expenditure on establishing and defending title to that property. It also includes royalties paid for the use of the intellectual property. Whether or not the expenditure is treated as capital expenditure in the financial statements is irrelevant, except that capital expenditure on tangible assets is specifically excluded.

b) The system provides that a 'tax debit' (normally an item of tax deductible expenditure) in respect of intellectual property can arise in five ways:

i) as expenditure written off as it is incurred;

a. as amortisation of capitalised intellectual property;

b. as a write-down following an impairment review;

c. as a reversal of a tax credit from a previous accounting period;

d. as losses on realisation of intellectual property.

c) A tax credit can arise on the following occasions:

i) receipts recognised in the profit and loss account as they accrue;

a. revaluations of intellectual property;

b. credits in respect of negative goodwill;

c. reversal of a tax debit in previous accounting periods;

d. gains on realisation of intellectual property.

d) The rules only apply to assets created or acquired after the 31st March 2002. These assets are called chargeable intangible assets. All other IFAs held by a company on the 1st April 2002 called existing assets, continue to be dealt with under the existing rules (i.e. mainly on a CGT basis) so long as the assets remain in the hands of the same 'economic family'.

e) Where the IFAs are not held for trade purposes, the taxable and relievable amounts are pooled to produce a net non-trading gain or loss.

Corporate Venturing Scheme

9. This scheme works for companies rather like the Enterprise Investment Scheme (EIS) works for income tax. It has been closed to new claims from 1 April 2011. Under this scheme, companies can obtain 20% corporation tax relief on amounts subscribed for new ordinary shares in small higher-risk trading companies which are held for at least three years. A gain on disposal of such an investment can be deferred where it is reinvested in another corporate venturing investment. A loss on disposal (net of the 20% relief) can be set against income.

A minimum proportion of the investee company's ordinary share capital must be held by individuals. The proportion is 20%. (Typically these individuals would be the founders/ managers of the investee company.)

The investing company's maximum stake in the investee company is 30%. Only ordinary share capital, and share and loan capital capable of conversion into ordinary share capital, will count towards this limit.

Only investments in unquoted companies qualify for relief, but relief will not be withdrawn if the company later becomes quoted, provided there were no arrangements in place or planned, at the time the investment was made, for seeking a listing.

Relief will not be withdrawn merely because the investee company goes into receivership.

Property income

10. Companies' property business income is measured on the same basis as the property of individuals, except that companies do not deduct mortgage interest on loans to purchase letting property specifically against the rental income, but treat it as a general non trade loan relationship deficit.

Other rules are similar to those for property business income of individuals, namely:

a) Rental income and expenses are computed on an accruals basis, with a deduction for all expenditure wholly and exclusively incurred for the letting business.

b) Furnished lettings, holiday and non-holiday, are taxed as income from property and the 10% wear and tear allowance is available as an alternative to claiming for renewals of furnishings and kitchen utensils etc.

c) Overseas property income is taxed as other income but computed as income from property.

d) Profits and losses on all lettings are pooled as the business is to be taxed as a single letting business.

e) The company intangible asset regime does not apply to intangible assets that bundle rights over land or buildings (i.e. typically leases, but also options over land): these assets have their own tax rules (see below).

f) Capital allowances where available (e.g. on landlord's fixtures, maintenance equipment for the property) are deducted as a business expense.

Rental losses after are relieved in the same way as management expenses, i.e. against current period total profits. They may also be surrendered as group relief or carried forward against future property income. This provides companies with a broader scope of property loss relief than is available for individuals.

Lease premiums

12. One way of looking at lease premiums is to regard them as a capitalised part of future rental income which would otherwise have been received by way of annual rent. They include any sum whether payable to the immediate or a superior landlord, arising in connection with the granting of a lease, but not arising from an assignment of an existing lease.

(Under an assignment the lessee takes the position of the original lessee, with the same terms and conditions.)

Where a new lease is granted (but not when an existing lease is assigned) at a premium for a period not exceeding 50 years, then the landlord is deemed for income tax or corporation tax purposes to receive rental income equal to the premium, less an allowance of 2% of the premium for each complete year of the lease remaining, excluding the first 12 month period.

Example

B Ltd granted a lease for 24 years of its warehouse to a trader on the following terms:

A lease premium of £12,000 to be paid on 1.1.2011 and an annual rent of £1,000;

Allowable letting expenditure for accounting period ended 31st December 2011 was £5,800.

Corporation Tax AP 31.12.2011

	£	£
Lease premium received	12,000	
Less 2% × 12,000 × (24 – 1)		
i.e. 1/50 × 12,000 × 23	5,520	6,480
Annual rent		1,000
		7,480
Less allowable expenses		(5,800)
Property income liable to corporation tax		1,680

In effect the lease premium is discounted by reference to its duration, and the longer the unexpired portion, the greater the discount. Thus if a lease had 49 years to run the discount would be:

$$(49 - 1) \times 2\% \text{ i.e. } 96\%.$$

The amount of the taxable premium may also be determined by use of the formula:

$$P - \frac{(P \times Y)}{50}$$

P = amount of premium paid; Y = number of completed 12 months other than the first.

Lease premiums and the lessee

13. Where the lessee makes a payment of a lease premium at the start of a lease, then a proportion of that premium may be set against the following:

a) any trading income, providing the premises are used for business purposes.

b) any rental income or lease premium received from any sub-lease granted by the lessee.

In effect the amount of the premium assessed as income of the lessor can be charged as an expense of trading by the lessee, the deductible expense being spread over the remaining life of the lease.

Example

S Ltd is granted a lease of premises to be used for trading purposes, for a period of 20 years, at an annual rent of £6000 p.a. plus an initial lease premium of £32,000.

	£
Lease premium	32,000
Less 2% × 32,000 × (20 – 1) i.e. 38% × 32,000	12,160
Lease premium taxed on lessor as income	19,840

Relief available to S Ltd for notional rent for trade purposes $= \frac{19840}{20}$ i.e.£992 p.a.

Overseas income

14. Income from overseas activities of UK companies is not directly covered in this text but some awareness points on international issues for companies are mentioned in Chapter 25.

Capital gains tax

15. Companies are not liable to capital gains tax as such, but they are liable to corporation tax on chargeable gains which must be computed in accordance with the appropriate CGT rules, as outlined in Chapters 26 to 33.

All chargeable gains are taxed at the relevant corporation tax rate which for FY 2011 is:

Company's profits > £1,500,000	26%
Small company profits < £300,000	20%

(With marginal relief where appropriate)

Example

K Ltd has corporation tax trading profits of £1,500,000 for its accounting year ended 31st March 2012, and a chargeable gain of £500,000.

Compute the corporation tax payable.

Solution: K Ltd corporation tax computation. AP to 31.3.2012

	£
Corporation tax trading profits	1,500,000
Chargeable gain	500,000
Taxable total profits	2,000,000
Corporation tax @ 26%	520,000

Comprehensive example – adjustment of trading profit for a company

16. S plc has the following results in respect of the year ended 31st March 2012.

		£	£
Sales			283,165
Factory cost of sales			(127,333)
Factory profit			155,832
Expenses:	General administration	37,021	
	Marketing	28,197	
	Distribution	16,031	
	Financial	22,000	(103,249)
			52,583
Non-sales revenue			14,723
Profit before tax			67,306
Corporation tax			(30,000)
Profit after tax			37,306

Additional information:		£
Factory cost of sales includes:		
Depreciation		17,832
Permanent partitioning of works office		3,179
Repairs to new premises to make usable		1,621
General expenses include:	Legal costs of tax appeal	627
	Legal costs of share issue	175
	Stamp duty – property	1,200
	Fines on employees for parking tickets	250

		£
Marketing expenses include:	Trade debts written off	1,211
	Loan to ex-employee written off	250
	Increase in general bad debt provision	5,000
	Increase in specific bad debt provision	1,000
	Promotional gifts, £45 each	1,800
	Advertising on TV	6,000
Financial expenses include:	Bank interest	1,100
	Bank charges	238
	Donation to political party	250
	Subscriptions to trade associations	1,250
	Redundancy payments	11,000
Non-sales revenue comprises:	Profit on sale of assets	323
	Bad debts recovered	1,700
	Agency commission	12,700

Compute the adjusted profits for corporation tax purposes, ignoring capital allowances.

Solution: S plc adjustment of profits. Accounting period to 31st March 2012

	£	£
Profit before tax		67,306
Add back items disallowed:		
(see notes):		
Depreciation	17,832	
Partitioning	3,179	
Repairs	1,621	
General administration:		
Legal expenses	627	
Legal expenses	175	
Stamp duty – property	1,200	
Marketing expenses:		
Loan to ex employee written off	250	
Increase in general bad debt provision	5,000	
Financial expenses:		
Political donation	250	
		30,134
Less profit on sale of fixed assets		(323)
Adjusted trading profit		97,117

Notes

1. Depreciation £17,832 – added back, capital allowances claimed in lieu.
2. Partitioning £3,879 –plant and machinery, see Jarrold v Johnson & Sons 1962 40 TC 681.
3. Repairs £1,621 – see Law Shipping Co. Ltd, and Odeon Theatres Ltd cases.
4. Legal expenses £627 – expenses of tax appeal not allowed.
5. Legal expenses £175 – capital expenditure (because it relates to a share issue) - This would be allowable if on a bond/loan stock issue.
6. Stamp duty £1,200 – capital expenditure not revenue.
7. Loan to ex-employee written off £250 – making loans to individuals is not the company's trade so this is not a trading expense. (customer bad debt write-offs are part of the trade, and loans to current employees that are waived would fall under the category of staff pay)
8. Increase in general provision for bad debts £5,000.
9. Donation to political party £250 – not an expense of trading.
10. Profit on sale of fixed assets £323 – this is not a taxable revenue receipt; in effect it is negative depreciation. No taxable capital gain will arise if the assets qualified for capital allowances and were sold for less than cost, or if they were chattels below £6,000, or cars.

See Chapter 10, section 7 for more details of the case law on disallowable expenses.

Student self-testing question

1. T Ltd has the following results for the year ended 30th June 2011

	£	£
Sales		160,000
Cost of sales		(40,000)
Gross profit		120,000
Wages and salaries	42,000	
Rent and rates	4,287	
Insurance and telephone	1,721	
Repairs and renewals	35,000	
Heating and lighting	2,897	
Professional charges	3,250	
Bank interest payable on business overdraft	1,155	
Subscriptions and donations	1,200	
Directors' remuneration	22,000	
Patent renewal fees	1,000	
Bad debts	1,250	
Sales commission	5,680	
Loss on sale of assets	1,000	
Miscellaneous expenses	7,251	(129,691)

Net Trading loss		(9,691)
Other income:		
Discounts received	1,123	
Foreign exchange surplus	12,107	
Dividends received	1,620	
Rents receivable less outgoings	651	15,501
Trading profit before taxation		5,810

Additional information:

Repairs and renewals:	£
Repairs to newly acquired premises of which £10,000 was necessary to make them usable	27,000
Furnace relining – provision for future expenditure	8,000
Professional charges:	
Audit and accounting	1,250
Architect's fees for new factory design	1,750
Legal costs for renewal of short lease	250
Subscriptions and donations:	
Donation to golf club used by staff	500
Subscriptions to trade associations	150
Gift aid payment to charity	550
Wages and salaries of staff:	
Salaries and national insurance	32,000
Staff Bonuses (paid in May 2012)	10,000
Directors' remuneration:	
Salary paid in year	14,000
Pension scheme accrued payment due at year-end (paid 31.8.11)	4,000
Bad debts:	
Trade debts written off	250
Increase in general provision	1,000
Entertaining:	
Office party	410
Theatre tickets for foreign customers	991
Removal expenses of new managing director	850
Compensation to customers for damage from company's product	5,000
Exchange surplus:	
Profit from currency dealings arising from trade	12,107
Rents receivable less outgoings:	
Net rents from letting part of factory	1,000
Deficit on property let to retired employee at a nominal rent	(349)

Compute the trading profits for taxation purposes for the AP to 30th June 2011.

Solution: T Ltd accounting period to 30th June 2011

	£	£
Trading profit per accounts		5,810
Add items disallowed:		
Repairs and renewals	18,000	
Professional charges	1,750	
Donation to golf club	500	
Gift aid to charity	550	
Pension provision unpaid at year end	4,000	
Bad debt provision (general)	1,000	
Loss on sale of asset	1,000	
Theatre tickets - entertaining	991	
Staff bonuses (unpaid after 9 months)	10,000	37,791
		43,601
Less dividends received (not taxable in hands of a company)	1,620	
Rents receivable (not trade income)	651	(2,271)
Trading profit for taxation purposes		41,330

Notes to answer

1. Repairs to make the premises initially usable are not allowable. Round sum provision for future costs is also disallowed.

2. Architect's fees for new factory are capital expenditure on the factory building.

3. Donation to golf club, although used by staff, is not welfare or sports expenditure.

4. The gift aid to the charity is not allowed as a trading expense, but is deducted as a qualifying charitable donation from total profits in the taxable total profits computation.

5. Pension contributions are not allowed unless actually paid in the AP.

6. The increase in the bad debt provision is general and therefore not allowed until applied to write off specific bad debts.

7. Losses on the sales of fixed assets are not trading expenses.

8. The theatre tickets are disallowed entertaining expenses.

9. Dividends received by a company are not liable to corporation tax.

10 Rents receivable are taxable as income from land and buildings.

11. As the exchange surplus has arisen through trading, it is taxable as a trading receipt.

12. As the staff bonus was paid more than nine months after the year end, it is not allowed against taxable profits until the next accounting period.

Questions without answers

1. Z plc has the following results for the year ended 31st March 2012.

	£	£
Trading profits		1,900,000
Bank deposit interest (gross)	1,500	
Building society interest (gross)	1,700	3,200
		1,903,200
Less allowable expenses	50,000	
Director's remuneration	25,000	
Depreciation	8,000	(83,000)
Profit before tax		1,820,200

Compute the taxable total profit, showing each separate category of income, and the corporation tax payable.

2. Carrot Limited, a company resident in the United Kingdom, makes up accounts annually to 30 September. The information listed below relates to Carrot Ltd's twelve month accounting period ended 30 September 2011.

INCOME	£
Trading profit (already adjusted for tax purposes)	1,120,000
Rents receivable	40,000
Dividends received from non-group companies	138,600
Building Society interest receivable	48,000
Capital gains	148,000

Requirement: Compute the TTP for Carrot Ltd and the corporation tax payable.

3. P Ltd's accounts for the 12 months to 31st December 2011 showed the following:

	£	£
Revenue		442,100
Less: Cost of sales		(214,000)
Gross profit		228,100
Net rents receivable on let property		750
Profit on sale of plant items		5,500
		234,350
Less: expenses		

Wages and salaries	90,500	
Rent, rates and insurance	6,000	
Motor expenses	2,000	
Legal expenses	2,000	
Directors' remuneration	35,000	
Audit charges	2,500	
Miscellaneous	1,300	
Depreciation	6,000	
Amortisation of purchased goodwill	14,000	
		(159,300)
Net profit		£75,050

Notes

i) Legal expenses comprise:

	£
Debt collection	600
Advice on staff service agreements	250
Issue of debentures	1,150
	2,000

ii) Miscellaneous expenses comprise:

		£
Subscriptions :	trade associations	150
	political party	440
Staff outing		710
		1,300

iii) On 1st January 2011 the company acquired the Goodwill of an unincorporated business for £140,000, which it has decided to write off over 10 years.

iv) Capital allowances for the accounting period to 31.12.2011 have been agreed at £33,230 and are deductible in computing trading income.

v) Gross profit has been computed after deducting £50,000 paid in December 2011 under a threat of blackmail of the chief executive.

Calculate the liability to corporation tax for the AP to 31st December 2011.

4. Valerie Limited's accounts for the 12 months to 31 December 2011 showed the following:

		£
Sales turnover		729,150
Less: cost of goods sold		401,000
Gross profit		328,150
Net rents		1,000
Capital gain on sale of plant		2,500
		331,650
Less expenses:		
Wages & salaries	140,000	
Rent, rates and insurance	6,000	
Motor expenses	4,000	
Miscellaneous expenses (1)	2,000	
Director's remuneration	40,000	
Bad debts (3)	3,650	
Audit fee	2,000	
Depreciation	5,000	
Premium on lease, written off (2)	14,000	
		216,650
Net profit		£115,000

Notes

(1) Miscellaneous expenses comprise:	£
Staff outing	600
Penalty for late VAT return	400
Wine given to customers	1,000

(2) On the 1st July 2011 Valerie Ltd was granted the lease of additional factory premises for a period of 7 years on payment of a premium of £14,000.

(3) Bad debts expense account comprises the following:	£
Specific provision	2,000
Loan to an ex-employee, written off	650
Increase in general bad debt provision	1,000

Requirement: Calculate TTP for the accounting period to 31 December 2011.

20 Capital allowances

Introduction

1. The capital allowance system, described in Chapter 13 in connection with income tax, is essentially the same for corporation tax. There is a difference in computing maximum writing down and annual investment allowances for a long period of account, as a CT accounting period cannot last longer than twelve months.

Another difference is that companies do not have private use assets.

Main features

2. a) Capital allowances are available in respect of qualifying expenditure incurred in an accounting period, which is the basis period.

b) Capital allowances are deducted as an expense in arriving at the trading income. A balancing charge is treated as trading income.

c) The pool system for plant and machinery and other assets is the same for companies as for individuals, but there is no disallowance for private use of a company asset.

d) A writing down allowance or a FYA for plant and machinery can be disclaimed by a company.

e) If capital allowances effectively create or increase a trading loss then they are carried forward as an integral part of the trading loss.

f) Where the accounting period is more than 12 months' duration then the capital allowances are computed for each separate period and not 'scaled up' as for income tax purposes.

g) A 100% first year allowance is available to assets qualifying for enhanced allowances just as for individual sole traders on the following expenditure:.

- i) Approved Energy-saving and Water-saving plant and equipment
- ii) Low-emission cars – the limit for these has now been set at 110g CO_2 per km emissions

h) The Writing Down Allowance is 20% per year (reducing balance) on the general pool of plant and machinery, including cars with CO_2 emissions of 160 g/km or less.

i) The Writing Down Allowance is 10% per year (reducing balance) in the special rate pool . which covers "features integral to a building", "long life assets", and cars with CO_2 emissions above 160 g/km.

Features integral to a building can broadly be defined as:

i) electrical systems (including lighting systems);

ii) cold water systems;

ii) space or water heating systems, powered systems of ventilation, air cooling or air purification, and any floor or ceiling comprised in such systems;

iv) lifts, escalators, and moving walkways;

v) external solar shading; and

vi) active facades

j) Annual Investment Allowance (AIA) may be claimed by companies for expenditure on general pool or special rate pool assets, other than cars. This AIA is given in addition to (and before) the normal writing down allowance on the same expenditure,

The AIA for a full twelve month period is currently £100,000 a year. The Government has announced as a policy intention that AIA maximum will fall to £25,000 a year from April 2012 and the writing down allowance rates will fall from 20% and 10% to 18% and 8% respectively. . However, examples in this book adopt the approach of ignoring such future changes until they are enacted, in order to keep examples simple.

If there is a group of companies under common control, sharing a similar trade or having the same trading premises, then only one AIA limit applies between them all. The AIA may be allocated to any company or companies but HMRC must be told how total AIA claims within the group have been allocated. This rule is to prevent groups of similar companies under common control benefiting from multiple AIAs. In general in the examples in this book it may be assumed that AIA is available to the company being looked at.

k) Companies can elect to "de-pool" Short life assets, namely plant from the general pool which will be used for less than 8 years (increased from 4 years in April 2011) in the trade and where the directors expect the residual value to be lower than the tax written down value when the assets are sold or scrapped.

De-pooled short life assets receive the same allowances during their ownership as they would have done if left in the general pool. The difference comes when they are sold or scrapped as a balancing allowance or charge arises on the difference between the disposal proceeds and the written down value, which would not be the case if they had not been de-pooled .

Example

K plc has the following data relating to its accounting period ended 31st March 2012.

	£
Trading profits for tax purposes	1,865,550
Profit from land and property	173,200
Plant and machinery pool at 1.4.2011	88,000
Additions 1.8.2011 (general plant and machinery)	27,000

Compute the capital allowances and the corporation tax liability for the CTAP to 31st March 2012.

Solution

Capital allowances: plant and machinery

	Pool
	£
Written down value b/f	88,000
Additions qualifying for AIA	27,000
AIA within £100,000 annual limit	(27,000)
	88,000
Writing down allowance @ 20%	(17,600)
Balance	70,400
Written down value c/f on general pool	70,400

Total allowances (27,000 + 17,600) = £44,600

Corporation tax computation CTAP 31.3.2012

	£
Trading profits	1,865,550
Less capital allowances	(44,600)
Net Trading profits	1,820,950
Income from land and buildings	173,200
Taxable Trading Profit	1,994,150
Corporation tax payable £1,994,150 @ 26% FY 2011	498,537

Example

Minty plc starts in business on 1 May 2011 making up accounts to 31 December 2011.

Additions to plant and machinery:		£
1 May 2011	BMW car CO_2 140 g/km	25,000
5 May 2011	Air cooling system	120,000
6 May 2011	Water saving plant	12,000
8 May 2011	Toyota car CO_2 105 g/km	15,000
9 May 2011	Photocopier	7,000
10 October 2011	VW car CO_2 190 g/km	16,000

Required: Calculate capital allowances for the accounting period 1 May to 31 December 2011.

Solution

		Workings	General pool	Special rate pool	Allowances
		£	£	£	£
Additions for 100% ECA					
Water saving plant		12,000			
Toyota car	Low emissions	15,000			
		27,000			
ECA 100%		(27,000)	0		27,000
Additions for AIA					
Air cooling system		120,000			
Max £100k x 8/12		(66,667)		53,333	66,667
Photocopier			7,000		
Additions not for ECA or AIA					
BMW car	<160g/km		25,000		
VW car	>160g/km			16,000	
			32,000	69,333	
WDA @ 20%	6,400 x 8/12		(4,267)		
WDA @ 10%	6,933 x 8/12			(4,622)	
					£93,667
WDV	31/12/2011		27,333	64,711	

Example

Minty plc has the following disposals of plant and machinery for the year to 31 December 2012:

1 August 2012	VW car (cost £16,000)	£12,000
10 October 2012	Photocopier (cost £7,000)	£ 9,000

Required: Calculate capital allowances for the year to 31 December 2012.

Solution

			General pool	Special rate pool	Allowances
			£	£	£
WDV	01/01/2012		27,333	64,711	
Disposals					
VW car	proceeds			(12,000)	
Photocopier	proceeds	9,000			
	max cost		(7,000)		
			20,333	52,711	
WDA @20%			(4,067)		4,067
WDA @10%				(5,271)	5,271
					£9,338
WDV	31/12/2012		16,266	47,440	

Student self-testing question

1 Cinders Ltd has a general pool balance brought forward of expenditure of £200,000 at 1 May 2010, and makes up its accounts to 30 April each year.

On 5 June 2010 the company buys a laser cutter costing £170,000 and elects for it to be treated as a short life asset.

On 30 September 2012 the laser cutter is sold for £24,000.

Required: Calculate capital allowances for the years to 30 April 2011, 2012, and 2013

Solution

y/e 30/04/11			General pool	Short life asset	Allowances
			£	£	£
WDV b/f			200,000		
Addition	Cutter	170,000			
AIA		(100,000)		70,000	100,000
WDA 20%			(40,000)		
WDA 20%				(14,000)	54,000
					154,000
WDV	30/04/11		160,000	56,000	
y/e 30/04/12					
WDA 20%			(32,000)	(11,200)	43,200
WDV	30/04/12		128,000	44,800	
y/e 30/04/13					
Disposal				(24,000)	
Balancing Allowance				(20,800)	20,800
WDA 20%			(25,600)		25,600
					46,400
WDV	30/04/13		102,400	0	

Question without answer

1. Wineglass Ltd purchased the following assets in respect of the six-month period ended 31 March 2012:

	£
1 October 2011 Office equipment	3,400
5 October 2011 Machinery	62,200
11 October 2011 Installation of cold water system	64,700
18 February 2012 Motor car	10,600
with CO_2 emissions 140g/km	

The motor car purchased on 18 February 2012 is used by the sales manager, and 15% of the mileage is for private journeys.

The cold water system is a "feature integral to a building".

There was no pooled expenditure brought forward at 1 April 2011.

Required: Calculate capital allowances available to Wineglass Ltd for the period to 31 March 2012.

21 Company Gift Aid /quarterly returns

Introduction

1. This chapter is concerned with the quarterly return system under which companies may have to collect and account for income tax on behalf of other taxpayers.

It also covers relief for qualifying charitable donations of companies, formerly known as relief for non-trade charges on income, and still alternatively called Company Gift Aid.

2. Qualifying charitable donations are allowed as a deduction in computing the profits chargeable to corporation tax for an accounting period. In equation form:

Taxable total profit	=	Profits – Trading losses etc.
		– Qualifying charitable donations
		– Group relief

Qualifying charitable donations are therefore deducted from total profits after trading losses etc. and before group relief.

Gift aid payments

3. Payments made by a company to a charity are covered by the Gift Aid Scheme. Under these rules:

i) The company does not deduct income tax at the basic rate when making the payment.

ii) The payment does not enter the quarterly CT61 scheme.

iii) The payment is treated as a qualifying charitable donation.

iv) The charity recipient cannot recover any income tax in respect of the amount it receives as this is the full amount of the donation.

v) There is no limit on the amount of charitable donations that could be made in this way by a company but if it pays more than its net total profits (After deductions and reliefs), the CT relief may be lost. Relief for charitable donations cannot be carried forward or back to another accounting period. However it can be surrendered as part of group relief (see chapter 24). It is also likely under company law that a company would require the consent of its shareholders to any significant charitable donations.

Qualifying donations – additional relief

4. Companies (other than close companies) can also treat as qualifying charitable donations gifts to a charity up to a maximum of $2^1/_2\%$ of dividends paid on ordinary share capital, during the company's accounting period.

The above relief is in addition to any gifts made by way of Gift Aid payments.

Eligible deductions

5. To be eligible for deduction from profits the qualifying charitable donations must comply with the following conditions.

a) They must be actually paid in the accounting period, and not accrued - except for a covenanted donation by a charity trading company to a charity which is its parent.

b) The payments must be ultimately borne by the company making the payment.

c) They must be paid out of the company's profits brought into charge to corporation tax.

Adjustment to accounts

6. As the normal company accounts do not distinguish between qualifying charitable donations and other charitable expenses it is necessary to 'add back' qualifying charitable donations, because only qualifying charitable donations actually paid in the accounting period are allowed, whereas for accounts purposes an element of accrual might have been made. If the payments relate to an earlier accounting period, they are nevertheless allowed as a qualifying charitable donation in the accounting period when the payments are made.

Collection of income tax on payments which are not distributions

7. The principles of the system for the collection of income tax that must be withheld by a company when it makes certain payments, and must later be accounted for to HMRC, are as follows.

Return periods

a) A company must make returns to HMRC in respect of each of its accounting periods of any payments made to others (not accruals) subject to the deduction of income tax at source, and of any income received (not accrued) which has been taxed at source.

b) The returns must be made for a quarter and the dates prescribed are 31st March, 30th June, 30th September, and 31st December. These are known as standard return periods, and if a company's accounting period does not coincide with any of the quarterly dates, then an additional return is required at its year-end.

Income tax is deductible from the following payments made by companies:

Yearly interest (paid to an individual)

Property Rents paid directly to non-UK resident landlords (including a non UK resident company): however, this requirement is lifted if the rent is paid via a UK agent

Interest paid on deposit or savings accounts held by individuals with banks/ buildings societies

Payment to an individual of the income element of an annuity

Patent royalties paid to individuals

Note: Payments of interest, royalties, annual payments and annuities to companies by other companies are made gross without any tax deduction so long as the recipient company is within charge to corporation tax.

Example

S Ltd has an accounting year ending on the 30th November 2011. The return periods relating to that accounting period are as follows:

2010	1st December to 31st December
2011	1st January to 31st March
	1st April to 30th June
	1st July to 30th September
	1st October to 30th November

The company here has five return periods and each return must be submitted within fourteen days of the end of the return period. If there are no transactions in the period a nil return is not required.

c) The return forms must show particulars of payments made in the period, and income tax deducted is due on the return date without the making of any formal assessment. Particulars of any income must also be included on the returns, and any income tax suffered at source is offset, on the company quarterly returns, against any income tax the company has retained, under legal obligation, from payments of the types listed at 7(b).

The position at the end of a return period

8. a) If the income tax suffered in a return period exceeds the income tax retained from payments made then no income tax need be paid over for the quarter. The net excess of income tax suffered at source on income may be carried back and set against any income tax accounted for and paid on earlier quarterly returns in the same accounting period. This generates a repayment which cannot exceed the amount of income tax already accounted for and paid over relating to net-of-tax payments made in the accounting period.

b) If (as is generally the case) cumulative income tax suffered by the company on taxed income does not exceed its income tax retained on payments made, then the net amount of income tax withheld on payments, less any suffered on income, is payable to HMRC on the due date.

c) Once all quarterly returns required have been submitted, and if income tax retained by company on payments to others has all been offset within he same AP against income tax suffered at source by the company itself, then any net income tax which the company has suffered on income received may be treated as CT already paid. Therefore, net income tax suffered is set off on the submitted CT return against the company's final CT liability for the accounting period (see last part of specimen computation at end of chapter 18).

Example

F Ltd has an accounting period ended 31st March 2012 and during the year the following transactions took place.

2011	April 11th	Debenture interest paid to individuals	8,000
	June 30th	Interest received (net)	4,000
	August 7th	Bank interest paid	12,000
	October 11th	Debenture interest paid to individuals	8,000
2012	January 1st	Interest received (net)	4,000

All transactions are shown net as entered in the company's bank account.

Show the quarterly returns for the year to 31st March 2012.

Solution

Quarter	Gross paid	Income tax retained (20%)	Gross received	Income tax suffered (20%)	Net income tax paid or repaid
	£	£	£	£	£
30.6.11	(10,000)	2,000	5,000	(1,000)	1,000
30.9.11	–	–	–	–	–
31.12.11	(10,000)	2,000	–	–	2,000
31.3.12	–	–	5,000	(1,000)	(1,000)
Total	(20,000)	4,000	10,000	(2,000)	2,000

Notes

i) In the fourth quarter, the excess of income tax suffered can be set against the payment made in quarter 1 or 3. This generates a repayment of £1,000 of income tax (previously accounted for and paid over) to the company for the 4th quarterly period.

ii) Interest paid by companies on bank borrowings is not subject to deduction of income tax and is, therefore, excluded from the quarterly return system.

iii) The 'total' line shows the company's cumulative position for the whole AP.

The position at the end of an accounting period

9. This may be summarised as follows.

a) Income tax suffered on income received net > income tax paid on outgoing net payments.

i) Excess can be set against corporation tax payable on the profits of the accounting period.

ii) If the excess is greater than the corporation tax payable then a cash repayment can be obtained.

b) Income tax deducted from income received net < income tax paid on outgoing net payments.

i) In this case since the excess has already been paid over within the quarterly return system, no further adjustment is necessary.

ii) Note that as stated in chapter 18, a UK trading company is not liable to Income tax (IT) on its own income, as it pays Corporation Tax.

Any BRIT paid over by companies on the quarterly returns is income tax paid out of the gross payment, on behalf of either individuals or non-resident companies.

That a company may deduct, from the basic rate income tax due on net payments it has made, any basic rate tax suffered at source on its own income in the same AP, is a cash flow convenience.

An individual, or a non-resident investment company, that receives interest, royalties or rents net from a UK company should also receive a tax certificate from the company showing the amount of tax withheld by law at 20%. This tax suffered is then creditable against the recipient's own income tax liability, whether the certifying company actually paid the tax to HMRC or simply offset it against the tax suffered at source on its own income.

Example

B Ltd has an accounting period ended 31st March 2012 and during that year, the following transactions took place.

2011	June 10	Interest on unsecured loan stock paid – individuals (net)	1,600
	July 19	Interest received (net)	2,000
	Aug 31	Building society interest received (gross)	2,500
	Dec 10	Interest on unsecured loan stock paid – individuals (net)	1,600
2012	Jan 19	Interest received (net)	2,000

The adjusted trading profits for the year ended 31st March 2012 amounted to £1,795,300 before any adjustment for loan interest paid. The unsecured loan interest is used for trade purposes. Property income in respect of the same period was £1,200.

Show the quarterly returns for the year to 31st March 2012 and the corporation tax computation for the same period.

Solution

Quarter	Gross paid	Income tax retained (20%)	Gross received	Income tax suffered (20%)	Net tax paid or repaid	Net tax suffered at source, c/fwd
	£	£	£	£	£	£
30.6.11	(2,000)	400	–	–	400	–
30.9.11	–	–	2,500	(500)	(400)	(100)
31.12.11	(2,000)	400	–	–	300	–
31.3.12	–	–	2,500	(500)	(300)	(200)
Total	(4,000)	800	5,000	(1,000)	–	–

Corporation tax computation AP to 31.3.2012

Trading profits (1,795,300 – 4,000)	1,791,300
Property income	1,200
Income taxed at source	5,000
Building society interest	2,500
Taxable trading profit	1,800,000
Corporation tax @ 26%	468,000
Less excess income tax as above	(200)
	467,800

Notes

i. The repayment of £400 for quarter 2 is limited to the amount of IT already paid for quarter 1. The £100 balance (500-400) of unrelieved tax suffered on net income in q2 is carried forward to q3. In quarter 3, this £100 is offset against the £400 of IT retained on net payments made, meaning that only £300 of tax has to be paid over with the 3rd quarterly return.

ii) The £300 paid over for quarter 3 is then all refunded in quarter 4, following receipt of net-of-tax interest on which £500 of IT has been withheld. After the £300 repayment claimed for the fourth quarter, a net £200 of income tax suffered on income over the 4 quarters remains unrelieved. This net £200 is relieved by offset against the CT liability.

iii. As there was an excess of taxed income suffered, the income tax unrecovered is set against the corporation tax payable. From a cash flow point of view, the benefit will not be felt until the corporation tax becomes payable.

Student self-testing question

K Ltd has the following data relating to its accounting period ended 31st March 2012.

	£
Trading profits	1,548,000
Building society interest receivable and received (gross)	2,000
Private loan interest receivable (received but net of 20% tax)	10,000
Gift aid payment made	40,000
Debenture interest payable and paid (gross), to investors who are not individuals, on a trade loan	20,000

Compute the corporation tax payable for the AP to 31st March 2012.

Solution

Corporation tax computation AP to 31.3.2012

	£
Trading profits (1,548,000 – 20,000 trade interest payable)	1,528,000
Surplus on non trade loan relationships:	
Interest receivable (10,000 + 2,000)	12,000
Total profits	1,540,000
Qualifying charitable donation	
Gift aid payment	(40,000)
Taxable total profit	1,500,000
Corporation tax liability	
1,500,000 @ 26%	390,000
Less relief for income tax suffered on loan interest received	(2,000)
Corporation tax payable	388,000

Notes

i) A Gift Aid payment by a company is made gross to the charity, not under tax deduction.

ii) There were no payments made in the year from which K Ltd did have to deduct income tax and therefore the tax suffered on the loan interest received has not been reclaimed through the quarterly return system by the end of the accounting period. .

iii) It is likely that K Ltd's private loan debtor withheld basic rate tax from interest if it was unsure about K Ltd's UK corporation tax status. The normal pattern for companies such as K Ltd is to receive bank interest gross, and other interest may be paid to companies gross as long as the payer has proof that the recipient company is within the charge to UK CT.

22 Relief for losses

Introduction

1. This chapter examines the various forms of loss relief available to a company which is not a member of a group of companies. The main emphasis is given to loss reliefs available in respect of trading losses. Non-trading loan relationship deficits are covered. Relief available in connection with property business losses and chargeable gains is also covered.

A company can claim to set a trading loss against other income in several ways. In summary form they may be depicted as follow:

Set against profits (income and gains) of the same period. Sec 37

Carried back and set against profits (income and gains) of the previous year*. Sec 37

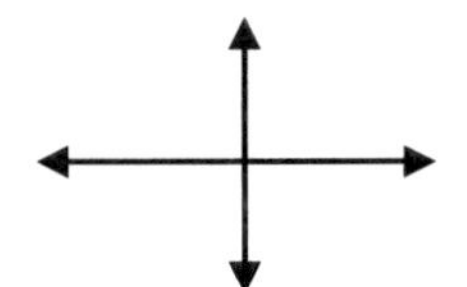

Carried forward and set against future trading income from the same source. Sec 45

Surrendered as group relief. Sec 130 (current year)

*Note: For APs ending between 24th November 2008 to 23rd November 2010, companies could carry back trading losses up to three years with a maximum of £50,000 in the earliest two years, in total. The temporary extended loss claim is not covered further here as it has ceased.

List of loss reliefs

2. i) Trade losses – set against taxable total profit of the same accounting period. Sec 37.

ii) Trade losses – set against taxable total profit of the previous year. Sec 37. (Also see Note above)

iii) Trade losses – carried forward and set against future trade income. Sec 45.

iv) Trade losses – terminal loss relief. Sec 39.

v) Trade losses – surrendered to a 75% subsidiary (and consortium company) by way of group relief. See Chapter 24.

vi) Trade losses – transfer to successor company along with trade.

vii) Non-trading loan relationship deficit – set against total profits.

viii) Pre-trading expenditure – treated as expenditure on 1st day of trading.

Trade losses

3. It is perhaps worth recalling that a trading loss is arrived at after deducting capital allowances which sometimes differ from accounting depreciation expensed. Either large capital allowances, or interest costs arising from a **trading** loan relationship may turn an 'operating profit' in the financial accounts (stated before borrowing costs) into a trading 'loss' for tax purposes.

Trade losses Section 37

a) Under this section a company which has incurred a loss in its trade (excluding any loss brought forward) in any accounting period, may claim to set off that loss against total profits (i.e. including chargeable gains) of the same accounting period.

b) Any balance of loss remaining after this set off in the current period can be set off against total profits of APs falling within the previous twelve months.

c) A total profits claim for the current year must be made before claiming total profits relief for any preceding year.

d) A claim under this section must be made within two years of the end of the accounting period in which the loss is incurred, or within such longer period as HMRC may allow.

e) Relief for the loss under Section 37 appears in the computation before Gift Aid donations and group relief are deducted.

f) Even if the accounting period of the loss is less than 12 months' duration, the loss can nevertheless be carried back 12 months, so long as a current period claim is made first.

Example

Q Ltd has the following corporation tax profit/loss for its accounting years ended 31st March 2011 and 2012 and makes both the available claims for loss relief under Section 37.

Show the computations.

Q Ltd

	31.3.11	**31.3.12**
	£	**£**
Trading profit/(loss)	–	(30,000)
Income from property	10,000	11,000
Chargeable gains	9,000	2,100
Non-trading loan relationship deficit	–	(2,000)

Solution

Claim for relief under Section 37

	£	£
Trading profit	80,000	
Income from property	10,000	11,000
Chargeable gains	9,000	2,100
Non-trading loan relationship deficit	-	(2,000)
Total profits	99,000	11,100
Less Section 37 loss claim	(18,900)	(11,100)
Assessment	80,100	-

Loss memorandum	£
The trading loss of £30,000 has been utilised as follows:	
Set against total profits for the year to 31.3.2012	11,100
Set against total profits for the year to 31.3.2011	18,900
	30,000

Notes

i) After making a claim under Section 37 for the year to 31st March 2012 it is not obligatory also to make the second claim to carry the losses back to the previous AP to March 2011.

ii) However, the carry-back relief, if claimed, is only available after a current period loss claim has been made.

iii) It is not possible to claim a partial relief for the year to 31st March 2012 and also claim relief for the period to 31st March 2011.

iv) The non-trading loan relationship deficit is deducted before the loss relief – see 8 below.

Trade losses carried forward against future trade profits, Section 45 CA 2010

4. Where a company incurs a trading loss in any accounting period, then if no other claim for relief is made by the taxpayer (e.g. under Section 37), the loss will be dealt with as follows:

a) It will be carried forward to succeeding accounting periods so long as the company continues to trade.

b) A loss carried forward is only deductible from future trading income, not from total profits.

c) The trading income/profit of a succeeding period is automatically treated as being reduced by trading losses brought forward.

d) A claim under this section must technically be made within four years (or before FY 2010, six years) of the end of the accounting period in which the loss was incurred. In practice section 45 relief is given automatically by the self assessment system to the extent optional loss relief claims are not made which would take priority (including a group relief loss surrender – see chapter 24).

e) Anti-avoidance legislation provides that there may be a disallowance of trading losses carried forward if there is a change of ultimate ownership of the company and also a major change in the nature or conduct of the trade within three years either side of the change of ownership .

Example

D Ltd has the following results for the two years ended 30th June 2012.

	30.6.11	**30.6.12**
	£	**£**
Trade profits/(loss)	(120,000)	70,000
Interest income	30,000	40,000
Chargeable gain	60,000	10,000

The company makes a claim under Sections 37 and 45 CTA 2010.

Compute the taxable total profit after loss reliefs.

Solution

	30.6.11	**30.6.12**
	£	**£**
Trade profits	–	70,000
Less Section 45 (second claim, in order of priority)	–	(30,000)
	–	40,000
Interest income	30,000	40,000
Chargeable gain	60,000	10,000
Total profits	90,000	90,000
Less Section 37 (first claim, in order of priority)	(90,000)	
Taxable total profit	–	90,000

Notes

i) The trading loss of £120,000 incurred in the accounting period to 30th June 2011 has been utilised as indicated below.

		£
Accounting period to 30.6.11	Section 37	90,000
" " " 30.6.12	Section 45	30,000
		120,000

ii) The trading loss carried forward to 30.6.12 is deducted from trading profits and not total profits.

Terminal loss relief Section 39 CTA 2010

5. Trading losses arising in the twelve months prior to the cessation of trading can be carried back against total profits of the previous thirty six months on a LIFO basis.

A claim for relief must be made within two years of the end of the accounting period in which the loss is made or within such later period as HMRC may allow.

Note that:

(a) there is no limit on the amount of losses that can be carried back under section 39 as long as they relate to the last twelve months of trading. ;

(b) the company must have ceased trading before this claim can be made;

(c) the loss available for carry-back is computed for exactly twelve months , which may involve more than one accounting period and apportioning the loss of the earlier one.

Example

Z Ltd has the following data for the four years ended 31st March 2012 when it ceased trading.

	31.3.09	**31.3.10**	**31.3.11**	**31.3.12**
	£	£	£	£
Trading profits	55,000	30,000	65,000	(180,000)
Income from property	7,000	8,000	9,000	9,000
Capital gains				1,000

The company makes a claim for loss relief under sections 37 (current period) and 39.

Show the final taxable profits.

Solution: Z Ltd APs ended 31st March

	2009	**2010**	**2011**	**2012**
	£	£	£	£
Trading profits	55,000	30,000	65,000	loss
Income from property	7,000	8,000	9,000	9,000
Capital gains	–	–	–	1,000
Total profits	62,000	38,000	74,000	10,000
Less section 37 claim				(10,000)
Section 39 claim (LIFO)	(58,000)	(38,000)	(74,000)	-
Taxable profits	4,000	–	–	-

Note

Loss Memorandum:	**£**	**£**
Trade loss to 31.3.2012		180,000
Section 37 31.3.12	10,000	
Section 39 31.3.11	74,000	
Section 39 31.3.10	38,000	
Section 39 31.3.09	58,000	180,000

Transfer of losses

6. When a company ceases trading and another company takes over the same trade, unrelieved trade losses can be carried forward to the successor company providing that certain conditions are met, which are:

a) On or at any time within two years after the succession and within one year prior thereto, at least 75% of the interest in the trade is held by the same persons. This means that three quarters of the ordinary share capital in both companies must be held by the same persons throughout the three-year period. Throughout the same period the same trade must be carried on by a company in charge to corporation tax.

b) It follows from this provision that the transfer of a trade from an individual to a company precludes the transfer of trading losses between the entities. However, in that case under Section 86 ITTOIA 2005 some relief for an individual is available whereby part of a business loss may be set against income which he or she receives from the company. See Chapter 14.

Where there is a transfer of trade then the following applies.

a) The trade is not treated as if it had been discontinued and a new one started.

b) Loss relief under Section 39 is not available to the company ceasing to trade. If the second company ceases to trade within four years of the succession, then loss relief can be carried back, where appropriate, to the first company.

c) Relief under Section 45 for the carry forward of losses is available, subject to any claim by the company ceasing to trade, under Section 37 i.e. set off against total profits .

   Where a trade or part thereof is transferred between two companies, then relief to the successor for losses brought forward is restricted where the amount of the 'relevant liability' immediately before the transfer exceeds the open market value of the 'relevant assets' at that time.

d) No capital allowances balancing adjustments are raised on the transfer.

e) Unused capital allowances can also be carried forward.

f) Losses cannot be carried forward where at any time before the change in ownership the scale of activity becomes small or negligible and the change takes place before any considerable revival has occurred.

g) Other losses or capital losses cannot be transferred.

Non-trading loan relationship / foreign exchange deficit

7. Interest incurred and receivable plus any other debits and credits relating to non-trade borrowing and lending must be pooled to produce either a non-trading credit or deficit for the period. This also includes any non-trading foreign exchange debt differences.

A net non-trading credit is included as interest income.

A net non-trading deficit is relieved by one or more of the following methods:

i) By offset against the company's taxable profits (in whole or part) for the same period. A current year non-trading deficit is deducted against taxable profits before: any current year trading loss offset under Section 37; charges on income; and a non-trading deficit carried back from a subsequent period.

ii) Against the taxable profits of fellow group members under the group relief provisions.

iii) By carry-back (in whole or part) against the company's interest income loan relationships profits falling within the previous 12 months.

iv) By carry-forward for offset against the company's non-trading profits for the next accounting period. (For this purpose, non-trading profits represent the company's total profits except those constituting trading income.)

The above reliefs must be claimed within two years of the end of the relevant accounting period or such further period as HMRC may allow. Any surplus non-trading deficit remaining after the above claims is automatically carried forward as a non-trading debit for the next accounting period.

Example

Q Ltd has the following data relating to the year ended 31st December 2011.

	£
Adjusted trading profit	93,000
Income from property	5,000
Non-trade interest cost incurred	65,000
Non-trade interest received	15,000

Compute the taxable total profits for the AP to 31st December 2011.

Solution: Q Ltd corporation tax computation AP 31.12.11

	£
Trading profits	93,000
Income from property	5,000
	98,000
Non-trading deficit	50,000
TTP	48,000

Notes

i) The non-trade LR deficit comprises:

non-trade interest paid	65,000
less non-trade interest received	15,000
	50,000

ii) The excess non-trade LR deficit is deducted from total profits and taken off before group relief. (Refer to specimen CT computation at end of chapter 18)

Pre-trading expenditure

8. Relief is available for expenditure by a company in the seven years before it commences to carry on a trade.

a) The expenditure must be allowable trading expenditure which would have been deducted in computing trading income if incurred after commencement of trading.

b) Such expenditure is treated as a trading expenditure on the first day on which the trade commences.

c) The relief does not apply to pre-trading purchases of inventory (trading stock).

Chargeable gains

9. The amount of any chargeable gain arising in an accounting period is reduced by any allowable capital losses of the same accounting period and then by those brought forward from a previous period. A company can never carry any capital losses back to an earlier accounting period.

Example

R Ltd has the following data relating to its AP to 31st March 2012.

	£
Capital losses brought forward 1.4.11	3,000
AP to 31.3.2012	
Trading profits	41,000
Chargeable gains	22,000

Compute the corporation tax payable.

Solution: R Ltd AP to 31st March 2012

	£	£
Trading profits		41,000
Chargeable gains	22,000	
Less capital losses b/f	(3,000)	19,000
Total profits/ Taxable total profit		60,000
Corporation tax payable: 60,000 @ 20%		12,000

Other Non-trading losses – relief

10. Non-trading loan relationship deficit

See section 7 above

Loss on property business

Relief can be taken for losses against current year total profits. See Chapter 19.

Capital losses

May be set against chargeable gains of same AP, or carried forward. They cannot be set against total profits.

Management expenses

Relief for expenses of management may be claimed where a company has a recognised business activity of managing investments. Excess management expenses may be set against total profits.

Student self-testing questions

1. Trailer Limited has the following results for the two years to 31 August 2011

	y/e 31.8.10	y/e 31.8.11
	£	£
Trading profit/(loss)	(21,000)	17,000
Interest income - non trade relationship	6,000	9,000
Capital loss	(2,000)	
Chargeable gains		7,000

Requirement: Calculate TTP for the 2 periods, assuming that the loss is relieved under S45 and showing any losses carried forward at 1 September 2011.

Suggested solution

	31/8/10	31/8/11
	£	£
Trading profit	-	17,000
Less : S45 relief		(17,000)
		NIL
Interest income	6,000	9,000
Chargeable gains (£7,000 - £2,000)		5,000
	6,000	14,000
TTP	6,000	14,000

Loss memorandum

	£
Loss for year ended 31/8/10	21,000
Relieved year ended 31/8/11 (S45)	(17,000)
Available for carry forward under S45	4,000

2. Caravan Limited has the following results for the accounting years ended 31 March 2011 and 31 March 2012.

	Year to 31/3/11	Year to 31/3/12
	£	£
Trading profit/(loss)	39,000	(49,700)
Income from property	2,000	1,500
Qualifying charitable donations (gross)	500	500

Requirement: Calculate TTP for both periods, assuming that relief under S37 is claimed for the loss in the period ended 31 March 2012. Show any losses available to carry forward at 1 April 2012.

Suggested solution

Caravan Limited: TTP computation for 2 years ending 31 March 2012

	Year ended 31/3/11	Year ended 31/3/12
	£	£
Trading profit	39,000	-
Income from property	2,000	1,500
TP	41,000	1,500
S37 relief	(41,000)	(1,500)
TTP	-	-
Unrelieved Gift Aid payments	500	500

Loss memorandum	£
Loss for the year ended 31/3/12	49,700
Less S37 year ended 31/3/12	(1,500)
S37 year ended 31/3/11	(41,000)
Loss to carry forward	7,200

3. Buttercup Limited made up accounts to 30 September and ceased to trade on 31 March 2012. Results have been as follows:

	30/9/09	30/9/10	30/9/11	Period ended 31/3/12
Trading profit/(loss)	5,200	4,700	3,200	(30,500)
Income from property	2,000	1,800	1,900	500
Interest income - non trading	750	900	840	400
Chargeable gains	3,000	-	2,000	-

Qualifying charitable donations:				
-Gift Aid payment	300	300	300	300

Requirement: Show the TTP for all years, assuming the loss is relieved under S39 terminal loss relief.

Suggested solution

	30/9/09	30/9/10	30/9/11	31/3/12
	£	£	£	£
Trading profit	5,200	4,700	3,200	-
Income from property	2,000	1,800	1,900	500
Interest income	750	900	840	400
Chargeable gains	3,000	-	2,000	-
Loss relief in aggregation (see W)			(1,600)	
Less S39 loss offset (see W)	(10,950)	(7,400)	(6,340)	(900)
TP	0	0	0	0
Gift Aid	-	-	-	-
TTP	Nil	Nil	Nil	Nil
Unrelieved Gift Aid Payment	300	300	300	300

Terminal loss memorandum :	£
Trade Loss of final 6 months 31/3/12	(30,500)
Less trade profits of prior 6 months (3,200 x 6/12)	1,600
= terminal trade loss of final 12 months	(28,900)
Set against other profits, LIFO:	
6 months to 31/3/12	900
6 months to 31/3/11 (balance of 7,940)	6,340
y/e 30/9/10	7,400
y/e 30/9/09	10,950
Loss remaining unrelieved	(3,310)

Questions without answers

1. Uncut Undergrowth Limited (UUL) is a United Kingdom resident company which has been manufacturing garden machinery since 1999. It has no associated companies. The company results are summarised as follows:

	Year Ended 30/6/11	6 months to 31/12/11	Year Ended 31/12/12	Year Ended 31/12/13 (forecast)
	£	£	£	£
Trading Profit/(Loss)	25,000	(51,000)	(362,500)	87,000
Non-trade loan interest received (gross amount)	-	15,000	22,000	-
Bank interest received -non trade relationship	-	-	-	10,000
Income from property	25,000	-	-	-
Chargeable gains	-	-	30,000	-
Gift Aid payment to charity	1,000	1,000	1,000	1,000

On 1 July 2010 there were no trading losses brought forward but £40,000 of capital losses were available.

Requirements

(a) Calculate the corporation tax liabilities for all years in the question after giving maximum relief at the earliest time for the trading losses sustained and any other reliefs. (11 marks)

(b) Show any balances carried forward. (5 marks)

NB: All apportionments may be made to the nearest month.

Note Use FY 2011 tax rates for all years. (ACCA December 1997 amended)

4. Loser Ltd's results for the year ended 30 June 2011, the nine month period ended 31 March 2012, the year ended 31 March 2013 and the year ended 31 March 2014 are as follows:

	Year ended 30 June 2011	Period ended 31 Mar 2012	Year ended 31 Mar 2013	Year ended 31 Mar 2014
	£	£	£	£
Trading profit/(loss)	90,200	(33,000)	34,600	(85,500)
Income from property	(3,600)	4,500	8,100	5,600
Gift Aid payments (gross)	(1,400)	(800)	(1,200)	(1,100)

Required:

(a) **State the factors that will influence a company's choice of loss relief claims. You are not expected to consider group relief.**
(3 marks)

(b) **Assuming that Loser Ltd claims relief for its losses as early as possible, calculate the company's Taxable Total Profits for:**

the year ended 30 June 2011,

the nine month period ended 31 March 2012,

the year ended 31 March 2013 and

the year ended 31 March 2014.

Your answer should show any amount of unrelieved losses as at 31 March 2014. **(10 marks)**

(c) **Explain how your answer to (b) would have differed if Loser Ltd had ceased trading on 31 March 2014.** **(2 marks)**

(15 marks)

(ACCA December 2002 updated)

Student note: Some of these questions contain brief elements of tax on the capital gains of companies, and this topic is covered in Chapters 26-33.

23 Corporation tax rates and the small (profits) company

Introduction

1. This chapter is concerned with the taxation of "small profits companies", known until 1 April 2010 simply as "small companies" for corporation tax rate purposes. The new name was introduced by the Corporation Tax Act 2010 to reflect the fact that a company with "small" profits, as defined, in a particular year may in all other respects be quite a "large" company.

This chapter begins with a reminder of the small profits rates and the meaning of profits for "small profits rate" purposes.

The profits in this sense are the augmented profits as defined by CTA2010, that is to say the taxable total profit plus FII but not group FII.

The UK government has made many changes in the rates of corporation tax for "small (profits) companies" over recent years. Before FY2006 there were special rules for companies with profits under £50,000. There was a 0% starting rate, marginal relief for very small profits from £10,000 to £50,000, and a "non-corporate distribution rate" to tax profits more highly where dividends were paid to individuals than where they were left in the company.

All of these special rules for profits under £50,000 were abolished for FY 2006 onwards. The Labour Government then announced an intention to raise the small companies rate in stages to 22% but the final stage of this staged increase was never implemented due to the 2008 recession.

The small profits rate of CT will be 20% from FY 2011. This is the same as the basic rate of income tax.

This chapter will show the effect of the change in the small profits CT rate during an accounting period.

Basic rates

2. Rates	**Financial years**	
	2010 to 31.3.2011	**2011 to 31.3.2012**
Small company augmented profits level	0-300,000	0-300,000
Small profits rate	21%	20%
Marginal relief band	300,001–1,500,000	300,001–1,500,000

Augmented Profits between £0 and £300,000 are taxed at the small profits rate of 20%. Profits in between £300,000 and £1,500,000 are taxed at the main rate of corporation tax, subject to marginal relief (see section 4). These profits limits are subject to adjustments for associated companies, examined in the next chapter.

Definition of profits

3. The definition of profits for the small profits rate is the sum of:

a) taxable total profit, i.e. total profits less allowable deductions and group relief, **plus**

b) franked investment income, excluding FII from group companies.

Example

Beta Ltd has the following data relating to the year ended 31st March 2012.

Trading profits	£3,500
Chargeable gains	£4,700

Calculate the corporation tax payable for the AP to 31st March 2012.

Solution: Corporation tax computation AP to 31.3.2012

	£
Trading profits	3,500
Chargeable gain	4,700
Total profits/Taxable total profit/Augmented Profits	8,200
Corporation tax payable £8,200 @ 20%:	1,640

Example

AP Ltd has the following income and charges relating to the year ended 31st March 2012.

	£
Trading profits	127,000
Chargeable gain	3,500
Gift Aid donations	1,500
Dividends received	14,400

Calculate the corporation tax payable for the AP to 31st March 2012.

Solution: Corporation tax computation AP to 31.3.12

	£
Trading profits	127,000
Chargeable gain	3,500
Total profits	130,500
Less qualifying charitable donations	1,500
Taxable total profit	129,000
Add franked investment income 14,400 + (10/90 × 14,400)	16,000
Augmented profits	145,000
Corporation tax payable:	
£129,000 @ 20%	25,800

Marginal relief – small profits rate

4. Where the augmented profits exceed the lower relevant amount of £300,000, but fall below the upper relevant amount of £1,500,000, then the position is as follows:

a) First tax is computed on TTP at the full rate of 26%.

b) Then Marginal relief is deducted (a relief in terms of tax) using the formula:

$$(U - A) \times {}^{N}/_{A} \times \text{the fraction}$$

U = Upper relevant amount i.e. £1,500,000. FY11 to 31.3.12.

A = Augmented profits = taxable total profits + non-group FII

N = Taxable total profits i.e. all profits chargeable to corporation tax.

c) The fraction is determined with respect to financial years, and the recent years to 31.3.2009 are as follows:

Financial years	Marginal relief fraction
FY2007 to 31.3.2008	1/40
FY2008 to 31.3.2009	7/400
FY2009 to 31.3.2010	7/400
FY2010 to 31.3.2011	7/400
FY2011 to 31.3.2012	3/200

The fraction is set so as to achieve a smoothly increasing average rate of CT on profits between the defined lower and upper relevant amounts, with both those limits being reduced by any non-group FII.

d) Thus in respect of accounting periods for the financial year to the 31st March 2012 the formula is:

$$(1{,}500{,}000 - A) \times \frac{N}{A} \times \frac{3}{200}$$

Example – marginal relief

Z Ltd has the undermentioned data relating to its accounting year ended 31.3.2012.

	£
Trading profits	453,100
Chargeable gains	2,250
Gift Aid donations	5,350
Dividend received	1,800
Dividend paid	24,000

Compute the corporation tax liability.

Solution: Calculation of augmented profits:

	£	
Trading profits	453,100	
Chargeable gain	2,250	
	455,350	
Less qualifying charitable donations	(5,350)	
Taxable total profit	450,000	(N)
Add franked investment income	2,000	
Augmented profits	452,000	(A)

Computation of marginal relief:

$$(1{,}500{,}000 - 452{,}000) \times \frac{450{,}000}{452{,}000} \times 3/200$$ 15,650

Z Ltd Corporation tax computation AP 31.3.2012

	£
Trading profits	453,100
Chargeable gains	2,250
Total profits	455,350
Less qualifying charitable donations	(5,350)
Taxable total profit	450,000
Corporation tax @ 26% ×450,000	117,000
Less marginal relief (above)	(15,650)
Corporation tax payable	101,350

Notes

i) From this example it can be seen that the marginal relief is a calculated amount which is deducted from the tax on taxable profits computed at the full rate of 26%.

ii) As A > £300,000 and < £1,500,000, marginal relief should be claimed.

Marginal rates of corporation tax

5. The marginal rate of corporation tax refers to the rate of corporation tax borne on profits in between £300,000 and £1,500,000, and for the financial year to 31st March 2012 this is 27.5% (year to 31 March 2011 29.75%).

If the difference between the full and small profits rates reduces then the marginal rate between the defined profit limits goes down too (assuming the profits limits do not alter).

This can be demonstrated as follows:

	£ FY2010	£ FY2011
Tax on £1,500,000	at 28%420,000	at 26% 390,000
Less tax on (£300,000)	at 21% 63,000	at 20% (60,000)
Subtracting		
Difference		
= tax on £1,200,000	357,000	330,000
	29.75%	27.5%

Example for FY 2011

B Ltd has profits chargeable to corporation tax of £400,000 for the year ended 31st March 2012. Calculate the corporation tax payable and show the marginal rate of tax.

Solution

	£
Taxable total profits	400,000
Corporation tax @ 26%	104,000
Less marginal relief	
(1,500,000 – 400,000) × 3 / 200	16,500
	87,500

Corporation tax liability

Although the statutory formula must be used in submitted CT computations involving marginal relief, when carrying out projected income calculations, or for tax planning purposes, a CT liability at marginal rates on £400,000 of taxable profit can be viewed as equivalent to:

£	£
300,000 @ 20%	60,000
100,000 @ 27.5% (marginal rate)	27,500
400,000	87,500

The marginal rate of 27.5% on company profits in the marginal rate band compares with a marginal rate of income tax for 2011/12 of 40% (the higher rate) or 50% (the additional rate) for the proprietor of a successful unincorporated business (plus, usually, 2% Class 4 NIC).

Associated companies

6. A company is treated as an associate of another at a given time, if at that time, or at any time within one year previously, either one of the two has control over the other, or both are under the same control. Control is generally established with a shareholding of more than 50%. Control is also established if the parent company is entitled to acquire:

a) the greater part of the share capital or issued share capital, or voting power of the associate company.

b) such part of the issued share capital as would entitle the parent company to receive the greater part of the income of the associate company if it were distributed amongst the participators, ignoring the rights of loan creditors.

c) such rights as would on a winding up of the company, or in any other circumstance, entitle the parent company to the greater part of the assets of the company, available for distribution among the participators.

If a company has one or more associated companies in the accounting period, then the upper and lower relevant maximum and minimum amounts are divided equally between the company and the number of associates. Thus a company with two associates would have to allocate the relevant amounts threefold:

FY 2011, to 31.3.2012	**Lower level**	**Upper level**
	£	£
The company	100,000	500,000
First associate	100,000	500,000
Second associate	100,000	500,000
	300,000	1,500,000

In determining the number of associated companies the following points should be noted.

a) An associated company which has not been active at any time in the accounting period (i.e. a dormant company) is disregarded.

b) A company which is only an associate for part of an accounting period is counted.

c) All active companies are counted separately in the total, even if they were associated companies for different parts of the accounting period.

2. Overseas companies are included in determining the number of associates.

Example

D Ltd, a company resident in the United Kingdom, owns 80% of the equity share capital of S Ltd., 52% of the ordinary share capital of J Ltd. and 25% of the ordinary share capital of N Ltd. The company prepares accounts to the year ended 31 December and provides the following information in respect of its accounting period of twelve months ended 31 December 2011:

INCOME	£
Trading profits	260,000
Bank interest	140,000
Capital gains	50,000
Rental income	200,000

Requirement: Compute the corporation tax liability for the above accounting period.

Solution

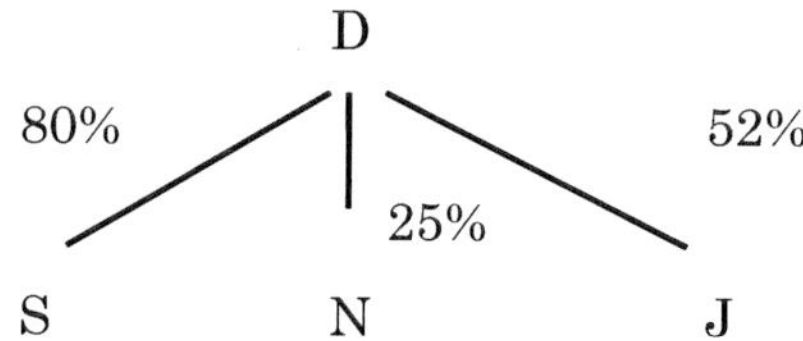

S & J are associates for the purposes of tax

Divide upper & lower limits by 3 :-

£300,000 / 3	Lower £100,000
£1,500,000 / 3	Upper £500,000

Calculation of TTP

Trading profits	260,000
Interest income	140,000
Income from property	200,000
Capital Gains	50,000
TTP	650,000

The company is taxed at full rate because 'profits' are £650,000 ('profits' = TTP as there are no dividends). The CT liability would need to be apportioned:

FY10	
1.1.2011 to 31.3.2011 3/12 x £650,000 x 28%	45,500
FY11	
1.4.2011 to 31.12.2011 9/12 x £650,000 x 26%	126,750
Total corporation tax liability	172,250

Accounting periods of less than 12 months

7. As already indicated, for corporation tax purposes a company's accounting period cannot exceed 12 months in duration. If the accounting period is less than 12 months in length then the relevant profits amounts are reduced accordingly.

Thus with an accounting period of three months' duration ending in the financial year to 31.3.2012 the lower profit level would be £300,000/4 i.e. £75,000, and the upper profit level would be 1,500,000/4 i.e. £375,000.

If the situation arises where a company has an accounting period of less than 12 months' length, and has an associated company, then the respective profit levels are first divided by the number of companies and then reduced in proportion to the length of the short accounting period.

Student self-testing questions

1. Harold Limited has the following results for the year ended 31 March 2012.

TTP	150,000
Dividend received on 1 September 2012	15,000

Requirement: Calculate the corporation tax liability for the year ended 31 March 2012.

Solution

	£
TTP	150,000
FII (£15,000 x 100/90)	16,667
Profits	166,667

Less than £300,000 therefore tax at small profits rate

	£
FY11	
150,000 x 20%	30,000

2. Hannah Limited has the following results for the year ended 31 March 2012.

TTP	250,000
Dividend received on 1 September 2011	50,000

Requirement: Calculate the corporation tax liability for the year ended 31March 2012.

Solution

	£
TTP	250,000
FII (£50,000 x 100/90)	55,556
Profits	305,556

Therefore marginal relief band

	£
FY11	
250,000 x 26%	65,000
(1,500,000 - 305,556) x 250,000/305,556 x 3/200	(14,659)
	50,341

3. Freddie Limited makes up accounts to the year ended 31 December. For the year ended 31 December 2011 the profit and loss account was as follows:

TTP	200,000
Dividend received on 1 September 2011	50,000

Requirement: Calculate the corporation tax liability for the year ended 31 December 2011

Solution

	£
TTP	200,000
FII (£50,000 x 100/90)	55,556
Augmented Profits	255,556
Tax liability	£
FY10	
200,000 x 3/12 x 21%	10,500
FY11	
200,000 x 9/12 x 20%	30,000
	40,500

4. K plc has the undermentioned data relating to its accounting period ended 31st March 2012.

	£
Trading profits	327,000
Income from property	13,000
Chargeable gains	45,000
Gift Aid donations paid	10,000
Dividend received 31.12.11	18,000
Dividend paid 31.12.11	24,000

Calculate the corporation tax liability for the AP to 31st March 2012.

Solution: Corporation tax computation AP to 31.3.2012

	£	
Trading profits	327,000	
Income from property	13,000	
Chargeable gains	45,000	
	385,000	
Less qualifying charitable donations	(10,000)	
Taxable total profit	375,000	= N
Corporation tax at full rate	£	
£375,000 @ 26%	97,500	
Less marginal relief	(15,736)	
Corporation tax payable	81,764	

Note: Marginal relief computation.

N = 375,000

A = N + FII = 375,000 + 20,000 = 395,000

$$(1{,}500{,}000 - 395{,}000) \times \frac{375{,}000}{395{,}000} \times 3/200$$

$$= \quad 1{,}105{,}000 \times \frac{375}{395} \times 3/200 \quad = \quad 15{,}736.$$

Questions without answers

1. James Limited has 2 associated companies and a TTP for the year ended 31 March 2012 of £200,000.

Requirement Calculate the corporation tax liability in respect of the year ended 31 March 2012.

2. D Ltd has the following data relating to its accounting year ended 31st March 2012.

	£
Trading profits	440,000
Other income	10,000
Income from property	20,000
Chargeable gain	20,000
Debenture interest paid (gross) trading in nature	10,000
Dividend received 31.12.11	4,500
Dividend paid 31.12.11	24,000

Compute the corporation tax liability for the AP to 31st March 2012.

3. The following information has been extracted from the records of Nerston Ltd, a UK resident company, for its trading year to 31st March 2012.

	£
Operating profits	18,000
Income from property	20,000
Debenture interest paid: trading purposes	3,200
Chargeable gain	2,400
Dividends paid in the year	30,000

Dividends were paid 1st December 2011.

Compute corporation tax payable for the accounting period to 31st March 2012.

4. N Ltd has owned 60% of the share capital of D Ltd for several years. Both companies are trading companies resident in the UK.

The following information relates to the ten month accounting period to 30 September 2011 of N Ltd:

INCOME	£
Adjusted trading profit (before capital allowances)	77,000
Bank interest receivable - non trading	5,000
Capital gains	10,000
Rental income	5,000

The balances brought forward at 1 December 2010 for capital allowances purposes were as follows:

General pool	Car pool all 145g/km	Post-31.3.09 Renault Car CO_2 165g/km
£38,000	£16,000	£14,000

During the above period machinery was sold for £10,000 (original cost £11,000) and new desks were bought for £6,000 on 1st May 2011. The Renault car with CO_2 emissions of 165g/km was traded in for £10,000 against the cost of a new Skoda car with CO_2 emissions of 170g/km costing £12,000 on 1st June 2011.

Requirement

(a) Compute the maximum capital allowances which N Ltd may claim for the ten month accounting period to 30 September 2011.

(b) Compute N Ltd's corporation tax liability for the ten month accounting period.

5. DLT Ltd is a resident in the United Kingdom. It has one associated company. The board decided to alter the company's accounting date and prepared accounts for the fourteen months from 1 January 2011 to 28 February 2012. The following relates to this period.

INCOME	£	£
Trading profit (before capital allowances)		420,000
Rents receivable		
- February 2011	52,000	
- February 2012	25,000	
		77,000
Bank interest receivable, received July 2011		48,000
Capital gains		
- October 2011	120,000	
-February 2012	150,000	
		270,000

The written down balances for capital allowances purposes brought forward at 1 January 2010 were:

	£
General pool	160,000
Citroen car CO_2 180g/km	18,000

Capital transactions during the above period were as follows:

Purchases:		
10/10/11	Lorry	24,000
05/01/12	Machinery	12,000
Disposals		
02/01/12	Citroen car sold for	11,000

*The bank interest wholly relates to the year ended 31/12/11 in a non-trading loan relationship.

Requirement: Compute the corporation tax liability payable in respect of the above accounting profits.

6. Upbeat Ukuleles Limited is a United Kingdom resident company, which has been manufacturing musical instruments for many years. It has no associated companies. The company has previously made up accounts to 30 June but has now changed its accounting date to 30 September.

The company's results for the 15 month period to 30 September 2011 are as follows:

	£
Trading profits (as adjusted for taxation before capital allowances)	1,320,000
Debenture interest receivable (notes 3)	20,000
Bank interest receivable (note 4)	6,000
Chargeable gain (notes 5 and 6)	10,000
Gift aid payment (note 7)	5,000
Dividends received from UK companies (note 8)	30,000

Notes

1. Capital allowances

   On 1 July 2010 the tax written-down value of the plant and machinery in the capital allowances pool was £100,000. There were no additions or sales in the period of account to 30 September 2011.

2. On 1 July 2010 the company had trading losses brought forward of £800,000.
3. The debenture had been acquired in July 2011.
4. Bank interest receivable (non trading relationship)

	£
30.11.10 received	3,000
30.5.11 received	1,000
30.9.11 accrued	2,000
	6,000

5. Chargeable gain. The chargeable gain of £10,000 is in respect of shares disposed of on 31 December 2010.

6. On 1 July 2010 the company had capital losses brought forward of £12,500.

7. Gift Aid Payment. £5,000 was paid to a charity on 31 December 2010.

8. Dividends received

	£
25.4.11	18,000
29.9.11	12,000
	30,000

Requirement: Calculate the corporation tax liabilities for the 15 month period ended 30 September 2011.

Note. All apportionments may be made to the nearest month. **(22 marks)**

(ACCA December 1996 updated)

7. Chandler Ltd has, for many years, prepared accounts to 30 September, but changes its accounting date to 31 December by preparing accounts for the 15 months ended 31 December 2011. The accounts show a profit, as adjusted for tax purposes (but before deducting capital allowances) of £200,000.

The tax written down value of the general pool was £18,000 at 1 October 2010. During the period ended 31 December 2011, the following transactions took place.

14 November 2010	Purchased machine at a cost of £17,500
3 February 2011	Sold a machine, purchased in 1993 for £2,500 realising proceeds of £3,000
11 November 2011	Purchased motor van, cost £10,000

The company also realised other income and capital gains in the period as follows:

Bank Interest received:	31 December 2010	£50
Non-trade loan relationship:	30 June 2011	£900
	31 December 2011	£800
Capital Gain: Disposal	15 December 2011	£25,000
UK Dividends received:	18 April 2011	£11,000
	3 November 2011	£14,865

Chandler Ltd has no associated companies.

Requirement: Calculate the mainstream corporation tax liabilities for this 15 month period of account.

Student note: Some of these questions contain brief elements of capital gains tax and this topic is covered in chapters 26-33.

24 Groups and consortia

Introduction

1. This chapter considers the main aspects of corporation tax where a company is a member of a group or consortium. It begins with a summary of the topics to be examined, each of which is considered in detail subsequently.

Topics to be considered

2. a) Group relief (75% subsidiaries and consortia)	The set-off of trading losses against profits within a group, known as group relief.
b) Inter-company transfer of assets (75% subsidiaries)	The transfer of assets between group companies without any chargeable gain or loss arising.
c) Company reconstructions	Without change of ownership.
d) Change in ownership	Disallowance of trading losses.

Group relief (groups and consortia) Section 130 CTA 2010

3. Group relief is a very flexible loss relief option within groups of companies. One company in a qualifying group of companies may surrender any specified amount(s) of its trading losses, excess charitable donations, non-trade loan deficits, or surplus management expenses, and other companies in the same group may claim the amounts to reduce their own taxable profits for UK CT. The provisions on group relief are now found in the CTA 2010, Sections 130 onwards.

Meaning of group – world wide

4. Two companies are members of the same group relief group if the following four conditions all prevail.

a) One is the 75% subsidiary of the other, or both are 75% subsidiaries of a third company. A 75% subsidiary is defined under Section 838 TA 1988 in terms of the direct or indirect ownership of not less than 75% of the ordinary share capital, ordinary shares meaning all shares other than fixed rate preference shares. For the FY 2009 under the Finance Act 2009 an amendment to the 75% rule has been introduced to remove the reference to fixed rate preference shares. This is to ensure that corporations issuing new preference shares to external investors do not lose the right to group relief. The term 'fixed rate preference shares' is replaced with 'relevant preference shares'.

b) The parent company is beneficially entitled to not less than 75% of the profits available for distribution to equity holders of the subsidiary company. An equity holder is any person who holds ordinary shares or is a loan creditor in respect of a loan which is not a commercial loan. Loan creditor has the same meaning as that used in connection with close companies except that the proviso in favour of bank normal borrowings is not excluded and therefore is within the definition for the purposes of these conditions. A normal commercial loan is one which carries a reasonable rate of interest, with no rights to conversion.

c) The parent company would be entitled beneficially to not less than 75% of any assets of the subsidiary company available to its equity shareholders on a winding up.

d) The meaning of "group" for group relief includes non UK subsidiaries, and UK branches of overseas companies. This means that control for group relief can be traced through non-UK intermediate companies.

However in general there is no point in seeking to include non UK companies in a group relief claiming relationship if they are not within the charge to UK corporation tax..

As regards overseas companies surrendering losses to the UK, following the European Court of Justice Judgement in the Marks and Spencer case a small extension to the group relief rules was made from FY 2006. Relief may be claimed for losses from subsidiaries within the European Economic Area (EEA) or having a permanent establishment within the EEA (including indirectly held subsidiaries) if the tax loss cannot ever be relieved in the country of the loss. The loss surrender must be computed in line with UK tax rules. In practice few companies with loss-making overseas subsidiaries will satisfy these tight conditions (in the M&S case the loss-making Italian and French subsidiaries had actually closed and this made it impossible for them to relieve their losses by local carry-forward against profits).

Example of applying the 75% control rule to see if a GR relationship exists

B Ltd owns 75% of the ordinary share capital of W Ltd, which in turn owns 75% of the ordinary share capital of Z Ltd.

Since B Ltd would only be entitled to 56.25% of the profits available for distribution by Z Ltd the three companies do not constitute a group for the purposes of group relief. B Ltd and W Ltd however would constitute a group, as would W Ltd and Z Ltd. So B cannot surrender GR losses to Z and Z cannot surrender GR losses to B. But W can surrender or claim losses from either of the other two.

Example

T Ltd is the UK parent of two 100% subsidiaries, A Inc and B Inc, both being USA resident companies. B Inc owns 75% each of two UK companies, D Ltd and E Ltd.

T Ltd and its USA subsidiaries, and the sub-subsidiaries D and E, all constitute a group relief group for tax purposes. Therefore GR losses could be surrendered from T Ltd, D Ltd and E Ltd to either of the other two UK resident companies. As A Inc and B Inc are outside the European Economic Area they cannot partake in GR surrenders, even under the limited scope introduced after the M & S case. However they are members of the group for control purposes.

Meaning of consortia – world wide

5. A company is owned by a consortium if 75% or more of its ordinary share capital is beneficially owned by companies, none of which:

a) beneficially owns less than 5% of the ordinary share capital,

b) would be entitled to less than 5% of any profits available for distribution to equity holders,

c) would be entitled to less than 5% of any assets available to equity holders on the wind up.

6. Group relief is also available to a consortium of companies in the following circumstances:

a) Where the company surrendering the loss is a trading or holding company owned by a consortium (not being a 75% subsidiary of any company) and the claimant company is a member of the consortium. A loss may also be surrendered from a member of the consortium to the trading or holding company.

b) Where a trading company is the 90% subsidiary of a holding company, which itself is owned by a consortium.

Example

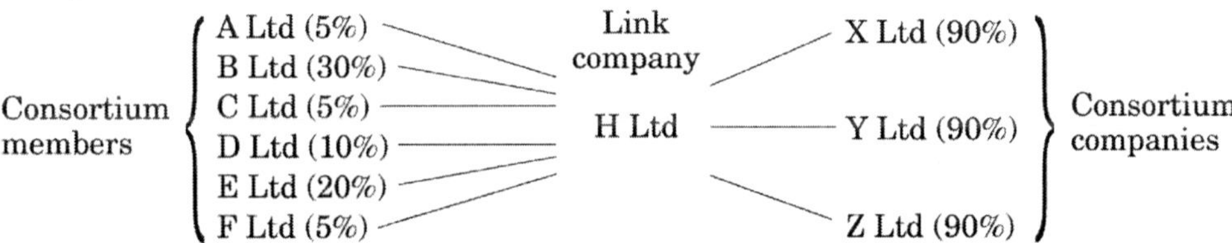

A loss in X, Y or Z could be transferred to the consortium members in proportion to their interests. In addition a loss by any of the consortium members could be claimed by X, Y or Z, and in this case the amount would be restricted to the profits of each claimant proportionately. However, see Section 12 below.

What may be surrendered as group relief

7. The following may be given by a surrendering company as group relief:

a) trading losses computed as for set off in accordance with Section 37 i.e. excluding any losses brought forward, but after claims for capital allowances.

b) any excess of capital allowances normally given against income of a special class, such as agricultural buildings allowances.

c) any charitable donations not relieved against total profits

d) any excess of management expenses of an investment company, other than a close investment holding company.

e) a net loss arising from a loan relationship.

No amounts arising from earlier or succeeding accounting periods can be surrendered.

The surrendering company does not have to make any claim for loss relief, e.g. under Section 37, before surrendering losses to GR claimants, although this is frequently done in practice.

The claimant

8. In the accounting period of the claimant company, the surrendered loss may be set against the claimant's total profits including chargeable gains determined as follows:

a) After taking into consideration any relief for losses from trading brought forward from previous years under Section 45. These would be deducted in arriving at the normal trading profits.

b) After taking into consideration any loss relief under Section 37 for the current accounting period, whether claimed or not.

c) Before any loss relief under Section 37 in respect of a loss brought back from a subsequent accounting period.

d) After deducting qualifying charitable donations .

e) Group relief is only available to companies resident in the UK or trading here through a branch.

Relief is to be set against the current profits of the claimant, and it cannot be either carried forward or backward to other accounting periods.

General points

9. a) Group relief is limited to the smaller of the surrendering company's losses relief, or the claimant company's profits available for group relief. Where the surrendering company's losses are greater than the claimant's available profits then the excess cannot be carried forward or backward as group relief. This does not prevent any other form of loss relief being obtained by the surrendering company, e.g. carry forward under Section 45.

b) More than one company in the group may make a claim relating to the same surrendering company.

c) If any payment takes place between the claimant and the surrendering company, and such a payment is not necessary to support a claim, then this transaction is:

   i) ignored for all corporation tax purposes as regards both payer and recipient

   ii) not treated as a distribution.

Example

H Ltd has a wholly owned subsidiary company M Ltd and the results of both companies for their current accounting period of the same 12 months are given below:

	H Ltd	M Ltd
	£	£
Trading profits	(75,000)	70,000
Less loss b/f under Section 45	–	30,000
	(75,000)	40,000
Interest income	15,000	–
Chargeable gain	10,000	5,000
Gift Aid donations	–	25,000

H Ltd decides to make a claim for loss relief under Section 37 and to surrender as much as possible of the balance of its loss to M Ltd.

Show the effects of the claims on H Ltd and M Ltd.

Solution

H Ltd

	£	
Interest income	15,000	
Chargeable gain	10,000	
	25,000	
Less Section 37 claim	(25,000)	
Taxable total profit	–	
Utilization of losses		
Available trade loss	75,000	
Less Section 37	(25,000)	
Available for group relief	50,000	
Less surrendered to M Ltd under Section 130	(20,000)	
Carried forward under Section 45	30,000	Smaller amount taken for group relief

M Ltd

	£
Trading profits	40,000
Chargeable gain	5,000
	45,000
Less qualifying charitable donations	25,000
Profits before group relief	20,000
Group relief claimed under Section 130	(20,000)
Taxable profits after group relief	0

Notes

i) In this example the group relief is limited to the claimant's profits of £20,000, as these are the lower amount.

ii) Group relief is deducted after qualifying charitable donations by the claimant.

Overlapping periods

10. Where the accounting periods of the surrendering company and the claimant company do not coincide, but they have been members of the same group throughout their respective accounting periods, then the group relief is in effect restricted to the proportion of the loss/profit of the overlapping period. This may, in fact, cover two accounting periods of either company.

Example

X Ltd has a 75% subsidiary, Y Ltd, and the results of both companies for the last two accounting periods are as follows:

X Ltd

AP to 31.3.2011 Trading profit	10,000
AP to 31.3.2012 Trading profit/(loss)	(16,000)

Y Ltd

AP to 31.12.2011 taxable profits	6,000
AP to 31.12.2012 taxable profits	24,000

Compute the group relief available.

Solution

In this example the period of the loss by X Ltd covers two accounting periods of Y Ltd and it will be necessary to determine the lower of the profit or loss in each corresponding period.

Group relief available

Overlapping period 1.4.2011 to 31.12.2011	£	£
X Ltd (3/4 × 16,000)	(12,000)	
Y Ltd (3/4 × 6,000)	4,500	
Restricted to the lower amount		4,500
Overlapping period 1.1.2012 to 31.3.2012	£	£
X Ltd (¼ × 16,000)	(4,000)	
Y Ltd (¼ × 24,000	6,000	
Restricted to the lower amount		4,000
Total		8,500

a) An overlapping period is the period throughout which both the claimant and the surrendering companies meet the qualifying conditions for group relief (as to membership of the group or consortium) and which is a common period within the corporation tax accounting periods of both companies.

b) The maximum loss to be surrendered is the smaller of the unused part of the total available or the unrelieved part of the total profit of the claimant company in the overlapping period.

c) The unused part of the loss is the part remaining after prior surrenders of loss. This assumes that the total loss available for the overlapping period is computed and successive surrenders of loss are deducted from that total until the whole of the loss for the overlapping period is exhausted.

d) The unrelieved part of the total profit assumes an apportionment of the total profit for the entire accounting period between the amount for the overlapping period and the balance. The profit for the overlapping period is then taken and successive group relief claims are deducted from it until, cumulatively, the profit is exhausted.

Companies joining or leaving a group

11. Group relief is generally only available if the claimant and surrendering companies are members of the same group (or fulfil the conditions relating to a consortium) throughout the accounting periods of both companies. However, when a company either joins or leaves a group or consortium, then some relief is available and a new accounting period is deemed to end or commence on the occurrence of that event.

Normally the profits/losses are apportioned on a time basis. However, if it appears that such an apportionment would produce an unreasonable result, then a more reasonable basis must be used.

Example

D Ltd, a trading company, acquires a 100% interest in W Ltd on the 30th June 2011. Both companies have the same year end and the results for the year to 31st December 2011 are as follows:

	D Ltd	W Ltd
	£	£
Trading profit	12,000	(40,000)
Interest income	3,000	–
Chargeable gain	15,000	–
Chargeable loss	–	(10,000)

Compute the amount of group relief available.

Solution

On the acquisition of W Ltd who then with D Ltd forms a group, there is deemed to be a commencement of an accounting period for group relief purposes.

	£
Loss to be surrendered by W Ltd	
Loss for 12 months to 31.12.2011	40,000
Proportion for deemed accounting period from	
1.7.2011 to 31.12.2011 $^{6}/_{12} \times 40{,}000$	20,000

Loss to be claimed by D Ltd

Trading profit	12,000
Interest income	3,000
Chargeable gain	15,000
	30,000
Proportion from 1.7.2011 $^{6}/12 \times 30{,}000 =$	15,000

Since this is smaller than the amount of the loss of the surrendering company, this is the maximum available for group relief.

The computations for the year to 31st December 2011 are:

	£
D Ltd	
Taxable profits as above	30,000
Less group relief	(15,000)
Taxable total profit after group relief	15,000
W Ltd	
Trading loss	40,000
Less surrendered	(15,000)
Unused loss	25,000

Notes

i) The balance of the loss of W Ltd is not available for future group relief, but it can be used by W Ltd under Section 37 or 45.

ii) The capital loss of W Ltd may not be set against the chargeable gain of any other company.

Similar provisions apply when a company leaves a group, and the profits and losses up to the date of the departure must be apportioned to determine the amount of any group relief available.

Consortium relief

12. Where there is a consortium of companies as defined in section 6 above, the following relief may be available:

a) surrender to consortium members

b) surrender by the consortium members

c) a mixture of group/consortium relief

d) relief through a link company.

Relief is only available to a UK member of a consortium which can include overseas members.

Surrender to a consortium member

13. K Ltd is owned by four companies A Ltd (20%), B Ltd (30%), C Ltd (10%) and D Ltd (40%).

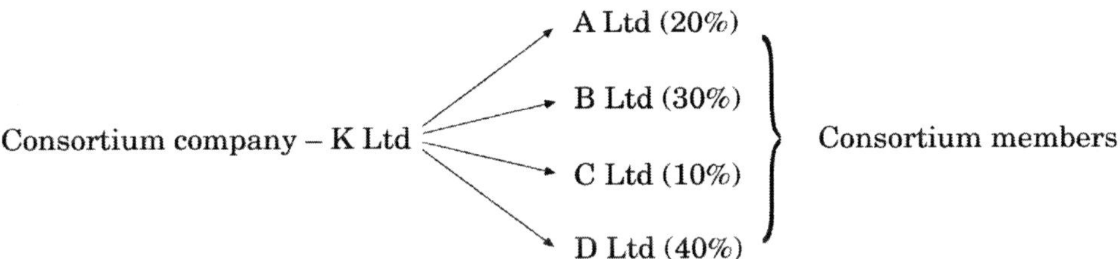

If K Ltd incurs a trading loss it may be surrendered to the consortium members A, B, C, D in proportion to their shareholding in K Ltd. Thus if K Ltd makes a loss of £20,000, the amount that can be surrendered to the consortium members is:

		£
A Ltd	20% × 20,000	4,000
B Ltd	30% × 20,000	6,000
C Ltd	10% × 20,000	2,000
D Ltd	40% × 20,000	8,000
		20,000

The amount of the loss that can be surrendered by K Ltd is reduced to the extent that it has profits of the same accounting period available to relieve the loss under Section 37. It should be noted that K Ltd does not have to make the claim under Section 37 but the consortium relief is restricted as though this had taken place whereas with group relief this restriction does not apply.

Surrender by the consortium members

14. Where a consortium member makes a loss then this can be surrendered to the consortium company. However, in this case the amount that can be surrendered is limited to the percentage of the profits of the consortium company.

Example

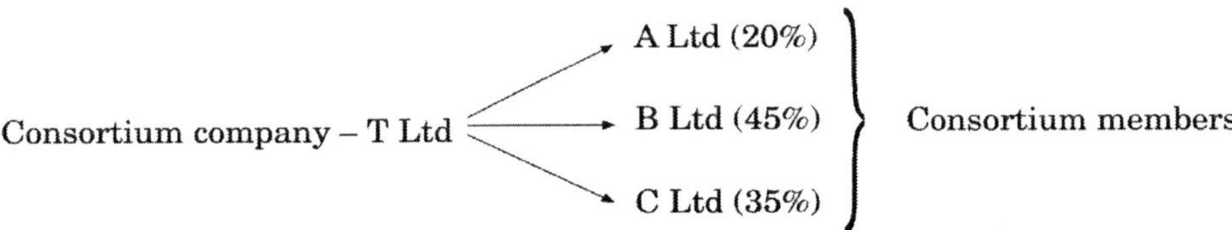

If C Ltd makes a loss then the amount that can be surrendered to T Ltd is restricted to 35% of the profit of T Ltd.

For example, if C Ltd makes a loss of £25,000 and T Ltd has profits of £50,000 then the amount of the loss that can be surrendered is limited to 35% x £50,000 i.e. £17,500.

In this case it is not necessary for C Ltd to consider any other profits available for set-off under Section 37.

A mixture of group/consortium relief

15. The position is as follows.

a) Where a consortium owned company is also a member of a group of companies then that company is known as a 'group/consortium company'.

b) If a group/consortium company incurs a loss then the amount that can be surrendered pro rata to the consortium members must first be reduced by:

   i) any potential claim under Section 37 (set-off against other profits of the same period)

   ii) any potential group relief claims that could be made under Section 130.

   The potential loss claims do not have to be made, but their availability restricts the loss to be surrendered by the group/consortium company.

c) Where the group/consortium company has taxable profits and wishes to claim loss relief from any of its consortium members , then the available profits must first be reduced by any potential group loss claims within the group/consortium company's own group.

d) If the accounting periods of the members of the group/consortium are not co-terminous then an overlapping period arises and the relief claimed cannot be more than the consortium members' proportionate share in the equity of the consortium subsidiary.

Example

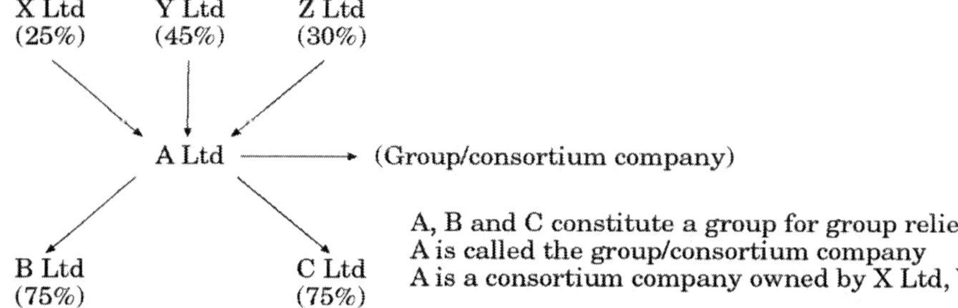

The following results relate to the year ended 31.12.2011.

		£
A Ltd	Trading loss	80,000
	Chargeable gain	12,000
B Ltd	Trading profits	25,000
C Ltd	Trading loss	10,000
	Chargeable gains	3,000

Compute the amounts that could be surrendered to X Ltd.

Solution

		£	£
a)	A Ltd trading loss		80,000
	Less potential reliefs:		
	Section 37 A Ltd	12,000	
	Section 130 B Ltd	25,000	
	Section 130 C Ltd	3,000	40,000
			40,000
	25% × 40,000 =		10,000
b)	A Ltd trading loss		80,000
	Less potential reliefs:		
	Section 37 A Ltd	12,000	
	Section 130 B Ltd	18,000	30,000
			50,000
	25% × 50,000 =		12,500

Notes

i) In (a) the intra-group relief claimable by B & C and the possible claim under Section 37 by C has not been exercised.

ii) In (b) the amount of potential group relief is after taking:

C Ltd Section 37	£10,000 – £3,000	=	£7,000 loss
B Ltd group relief with C Ltd	£25,000 – £7,000	=	£18,000 profit.

Relief through a link company

16. A link company is defined as a company which is a member both of a consortium and of a group.

Example

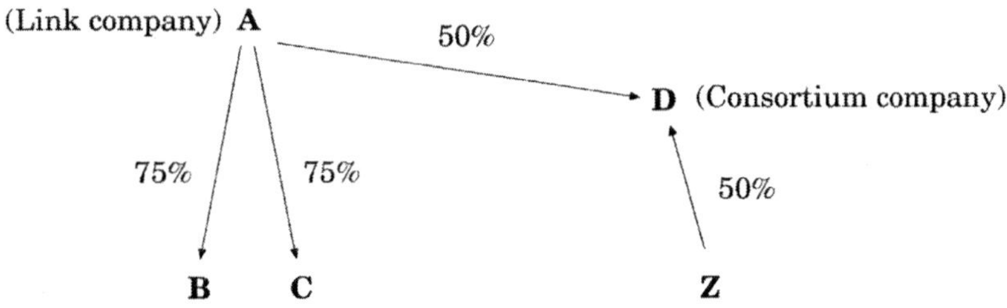

A, B and C constitute a group for group relief purposes.

A and Z jointly own the consortium company D.

A is a member of a group and a consortium.

Example

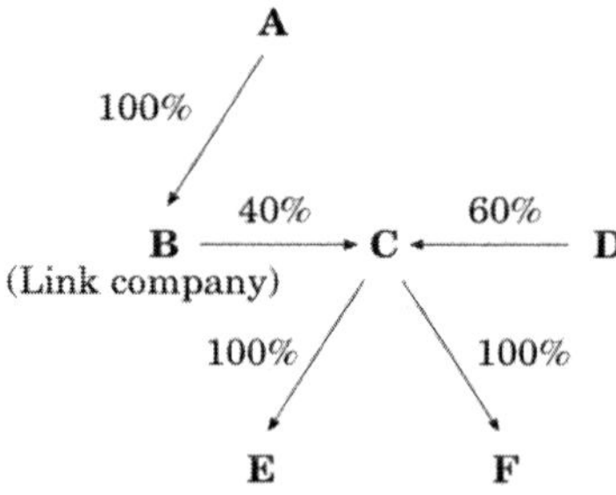

A and B constitute a group. C, E and F constitute a group. C is owned by a consortium of two members B and D. C is also a group consortium company.

In respect of the year ending 31st December 2011 the companies have the following results:

	£	
A Ltd	100,000	
B Ltd	(30,000)	loss
C Ltd	(20,000)	loss
D Ltd	Nil	
E Ltd	12,000	
F Ltd	(4,000)	loss

Calculate the possible claims for group relief and consortium relief.

Solution: AP to 31st December 2011

E Ltd Profits before relief			12,000
	Less Group relief surrendered by F	4,000	
	do. C	8,000	12,000
Assessment			–
A Ltd	Profits before relief		100,000
	Less Group relief surrendered by B	30,000	
	Consortium relief C:		
	40% × (20,000 – 8,000)	4,800	34,800
	Profits chargeable to corporation tax		65,200

Notes

The consortium relief available to A Ltd from C Ltd is the lower of:

A Ltd profits after group relief i.e.	100,000 – 30,000	=	70,000
B Ltd share of C Ltd loss i.e.	40% (20,000 – 8,000)	=	4,800

Group payments of interest etc. – intercompany transactions

17. Payments of interest, royalty payments and annual payments and annuities, are made without the deduction of income tax where the companies concerned are within charge to UK corporation tax, or in the case of interest and royalty payments, where the recipient is an EU company. Unlike the treatment of intra-group payments for consolidated accounting purposes, all companies in a group are charged o separate CT on an entity basis.

Group Chargeable Gains rules including transfer of assets between group companies

18.

a) Until recently there was no kind of "group relief" for chargeable gains and capital losses between different members of a group of companies. This situation has changed recently.

b) Where one member of a CGT group makes a chargeable asset disposal, the company actually disposing of the asset and another company in the group can elect that the asset disposal outside the group be treated as being made by the other company. The election must be made within two years after the end of the accounting period in which the actual disposal is made. This can achieve the offset of chargeable gains against brought forward capital losses in a different company. However there are anti avoidance rules relating to "pre entry" losses, i.e. losses realised or accruing before a company joined the CGT group, which cannot be used in this way. The further rules in this field are too complex for a book at introductory level, although they are due to be simplified slightly in 2011.

c) The most important point to note on CGT and groups is that as a general rule, when a company disposes of a chargeable asset outside the CGT group, it makes a chargeable gain or loss on normal principles. However, if a chargeable asset disposal is made by one member of a CGT group to another group company, that transaction automatically takes place for tax purposes at **no gain and no loss**. This applies regardless of actual payment made for the asset by the acquirer.

d) A no gain no loss (NGNL) disposal is achieved by deeming the consideration for the disposal of the asset to be an amount at which neither a gain nor a loss accrues to the company disposing of the asset. Normally this means that the amount paid between the companies is deemed for CGT to be the original cost, plus enhancement expenditure, plus all indexation allowance to date.

When the asset is ultimately disposed of outside the group, the liability to corporation tax on any gain would arise in the company that actually sold the asset (or another group company, if the election at (b) above is made). The allowable cost would be the deemed cost at which the asset was acquired intra-group.

Companies defined as being in the same "CGT group "

19. a) A Capital Gains Tax group comprises a principal company and all of its 75% subsidiaries. Unlike with section 130 group losses relief, a company cannot be a member of more than one "CGT group" at the same time.

b) A 75% subsidiary means a company whose ordinary share capital is owned by another company either directly or indirectly to the extent of at least 75%. Again ordinary share capital comprises all shares other than relevant preference shares.

c) A company which is itself a 75% subsidiary of another company cannot be the principal company of a CGT group. It is the 75% parent company which is the principal company. This may have an impact on which other companies further down a group are counted in the same CGT group : a sub-subsidiary which is not in a ≥50% indirect relationship with the principal company (one particular company, as defined), as well as a ≥ 75% relationship with its own holding company, is excluded from the CGT group.

d) Members of a consortium are not eligible for treatment as a CGT group, nor are close investment holding companies, unless the transfer is between two close investment holding companies.

Assets available for group treatment

20. The disposal of any chargeable asset between group companies should attract no gain or loss treatment, but there are some exceptions given in the Act which are as follows.

a) Where the disposal is of redeemable preference shares in a company (these are normally not chargeable assets in the hands of a company anyway, if accounted for as debt instruments).

b) Where the disposal is of a debt due from a member of a group (now superseded by the loan relationships rules under which debts are not chargeable assets for companies).

c) Where the disposal arises from a capital distribution on the liquidation of a company.

d) Where the company is a dual resident member of a group of companies and any gain made by that company on the disposal would be exempt from tax under a double tax treaty.

If the transfer is of an asset which the recipient company appropriates to its inventory (trading stock), then that company is deemed to have received a capital asset and immediately transferred that asset to its inventory (trading stock). There would thus be no capital gain or loss arising on the inter-company transfer, as it would fall within the provisions noted above.

Where the asset transferred to a group company was inventory (trading stock) of the transferor company, then the latter is treated as having appropriated the asset as a capital asset immediately prior to the disposal. The value placed on the asset for trading purposes under Section 161 TCGA 1992 would be the transfer value giving rise to a 'no gain or loss' situation.

Other points

21. a) When an asset is disposed of by a group company to a company outside the group, then any capital allowances granted to any member of the group relating to the asset are taken into consideration in computing any gain or loss.

b) If a company to which an asset has been transferred at no gain and no loss ceases to be a member of a group within six years of the date of the transfer the position is as follows.

i) At the date of the acquisition of the asset by the company leaving the group , or if later the beginning of the accounting period when the company left the group, it is deemed to have sold and reacquired the asset at its market value at the date when it acquired the asset from the other group member.

ii) There will therefore, be a chargeable gain or loss on the difference between the market value at the time of the intra-group asset transfer, and the original cost to the group of the asset.

This provision does not apply if a company ceases membership of a group by being wound up.

c) The provisions of Section 152 TCGA 1992 (rollover relief) are extended to CGT groups which enables all trades carried on by the group to be treated as one for the purposes of the sale of assets "used in the trade" and purchase of replacement assets "used in the trade".

For further details see Chapter 33.

Student self-testing questions

1. The results of A Ltd and its wholly owned subsidiary B Ltd for the three years ended 31st March 2012 are as follows:

		31.3.2010	**31.3.2011**	**31.3.2012**
		£	**£**	**£**
A Ltd	Trading profit/(loss)	1,200	(7,500)	4,800
	Income from property	500	500	500
B Ltd	Trading profit	2,500	3,500	5,000

A Ltd makes a claim for loss relief under Section 37 and then claims group relief under Section 130.

Show the computations of taxable total profit.

Solution:

	31.3.2010	31.3.2011	31.3.2012
A Ltd	£	£	£
Trading profit	1,200	–	4,800
Less Section 45	–	–	1,800
	1,200	–	3,000
Income from property	500	500	500
	1,700	500	3,500
Less Section 37	(1,700)	(500)	–
Taxable total profit	–		–3,500
B Ltd			
Trading profit	2,500	3,500	5,000
Less group relief Section 130	–	(3,500)	–
Taxable total profit	2,500	–	5,000

Loss memorandum		£	£
Loss year to 31st March 2010			7,500
Section 37	31.3.2010	500	
Section 37	31.3.2009	1,700	
Section 37	31.3.2011	1,800	
Section 130	31.3.2010	3,500	
(group relief surrendered to B Ltd)			(7,500)

Note. The maximum amount has been surrendered to B Ltd.

2. Arch Ltd owns 100% of the share capital of Bow Ltd and Can Ltd. The results of each company for the year ended 31 March 2012 are as follows:

	Arch Ltd	Bow Ltd	Can Ltd
	£	£	£
Tax adjusted trading profit/(loss)	(125,000)	650,000	130,000

Required

a) Explain the group relationship that must exist in order that group relief can be claimed. (3 marks)

b) Explain how group relief should be allocated between the respective claimant companies in order to maximise the potential benefit obtained from the relief. (4 marks)

c) Assuming that reliefs are claimed in the most favourable manner, calculate the corporation tax liabilities of Arch Ltd, Bow Ltd and Can Ltd for the year ended 31 March 2012. (8 marks)

ACCA Pilot updated

Solution

(a) (1) One company must be a 75% subsidiary of the other, or both companies must be 75% subsidiaries of a third company

(2) The holding company must have an effective interest of at least 75% of the subsidiary's share capital, excluding relevant preference shares.

(3) The holding company must have the right to receive at least 75% of the subsidiary's distributable profits and net assets on a winding up.

(b) (1) Group relief should be allocated to the company(s) with the highest marginal rate of tax first. The upper and lower limits for marginal relief for this group are £1,500,000 / 3 = £500,000 and £300,000 / 3 = £100,000. Profits of between £500,000 and £100,000 are taxed at the marginal rate of 27.5%. Next those companies that are taxed at the 26% rate should be given relief.

(c)	£	£	£
	Arch Ltd	Bow Ltd	Can Ltd
Trading profit	-	650,000	130,000
Less group relief	-	(95,000)	(30,000)
TTP	-	555,000	100,000
Tax @ 20%			20,000
Tax @ 26%		144,300	

Questions without answers

1. Z Ltd, a UK trading company, acquired a 75% interest in Q Ltd on the 30th September 2011. Both companies have the same year end and their results for the AP 31.3.2012 are as follows:

	Z Ltd	**Q Ltd**
	£	**£**
Trading profit/(loss)	75,000	(30,000)
Income from property	15,000	–
Chargeable gain	10,000	–
Debenture interest paid (gross)	5,000	5,000

Compute the amount of group relief available for the AP to 31st March 2012, and show the corporation tax computations.

2. Straight plc is the holding company for a group of companies. All of the companies in the group have an accounting date of 31 March. The group structure is as follows:

Straight plc > 100% > Arc Ltd > 80% > Bend Ltd > 75% > Curve Ltd

For the year ended 31 March 2012 Straight plc has a trading profit of £185,000. As at 31 March 2011 the company had unused trading losses of £15,000 and unused capital losses of £10,000.

Straight plc sold a freehold office building on 20 June 2011 for £350,000, and this resulted in a capital gain of £80,000.

During the year ended 31 March 2012 Straight plc received dividends of £18,000 from Arc Ltd, and dividends of £9,000 from Triangle plc, an unconnected company. These figures are the actual amounts received.

Arc Ltd sold a freehold warehouse on 10 March 2012, and this resulted in a capital loss of £40,000.

i) **Explain why Straight plc, Arc Ltd, Bend Ltd and Curve Ltd form a group for capital gains purposes, and why Curve Ltd would be excluded from the group if Straight plc's holding in Arc Ltd were only 80% instead of 100%.**

ii) **Before taking into account any notional transfer of assets, calculate the corporation tax payable by Straight plc for the year ended 31 March 2012.**

(ACCA updated)

3. Animal Ltd is the holding company for a group of companies. The results of each group company for the year ended 31 March 2012 are as follows:

	Tax adjusted trading profit/(loss)	**Income from property**	**Franked Investment Income**
	£	£	£
Animal Ltd	450,000	5,000	20,000
Bat Ltd	65,000	15,000	–
Cat Ltd	85,000	–	–
Dog Ltd	100,000	–	–
Elk Ltd	–	–	–
Fox Ltd	60,000	–	5,000
Gnu Ltd	(200,000)	–	–

Animal Ltd owned 100% of each subsidiary company's ordinary share capital throughout the year ended 31 March 2012 with the following exceptions:

(1) Animal Ltd only owned 90% of Bat Ltd's ordinary share capital.

(2) Animal Ltd's shareholding in Cat Ltd was disposed of on 31 December 2011.

The trading profit of £85,000 is for the year ended 31 March 2012.

(3) Animal Ltd's shareholding in Dog Ltd was acquired on 1 January 2012. The trading profit of £100,000 is for the year ended 31 March 2012.

(4) Elk Ltd was a dormant company throughout the year ended 31 March 2012.

Required:

(a) Explain the group relationship that must exist in order that group relief can be claimed. (3 marks)

(b) Explain why there are six associated companies in the Animal Ltd group of companies. Your answer should identify the six associated companies. (3 marks)

(c) Assuming that relief is claimed for Gnu Ltd's trading loss of £200,000 in the most favourable manner, calculate the profits chargeable to corporation tax of Animal Ltd, Bat Ltd, Cat Ltd, Dog Ltd and Fox Ltd for the year ended 31 March 2012. (9 marks)

(15 marks)

(ACCA June 2003 updated)

Student note: Some of these questions contain brief elements of capital gains tax and this topic is covered in chapters 26-33.

25 International aspects

Introduction

1. This chapter deals at an awareness level with some aspects of corporation tax arising from overseas or international operations under the following main headings:

Income from overseas sources

Relief for Withholding taxes suffered on income or gains

Double tax relief – general OECD principles

Foreign dividends received after 1 July 2009 / 23 November 2008

Foreign tax credit relief and loss relief

Controlled foreign companies.

Transfer pricing.

Tax Differences between Foreign Branch and Foreign Subsidiary

"Worldwide debt cap" restriction on UK allowable interest costs from January 2010

Income from overseas sources

2. Income from overseas sources is liable to CT in the same way as all other income of a UK resident company. All interest receivable is within the loan relationship arrangements, and any profit on overseas loans is taxed as loan relationship surplus. Trading income from foreign branches (permanent establishments) is under the CTA2009 included in normal trade profits and not treated as a separate source of income (this was a minor legislative change from 1 April 2009). Income from overseas rentals is treated in the same way as UK property income. Chargeable gains realised on overseas assets are computed in the same way as other gains and liable to UK corporation tax (subject to double tax relief for overseas tax – see below).

Income from overseas sources that is passed over in cash may be received under deduction of local withholding taxes, charged on the payment (e.g. rents, royalties, licence fees or dividends paid). In the case of rent and royalties, etc, the income liable to UK corporation tax must be grossed up for the foreign withholding tax. Full relief is available for the withholding tax against UK CT, provided it has not been suffered at a higher effective rate than the UK CT on the same income.

However, foreign dividends are not grossed up for actual foreign withholding taxes deducted, because they are not taxable income in the hands of a UK company. Instead the net dividend is grossed up by the UK notional tax credit for dividends of one-ninth. See section 4 below.

Example

K Ltd has the following data relating to the 12 months AP to the 31st March 2012.

	£
Trading profits	1,280,000
Interest income:	
(foreign interest after 15% withholding tax)	85,000
Chargeable gains	250,000

Calculate the CT payable for the AP to 31st March 2012.

Solution

K Ltd corporation tax computation AP 31.3.2012

	£
Trading profits	1,280,000
Interest income (gross) $\frac{85,000}{85} \times \frac{100}{1}$	100,000
Chargeable gains	250,000
Total profits/taxable total profit	1,630,000
Corporation tax	£
1,630,000 @ 26%	423,800
Less double tax relief – withholding tax suffered	(15,000)
Corporation tax liability	408,800

Note

The double tax relief is the lower of the following:

Foreign income	100,000
UK tax @ 26%	26,000
Foreign tax	15,000

Double tax relief – general OECD principles

3. Double Taxation Agreements (Tax Treaties) provide negotiated means of determining the taxing rights of any two competing Governments (Taxing States), where the domestic tax rules of both States charge tax on the same income or gains.

The UK has an extensive network of Double Tax Treaties at Government level. These have been drafted so as to follow the OECD (Organisation for Economic Cooperation and Development) guidelines on Double Tax Treaties.

If there is no Double Tax Treaty with the relevant State, unilateral double taxation credit relief, which works on a similar basis to the commonest type of Tax Treaty credit relief, is given by the UK Taxes Acts for foreign tax shown to have been suffered on income or gains theta re also chargeable to tax in the UK.

The OECD principles state that the profits of a permanent establishment in another Taxing State should be primarily taxable in that other Taxing State. A permanent establishment covers a branch operation if there is the capacity for employees to conclude contracts there which bind the UK company. It also covers an appointed general agent (i.e. not an employee of the UK company) who has authority to conclude binding contracts in the foreign territory on behalf of the UK company.

Another OECD principle of double tax relief is that, in giving relief in the second Taxing State for tax suffered in the first, the second State may limit that relief to the amount of tax that would be paid on the same income in the second country. This principle is illustrated by the DTR calculations in the example at section 2 above. If the withholding tax had been 30% (£30,000), then only £28,000 would have been available for offset against the UK tax liability.

Foreign dividends received after 1 July 2009/ 23 November 2008

4. The Finance Act 2009 introduced a very important change to the tax treatment of dividends received by a UK company from companies resident outside the UK.

Formerly non-UK dividends were treated as taxable overseas investment income. From 1 July 2009 (23 November 2008 for companies in the European Economic Area) such dividends are treated the same way as UK dividends. Thus they are not taxable income in the hands of the UK recipient company. However, they do count as FII (if they are not paid by subsidiaries) for the purposes of determining the augmented profits of the UK company. For his purpose the FII value is found by adding a notional 1/9 tax credit to the net dividend received.

Before those dates, FII treatment only applied to dividends from UK resident companies and foreign dividends counted as taxable investment income.

To avoid disadvantaging some international corporate structures, the treatment of foreign dividends as tax-exempt FII from July 2009 may be waived by a UK corporate taxpayer, if the older UK treatment (as taxable foreign investment income) is more beneficial under a Tax Treaty in the particular circumstances. The implications of this are not considered further here.

Foreign tax credit relief and loss relief

5. Where a UK company has foreign income, then in order to preserve the maximum amount of DT relief, loss relief claims should be considered carefully.

Example

W Ltd and its wholly owned UK subsidiary X Ltd have the following results for the year ended 31st March 2012.

	W Ltd	X Ltd
	£	£
Trading profits	(30,000)	80,000
Overseas Royalties	16,000	
(gross before withholding tax of 15%)		
Chargeable gains	2,000	1,000

Calculate the corporation tax payable in the following situations:

a) **W Ltd claims loss relief under Section 37 and surrenders the maximum loss to X Ltd.**

b) **W Ltd makes no claim under Section 37 and surrenders as much loss as possible to X Ltd.**

Solution

(a) **Corporation tax computations AP 31.3.2012**

	W Ltd	X Ltd
	£	£
Trading profits	–	80,000
Overseas royalties	16,000	–
Chargeable gains	2,000	1,000
	18,000	81,000
Less Section 37 (current year offset)	(18,000)	
Section 130 (group loss surrender)		(12,000)
Profits chargeable to CT	–	69,000
CT Payable @ 20%	–	13,800
Unrelieved foreign tax =	£2,400	

	W Ltd	X Ltd
	£	£
(b) **Trading profits**	–	80,000
Overseas income	16,000	–
Chargeable gain	2,000	1,000
	18,000	81,000
Less Section 130 group loss surrender	–	(30,000)
Profits chargeable to CT	18,000	51,000
CT payable @ 20%	3,600	10,200
Less DTR	(2,400)	–
CT	1,200	10,200

Notes

i) By X not claiming loss relief under Section 37 the full DT relief of £2,400 has been obtained by X.

Controlled foreign companies

6. UK resident companies with interests (even non controlling interests) in a profitable "controlled foreign company" (CFC) that is resident in a low-tax area may be charged to additional UK corporation tax on an apportionment of the profits of the CFC on an arising basis.

The present rules about CFCs date originally from 1984 and notice has already been given by the Government of substantial reforms to the CFC system from April 2012. Various proposals have been issued and debated (See "Foreign profits Consultation" on the HMRC website) but the final rules and exceptions are still not decided. Meanwhile the older tax regime continues for FY2011 but with certain limitations in practice as some of the original rules have been deemed incompatible with EU and international obligations.

The present rules require a UK company to declare on its CT self-assessment form any apportioned non-UK profits of a CFC which it has an interest, and to pay tax on these profits in the UK. A CFC is defined as:

a) an overseas resident company which is under the control of persons resident in the UK, and,

b) the overseas resident company is subject to a lower level of taxation in its country of residence than it would be in the UK. "Lower" in this case means that the tax paid in the country of residence $<$ 75% of the tax bill, had the company been resident in the UK.

c) "Control" is deemed to exist where $\geq$40% of the CFC is owned by a UK company.

d) The CFC regime includes UK incorporated companies that are not UK tax-resident.

e) On the 12th March 2008 additional anti-avoidance measures were introduced to extend the CFC regime to corporations classified as Special Purpose Vehicles (SPV's) set up with the sole intention of avoiding UK corporation tax.

Tests of exclusion

7. No direction will be made to apportion the profits of the CFC if that company satisfies any one of the following tests of exclusion.

a) Until 1 July 2009 only, "the CFC pursues an acceptable distribution policy". This ground for exclusion was removed when foreign dividends became exempt from UK corporation tax. Before that date the test meant that a trading CFC must have paid to UK residents by way of dividends at least 90% of its "available profits", within a certain time after earning them. For non-trading CFCs, 90% of taxable profits less capital gains and foreign tax must be distributed.

b) "The CFC is engaged in exempt activities"
A CFC is engaged in exempt activities if it has, throughout the accounting period, a business establishment in its territory of residence and its business affairs are effectively managed there. The latter is evidenced, amongst other things, if it has a sufficient number of employees in the territory to deal with its volume of business locally. Certain non-trading activities have to meet other criteria to benefit under this heading.

c) "The CFC fulfils the public quotation condition"
This is met where the CFC has at least 35% of its shares which have voting power, quoted on a recognised stock exchange in the country of residence. As for close companies in the UK, this requirement is not met where 85% of the company's voting power is in the hands of its principal members.

d) "The CFC satisfies the motive test"
There are two conditions to be met if the CFC is to satisfy the motive test.

i) The existence of the CFC was not made mainly for the purposes of achieving a diversion of profits from the UK, and

ii) Any reduction of UK tax resulting from transactions is either minimal or is not the main reason for undertaking those transactions.

e) "The CFC has chargeable profits <£50,000"
Where the chargeable profits (calculated on the same basis as UK taxable total profits) of the CFC are less than £50,000 for a 12 month accounting period then it is excluded from apportionment.

Assessable profits

8. a) The CFC profit brought into UK taxable profits is the apportioned amount of the CFC's chargeable profits, computed on UK tax principles. Any overseas tax paid that is attributable to the apportioned profits is eligible for Double Tax Relief.

b) Deductions can be made against apportioned CFC profits where the UK company has reliefs which have not been fully utilised against its UK taxable profits. The reliefs are:

i) relief for trading losses

ii) group relief

iii) relief for management expenses

c) No self-assessment need be made unless the amount apportioned to a UK company and its associates of the CFC's chargeable profits amount to at least 10% of the CFC's chargeable profits.

HMRC press releases have provided a list of what are known as 'excluded countries'. Where a company carries on a trade in one of these countries it is deemed to fall outside the charging provisions noted above.

CFCs – self-assessment

9. The CTSA rules – i.e. corporation tax self-assessment rules – apply to CFCs. This means that UK companies now have to include in their tax returns (Form CT600B) their share of a CFC's profits in accordance with the CFC rules. It is not necessary for HMRC to make a direction regarding a CFC but HMRC do maintain information about possible CFCs and the UK companies believed to have controlling interests in them, so HMRC could initiate an enquiry if non-exempt CFC profits were not shown on the CT return.

International transfer pricing – tax issues

10. A UK company is required to calculate its taxable income on an arm's length basis for transactions with connected companies or businesses (e.g. a branch), where this would increase the amount of UK taxable income.

The transfer pricing rules basically state that if any transaction is made with a related company (whether a trading supply of goods services or raw materials, a charge for rent, interest or a charge for management services) at a price that is not the level which would be reached between two unrelated parties negotiating at arm's length, and as a result the UK company (i.e. the company within the charge to UK tax) pays a higher amount of cost, or receives a lower amount of income, than would have applied under an arm's length pricing basis, then for tax purposes the arm's length transfer price (as agreed with HMRC) must be substituted.

The following additional rules apply

i) The transfer pricing tax rules do not apply to Small and Medium sized Enterprises, except in relation to transactions with a related business in a territory which does not have a double tax treaty with the UK containing a suitable non-discrimination article.

ii) For large groups (not SMEs), transfer pricing tax rules apply between related group companies resident in the UK, as well as to international transactions.

iii) In exceptional circumstances a medium-sized company may be required by HMRC to apply transfer pricing adjustments.

In practice HMRC will enter into "advance pricing agreements" with multinational companies, typically lasting six years at a time These will agree the basis on which work in progress, raw materials or components, or other goods or services are to be priced when supplied to or purchased from a related non UK company under the same ultimate control.

Advance pricing agreements are very important for multinational groups to be sure that their methods of arriving at group internal transfer prices and entity profits on sales to related companies are acceptable to the taxing authorities in all the countries involved.

Most developed tax systems are introducing similar transfer pricing review rules for profits taxation, in order to prevent the global profits of multinationals being disproportionately recognised in those countries with the lowest tax rates.

The largest settlements of transfer pricing tax enquiries to date have been made by pharmaceutical companies. In June 2010, a transfer pricing out-of-court settlement with UK HMRC of £505 million in back taxes by Astra Zeneca plc was announced, covering Astra Zeneca's business in the years 1995-2010.

Foreign branches of UK companies

11. Where a UK company carries on part of its trade through a foreign branch then the following rules apply:

a) The trade of the overseas branch is subject to UK corporation tax: the branch profits are taxed as part of the company's trading profits.

b) If the overseas branch is subject to foreign taxation (i.e. direct tax on its profits) then this is taken into consideration for double tax relief against UK tax on total profits.

c) The OECD principles allow the other Taxing State to tax the branch profits first, if the branch is a permanent establishment, as defined.

d) The transactions of the foreign branch with the UK parent should be priced on a "separate enterprise" principle when computing the profits of the branch, and of the UK parent, for the purpose of DTR , i.e. when comparing overseas tax on the branch profits with UK tax on the same profits.

d) Capital allowances are available in the UK tax computations for plant and machinery purchased by the overseas branch

e) Net trading losses of the overseas branch are in effect relieved against the UK profits without the need for a formal claim, since both results are combined.

f) The existence of a foreign branch does not increase the number of associated companies for the purposes of the small profits rate of CT.

g) It is generally straightforward for income flows to pass between the branch and the parent HQ, unless exchange control restrictions exist in the foreign country. There is no need for formal declaration of a dividend or any specific transaction for the branch to send profits to the UK.

h) Branch net profit is taxable in the UK, whether or not it is remitted to the UK.

As noted in chapter 18, Finance Bill 2011 contains a new election, allowing a UK company to opt out of having its overseas branches' income and expenses included in its taxable worldwide profits. If the opt-out is made it is irrevocable. It also means the losses of overseas branches can no longer reduce UK profits by aggregation and that overseas tax paid by the branch will not be available for DTR. Capital allowances will no longer be available on branch assets.

This new election will alter the commercial and financial choices from 2011 available to companies that have to choose between expanding overseas using a trading branch, and expanding by means of a newly-incorporated or purchased subsidiary company.

Foreign subsidiaries of UK companies

12. The above tax features of trading through a foreign branch may be contrasted with the position where a separate foreign company is incorporated or acquired by a UK company to handle its trade in a foreign country. In that case:

a) The profits of the overseas company will not be subject to UK corporation tax, unless it establishes a taxable presence in the UK (or it is a CFC – see (h) below).

b) Any foreign taxation paid by the overseas company on its profits (i.e. direct taxes) is not relievable in the UK against UK tax.

c) Any dividends paid by the subsidiary out of taxed profits will be tax free dividend income of the parent in the UK, but not augmented profits (because it is group FII).

d) The transactions of the foreign subsidiary with the UK parent may be subject to tax transfer pricing rules to prevent distortion of profits (but not to UK rules, if the companies count as SMEs).

d) Capital allowances are not available in the UK for plant and machinery of the subsidiary company.

e) Net tax losses of the overseas subsidiary cannot be surrendered as group relief (except under the limited circumstances of the Marks and Spencer case if it is located in the EEA.) (See chapter 24, section 4.)

f) The subsidiary company will count as an extra associated company for the purposes of the small profits rate of CT.

g) Payments from the subsidiary company to the UK parent in the form of purchases of goods and services, management charges, rent or interest payments will be taxable income in the UK. However they will probably be allowable costs in the foreign country against profits taxed there.

h) If the subsidiary is located in a low tax area as defined, then it may be a CFC unless one of the exempting tests is satisfied.

Restrictions for UK companies on allowable interest – "worldwide debt cap" rules

13. The UK tax authorities have become concerned that global groups can take advantage of the leading role of London as a centre for debt finance, and the higher rates of CT in the UK than in some other countries, to borrow money in London which the group does not actually need to borrow, viewed at the world level.

In theory, surplus funds could be borrowed in the UK, with full UK tax relief on the interest at 26%, and then advanced to group companies outside the UK at a lower rate of interest than is being paid in the UK. The borrowed funds, or the profits and trading returns that they generate, may never come back to the UK but may remain as group cash deposited in a low tax country.

To deal with this, concern, UK companies belonging to groups over a certain size are subject to a new "worldwide debt cap" test on their UK interest costs, effective from the first accounting period beginning on or after 1 January 2010. The final UK debt cap rules were enacted in 2009, after extensive consultation. It is likely that they will be further amended as the system beds down.

The basic rule is that a UK company over a certain size, and with over a certain level of borrowings, will not be able to deduct its borrowing costs in UK corporation tax computations to the extent that these costs exceed the total borrowing cost of the group worldwide for the same period, as shown in the consolidated accounts of the group.

There are exceptions for banks and insurance companies and other detailed additional rules.

Like the CFC rules discussed at 8 above it is likely that the new "debt cap" rule for UK-deductible interest will act more as a deterrent to certain group financing structures than as a measurable revenue raiser for the UK Government.

Student self-testing questions

1. Dingbat Ltd forecasts a tax-adjusted trading profit of £1,200,000 for the year ended 31 October 2012. Its directors are not expecting that it will earn any non-trading income or gains in the year. It has no associated companies.

Dingbat Ltd is planning to set up an overseas trading operation. The directors are unsure whether to set up a branch of Dingbat Ltd or a separate wholly-owned overseas company. In either case, the profit in the first accounting period would be the same, £140,000, and the overseas tax due on this profit would be £35,000. The overseas company would remit a dividend of half of its profit after tax.

Required:

Calculate the projected UK corporation tax liability of Dingbat Ltd and show the total tax paid out of the overseas profits (foreign and UK) for the year to 31 October 2012, after any available double tax relief:

(a) if the new operation is set up as an overseas branch, but no election is made to exclude the branch from Uk taxation;

(b) if the operation is set up as an overseas subsidiary.

(Assume that corporation tax rates and limits will be the same in Financial Year 2012 as in Financial Year 2011.)

Solution:

(a) Overseas branch: Corporation tax liability of Dingbat Ltd:

		£
Trading profits	UK operation	1,200,000
	Branch operation	140,000
Taxable total profit		1,340,000
Upper limit (12 mths)	1,500,000	
Lower limit (12 mths)	300,000	
Corporation Tax	At 26% x £1,340k	348,400
Less Marginal relief	(1.5m-1.34m) x 3 / 200 x 1	(2,400)
UK CT	(effective rate 346/1340 = 25.8%)	346,000
Less double tax relief :	Check : 35k/140k = 25% which is less than 25.8% so no restriction on DTR	(35,000)
UK CT liability		311,000
Additional overseas tax liability		35,000
		346,000
Total tax on overseas profits	(25.8% x 140,000))	36,120

(b) Overseas subsidiary: CT liability of Dingbat Ltd

		£
Trading profits	UK company	1,200,000
	[Foreign dividend income is exempted]	
Taxable total profit		1,200,000
Upper limit (2 cos)	750,000	
Lower limit	150,000	
UK Corporation Tax	26% x £1200k	312,000
Additional overseas tax liability		35,000
		347,000
Total tax on overseas profits		35,000

Questions without answer

1. T Ltd, a UK company, owns 20% of A Inc, a foreign resident company. T Ltd has the following results for the year ended 31st March 2012:

	£
Trading profits	2,000,000
Chargeable gains	66,000
Overseas income :	
Dividend received from A Inc, net of 15% withholding taxes	85,000
Interest received from A Inc, net of 20% withholding taxes	160,000
Debenture interest paid (trading, gross)	140,000
Dividend paid	500,000

Compute the CT payable by T Ltd for the AP to 31st March 2012.

2. Wash plc is a UK resident company that manufactures kitchen equipment. The company's trading profit for the year ended 31 March 2012 is £1,600,000. Wash plc has a 100% owned subsidiary, Dry Inc. that is resident overseas. Dry Inc. sells kitchen equipment manufactured by Wash plc. The results for Dry Inc. for the year ended 31 March 2012 are as follows:

	£	£
Trading profit		580,000
Corporation tax		160,000
		420,000
Dividend paid – net	270,000	
– withholding tax	30,000	300,000
Retained profits		120,000

Dry Inc.'s dividend was paid during the year ended 31 March 2012. The company's overseas corporation tax liability for the year ended 31 March 2012 was £8,000 more than that provided for in the accounts.

All of the above figures are in pounds sterling.

i) **Calculate Wash plc's corporation tax liability for the year ended 31 March 2012.**

ii) **Explain the tax implications if Wash plc were to invoice Dry Inc. for the exported kitchen equipment at a price that was less than the market price.**

(ACCA)

End of section questions and answers

1. Threadbare Ltd is a manufacturer of quality clothing which makes its accounts up to the 31st March each year.

Its trading and profit and loss account for the year ended 31st March 2012, its centenary year, is as follows:

	£	£
Sales		7,873,150
Cost of sales		7,311,180
Gross profit		561,970
Add miscellaneous income		51,420
		613,390
Less expenses:		
Salaries	47,050	
Rent rates and insurance	16,500	
Lighting and heating	12,910	
Motor expenses	74,020	
Repairs and renewals	100,110	
General expenses	81,170	
Depreciation	54,830	
Debenture interest paid (trading, gross)	75,000	
		461,590
Profit before taxation		151,800

You are given the following information:

1. Miscellaneous income comprises:

	£
Profit on sale of plant and machinery	15,420
Dividend from UK non group company received 15.6.11	9,000
Building society interest received gross, non trade	18,000
Bank interest received gross, non trade	9,000
	51,420

2. Repairs and renewals comprise:

	£
Repairs to new premises, needed to make them usable	25,020
Portable office partitioning	25,090
New photocopiers	50,000
	100,110

3. General expenses comprise:

	£
Bad debts written off	11,230
Increase in general bad debt provision	10,000

Legal costs of renewal of lease for 20 years	5,570
Entertaining	15,320
Promotional gifts of bottles of wine	20,550
Gift aid payment	1,000
Theatre outing for staff	17,500
	81,170

4. Capital allowances in respect of all qualifying expenditure have been agreed at £18,190.

5. The debenture interest received is in respect of a trade loan.

   a) Compute the Taxable Total Profit.

   b) Calculate the Corporation Tax liability.

Solution: Threadbare Ltd AP to 31st March 2012

Adjustment of trading profits	**£**	**£**
Profit before taxation		151,800
Add back:		
Repairs to make premises usable	25,020	
Office partitioning	25,090	
New microcomputers	50,000	
Increase in general bad debt provision	10,000	
Entertaining	15,320	
Promotional gifts of wine	20,550	
Gift aid	1,000	
Depreciation	54,830	
Debenture interest	75,000	276,810
		428,610
Less non-trading income		(51,420)
		377,190

Corporation tax computation AP to 31st March 2012

	£	**£**
Adjusted trading profits	377,190	
Less: capital allowances	(18,190)	359,000
Non-trading loan deficit (75,000 – 27,000)		(48,000)
Total profits		311,000
Qualifying charitable donations: Gift aid		(1,000)
Taxable total profit		310,000
Corporation tax payable:		
310,000 @ 26 %		80,600
Marginal relief		
(1,500,000 – 320,000) x 310,000 / 320,000 x 3/200		(1,171)
		£79,429

Notes

i) Non-trading loan deficit is:

Debenture interest payable	75,000
Less interest receivable	(27,000)
	48,000

ii) F11 of £10,000 (9,000 x 10/9) makes the augmented profits £320,000 so marginal relief applies.

2. Andrell Ltd was incorporated on 1st April 1991 and has always prepared accounts to the 31st March each year. The directors have now decided to change the accounting date to the 30th June and the accounts for the 15 months to the 30th June 2011 are as follows:

	£	£
Sales		485,000
Cost of sales		(307,690)
Gross profit		177,310
Add: Bank deposit interest receivable (note 1)	3,450	
Rents receivable (note 2)	1,000	
Profit on sale of plant (note 3)	6,000	10,450
	187,760	
Deduct: Wages and salaries	43,000	
Light and heat 23,000		
Legal and professional charges (note 4)	1,860	
Depreciation 3,000		
Bad debts (note 5)	4,600	
Debenture interest (gross) (note 6)	11,250	
Rent and rates 10,000	96,710	
	91,050	

Andrell Ltd has no associates and the following information is given in relation to the above accounts.

1. The bank short-term interest was earned quarterly and received on the following dates:

	£
30th June 2010	1,200
31st December 2010	1,850
30th June 2011	400

2. On the 1st June 2011 the company negotiated to rent out part of its storage facilities, the annual rent of £1,000 being payable in advance on the 10th June. Due to an industrial dispute however, the first rent payment was not received until the 10th July 2011.

3. An extract from the asset disposal account relating to the sale of plant showed:

	£
Cost (purchased 1st March 2010)	12,000
Less accumulated depreciation	2,500
	9,500
Sale proceeds (sold 12th February 2011)	15,500
Profit on sale	6,000

The chargeable gain on the plant sale has been computed at £2,300.

4. The legal and professional charges were made up of:

	£
Accountancy charge re annual audit	1,500
Accountancy charge for negotiating successful tax appeal	150
Legal charge for negotiating successful rates appeal	210
	1,860

5. Bad debts account comprises:

	£
Increase in specific provision	1,800
Increase in general provision	2,000
Bad debts written off	1,200
	5,000
Less bad debts recovered	(400)
	4,600

6. The debenture interest payable related to an issue of debentures for trade purposes, the interest on which is payable half yearly on 30th June and 31 December and the accounts include an accrual of £2,500 as at the 30 June 2011.

The company had a pool balance brought forward for plant and machinery of £276,000 and the only capital additions during the period of account were:

	£
1st December 2010 purchased new plant	3,000
1st May 2010 purchased 16 cars for use by the company salespeople, each car costing £12,000	192,000

(CO_2 emissions of all cars <160g/km)

The salespeople are allowed to make private use of their cars.

Compute the corporation tax payable. Assume that all allowances and reliefs are claimed as early as possible.

Solution: Andrell Ltd period of account 15 months to 30.6.2011

Adjustment of profits	**£**	**£**
Net profit per accounts		91,050
Add back: Legal and professional fees	150	
Depreciation	3,000	
Bad debts	2,000	
		5,150
		96,200
Less non-trading income:		
Bank deposit interest	3,450	
Rents receivable	1,000	
Profit on sale of plant	6,000	(10,450)
Trading profit before capital allowances		85,750

Corporation tax computation

	CTAP	
	12 months to 31.3.2011	**3 months to 30.6.2011**
	£	**£**
Adjusted profits 12/15 × 85,750	68,600	
3/15 × 85,750		17,150
Less capital allowances(see working)	(55,800)	(20,160)
Trading profits/(loss)	12,800	(3,010)
Interest income	3,050	400
Income from land and property	–	1,000
	18,850	1,400
Chargeable gain	2,300	-
Total profits	18,150	1,400
Less Section 37 claim (total 3,010)	(1,610)	(1,400)
Taxable total profits	16,540	NIL
Corporation tax @ 21% FY 2010	3,473	

		AP to 31.3.11	AP to 30.6.11
		£	£
Capital allowances			
Pool balance b/f		276,000	211,200
Proceeds of sale (restricted to cost)/additions		(12,000)	192,000
		264,000	403,200
WD allowance 20%	52,800	20% × $\frac{1}{4}$	20,160
		211,200	
AIA addition	3,000		
AIA 100%	3,000	nil	
Balance c/f		211,200	383,040

Summary of allowances		**AP 31.3.11**	**AP 30.6.11**
Plant and machinery WDA		52,800	20,160
	AIA	3,000	–
Motor cars	WDA	–	–
		55,800	20,160

Notes

i) The loss of £3,010 is partly carried back to the accounting period to 31.3.2011 under Section 37.

ii) As the motor vehicles have a CO_2 rating of <160 g/km each they belong in the general pool (private use is irrelevant for the company's capital allowances but could impact on the salesmen's own income tax position).

iii) Debenture interest payable for trade purposes is allowed in computing trading income.

iv) Only the adjusted profit **before** capital allowances is time-apportioned.

3. XYZ Ltd has a 100% subsidiary, PQR Ltd, and each company prepares its accounts annually for the year ended 31st March.

The following are summarised results of each company for the year ended 31st March 2012:

	XYZ Ltd	**PQR Ltd**
	£	£
Adjusted trading profit/(loss) before capital allowances	279,600	(112,000)
Deposit interest received	4,000	2,000
Chargeable gains/(losses)	7,900	(4,000)
Capital allowances	2,400	1,800

XYZ Ltd has a capital loss brought forward of £2,700.

a) Show how the losses of PQR Ltd may be most effectively utilised, assuming that it is not expected to make a profit for several years.

b) Calculate the corporation tax payable by XYZ Ltd.

c) State with reasons what tax benefit if any could may be obtained by ABC Ltd from the capital loss of PQR Ltd. (CIMA, adapted)

Solution

a) **Corporation tax computation AP. 31.3.2012**

	£	XYZ Ltd £	PQR Ltd £
Adjusted Trading profit	279,600		–
Less capital allowances	(2,400)	277,200	
Interest income		4,000	2,000
		281,200	2,000
Chargeable gain	7,900		
Less losses b/f	(2,700)	5,200	–
		286,400	2,000
Total profits before loss reliefs		286,400	–
Less S37 claim			(2,000)
Less group relief Section 130		(111,800)	
Taxable total profit		174,600	–

b) **Corporation tax payable by ABC Ltd:**

£174,600 @ 26% =	45,396
Less Marginal relief:	
(750,000 – 174,600) x 1 (=174,600/174,600) × 3/200	
= 575,400 × 3/200	(8,631)
CT Liability	36,765
Loss memorandum: PQR Ltd	
Trading loss	112,000
Add capital allowances	1,800
	113,800
S37 current year own claim	(2,000)
Group relief to ABC Ltd	(111,800)

Notes

1) Small profits limits for two companies : 1,500,000/2 = 750,000 and 300,000/2 = 150,000

2) The capital loss incurred by PQR Ltd cannot be surrendered to XYZ Ltd as group relief. It can either be carried forward and set against future gains incurred by PQR Ltd, or else, as there is a CGT group relationship it would be possible for the two companies to elect for the matching of the gain in XYZ Ltd against the loss in PQR Ltd. The position would then be :

	£
ABC Ltd Net gains per computation	5,200
Transferred by election to PQR Ltd	(4,000)
	1,200

Questions without answers

1. Zoom plc

Zoom plc is a manufacturer of photographic equipment. The company had profits chargeable to corporation tax of £860,000 for the year ended 31 March 2012. The summarised profit and loss account of Zoom plc for the year ended 31 March 2012 is as follows:

	£	£
Operating profit (note 1)		812,500
Other operating income (note 4)	16,400	
Income from investments		
Bank interest (note 5)	10,420	
Loan interest (note 6)	22,500	
Income from property (note 7)	44,680	
Dividends (note 8)	49,500	
Total other income		127,100
		956,000
Interest payable (note 9)		46,000
Profit before taxation		910,000

Note 1 – Operating profit

Depreciation of £48,100 has been deducted in arriving at the operating profit of £812,500.

Note 2 – Plant and machinery

On 1 April 2010 the tax written down values of plant and machinery were as follows:

	£
General pool	19,600
Motor car CO_2 180g/km (purchased 1 April 2010)	20,200
Short-life asset (2 years old)	36,000

The following transactions took place during the year ended 31 March 2012:

		Cost/(Proceeds) £
15 April 2011	Purchased equipment	4,600
19 June 2011	Purchased a computer	2,280
29 July 2011	Sold the motor car	(24,200)
31 July 2011	Purchased motor car CO_2 150g/km (1)	16,600

3 August 2011	Sold a lorry	(9,800)
22 December 2011	Purchased motor car CO_2 140g/km (2)	10,800
1 February 2012	Purchased motor car (3)	14,200
28 February 2012	Sold the short-life asset	(8000)

The motor car sold on 29 July 2011 for £24,200 originally cost £23,400. The lorry sold on 3 August 2011 for £9,800 originally cost £17,200. Motor car (3) purchased on 1 February 2012 is a low emission motor car (CO_2 emission rate of less than 110 grams per kilometre).

Note 3 – Corporation Tax information

Zoom plc made quarterly instalment payments in respect of its corporation tax liability for the year ended 31 March 2012.

Zoom plc has three associated companies.

For the year ended 31 March 2011, Zoom plc had profits chargeable to corporation tax of £780,000.

Note 4 – Other operating income

The other operating income consists of patent royalties that were received gross during the year ended 31 March 2012. They relate to a process that the company invented.

Note 5 – Bank interest received

The bank interest was received on 31 March 2012 and there was no accrual brought forward or carried forward. The bank deposits are held for non-trading purposes.

Note 6 – Loan interest receivable

The loan was made for non-trading purposes on 1 July 2011. Loan interest of £15,000 was received on 31 December 2011, and interest of £7,500 was accrued at 31 March 2012.

Note 7 – Income from property

Zoom plc lets out two unfurnished office buildings that are surplus to requirements.

The first office building was let from 1 April 2011 until 31 January 2012 at a rent of £3,200 per month. On 31 January 2012 the tenant left owing two months rent which Zoom plc was unable to recover. This office building was not re-let until May 2012.

The second office building was not let from 1 April 2011 to 31 July 2011. During this period Zoom plc spent £4,800 on advertising for new tenants, and £5,200 on decorating the office building. On 1 August 2011 the office building was let at an annual rent of £26,400, payable in advance.

Zoom plc insured its two office buildings at a total cost of £3,360 for the year ended 31 December 2011, and £3,720 for the year ended 31 December 2012. The insurance is payable annually in advance.

Note 8 – Dividends received

The dividends were all received from unconnected UK companies. The figure of £49,500 is the actual cash amount received.

Note 9 – Interest payable

The interest is in respect of a debenture loan that has been used for trading purposes. Interest of £23,000 was paid on 30 September 2011 and again on 31 March 2012.

Required:

(a) (i) Calculate the amount of capital allowances that Zoom plc can claim for the year ended 31 March 2012. (12 marks)

(ii) Prepare a computation for the year ended 31 March 2012 reconciling Zoom plc's profit before taxation with its profits chargeable to corporation tax. Your reconciliation should commence with the profit before taxation figure of £910,000, clearly identify the tax adjusted trading profit and the amount of profit from land and property, and end with the figure of profits chargeable to corporation tax. (8 marks)

(b) Explain why Zoom plc was required to make quarterly instalment payments in respect of its corporation tax liability for the year ended 31 March 2012. (3 marks)

(c) Calculate Zoom plc's corporation tax liability for the year ended 31 March 2012, and explain how and when this will have been paid. You should assume that the company's profits chargeable to corporation tax accrued evenly throughout the year. (3 marks)

(d) Explain how your answer to part (c) above would differ if Zoom plc had no associated companies. Your answer should include a calculation of the revised corporation tax liability for the year ended 31 March 2012. (4 marks)

(30 marks)

(ACCA December 2004 updated)

2. Scuba Ltd

Scuba Ltd is a manufacturer of diving equipment. The following information is relevant for the year ended 31 December 2011:

Operating profit

The operating profit is £162,400. The expenses that have been deducted in calculating this figure include the following:

	£
Depreciation and amortisation	45,200
Entertaining customers	7,410
Entertaining employees	2,470

Gifts to customers	
(diaries costing £25 each displaying Scuba Ltd's name)	1,350
Gifts to customers (food hampers costing £80 each)	1,600

Leasehold property

On 1 April 2011 Scuba Ltd acquired a leasehold office building that is used for business purposes. The company paid a premium of £80,000 for the grant of a twenty-year lease.

Plant and machinery

On 1 January 2011 the tax written down values of plant and machinery were as follows:

	£
General pool	47,200
Ford car CO_2 190g/km	22,400
Features integral to a building	105,000

The following transactions took place during the year ended 31 December 2011:

		(Cost/Proceeds)
		£
3 April 2011	Purchased machinery	7,300
10 April 2011	Purchased a computer	1,400
4 May 2011	Purchased a Skoda car CO_2 180g/km	10,400
18 August 2011	Purchased machinery	14,800
1 September 2011	Purchased a ventilation system (a feature integral to a building)	10,150
29 September 2011	Purchased computer software	1,100
15 November 2011	Sold a lorry	(12,400)

The Skoda car purchased on 4 May 2011 for £10,400 is used by the factory manager, and 40% of the mileage is for private journeys. The lorry sold on 15 November 2011 for £12,400 originally cost £19,800.

Income from property

Scuba Ltd lets a retail shop that is surplus to requirements. The shop was let until 31 December 2010 but was then empty from 1 January 2011 to 30 April 2011. During this period Scuba Ltd spent £6,200 on decorating the shop, and £1,700 on advertising for new tenants. The shop was let from 1 May 2011 to 31 December 2011 at a quarterly rent of £7,200, payable in advance.

Interest received

Interest of £435 was received from HMRC on 31 October 2011 in respect of the overpayment of corporation tax for the year ended 31 December 2010.

Profit on disposal of shares

On 8 November 2011 Scuba Ltd sold 5,000 £1 ordinary shares in Deep Blue Sea plc for £42,400. The shareholding had been purchased on 19 March 2007 for

£26,900. The retail prices index (RPI) for March 2007 was 204.4, and for November 2011 it was 236.8 (estimated).

Other information

Scuba Ltd has no associated companies and has always had an accounting date of 31 December.

Required:

(a) Calculate Scuba Ltd's tax adjusted trading profit for the year ended 31 December 2011. You should assume that no other adjustments are required to the operating profit except in respect of the expenses that have been deducted. (21 marks)

(b) Calculate Scuba Ltd's corporation tax liability for the year ended 31 December 2011. (6 marks)

(c) State the date by which Scuba Ltd must pay its corporation tax liability for the year ended 31 December 2011, and explain the implications for the company if this liability is paid three months late.

(3 marks)

(30 marks)

(ACCA December 2005 updated)

3. Tock Tick

Tock-Tick Ltd is a clock manufacturer. The company's summarised profit and loss account for the year ended 31 March 2012 is as follows:

	£
Gross profit	822,280
Operating expenses	
Bad debts (note 1)	9,390
Depreciation	99,890
Gifts and donations (note 2)	3,090
Professional fees (note 3)	12,400
Repairs and renewals (note 4)	128,200
Other expenses (note 5)	426,920
Total expenses	679,890
Operating profit	142,390
Profit from sale of fixed assets	
Disposal of office building (note 6)	78,100
Income from investments	
Loan interest (note 7)	12,330
	232,820
Interest payable (note 8)	48,600
Profit before taxation	184,220

Note 1 – Bad debts

Bad debts are as follows:	£
Trade debts recovered from previous years	(1,680)
Trade debts written off	7,970
Decrease in specific bad debt provision	(3,100)
Increase in general provision for doubtful debts	6,200
	9,390

Note 2 – Gifts and donations

Gifts and donations are as follows:	£
Gifts to customers (pens costing £45 each displaying Tock-Tick Ltd's name)	1,080
Gifts to customers (food hampers costing £30 each)	720
Long service award to an employee	360
Donation to a national charity (made under the gift aid scheme)	600
Donation to a national charity (not made under the gift aid scheme)	250
Donation to a local charity (Tock-Tick Ltd received free advertising in the charity's magazine)	80
	3,090

Note 3 – Professional fees

Professional fees are as follows:	£
Accountancy and audit fee	5,400
Legal fees in connection with the issue of share capital	2,900
The cost of registering the company's trademark	800
Legal fees in connection with the renewal of a 35-year property lease	1,300
Debt collection	1,100
Legal fees in connection with a court action for not complying with health and safety legislation	900
	12,400

Note 4 – Repairs and renewals

The figure of £128,200 for repairs and renewals includes £41,800 for replacing the roof of an office building, which was in a bad state of repair, and £53,300 for extending the office building.

Note 5 – Other expenses

Other expenses include £2,160 for entertaining suppliers; £880 for counselling services provided to two employees who were made redundant; and the cost of seconding an employee to a charity of £6,400. The remaining expenses are all fully allowable.

Note 6 – Disposal of office building

The profit of £78,100 is in respect of a freehold office building that was sold on 20 February 2012 for £276,000.

The office building was purchased on 18 November 2001 for £197,900. Assume the indexation allowance from November 2001 to February 2012 is £68,700.

The building has always been used by Tock-Tick Ltd for trading purposes.

Note 7 – Loan interest received

The loan interest is in respect of a loan that was made on 1 July 2011. Interest of £8,280 was received on 31 December 2011, and interest of £4,050 was accrued at 31 March 2012. The loan was made for non-trading purposes.

Note 8 – Interest payable

The interest payable is in respect of a debenture loan that is used for trading purposes. Interest of £24,300 was paid on 30 September 2011 and again on 31 March 2012.

Note 9 - Plant and machinery

On 1 April 2011 the tax written down values of plant and machinery were as follows:

	£
General pool	12,200
Renault car CO_2 170g/km (purchased May 2010)	20,800
Short-life asset	3,100

The following transactions took place during the year ended 31 March 2012:

	Cost/(Proceeds)
	£
28 May 2011 Sold the Renault car CO_2 170g/km	(34,800)
7 June 2011 Purchased a Honda car	14,400
1 August 2011 Sold the short-life asset	(460)
15 August 2011 Purchased equipment	6,700

The Renault car sold on 28 May 2011 for £34,800 originally cost £33,600. The Honda car purchased on 7 June 2011 is a low emission motor car (CO_2 emission rate of less than 110 grams per kilometre).

Required:

(a) Calculate Tock-Tick Ltd's tax adjusted Trading profit for the year ended 31 March 2012. Your computation should commence with the profit before taxation figure of £184,220. (19 marks)

(b) Calculate Tock-Tick Ltd's profits chargeable to corporation tax for the year ended 31 March 2012. (5 marks)

(c) State the effect on Tock-Tick Ltd's profits chargeable to corporation tax for the year ended 31 March 2012 if Tock-Tick Ltd had claimed the maximum possible group relief from a 100% owned subsidiary company that had made a trading loss of £62,400 for the year ended 31 December 2011. (4 marks)

(28 marks)

(ACCA June 2005 updated)

Part IV

Taxation of chargeable gains

26 General principles

Introduction and brief history

1. UK Capital Gains Tax was originally brought in from the 6th April 1965. However, due to subsequent reforms and simplifications, on a disposal of an asset held since before April 1982, there is now an effective discount from the gain liable to tax, to the extent that this gain is identified by CGT rules as having accrued before 1 April 1982. This date is the same for both individuals and companies.

The basic principle of capital gains tax has always been that when an asset is sold, exchanged or gifted, any gain represented by the excess of the realised value over the historic cost is considered to be a taxable capital gain.

In 1982 indexation relief was introduced to take account of rising prices which were seen as causing inflationary gains to be unfairly taxed. Until 1988 the gains tax rate was lower than the top rates of IT and CT but from April 1988, individuals' CGT rates were aligned with income tax rates, and corporate capital gains were made subject to full corporation tax.

In 1998, indexation relief was abolished for individuals (with existing indexation allowances being frozen at 1998 values). However the indexation allowance in its previous form continued to apply to reduce corporate capital gains.

From 1998, the indexation allowance for individuals was replaced by CGT taper relief, with a varying percentage reduction of the gain's value, depending on the length of ownership of an asset and whether it was a business or non-business asset.

In 2008/09 both frozen indexation allowances and taper relief were abolished for individuals and replaced with a flat rate of capital gains tax of 18%. This represented a major simplification. A new relief was given for "entrepreneurs", giving a lower effective CGT rate of 10% on up to £1 million of gains from qualifying businesses and shares.

The first Budget of 2010, in March, proposed no change to CGT rules for 2010/11, except for a doubling of the lifetime limit for gains qualifying for entrepreneurs' relief, to £2 million.

However the second "Emergency" Budget of June 2010 introduced a split-year treatment for personal capital gains in tax year 2010/11, with a flat rate of 18% applying to gains up to 22 June 2010 and a higher rate of 28% applying to gains from 23 June 2010 only if the taxpayer is a higher rate taxpayer for income tax in 2010/11.

From 23 June 2010, the lifetime limit for entrepreneurs' relief was increased to £5 million and the mechanism for giving this relief changed to a simpler method.

For tax year 2011/12 (the subject of this book), the only further change to CGT is that the lifetime limit for entrepreneurs' relief is now £10 million.

There are still two different CGT rates for "non-entrepreneur" gains (28% and 18%), but only one (10%) for "entrepreneur" gains. Companies pay tax on chargeable gains (reduced for inflation) at their CT rate. As CT rates have fallen for FY2011 the burden of CGT has been shifted in 2011 more towards individuals and away from companies.

The existence of different personal CGT rates on different types of disposal necessitates allocation of the annual exemption to specific gains. The same applies to capital losses offsettable against capital gains. The reduction of the basic rate income tax band limit to £35,000 (from £37,400 the previous year) in 2011/12 means more taxpayers are exposed to CGT liability at 28% if they realise gains above the annual exemption and their incomes remain constant.

Legislation on the detailed computation of chargeable gains is in the Taxation of Chargeable Gains Act 1992, as amended.

However it is important to recognise that for individuals the regime is now very different than for companies, even though the rules are found in the same Act. One main difference is that individuals do not get adjustment of their CGT-allowable costs by inflation even if they have owned an asset for a long time. Companies do get this relief in the form of the indexation allowance (assuming there is some inflation). This difference could be significant depending on the length of time an asset is owned and the rate of inflation over that time.

2. **For individuals, including sole traders and partnerships:**

a) For gains realised on or after 6th April 2008 the basic computation of the chargeable gain is made by reference to the disposal proceeds less any allowable costs.

b) For disposals on and after 23 June 2010, including all disposals in 2011/12, personal capital gains are taxed as follows:

   i) at 18%, to the extent that they fall in the part of the individual's personal basic rate band for income tax for the tax year that has not been set against taxable income;

   ii) at 28%, to the extent that they exceed this limit.

   When either an individual or a company disposes of less than a total holding of identical shares (or chargeable securities) acquired piecemeal, there are detailed matching and pooling rules to determine the respective CGT "costs" of the part disposed of and of the part retained. For companies only, indexation allowance is available on such share gains. However, it is computed on pooled shares by a continuous method, slightly different from IA calculations on other disposals. See chapter 29.

For incorporated entities in FY2011 the summarised position is as follows:

a) Chargeable gains are calculated by reference to the disposal proceeds, less any allowable costs, and to the extent it does not increase or create a capital loss, a related indexation allowance on those costs. The resulting gain (less any losses) is included in total profits and tax is calculated on taxable total profit at the corporation's effective tax rate. For a large corporation the rate will be 26%, for a small corporation the rate will be 20%. For those corporations in the marginal rate band, the effective tax rate will be between 20% and 26% for the financial year 2011, calculated by taxing at full rate and deducting marginal relief (See part III).

b) Shares and securities are 'pooled' together and a weighted average cost is used to determine the allowable cost on disposal.

Persons chargeable

3. The following classes of persons are chargeable to capital gains tax:

Individuals and personal representatives

Companies, who pay corporation tax at the appropriate company rate

Trusts and trustees.

Rates of tax on capital gains 2011/12

4. Person	Exemption	Rate of tax
Individuals	£10,600	18% or 28% (See detailed comments in section 2 above)
		Chargeable gains that qualify for Entrepreneurs' Relief are taxed at a rate of 10% on the first £10 million.
Companies	Nil	Chargeable gains taxed at company corporation tax rate, i.e. small profits rate, marginal rate or full rate.

Chargeable assets

5. Under Sections 21 and 22 of the TCGA 1992 "all forms of property are assets for the purposes of capital gains tax, whether situated in the UK or not", including:

a) options, debts, and incorporeal property in general

(see section 6 below regarding application to companies)

b) currency other than sterling

(see section 6 below regarding application to companies)

c) any form of property created by the person disposing of it, or coming to be owned without being acquired

d) capital sums derived from assets.

Property

6. For individuals this term includes anything capable of being owned, such as freehold and leasehold land, shares and securities, and other tangible assets and intangible assets such as purchased and non-purchased goodwill. It also includes legal claims that have a value.

For companies the term "property" in principle includes the same things as for individuals. However, having said that, the chargeable gains regime for companies specifically does not cover transactions involving such "property" that are dealt with for corporation tax under the loan relationships rules or the intangible assets regime.

Companies' intangible fixed assets acquired after 31 March 2002 are outside the chargeable gains regime, and their debt relationships, including financial options and foreign currency deposits, are taxed as loan relationships, not as capital assets.

Options

7. Where a person (the grantor) grants an option over a chargeable asset to another person (the grantee) then this is a disposal by the first person of a chargeable asset, or alternatively the derivation of a capital sum from an asset. If the option is later exercised, any consideration received is added to any made with the initial grant, to form a single disposal transaction. If it is not exercised then the capital sum is taxable proceeds.

Where some types of option are abandoned, then this is not a disposal by the grantee, so that he or she cannot establish a capital loss. However if the option was over equity shares or was an exchange-traded option (not held as part of a trading activity), TCGA allows a capital loss in certain circumstances. For companies, any transactions in options or other derivatives (eg swaps) relating to underlying debt arrangements are taxed as loan relationships. However equity share options come under the chargeable gains regime for companies.

Debts

8. The original CGT rules on debts are now limited to individuals in their application as no loan relationship can be a chargeable asset for a company.

An ordinary debt is not a chargeable asset in the hands of the original creditor, his or her personal representative or legatee.

However, an individual who acquires a debt for value, say by an assignment, obtains a chargeable asset and if it is later redeemed at a lower value a capital loss may be claimed.

Also, a loan to a UK resident trader, or a payment by way of guarantee of such a loan, if irrecoverable, can be claimed by an individual as an allowable capital loss.

UK Government securities (gilts and bonds) owned by individuals or trustees are specifically exempted from CGT.

Incorporeal property

9. This is other intangible property such as a tithe or easement, or a right to exploit a copyright. For companies the corporate intangible assets regime takes priority.

Currency

10. Any currency other than sterling is in principle a chargeable asset for an individual (the capital gain or loss arises from the exchange difference, compared with is sterling cost, when it is reconverted to sterling). However there is a useful exemption for foreign currency "acquired by an individual for personal use", so only holdings of an investment nature or unrelated to personal travel are chargeable assets in practice .

Created property – intangible fixed assets

11. For individuals this term includes such assets as goodwill, copyright, trademarks or know-how as chargeable assets. For the corporation tax treatment of intangible fixed assets see Chapter 18.

Patents are not chargeable assets since any excess over cost realised on a sale is taxed as patent income under ITTOIA 2005.

For an individual, business "know-how" is treated as a chargeable asset where disposed of along with any part of a trade, but not if disposed of alone when it gives rise to a trading receipt.

Capital sums

12. These are defined to include:

a) Any capital sums received by way of compensation for any kind of damage or injury to assets, or for the loss, destruction or dissipation of assets, or for any depreciation of an asset

b) Capital sums received under a policy of insurance of the risks of any kind of damage or injury to, or the loss or depreciation of assets.

c) Capital sums received in return for forfeiture or surrender of rights, or for refraining from exercising rights.

d) Capital sums received as consideration for use or exploitation of assets.

When a person derives any capital sum from an asset, then the part-disposal of the chargeable asset occurs. If any part of the amount received is used to restore or replace the original asset then special reliefs apply. (See Chapter 31).

Non-chargeable assets and exemptions

13. The following assets are either exempt assets, or chargeable assets on whose disposal there may not be a chargeable gain or loss because of specific circumstances.

a) Private motor vehicles.

This includes private cars and vintage cars purchased for investment.

b) Savings certificates.

All non-marketable securities are included under this heading such as National Savings Certificates, and Defence Bonds.

c) Gambling winnings.

This covers winnings from pools, lotteries, premium bonds and bingo prizes.

d) Decorations for valour.

These are exempt assets if disposed of by the individual to whom they were awarded, or their legatee. If purchased by anyone else they become chargeable assets.

e) Currency.

As already noted, foreign currency acquired for personal use is exempt.

f) Compensation.

Any compensation or damages obtained for any physical wrong or injury suffered by a person, or in connection with his or her profession or vocation.

g) Life assurance and deferred annuities.

No chargeable gain arises on the disposal of any rights under a life assurance policy or deferred annuity, providing the disposal is made by the original owner. The acquisition of such rights from an original owner gives an individual acquirer a chargeable asset

h) British government securities and "qualifying corporate bonds" are exempt when held by individuals. (The same investments held by corporate investors fall under the loan relationship rules).

i) Principal private residence of an individual . (See Chapter 28).

j) Chattels bought and sold for less than £6,000 . (See Chapter 28).

k) Assets gifted to a recognised charity.

l) Certain disposals conditionally exempt from IHT e.g. works of art.

m) Wasting chattels , ie Tangible moveable property with useful life of less than 50 years, not used for trade purposes.

Exempt persons

14. The under-mentioned persons are exempted from capital gains tax:

a) Pension funds approved by HMRC.

b) Registered charities providing the gains are used for charitable purposes.

c) Registered friendly societies.

d) Local authorities.

e) Scientific research associations.

f) Community amateur sports clubs.

Administration

15. A section of the self assessment tax return is available for individual taxpayers to notify HMRC of chargeable gains. Appeals against HMRC decisions can be made through the Tribunal System (See Chapter 3: 11).

Payment of tax

16. Capital gains tax is due when the final balancing payment is made under the income tax rules for self assessment, as described in Chapter 2. The due date is as follows:

2011/12	-	31st January 2013
2010/11	-	31st January 2012

It is possible to pay capital gains tax by instalments where the consideration is payable over a period exceeding 18 months, and payment of capital gains tax in one sum would cause undue hardship. Payment of tax by ten equal instalments is also available in respect of tax due on gifts not eligible for holdover relief (See Chapter 32).

Rebasing

17. Rebasing is only relevant to corporations that have held an asset prior to 31st March 1982, which was when the indexation system was introduced. The base date was changed from the 6th April 1965 to the 31st March 1982 and for disposals after the 5th April 1988 only gains or losses accruing from 31st March 1982 need be brought into charge to tax.

For assets held on 31st March 1982 re-basing means that the asset is assumed to be sold and immediately re-acquired on 31st March 1982 at that date.

In general, if the gain under the re-basing method is greater than it would be under the 'old rules' then the latter may be used. The taxpayer can make a once and for all election that all gains and losses acquired before 31st March 1982 are to be computed by reference to the 31st March 1982 re-basing method. In practice most assets that are re-valued with reference to the rebased amount will produce a lower gain, therefore the rebased amount will normally be used.

Indexation – Incorporated entities

18. Assets acquired before 31st March 1982 can be re-valued at 31st March 1982 and that value substituted for the initial cost plus incidental expenses, under the re-basing principle.

The indexation allowance is calculated by reference to changes in the Retail Prices Index which was re-based to 100 in January 1987.

Where an asset was held on the 31st March 1982 then indexation allowance is automatically based on the higher of the original cost or market value at 31st March 1982.

Indexation cannot be used to create or increase a capital loss.

Layouts for capital gain or loss computations – companies and individuals

19. I. Chargeable assets held by incorporated entities y/e 31.03.12 **FY 2011**

	£	£
Gross consideration or market value		–
Less: Incidental costs of disposal		–
Net proceeds of disposal		–
Allowable deductions:		
Initial cost of asset plus incidental purchase expenses	–	
Enhancement expenditure (not repairs)	–	
	–	
Unindexed gain		–
Less: Indexation Relief – On initial cost etc		–
On enhancement expenditure		–
(note: indexation relief cannot create or augment a capital loss)		
Chargeable gain added to TTP		–

		2011/12
		£
II. Chargeable assets held by individuals		
Gross consideration (or market value if connected party/gift)		
Less: Incidental costs of disposal		–
Allowable deductions–		
Initial cost of asset plus incidental expenses	–	
Enhancement expenditure (not repairs)	–	
		–
Chargeable gain subject to capital gains tax		

20. Retail Prices Index

RPI	Jan	Feb	Mar	April	May	June	July	Aug	Sept	Oct	Nov	Dec
1982	–	–	79.44	81.04	81.62	81.85	81.88	81.90	81.85	82.26	82.66	82.51
1983	82.61	82.97	83.12	84.28	84.64	84.84	85.30	85.68	86.06	86.36	86.67	86.89
1984	86.84	87.20	87.48	88.64	88.97	89.20	89.10	89.94	90.11	90.67	90.95	90.87
1985	91.20	91.94	92.80	94.78	95.21	95.41	95.23	95.49	95.44	95.59	95.92	96.05
1986	96.25	96.60	96.73	97.67	97.85	97.79	97.52	97.82	98.30	98.45	99.29	99.62
1987	100.00	100.4	100.6	101.8	101.9	101.9	101.8	102.1	102.4	102.9	103.4	103.3
1988	103.3	103.7	104.1	105.8	106.2	106.6	106.7	107.9	108.4	109.5	110.0	110.3
1989	111.0	111.8	112.3	114.3	115.0	115.4	115.5	115.8	116.6	117.5	118.5	118.8
1990	119.5	120.2	121.4	125.1	126.2	126.7	126.8	128.1	129.3	130.3	130.0	129.9
1991	130.2	130.9	131.4	133.1	133.5	134.1	133.8	134.1	134.6	135.1	135.6	135.7
1992	135.6	136.3	136.7	138.8	139.3	139.3	138.8	138.9	139.4	139.9	139.7	139.2
1993	137.9	138.8	139.3	140.6	141.1	141.0	140.7	141.3	141.9	141.8	141.6	141.9
1994	141.3	142.1	142.5	144.2	144.7	144.7	144.0	144.7	145.0	145.2	145.3	146.0
1995	146.0	146.9	147.5	149.0	149.6	149.8	149.1	149.9	150.6	149.8	149.8	150.7
1996	150.2	150.9	151.5	152.6	152.9	153.0	152.4	153.1	153.8	153.8	153.9	154.4
1997	154.4	155.0	155.4	156.3	156.9	157.5	157.5	158.5	159.3	159.5	159.6	160.0
1998	159.5	160.3	160.8	162.6	163.5	163.4	163.0	163.7	164.4	164.5	164.4	164.4
1999	163.4	163.7	164.1	165.2	165.6	165.6	165.1	165.5	166.2	166.5	166.7	167.3
2000	166.6	167.5	168.4	170.1	170.7	171.1	170.5	170.5	171.7	171.6	172.1	172.2
2001	171.1	172.0	172.2	173.1	174.2	174.4	173.3	174.0	174.6	174.3	173.6	173.4
2002	173.3	173.8	174.5	175.7	176.2	176.2	175.9	176.4	171.6	177.9	178.2	178.5
2003	178.4	179.3	179.9	181.2	181.5	181.3	181.3	182.6	182.5	182.6	182.7	183.5
2004	183.1	183.8	184.6	185.7	186.5	186.8	186.8	187.4	188.1	188.6	189.0	189.9
2005	188.9	189.6	190.5	191.6	192.0	192.2	192.2	192.6	193.1	193.3	193.6	194.1
2006	193.4	194.2	195.0	196.5	197.7	198.5	198.5	199.2	200.1	200.4	201.1	202.7
2007	201.6	203.1	204.4	205.4	206.2	207.3	206.1	207.3	208.0	208.9	209.7	210.9
2008	209.8	211.4	212.1	214.0	215.1	216.8	216.5	217.2	218.4	217.7	216.0	212.9
2009	210.1	211.4	211.3	211.5	212.8	213.4	213.4	214.4	215.3	216.0	216.6	218.0
2010	217.9	219.2	220.7	222.8	223.6	224.1	223.6	224.5	225.3	225.8	226.8	228.4
2011	229.0	231.3	232.5	234.4								

27 The basic rules of computation

Introduction

1. This chapter is concerned with the basic rules of computation used in the taxation of chargeable gains. It begins with an examination of the meaning of consideration and market price, and the allowable deductions (excluding any indexation relief), which apply to both individuals and incorporated entities. The chapter goes on to consider the computational rules on disposal of an asset by an individual in 2011/12. The chapter concludes with the somewhat different rules for taxing the disposal of an asset by an incorporated entity.

Consideration and market price

2. As a general principle a chargeable gain is computed by deducting from the total consideration obtained the initial cost of acquisition, any allowable expenditure, and (for corporate gains only) the 'indexation allowance'. Consideration is taken to be the gross sales price without any deduction for expenses of sale. However, in the following cases the disposal is deemed to be at market price:

a) where the disposal is by way of a gift or a part-gift (sale at undervalue)

b) where the transaction is not at arm's length, e.g. between connected persons (excluding connected persons who are husband and wife, civil partners, or CGT-grouped companies, where the disposal is deemed to be at a price giving "no-gain-and-no-loss") ;

c) where an asset cannot be readily valued, or is acquired in connection with a loss of employment

d) on a transfer into a settlement by a settlor.

3. Where the market value for a disposal is used, then the person who acquires the asset is also treated as acquiring at the market value.

Market value means the price which assets might reasonably be expected to fetch in a sale on the open market. There are a number of special rules which relate to particular assets, and these are noted below.

Deferred consideration

4. The general rules of computation are not affected where the consideration is payable by instalments as the whole of the consideration is brought into account with no discount for the future receipt of monies. Where all or part of the consideration is deferred because it cannot be quantified at the date of the original disposal, the value of the right to receive that additional amount is included with any ascertainable consideration at the date of the original disposal. The value of this right (known as a 'chose in action') is deducted from the deferred consideration when that is received at a later date.

Allowable deductions

5. The following may be deducted from the consideration:

a) The cost of acquisition, including incidental expenditure.

b) Any enhancement expenditure, but not repairs or maintenance.

c) Expenditure incurred in establishing or protecting the right to any asset.

d) Incidental costs of disposal (see below).

e) The indexation allowance for incorporated entities (see below).

6. Incidental costs include: fees, commission, or professional charges such as legal accountancy or valuation advice: costs of transfer and conveyance including stamp duty: advertising to find a buyer or seller. The following items of expenditure are specifically disallowed:

a) Costs of repair and maintenance.

b) Costs of insurance against any damage injury or loss of an asset.

c) Any expenditure allowed as a deduction in computing trading income.

d) Any expenditure recouped from the Crown or public or local authority.

Entrepreneurs' relief

7. For chargeable assets disposed of after 5th April 2008 by individuals or trustees, entrepreneurs' relief has been introduced which reduces the tax on certain qualifying gains.

Entrepreneurs' relief is available in respect of gains made by individuals on the disposal of:

a) all or part of a trading business the individual carries on alone or in partnership;

b) assets of the individual's or partnership's trading business following the cessation of the business (the relief is available for one year after cessation);

c) shares in (and securities of) the individual's "personal" trading company (or holding company of a trading group). The relief is given on gains on disposals of shares in (and securities of) a trading company (or the holding company of a trading group) provided that throughout a one-year qualifying period before the disposal, the individual making the disposal:

    i) is an officer or employee of the company, or of a company in the same group of companies; and

    ii) owns at least 5 per cent of the ordinary share capital of the company and that holding enables the individual to exercise at least 5 per cent of the voting rights in that company.

d) assets owned by the individual and used by his / her "personal" trading company (or group) or trading partnership.

e) The rules for entrepreneurs' relief are extended to assets held by trustees and personal representatives.

f) The aim of Entrepreneurs' relief is to create a charge to capital gains tax at an effective rate of 10%. For disposals after 22 June 2010 there is a separate rate of Entrepreneurs' Relief tax at 10% (For disposals up to 22 June 2010 the effective rate was achieved by 5/9ths of the gain being chargeable at 18%). There is a lifetime limit on entrepreneurs' relief gains of £1m from 6 April 2008, increasing to £2m from 6 April 2010, to £5m from 23 June 2010, and to £10m from 6 April 2011.

The basic computation for individuals

8. This section illustrates a basic computation for an individual.

a) The basic computation for an individual who disposes of an asset that does not qualify for entrepreneurs' relief is illustrated as follows:

Example 1:

Peter purchased a house that was not his main residence, in January 1987 for £50,000. He incurred legal fees and survey fees of £500 on the acquisition of this property. In September 1991 Peter added an extension to the property at a cost of £15,000. He sold the house on 1st May 2011 for £350,000, incurring legal fees and selling costs amounting to £2,000. Peter has no other disposals for the tax year 2011-2012. Peter's taxable income for 2011-12 is £32,000, and he made net contributions of £1,600 to a personal pension scheme.

Compute the chargeable gain and capital gains tax payable on the disposal.

Suggested solution

	£	£
Proceeds from sale		350,000
Allowable deductions:		
Initial cost	50,000	
Costs of acquisition	500	
Enhancement expenditure, September 1991	15,000	
Incidental costs of disposal	2,000	(67,500)
Chargeable gain		282,500
Less annual exemption		(10,600)
Gain subject to capital gains tax		271,900
Capital gains tax @ 18% of £5,000		£900
Capital gains tax @ 28% of £266,900		£74,732
Total CGT payable		£75,632

Working to support CGT rates above

Income tax basic rate band	35,000
Extension to basic rate band	
Grossed up personal pension contributions £1,600 x 100/80	2,000
	37,000
Taxable income	32,000
Basic rate band available for taxation of gains at 18%	£5,000

b) The basic computation for an individual who disposes of a business asset that qualifies for entrepreneurs' relief is shown in the following example:

Example 2:

Simon purchased a retail shop selling electrical goods in October 1985 for £85,000. He incurred acquisition costs of £1,500. In September 2000 the shop was extended and structurally improved at a cost of £30,000. Simon has been running this business as a trade since buying the shop. On 1st June 2011 Simon sold the shop and the trade for £750,000, incurring legal costs and other selling expenses of £3,500. Simon has no other capital gains during the tax year, and has made no previous claims for entrepreneurs' relief. Compute the chargeable gain and the capital gains tax payable.

Suggested solution	£	£
Proceeds from sale		750,000
Allowable deductions:		
Initial cost	85,000	
Costs of acquisition	1,500	
Enhancement expenditure, September 2000	30,000	
Incidental costs of disposal	3,500	120,000
Chargeable gain		630,000
Less annual exemption		(10,600)
Gain subject to capital gains tax		619,400
Capital gains tax @ 10%		61,940

Notes:

i) This is a sale of a trade, together with the main chargeable asset used for the trade, therefore both disposals qualify for entrepreneurs' relief. From a CGT computational point of view it is not critical to separate the disposal into the shop and the trade goodwill if both are sold together (though for stamp duty land tax purposes it is likely that this price allocation would be done in the legal documents). It is assumed none of the sale proceeds mentioned related to non-chargeable trade assets such as stock or trade debtors.

ii) Simon has used up £630,000 of his lifetime allowance for capital gains tax entrepreneurs' relief purposes. He therefore has a lifetime balance left for entrepreneurs' relief of £9,370,000 at 2 June 2011.

Part-disposals

9. On a part-disposal of an asset (other than a holding of shares or securities), the attributable cost of acquisition of the part disposed of is determined by the following general formula:

$$\text{Attributable cost} = \text{Cost of acquisition} \times \frac{A}{A + B}$$

A is the consideration for the disposal, excluding any expenses of sale.

B is the market value of the un-disposed portion.

Indexation allowance – Incorporated entities

10. For incorporated entities an indexation allowance applies in computing the gain.. The main general provisions relating to disposals are as follows.

a) The indexation allowance is calculated by reference to the change in the Retail Price Index between the date of the disposal and:

   i) the date of acquisition, or

   ii) the 31st March 1982 if that is later than the date of acquisition.

b) The indexation applies to the initial cost of acquisition and any enhancement expenditure but not to the incidental costs of disposal.

c) Where an asset was held on the 31st March 1982 indexation is automatically applied to the market value at that date or the actual allowable expenditure, whichever is the greater.

d) On a part-disposal, indexation allowance is calculated based on the fractional part of the total cost that was used in the calculation of the unindexed gain. The allowable cost carried forward for the part not disposed of is not indexed at that stage.

e) The indexation allowance cannot be used to create or increase a capital loss.

Calculation of indexation allowance

11. The 'indexation factor' is calculated according to the following formula, and rounded by statute to three decimal places. See the official RPI table provided at the end of chapter 26.

$$\frac{\text{RPI in month of disposal} - \text{RPI in month of acquisition (or if later } 31^{st} \text{ March 1982)}}{\text{RPI in month of acquisition (or if later } 31^{st} \text{ March 1982)}}$$

Example

Q Ltd purchased an office for use in its trading business for £10,000 in January 1983. Legal charges and other allowable costs of acquisition amounted to £500. In January 1984 an extension to the property was built for £3,000, and major repairs undertaken amounting to £1,000. The whole property was sold for £100,000 on 28th January 2011 with incidental costs of disposal of £1,500. RPI January 1983 = 82.61, January 1984 = 86.84, January 2011 = 229.0.

Compute the chargeable gain arising to Q Ltd on the disposal of the office.

Suggested solution

CGT computation			£	£
	Proceeds of sale			100,000
	Less: Expenses of disposal			(1,500)
				98,500
	Less:	Cost of acquisition (1983)	10,000	
		Expenses of acquisition (1983)	500	
		Enhancement expenditure (1984)	3,000	
				(13,500)
		Un-indexed gain		85,000
		Indexation allowance to January 2011 (See working)		(23,517)
	Chargeable gain added to TTP			61,483

Working : Indexation allowance:

On Cost January 1983	£10,500	
$\frac{229.0 - 82.61}{82.61} =$	1.772 × 10,500 =	18,606
On Enhancement cost January 1984	£3,000	
$\frac{229.0 - 86.84}{86.84} =$	1.637 x 3,000 =	4,911
Total indexation allowance		23,517

Notes:

i) The gain will be taxable at Q Ltd's corporation tax rate, which for FY 2010 was 28%.

Assets held on 31st March 1982 – rebasing

12. For assets held on 31st March 1982, the following rules apply when computing a chargeable gain

a) The gain on cost is compared with the gain which would apply if the asset is assumed to have been sold on 31st March 1982 and immediately re-acquired at its market value at that date. This is called the re-basing comparison.

b) For incorporated entities, indexation allowance is then deducted for the period from March 1982 up to disposal, but the factor is multiplied in both cases by the same figure, which is the **higher** of the 1982 market value and the actual cost.

c) As indexation allowance cannot be used to increase a loss on disposal, therefore the remaining indexation allowance is unavailable once a gain has been reduced to zero.

d) If both calculations result in a gain, the chargeable gain is the lower gain. If both of them give a loss, the allowable loss is the lower loss. If one gives a loss and the other a gain, or either of them gives a nil result, then the chargeable gain is nil.

e) The above comparison is not done if the taxpayer made a CGs rebasing election under Finance Act 1988 in which case all computations for pre-April 1982 assets are based only on market values at 31 March 1982 without any regards to the original cost records. A rebasing election has to be made during the 2 tax years after the first relevant disposal after 1/6 April 1988 of a chargeable asset owned since before 1 April 1982.

Example

X purchased a painting in 1979 for £10,000 which he sells for £85,000 in August 2011, after incurring expenses of disposal amounting to £5,000. The market value at 31st March 1982 was £36,000.

Calculate the chargeable gain and the CGT on it, assuming that X has no other gains in 2011/12, taxable income totalling £40,000.

Solution: Capital gains tax computation 2011/12

	Re-basing 31.3.82	**Original cost**
	£	**£**
Proceeds of sale	90,000	90,000
Cost of disposal	(5,000)	(5,000)
	85,000	85,000
Less cost of acquisition/	–	(10,000)
MV at 31.3.82	(36,000)	–
Gain	49,000	75,000

Take the lower of the two gains:	£49,000
Realised in August 2010 therefore 28% CGT could apply	
Less: Annual exemption	(10,600)
Chargeable gain subject to CGT	38,400
Remaining IT basic rate band	NIL
Subject to capital gains tax @ 28%	£10,752

Note

i) The smaller gain of £38,400 obtained from re-basing will be taken as the chargeable gain. Where the March 1982 value is greater then the original cost computation will not normally be required.

Indexation – losses

13. The Indexation allowance claimed by corporations cannot be used to turn a gain into a loss or to increase a loss.

Example

B Ltd owns freehold property which has a market value of £20,000 on 3rd March 1982. The property was sold on 30th January 2011 for:

a) £300,000 b) £50,000

Compute the chargeable gain/loss.

Solution: B Ltd chargeable gain/loss computation

a)	Proceeds of sale	300,000
	March 1982 value	20,000
	Unindexed gain	280,000
	IA $\frac{229.0 - 79.44}{79.44} = 1.883 \times 20{,}000 =$	37,660
	Chargeable gain	242,340
b)	Proceeds of sale	50,000
	March 1982 value	20,000
	Unindexed gain	30,000
	IA of £37,660 restricted to	30,000
	No gain/loss	nil

Disposals treated by law as no gain / no loss

14. The following transactions are treated as no gain/no loss disposals. Other no gain/no loss transactions, such as on certain company reconstructions, are outside the scope of this book.

i) Acquisitions of quoted securities before 6th April 1965 where the substitution of the market value at 6th April 1965 converts a gain into a loss or vice versa.

ii) Disposals between spouses or civil partners who were not permanently separated throughout the tax year in question. .

iii) Transfers of chargeable assets between companies in the same capital gains group. See chapter 33, section 6.

Student self-testing question

1. Z purchased a painting for £100,000 in August 1984 which he sold for £200,000 on the 3rd March 2012. Selling expenses amounted to £10,550.

Compute the capital gains tax payable on 31 January 2013, assuming no other chargeable disposals in the year , and that Z's 2011/12 taxable income is £49,000.

Suggested solution: Z CGT computation 2010/11

		£	£
Proceeds of sale			200,000
Less	cost of acquisition	100,000	
	Selling expenses	10,550	(110,550)
Gain			89,450
Annual exemption			(10,600)
Gain subject to CGT			78,850
Capital gains tax @ 28%			22,078

Question without answer

1. A shareholding qualifying for entrepreneurs' relief was acquired by an individual in February 1988 at a cost of £70,000. The individual has not made any disposals since April 2008. The shareholding was sold in January 2012 for sale proceeds of:

i) £5,500,000

ii) £850,000

Requirement

Compute the capital gains tax payable in each case, assuming the individual has £50,000 of taxable income for 2011/12.

28 Land and chattels

Introduction

1. This chapter deals with the CGT rules applicable to land and chattels under the following headings:

- Freehold/leasehold land and buildings
- Part-disposals of land
- Small part-disposals of land
- Disposals of short leases
- Granting a lease from a freehold interest
- Private residence
- Chattels

Freehold/long leasehold land and buildings

2. There are no special rules for the computation of capital gains arising on the disposal of assets under this heading.

A long lease is a lease with more than 50 years to run at the date of the transaction.

Land includes houses, hereditaments and buildings.

Where the property is also the main residence of an individual owner or joint owners, then the residence exemption is normally available. See below.

Part-disposals of land

3. Where there is a part-disposal of freehold or long leasehold land then unless the disposal is 'small', (see below) the normal part-disposal formula applies.

$$\text{Attributable cost} = \text{Cost of acquisition} \times \frac{A}{A + B}$$

$$\text{Attributable cost} = \text{Market value at 31.3.1982} \times \frac{A}{A + B} \quad \text{(Assets held on 31.3.82)}$$

Example

G purchased a plot of land of 10 acres for £22,000 in May 1987, and an adjacent further 2 acres for £10,000 in June 1990. In December 2011 a sale of 5 acres was made for £60,000, from the original 10 acres, the remaining 5 acres being worth £75,000 at that time. The land was not used for business purposes. Compute the capital gains tax payable, assuming no other disposals during the year and a taxable income for G of £55,000 in 2011/12.

Solution: CGT computation 2011/12

	£
Proceeds of sale	60,000
Cost $22{,}000 \times \dfrac{60{,}000}{60{,}000 + 75{,}000}$	(9,778)
Gain	50,222

Annual exemption	(10,600)
Chargeable gain subject to capital gains tax	39,622
Capital gains tax @ 28%	11,094

In this case, since the disposal was out of the first identifiable plot, there is no need to combine the acquisition costs of the two plots.

If the sale had been 5 acres out of the total of 12 acres with the remaining 7 acres being valued at £85,000 at the date of disposal then the computation would be:

Proceeds of sale	60,000
Cost $32{,}000 \times \dfrac{60{,}000}{60{,}000 + 85{,}000} =$	(13,241)
Gain	46,759
Annual exemption	(10,600)
Chargeable gain subject to capital gains tax	36,159
Capital gains tax @ 28%	10,124

Small part-disposals of land

4. There are some special rules which relate to land where:

a) the value of the part-disposal does not exceed £20,000; and

b) the part-disposal is small relative to the market value of the entire property, before the disposal. Small in this context means 20% of the value immediately prior to the disposal.

Given these conditions, then the taxpayer can claim to have any consideration received for the part-disposal deducted from the allowable expenditure of the whole property. In that case there would be no chargeable gain on the part-disposal.

The £20,000 exemption does not apply to a compulsory purchase by a public authority.

The taxpayer's total consideration for disposals of land in a tax year must not exceed £20,000, for him or her to be eligible to claim relief under this section.

Example

Z owns land which he acquired in April 1982 for £20,000 comprising some 10 acres. The costs of the acquisition amounted to £500. In August 2011 Z sells 1.5 acres for £13,500 incurring disposal costs of £750. At the date of sale the remainder of the land had a market value of £135,500.

Compute the chargeable gain arising in 2011/12. If Z makes a claim under Section 242 show the computations.

Solution: CGT computation 2011/12

		£	£
August 2011 proceeds of sale			13,500
Deduct – allowable cost	$\frac{13{,}500}{13{,}500 + 135{,}500} \times 20{,}500$	1,857	
Cost of disposal		750	2,607
Gain			10,893

Alternative treatment: Claim under Section 242 TCGA 1992

Cost of acquisition	20,500
Less proceeds of sale August 2011 (13,500 – 750)	12,750
Revised allowed cost	7,750

Notes

i) In this example, rather than claim relief under Section 242 it might be more advantageous to accept the chargeable gain since most of it falls within the exemption level of £10,600 for 2011/12 which might otherwise go unused.

ii) The election under Section 242 TCGA 1992 can be made where the proceeds of sale are less than 20% of the value of the entire property before the disposal.

$$\frac{\text{Disposable value}}{\text{Total value before sale}} = \frac{13{,}500}{13{,}500 + 135{,}500} \times \frac{100}{1} = 9\%$$

Private residence

5. Any gain accruing to an individual on the disposal of his or her principal private residence (PPR) can be exempt from capital gains tax. The exemption also extends to one other residence provided for a dependent relative before 6 April 1988, if the property is provided rent free and without other consideration, and has been occupied continuously since 6th April 1988.

Residence includes a dwelling house (or part) together with garden land up to half a hectare in area, or more if justified, and a mobile home.

Full exemption is available where there has been a continuous period of ownership since 1 April 1982, or since puchase, whichever falls later, and the property has been occupied as a PPR for all that time .

If there have been identifiable periods when the owner's principal residence was elsewhere, the following are to be taken into consideration in determining the total ownership period for which the time apportioned gain qualifies for PPR exemption.

a) Actual periods of occupation as PPR.

b) Any period of absence during the last three years of ownership providing that at some time the residence was occupied as the principal private residence of the taxpayer. This period of absence applies even where the original PPR occupancy was only before 31st March 1982.

c) Absences for whatever reasons, for periods which in total do not exceed three years and are both preceded and followed by occupation as the PPR. (see comment below)

d) Absence for any period of time during which the owner was in employment, carrying out duties abroad.

e) Absences amounting in total to not more than four years during which the owner:

   i) was prevented from living at home because of the distance to the place of employment.

   ii) lived away from home at the employer's request, in order to perform his or her employment more effectively.

Absences under items (c) to (e) above only qualify as deemed occupation if the owner actually occupies the home both before and after the period of absence, and there is no other house which counts as an alternative PPR during the absence period. However, if the owner is unable to resume residence at the end of a (d) or (e) qualifying absence period because employment forced him or her to work elsewhere, periods of absence under (d) and (e) can still qualify as periods of occupation.

Where the maximum period of absence under (c) and (e) is exceeded then only the excess is treated as giving rise to a chargeable gain.

Where the main residence qualifies for occupancy for a part of the period since 31st March 1982, the exempt gain is:

$$\frac{\text{Period of exemption as main residence}}{\text{Total period of ownership}} \times \text{Gain}$$

6. The following additional points should be noted.

a) If part of any house (eg an office or a consulting room) is used exclusively for business purposes, then the part of any gain attributable to the business portion is not eligible for any exemptions. Dual use of rooms for both business and private purposes is acceptable.

b) If a house, or part of it, is let for residential purposes, then the part of the gain attributable to that letting period can be exempt up to the smallest of:

   i) An amount equal to the gain already exempt by reason of owner occupation

   ii) £40,000

   iii) the gain attributable to the let period/ the let proportion.

Example

A purchased a house on 1st July 1987 for £25,806 in which he lived until the 31st March 1988. The property was then let for five years, followed by occupation by A until he sold the house for £600,000 on the 31st March 2012.

Compute the chargeable gain.

Solution: Computation 2011/12

		£
Proceeds of sale		600,000
Cost of acquisition		(25,806)
Total gain before exemption		574,194
Less exemption:		
Proportion of total gain 273/297 x 574,194		(527,794)
		46,400
Less let property exemption: Lowest of:		
maximum amount	40,000	
gain otherwise exempt	527,794	(40,000)
letting gain	46,400	
chargeable gain subject to capital gains tax		
(before annual exemption)		6,400

Notes

		Years	Months	Total months
Period of ownership	1.7.87 – 31.3.12	24	9	285
Period of absence	1.4.88 – 31.3.93	5	–	60
Periods of occupancy	1.7.87 – 31.3.88	–	9	9
1.4.93 – 31.3.12	19	–	216	

		Months
Last three years		36
Period of absence preceded and followed by occupancy		36
Occupancy additional to last three years		
1.7.87 – 31.3.88	9	
1.4.93 – 31.3.09	192	201
		273

c) A husband and wife or civil partners can only have one residence between them for the purposes of the PPR and letting exemptions.

In a tax year throughout which spouses are permanently separated or divorced, each qualifies individually for the PPR exemption.

d) In the absence of formal election, it is a question of fact which of several actual residences is the principal private residence of a couple, or of an individual. Election can be made to specify which is the PPR within 2 years of acquiring more than one possible PPR. If no election is made the decision as to which residence was the PPR can be made by HMRC.

e) Deemed occupation also applies to an individual who lives in job-related accommodation and who intends in due course to occupy a house owned by that individual, as his or her main residence. It also applies to self-employed people living in job-related accommodation.

Chattels

7. The chattels discussed here are personal chattels or tangible movable property, which for capital gains tax purposes are put into four categories.

a) Chattels which are specifically exempt from capital gains tax, e.g. private cars, or decorations for valour.

b) Chattels which are wasting assets.

c) Chattels, not being wasting assets, both bought and disposed of for £6,000 or less

d) all other chattels – which in general are subject to normal CGT rules but are subject to some special rules linked to a) to c) above .

Chattels which are wasting assets

8. A wasting asset is one with an estimated useful life of less than 50 years at the time of the disposal. A chattel which is a wasting asset is exempt from capital gains tax unless:

a) the asset has been used since first owned, for the purposes of a trade, profession or vocation, and capital allowances were available in respect of the expenditure, whether claimed or not, or

b) it consists of commodities dealt with on a terminal market.

Where capital allowances have been claimed, then no chargeable gain will arise unless the disposal value is greater than the original cost. If the proceeds are less than £6,000 then the exemption noted below can be claimed.

Chattels disposed of for £6,000 or less – marginal relief

9. Any gain arising on the disposal of a chattel, not being a wasting asset, is not a chargeable gain where the gross disposal value is £6,000 or less.

Marginal relief applies where the disposal value is greater than £6,000 and the cost less than £6,000. The marginal relief limits the gain to:

$$\frac{5}{3} \times (\text{gross proceeds} - £6{,}000)$$

Thus the maximum assessable gain is the lower of:

i) $\frac{5}{3} \times$ (gross proceeds – £6,000) or

ii) The actual gain i.e. gross proceeds less.

Example

H buys a piece of pottery for £800 in June 1982 which he sells in October 2011 for (a) £4,800, (b) £6,800.

Compute the chargeable gains.

Solution: H CGT computation 2011/12

a) As the proceeds of sale are less than £6,000 no chargeable gain arises.

b)

	£
Proceeds of sale	6,800
Less: cost of acquisition	(800)
Chargeable gain	6,000
Limited to $\frac{5}{3}$ (6,800 – 6,000)	1,333
Net chargeable gain subject to capital gains tax (before annual exemption)	1,333

Restriction of losses on chattels sold for less than £6,000

10. If a chattel which cost more than £6,000 is sold for less than £6,000 then the allowable loss is calculated by reference to gross proceeds of £6,000 and not the actual disposal value.

If both the disposal price and the cost price are less than £6,000 then the loss is not allowed at all.

Where two or more chattels form part of a set, then any disposal of part of the set to the same or connected persons is to be aggregated with any disposal of the other parts, and treated as a single transaction.

Student self-testing question

1. In March 2012, Neil sells an oil painting, which he had acquired in June 1992 for £10,000. He sells the painting for:

   a) £7,200 b) £5,700

   Compute the allowable loss in each of the above cases

Solution

a) The disposal is not exempt from CGT as the proceeds exceed £6,000. The allowable loss is therefore calculated in the normal way at £2,800 (£10,000 – £7,200).

b) The asset was acquired for more than £6,000 and therefore a loss is allowed. This is calculated by substituting £6,000 for the disposal proceeds. The allowable loss is therefore £4,000 (£6,000 – £10,000).

Questions without answers

1. James purchased a house in Oxford, 'Millhouse', on 1st July 1986 and took up immediate residence. The house cost £50,000. On 1st January 1989 he went to work and live in the United States where he stayed until 30th June 1991.

On 1st July 1991 James returned to the UK to work for his United States employers in Scotland where it was necessary for him to occupy rented accommodation. On 1st July 1992 his mother became seriously ill and James resigned from his job to go and live with her. His mother died on 30th September 1993 leaving her house to James. James decided to continue to live in his mother's house and finally sold 'Millhouse' on 30th June 2011 for £300,000.

Calculate the chargeable gain assessable on James for 2011/12. (ACCA)

2. Mr and Mrs Scott had the following transactions in assets in the year to 5 April 2012.

Mr Scott

Sold an antique for £7,250, incurring expenses of £250, on 1 December 2011, which he had bought on 19 April 1982 for £2,950, including expenses of purchase.

A holiday cottage, which had been bought for £31,000 on 3 April 1983, was sold on 1 November 2011. On 14 May 1984 an integral garage costing £3,000 was added. The net proceeds of sale were £80,000.

Sold a vintage Rolls Royce for £38,000 on 9 May 2011, which had cost £15,000 on 6 May 1982.

Mrs Scott

On 4 June 2011 sold an antique silver brooch for £4,800, incurring expenses of £54. It had cost £6,200, including expenses, on 5 April 1983.

Sold 5 acres of land on 14 October 2011 for £11,000, incurring expenses of £480. It was part of a 25 acre plot, which had been purchased on 14 March 1984 for £17,000, including expenses. The remaining 20 acres have been valued at £33,000.

Compute the capital gain accruing to Mr and Mrs Scott in each of the cases above. **15 marks**

3. Lord Scarlet carried out the following capital transactions in January 2012.

Sold a cricket bat, signed by the 1978 England test team, which he had bought at an auction in May 1982 for £1,400. The net proceeds, after paying auctioneer's fees of £520, were £11,520.

Sold £20,000 13.75% Treasury stock for £27,400. He had acquired the stock in September 1987 at par.

Sold an antique book for £3,000. He had bought it in May 1987 for £8,000.

Sold a one-third interest in a plot of land for £11,500. Lord Scarlet had acquired the land in June 1984 for £15,000. The value of the remaining two thirds interest in January 2012 was £28,000.

Compute the total capital gains tax payable by Lord Scarlet for 2011/12 if his taxable income for the year is £36,000. **8 marks**

29 Stocks and securities

Introduction

1. This chapter is concerned with the CGT rules applicable to stocks and securities and begins with the general method of computation following the changes introduced by the FA 2008; In line with other areas of capital gains tax, major changes have taken place in respect of the treatment of gains and losses in respect of stocks and securities transactions involving individuals. From 6th April 2008 the frozen indexation allowance and taper relief is abolished for individuals and a simplification of the cost apportionment of shares of the same class has been introduced. For corporations, gains and losses on transactions in stocks and securities remain broadly the same as the previous year, with indexation using the weighted average cost being available for the current year. This chapter commences with an overview of the rules for the current year for shares or securities of the same class and then examines bonus and rights issues and takeover bids.

FA 2008 – main changes for individuals

2. The following are the main provisions concerning stocks and securities introduced by the FA 2008:

a) The system of cost allocation on disposal of a shareholding by an individual were simplified for the FA 2008 year. The cost is calculated on a weighted average basis so that all shares of the same class purchased over a period of time are 'pooled' together. Anti avoidance rules are in place to prevent unlawful gains, such as insider trading, whereby same day acquisitions and buy backs within the next 30 days are treated as being the deemed cost for capital gains tax purposes. This is referred to as 'bed and breakfasting' of share and is considered in section c below.

b) If a shareholding qualifies as a business asset under the entrepreneurs' relief scheme, any gain arising on the first £10 million will be chargeable to capital gains tax at the reduced rate of 10%. The following conditions apply, provided that throughout a one-year qualifying period the individual making the disposal:

    i) is an officer or employee of the company, or of a company in the same group of companies; and

    ii) owns at least 5 per cent of the ordinary share capital of the company and that holding enables the individual to exercise at least 5 per cent of the voting rights in that company.

c) Shares and securities held at or prior to 31st March 1982 are valued at their 31st March 1982 market value for the computation of the capital gain on disposal.

d) When part of the share holding is disposed of, the cost of acquisition relating to the disposal is the proportionate part of the cost of all the shares in the holding. A weighted average cost is computed.

e) Shares that meet the income tax relief criteria as investments in the Enterprise Investment Scheme, Venture Capital Trusts and the Corporate Venturing Scheme are exempt from capital gains tax.

Share matching - individuals

3. When there is a part-disposal of some of the share holding of a particular type of share in a given company, the following matching rules apply to decide which shares were sold, and therefore what they cost:

1) Against any shares acquired on the same day as the disposal;
2) Against any shares acquired within the following 30 days, taking the earlier acquisitions before the later;
3) Against all other acquisitions with the cost calculated on a weighted average basis (the s104 holding).

Weighted average cost - individual

Example 1

Denis has the following transactions in the 25p ordinary shares of Z plc, a quoted trading company.

				£
6th May 1982	purchased	3,500	shares at cost	2,500
31st March 1984	purchased	1,000	shares at cost	1,500
3 rd April 1998	purchased	2,000	shares at cost	7,500

Calculate the value of the general pool at 6th April 2011.

Suggested solution

General pool Denis ordinary shares in Z plc

		Number of shares	**Qualifying expenditure**
		£	**£**
6.5.82	Purchased	3,500	2,500
31.3.84	Purchased	1,000	1,500
3.4.98	Purchased	2,000	7,500
Pool values at 6.4 2011		6,500	11,500

Notes:

i) If all the shares were sold the qualifying expenditure would be the full £11,500.

ii) In accounting terms, the average cost per share at this point is 11,500÷6,500 = £1.77. However, using a per-share average cost for CG computations involving many shares can introduce rounding errors. Also, TCGA 1992 deems the s.104 holding (post-1982 share poo) l to be a single asset (and the "1982 holding" to be another single asset), which means the average cost of a single share is not relevant for CGT unless only one share is sold. Therefore, in tax accounting exams, students should use the statutory method for share cost apportionment."

iii) If part of the holding is disposed of the allowable cost would be allocated on a pro-rata basis. For example, if 1,625 of the 6,500 shares are sold now, the apportioned cost for CGT is £2,875 (1625/6,500 x £11,500). The balance of cost (£8,625) is carried forward and averaged with future acquisitions (except any acquisitions not forming part of the s.104 holding, under the matching rules above).

Example 2

Colin has the following transactions in the 25p ordinary shares of K plc, a quoted trading company.

				£
1.6.1990	purchased	1,000	shares at cost	525
1.9.2000	purchased	500	shares at cost	575
2.1.2003	purchased	2,500	shares at cost	3,500
10.10.2011	sold	3,000	shares, proceeds	36,000

The shares do not qualify for entrepreneurs' relief.

Calculate the chargeable gain for 2011/12 before annual exemption.

Suggested solution

General pool K plc		**Number of shares**	**Qualifying expenditure**
			£
1.6.1990	Purchase	1,000	525
1.9.2000	Purchase	500	575
2.1.2003	Purchase	2,500	3,500
	Total	4,000	4,600
10.10.2011	Disposal	3,000	3,450
11.10.2011	Balance remaining in pool	1,000	1,150

Colin CGT computation 2011/12

	£
10.10.2011 Proceeds of sale of 3,000 shares	36,000
Allowable cost	3,450
Chargeable gain before annual exemption	32,550

Share matching rules - incorporated entities

4. The following rules apply in deciding which shares out of a holding of particular type of share in a given company were sold:

1) Against any shares acquired on the same day as the disposal;
2) Against a pool of any shares acquired in the previous 9 days, on a first in first out (FIFO) basis;
3) Against all other shares acquired on or after 1 April 1982 (the s104 pool);
4) Against a pool of any shares acquired between 6 April 1965 and 31 March 1982;
5) Against any shares acquired before 6 April 1965 on a last in first out (LIFO) basis.

Pooling rules - incorporated entities

The following are the main provisions which apply to shares or securities of the same class, where they are held by an incorporated entity.

a) Separate pools must be established as follows.
   i) Shares or securities acquired on or after the 1st April 1982 'the section 104 holding'. The s.104 holding indexation factor at each step is specifically not rounded to 3 decimal places like all other CGT indexation factors, but is left unrounded (due to the possibility for multiple small-step calculations in a fast changing shareholding)
   ii) Shares or securities acquired prior to 1st April 1982 are called the 1982 Holding.

b) The re-basing rules apply to shares and securities held at the 31st March 1982 and the market value at that date forms the basis of valuation of the 1982 Holding.

c) Disposals are first deducted from the Section 104 Holding and then from the 1982 Holding.

c) The weighted average cost plus indexation allowance is used to calculate the allowable cost against the sale proceeds.

d) Indexation cannot increase or create a loss.

e) The chargeable gain is added to the corporations TTP.

Example

V Ltd had the following transactions in the quoted shares of Z plc, a quoted trading company.

31.1.1983	Bought	8,000	shares costing	£15,600
31.5.1998	Bought	12,000	shares costing	£36,000
28.5.2011	Sold	5,000	shares for	£176,000

Compute the chargeable gain, assuming the value of the retail prices index for May 2011 was 234.5 (estimated). The RPI for May 1998 was 163.5.

Suggested solution

The first step is to construct the section 104 holding. In documenting a company's section 104 holding, 3 columns are required for the pooled cost records: an 'indexed cost' column is required as well as original (historic) 'cost'. Indexation must be calculated in the ' indexed cost' column between each pair of successive 'operative events'. An operative event means not only a chargeable disposal of any shares from the s. 104 holding, but also any addition of more shares to it, except an addition involving no actual or deemed cost to the shareholder (i.e. a bonus issue).

Section 104 holding	**Number of shares**	**Cost**	**Indexed pool**
		£	£
31.1.1983 Pool starts	8,000	15,600	15,600
IA to 31.5.98			15,275
163.5-82.61 x 15,600 (do not round) / 82.61			
31.5.1998 Purchase	12,000	36,000	36,000
IA to 28.5.2011 (next operative event)			66,875
234.5-163.5 x 66,875 / 163.5			29041
Total	20,000	51,600	95,016
28.5.2011 Disposal (15/20)	(15,000)	(38,700)	(71,937)
	5,000	12,900	23,979

V Ltd CG computation

	£
Sales proceeds (15,000 shares)	176,000
Allowable deductions:	
Cost (from share pool working)	(38,700)
Un-indexed gain	137,300
Indexation Section 104 pool (71,937 – 38,700)	33,237
Chargeable gain added to TTP	104,063

Notes:

i) The remaining balance will be held until the next 'operative event'.

ii) Indexation should be shown separately in case a loss on disposal is incurred. In the case of a loss the indexation allowance is restricted so as not to create or increase a loss on disposal. Thus if the shares in this example were disposed of for, say, £50,000, this would result in a gain of nil and no loss being allowed, with indexation restricted to £11,300 (sales proceeds less cost). A capital loss can only be allowed when the shareholding is sold for less than cost.

Bonus issues of similar shares

5. When a company makes a bonus or scrip issue of shares of the same class, then the average cost (or market value at 31.3.1982) of all the shares held is not affected, but their number is increased, and hence the average cost per share is reduced. The indexation allowance principle is not affected by a bonus issue, so that the normal rules for identification noted above apply in the case of incorporated entities. The number of shares in each pool is increased by the bonus issue.

Example

T Ltd makes a bonus issue of 1 for 5 in respect of its ordinary shares on 1st August 1984. Alex had acquired 500 ordinary shares in T Ltd on 1st May 1982 at a cost of £1,250. In June 2011 Alex sells 250 of the shares for £650. The shares do not qualify for entrepreneurs' relief.

Compute the chargeable gain.

Suggested solution

Cost of shares

		£
1.5.1982 cost of	500 ordinary shares	1,250
1.8.1984 cost of	100 bonus shares	–
	600	1,250

The deemed date of acquisition of the bonus shares is the date of the original purchases.

CGT computation 2011/12	£
Proceeds of sale June 2011	650
Cost of 250 shares sold as at 1 May 1982:	
$\frac{250}{600} \times 1{,}250$	521
Chargeable gain subject to CGT (before annual exemption)	129

Notes

i) The cost of the 250 shares sold, as at 1 May 1982, is 250 × £2.083 = £521 (£1,250 ÷ 600 = £2.083).

ii) The value of the 350 shares carried forward is £1,250 – 521 i.e. £729.

Example

AB Ltd makes a bonus issue of 1 for 10 on the 30th June 1997. John had acquired 10,000 ordinary shares in AB Ltd in April 1990 at a cost of £15,000. John sells 2,000 shares in May 2011 for £8,000. The shares do not qualify for entrepreneurs' relief.

Compute the chargeable gain.

Solution: CGT computation 2011/12

	£	£
Proceeds of sale – 2,000 shares		8,000
Cost: 10,000 @ £1.50 =	15,000	
$\frac{2000}{11000}$ × 15,000 (i.e. 2,000 × £1.364)	2,727	2,727
Chargeable gain subject to capital gains tax (before annual exemption)		5,273

Notes

i) **1982 holding:**

	Number	Cost
April 1990 cost	10,000	15,000
June 1997 bonus	1,000	Nil
	11,000	15,000

Cost of shares plus the bonus issue is $\frac{\pounds 15{,}000}{11{,}000}$ = £1.364 per share i.e. the price as adjusted for the bonus issue. 2,000 shares @ £1.364 = £2,727.

ii) The MV carried forward is £15,000 – £2,727 = £12,273.

Bonus issues of shares or debentures of a different class

6. A bonus issue of shares of a different class, or debentures, gives rise to two distinct classes of holdings, and the original cost of the shares must be apportioned. The method of apportionment is as follows:

a) Quoted investments. Apportionment by reference to the market value of the new holding on the first day a price is quoted on the stock exchange.

b) Unquoted investments. The part-disposal formula is applied as and when a disposal occurs.

Example

T plc, a quoted company, made a bonus issue on the 31st August 2011 of 1 new ordinary share for every 5 held, and £1.00 of 8% debenture stock for every 2 shares held. First day dealing prices on 1st September were 160p for the ordinary, and par for the debentures. Andrew acquired the shares from his father's estate on 1st July 1984: 1,000 ordinary shares in T plc value £1,500.

Compute the apportioned cost.

Solution

Calculation of apportioned cost		**£**	
After bonus issue of 1 for 5. 1,200 shares held at a cost of		1,500	
	Market value 1.9.2011	Apportioned cost	
	£	£	
1,200 ordinary shares @ 160p	1,920	1,190	see below
£500 8% debenture @ £100	500	310	
	2,420	1,500	

Ordinary shares:	$\frac{1,920}{2,420} \times 1,500$ i.e.	1,190
Debentures:	$\frac{500}{2,420} \times 1,500$ i.e.	310

Rights issues of the same class

7. Where a company makes a rights issue of the same class of shares as existing ones, and they are taken up, then for CGT purposes the following rules apply.

a) The consideration paid for the shares by way of the rights issue is deemed to take place at the time when the cost of the rights becomes due.

b) Each pool cost is increased accordingly.

c) For incorporated entities indexation from the date of the rights issue.

Example

T plc makes a rights issue on the 7th February 1984 of 1 new ordinary share for every 2 held, at a price of 125p per share. Jack acquired 1,000 ordinary shares in T plc for £1,300 on the 1st October 1982. He sells 750 shares for £10,000 on the 25th October 2011. The shares do not qualify for entrepreneurs' relief.

Compute the chargeable gain.

Solution: CGT computation 2011/12

Pool at October 2011	**Number of shares**	**Qualifying expenditure**
1.10.1982 Acquisition	1,000	1,300
7.2.1984 Rights issue	500	625
Pool value @ 25th October 2011	1,500	1,925
25.10.2011 Disposal 750 shares	750	
$\frac{750}{1,500} \times 1,925$		963
Value of pool c/f	750	962

CGT computation 2011/12	£
Proceeds of sale	10,000
Less pool cost at 25th October 2011	963
Chargeable gain subject to capital gains tax before annual exemption	9,037

Note
The rights issue of 1 for every 2 is 500 new shares at a cost of 125p per share i.e. £625.

Rights issues of a different class

8. Where the shareholder is offered shares of a different class, or securities, by way of a rights issue, then the same rules apply as for a bonus issue of shares of a different class, noted above. The different treatment for quoted and unquoted shares also applies to this type of rights issue. For indexation purposes the additional consideration becomes a separate asset as for rights issues in general.

Takeover bids

9. Where a company makes a bid for the shares of another company the following situations could arise.

a) The consideration is satisfied entirely by cash. In this case a shareholder who accepts the offer has made a chargeable disposal.

b) The consideration is a share for share exchange. In this case an accepting shareholder is deemed to have acquired the new shares at the date and cost of the original holding, or the 1982 value.

c) The consideration is either a partial cash settlement, or it consists of two or more shares or securities by way of exchange. In both cases it will be necessary to use the market value of the separate components of the bid, in order to apportion the original cost.

Example

Arthur owns 1,000 ordinary shares in P Ltd which he acquired for £1,500 on 27th June 1983. On the 30th May 2011 Z plc makes a bid for P Ltd on the following terms:

For every 200 shares: £30.00 in cash, 100 ordinary shares in Z plc, and £50.00 of 7% unsecured loan stock. MV when first quoted: ordinary 375p, 7% loan stock at par.

Compute the apportioned cost and CGT computation for 2011/12.

Solution

	Market value	Apportioned cost
	£	£
Cash 5 × 30	150	99
7% loan stock 5 × 50	250	165
500 ordinary share 500 × 375p	1,875	1,236
	2,275	1,500

CGT computation 2011/12	
Disposal cash receipt	150
Less apportioned cost	99
Chargeable gain subject to capital gains tax before annual exemption	51

Notes

i) The cost apportionments are as follows:

Cash	$\frac{150}{2,275} \times 1,500$	=	99
7% loan stock	$\frac{250}{2,275} \times 1,500$	=	165
Ordinary shares	$\frac{1,875}{2,275} \times 1,500$	=	1,236

ii) See 11 below for treatment of 'small' disposals. In this case $\frac{150}{2,275} = 6.5\%$.

Example

Using the data in the previous example Arthur sells all his 500 ordinary shares in Z plc for £10,000 on the 1st December 2011.

Compute the chargeable gains.

Solution: CGT computation 2011/12	£	£
Proceeds of sale 500 shares in Z plc	10,000	
Less cost of acquisition (as above)	1,236	
Chargeable gain subject to capital gains tax before annual exemption		8,764

Small capital distributions Section 122

10. Where a person receives cash by way of a capital distribution, e.g. on a takeover bid, in the course of a liquidation, or by the sale of any rights, then there is a part-disposal for capital gains tax purposes. However, if the cash received is small relative to the value of the shares, then it may be deducted from the cost of acquisition. Small here is taken to be the highest of 5% or £3,000 of the value of the shares, before the sale of rights and in other cases after the distribution is made.

Example

Terry acquired 5,000 ordinary shares in A Ltd at a cost of £3,750 on 8.2.1998. On the 12th June 2011 the company made a rights issue of 1 for 10 at a price of 25p, Terry sold his rights for 60p each on the 1st August 2011 when the market value of the 5,000 ordinary shares was £7,000.

Compute the allowed cost carried forward, and any CGT liability for 2011/12.

Solution: Terry CGT computation 2011/12

	£
Proceeds of sale of rights 500 × 60p	300
As this is less than 5% of the market value of the shares of £7,000, the cost of acquisition can be reduced for any future disposal:	
Cost of 5,000 ordinary shares	3,750
Less sale of rights	300
Allowed value carried forward	3,450

Note

i) As there is no part-disposal there is no CGT liability for 2011/12.

ii) 5% of MV of £7,000 = £350.

Example

Alex holds 100,000 ordinary shares in Beta plc which he bought in September 1988 for £50,000. In May 2011 there was a rights offer of 1 for 10 which Alex did not take up. The rights were sold for £20,000, paid when the ex rights price of the shares was £120,000.

Compute the chargeable gain for 2011/12.

Solution: Alex CGT computation 2011/12

Proceeds of sale of rights	20,000	
Allowable cost		
$50{,}000 \times \dfrac{20{,}000}{20{,}000 + 120{,}000}$	7,143	
Chargeable gain subject to capital gains tax before annual exemption		12,857

Note

5% × ex rights price £120,000 = £6,000 which is less than the proceeds of sale from the rights, therefore this gain cannot be deducted from the cost of the original acquisition.

Stock dividends

11. For capital gains tax purposes, if an individual shareholder elects to receive shares instead of cash, then on a subsequent disposal of shares the amount of the Cash Equivalent will be treated as the consideration given for the new shares.

The number of new shares to be allotted to electing shareholders is calculated by multiplying the number of shares on which an election has been made by the cash dividend per share and dividing by the cash equivalent share price, being the price determined using the average middle market quotation of an ordinary share in the company, as derived from the London Stock Exchange Daily Official List. New shares may be allotted up to the maximum whole number possible. Fractions of new shares cannot be allotted and any fractional entitlement will be dealt with in accordance with the notes below. The number of new shares to be allotted is calculated as follows:

$$\frac{(N \times D) + F}{P}$$

N is the number of shares on which the shareholder has elected to receive a scrip dividend

D is the cash dividend per share

F is the fractional entitlement carried forward from previous scrip dividends (where a standing election mandate has been given and not revoked); and

P is the cash equivalent share price of one new share

The issue of a stock dividend does not constitute a reorganisation of capital and accordingly the receipt is treated as a separate acquisition for CGT purposes, from the date they are issued.
Any taper relief starts from the date of the stock dividend and not from the date of the purchase of the original shares.

Student self-testing questions

1. Peter acquired the following shares in Hirst plc.

Date of acquisition	No. of shares	Cost
9/11/90	17,000	£25,000
4/8/05	7,000	£19,400
15/7/09	6,000	£19,000

He sold 24,000 shares on the 20th July 2011 for £80,000. The shares are not business assets for the purposes of entrepreneurs' relief. Calculate the chargeable gain arising.

Suggested solution

S.104 holding	Number of shares	Cost £
9/11/90 Acquisition	17,000	25,000
4/8/05 Acquisition	7,000	19,400
15/7/09 Acquisition	6,000	19,000
Total	30,000	63,400
20/7/11 sales (x 24/30)	(24,000)	(50,720)
Balance to carry forward	6,000	12,680

Peter CGT computation 2011/2012	£
Sale proceeds	80,000
Cost	(50,720)
Chargeable gain subject to capital gains tax before annual exemption	**29,280**

2. Paul had the following transactions in Super Ltd, in which he holds the position of Finance Director.

1.10.95	Bought 20,000 shares (10%) holding for £30,000
11.9.03	Bought 4,000 shares for £10,000
1.2.04	Took up rights issue 1 for 2 at £2.75 per share
14.10.11	Sold 10,000 shares for £40,000

Note: The shares meet the qualifying conditions for entrepreneurs' relief.

Compute the gain arising in October 2011 and the capital gains tax payable assuming Paul has no other gains during the year and a taxable income of £75,000.

Solution:

S.104 holding	Number	Cost £
1.10.95 purchase	20,000	30,000
11.9.03 purchase	4,000	10,000
Pool at 1.2.04	24,000	40,000
Rights issues 1.2.04	12,000	33,000
	36,000	73,000
14.10.11 sale	(10,000)	(20,278)
C/F	26,000	52,722

Paul CGT computation 2011/2012	**£**
Sale proceeds	40,000
Cost	(20,278)
Chargeable gain	19,722
Annual exemption	(10,600)
Chargeable gain subject to CGT (qualifying for ER)	9,122
CGT payable @ entrepreneurs' relief rate (10%)	912

3. Tony has the following transactions in the 10p ordinary shares of W plc, a quoted trading company.

30.04.1982	purchased	1,500	shares cost	£2,475
20.5.1983	sold	500	shares for	£1,000
25.10.1999	purchased	500	shares cost	£1,000
30.3.2012	sold	1,200	shares proceeds	£10,000

Compute the chargeable gain for 2011/12.

Solution: Tony CG computation 2011/12.

Section 104 holding :Pool working		**Number of shares**	**Qualifying expenditure £**
i) 30.4.1982	Purchase	1,500	2,475
20.5.1983	Sale (1/3)	(500)	(825)
25.10.1999	Purchase	500	1,000
		1,500	2,650
30.3.2012 Sale (4/5)		(1,200)	(2,120)
s 104 holding Pool carried forward		300	530

CG computation :

Sale proceeds	10,000
Allowable cost:	
Section 104 holding	(2,120)
Chargeable gain before annual exemption	**7,880**

Note : If Tony had been an incorporated taxpayer, the CG computation would have involved claiming indexation allowance on the share pool.

Questions without answers

1. Frank acquired 10,000 ordinary shares in Trent plc on 12th May 1982 for £1,500. On 15th December 1983, T plc made a rights issue of 1 for 5 at a price of 130p. Frank took up the rights and then sold half of his total holding on 10th May 2011 for £16,000.

   Compute the CGT liability of Frank for 2011/12 if his taxable income is £65,000. The shares do not qualify for entrepreneurs' relief.

2. Trevor has the following transactions in the 10p ordinary shares of Baker plc, a quoted company. Trevor has taxable income of £38,000 for 2011/12.

4.5.82	purchased	5,300	@	100p	£5,300
16.5.82	purchased	1,000	@	104p	£1,040
30.4.83	purchased	3,000	@	125p	£3,750
5.9.00	purchased	2,000	@	150p	£3,000
31.3.11	sold	9,000	@	180p	£27,000

Compute CGT liability for 2011/12. The shares do not qualify for entrepreneurs' relief.

30 Taxable persons

Introduction

1. This chapter is concerned with the persons who are liable to capital gains tax (as opposed to corporation tax on chargeable gains). It considers individuals (including spouses/civil partners), trustees and personal representatives.

Individuals

2. An individual is liable to capital gains tax if he or she is resident, or ordinarily resident in the UK in an income tax year, wherever he or she may be domiciled.

If domiciled outside the UK, then any capital gains tax arising from the disposal of foreign assets is only chargeable to the extent that the sums are remitted to the UK. For this purpose the terms residence, ordinary residence and domicile, have the same meaning as for income tax.

From 2008 a non-domiciled resident who claims UK taxation on the remittance basis does not benefit from a CGT annual exemption.

For other individuals, including non-domiciled residents taxed on the arising basis, the first £10,600 of net gains in the income tax year is exempt.

For most trustees the first £5,300 of net gains in the year is exempt (this limit is subject to reduction for multiple trusts created on the same day)

The following points should be noted.

a) In principle, for each tax year, chargeable gains and allowable losses for the whole year are first added together. Any annual exemption is deducted from the total net gains before considering losses brought forward which may also be deducted.

b) If a taxpayer has no taxable income for the year, unused income allowances and reliefs cannot be deducted from net chargeable gains.

c) The personal capital gains tax rate for 2011/12 is either 18% or 28% as already explained in chapter 26. Gains of up to a lifetime limit of £10m on disposals qualifying for entrepreneurs' relief are taxed at an effective rate of 10%.

   For UK personal representatives' and trustees' CGT rates and exemptions. (See section 6).

   The CGT rate for gains taxed on non-domiciled UK residents on the remittance basis is 28%. (See section 7.)

3. i) A capital loss can only be offset against a capital gain of the same or a later year. Losses of the current year must be set against gains of the current year before being carried forward. The annual exemption amount of £10,600 is deducted from the net gains.

ii) Losses brought forward can be set off against gains of the current year.

iii) Losses brought forward are only utilised to the extent that they are used to reduce any gains to the £10,600 level.

iv) The only time when capital losses can be carried back against gains of an earlier year is after death. (See section 6).

Example of loss offset – current year

Barry makes a chargeable gain from shares of £20,000 on 3 May 2011. He also incurred a capital loss in October 2011 of £2,500. The shares are not eligible for entrepreneurs' relief. Barry has taxable income of £48,000.

Compute Barry's CGT liability for 2011/12

Solution: Barry CGT computation 2011/12

	£
Chargeable gain	20,000
Less capital loss	2,500
Gain	17,500
Less annual exempt amount	(10,600)
Taxable gain	6,900
CGT payable 6,900 @ 28% =	1,932

Husband and wife

4. All husband and wife tax rules apply equally to registered civil partners from the tax year 2005/06. The following points should be noted regarding CGT.

a) Husband and wife are treated as separate individuals, each with a CGs annual exemption of £10,600 for 2011/12.

b) Chargeable gains are recorded by husband and wife in their respective Self Assessment Tax Returns (SATR).

c) The transfer of chargeable assets between husband and wife in any year of assessment does not give rise to any CGT charge where they are living together in the year of assessment; however the next owner takes on the previous one's exact CGT base cost at the date of transfer.

d) Losses of one spouse cannot be set against the gains of the other.

e) Where assets are jointly owned then in the absence of a declaration of beneficial interest, the 50–50 rule applies and each is treated as owning 50% of the assets.

f) Where a married couple live together they can have only one residence which can qualify as their principal private residence.

Example

Mr and Mrs Johnson have the following data relating to the year ended 5th April 2012:

	Mr J	Mrs J
	£	£
Capital gains	15,200	14,000
Capital losses	–	1,000
Taxable income	50,000	18,000

Entrepreneurs' relief is not available.

Compute the CGT liabilities for 2011/12.

Solution: CGT computation 2011/12

	Mr J	Mrs J
	£	£
Capital gains	15,200	14,000
Less losses	–	(1,000)
Net gains	15,200	13,000
Less annual exemption	(10,600)	(10,600)
Chargeable gains	4,600	2,400
CGT payable @ 28% / 18%	1,288	432

Trading losses set against chargeable gains

5. Where a trading loss is incurred in the year then to the extent that it has not been fully relieved against total income of the same or prior tax year, a claim for relief against any chargeable gain can be made. The amount to be claimed cannot exceed the chargeable gain for the year, before deducting the exemption amount of £10,600.

Example

Nick, who is single, has the following data relating to the year 2011/12:

	£
Trade profits 2011/12 (year to 31.3.2012)	15,000
Chargeable gains	12,500

In the year to 31st March 2013 Nick has a trading loss of £16,000, and no other income.

Compute the income tax liability and CGT liability for 2011/12.

Solution

Nick Income tax computation 2011/12

	£
Trade profits	15,000
Less loss relief (see Chapter 14)	(15,000)
Assessable income	–

CGT computation 2011/12

	£
Chargeable gains	12,500
Less trading loss claimed against current year gain	(1,000)
Chargeable gains	11,500
Less annual exemption	10,600
	900
CGT payable @ 18%	162

Notes

i) Nick's personal allowance of £7,475 would be wasted.

ii) The trading loss of £16,000 has been dealt with as follows:

	£
Carry back 2011/12	15,000
Capital gains 2011/12	1,000

The trading loss for the year ended 31st March 2013 can be used in either 2011/12 or 2012/13. However, since there is no other income in the period to 31st March 2013 the carry back has been used. Nick could also have decided to carry the loss forward against future trading income (see Chapter 14).

Personal representatives and trustees

6. The executor or administrator of a deceased person's estate is deemed to have acquired all the chargeable assets at the market value at the date of death, but there is no disposal. Legatees are also deemed to have acquired assets passing to them, at their market value at the date of death, so that any transfer to a legatee is not a chargeable disposal.

Rates The first £10,600 of net gains is exempt in the year of assessment in which the death occurs and the subsequent two years of assessment.

Any balance within the time scale noted above, at 18%.

Losses Losses of the personal representative cannot be set against previous gains of the deceased.

Losses of the deceased in the year of his or her death can be carried back against gains of the previous three tax years.

Within the time scale of the year of death and the next two years, losses need only be utilised to the extent that they reduce the net gains to the exempt amount.

The 2011/12 CGT rate for personal representatives (trustees administering the estates of deceased people) should be 18% for the first £10,000 of gains, then 28%.

The 2011/12 rate for Trustees who are not personal representatives of a deceased person is 28%.

Overseas aspects

7. Non-domiciled individuals

An individual who is resident or ordinarily resident in the UK, but who is not domiciled in the UK, is only charged on gains in foreign assets to the extent that the proceeds from those gains are remitted to the UK. As there is no equivalent concept of remitting loss, there is no relief for losses realised by a non-domiciled individual on foreign assets.

Gains are computed at the date of disposal in accordance with normal computational rules. It is the individual's domicile status at the date of the disposal, not the date of the remittance, which determines the treatment of the gain.

The CGT rate for gains taxed on non-domiciled residents on the remittance basis is 28%. Persons taxed on the remittance basis get no annual exemption.

Temporary non-residents

The following rules apply to individuals who become non-UK resident and non-UK ordinarily resident after 16th March 1998 but who are abroad for less than five complete tax years. Such individuals are still liable to UK CGT on certain gains made during that period of temporary non-residence.

A gain or loss of the tax years between the years of departure and return ('the intervening years') in the UK will be taxed as a gain or allowed as a loss of the year of return provided that:

a) the individual was resident or ordinarily resident for at least four out of seven tax years before the tax year of departure; and

b) the intervening years do not exceed five tax years; and

c) the gain or loss arose on an asset acquired by the individual before actual departure from UK.

Splitting the tax year where residence changes

Normally, an individual's residence status is determined for a complete tax year. However, where a person comes to or leaves the UK, the tax year can in certain circumstances be split into resident and non-resident periods under Extra Statutory Concession D2 (ESC).

This concession applies when the individual:

1) comes to the UK to take up permanent residence or to stay for at least two years; or

2) ceases to reside in the UK if he has left for permanent residence abroad.

It is also extended to the situation where an individual goes abroad to work under a full-time employment contract and:

1) the absence and the employment both extend over a period covering a complete tax year; and

2) interim visits to UK during period do not exceed 183 days in any year or 91 days on average, so that the individual is regarded as not resident and not ordinarily resident for the whole of the contract. However, the concession is restricted where any individual ceases to be resident or ordinarily resident in the UK on or after 17th March 1998 or becomes resident or ordinarily resident in the UK on or after 6th April 1998.

Where an individual arrives in the UK, the year of arrival can be split into resident and non-resident periods, but only if the individual has been non-resident and non-ordinarily resident in the UK throughout the whole of the preceding five tax years. Gains made between the previous 6th April and the day before arrival are not charged to tax in this case.

Where an individual is leaving the UK, the year of departure can be split into resident and non-resident periods, but *only* if the individual was not resident and not ordinarily resident in the UK for at least four out of the seven preceding tax years. Gains made between the day of departure and the following 5th April are not charged to tax in this case.

An important case is R v HMIT ex parte Fulford-Dobson 1987 STC 344 which was on ESC D2 and established that a taxpayer could not use an ESC for tax avoidance.

Partners

8. A partner is assessed as an individual in respect of his or her share of any chargeable gains accruing from the disposal of partnership assets. Accordingly any personal chargeable gains can be set against his or her share of any partnership capital losses, and vice versa.

Student self-testing question

Roger bought a painting for £15,000 in June 2008 which he sold for £65,000 on the 8th May 2011. Incidental costs of acquisition amounted to £200, costs of disposal £2,200. Roger has taxable income of £52,000 for 2011/12.

Roger's wife Vanessa has capital losses of £3,500 for 2011/12.

Compute Roger's 2011/12 CG liability.

Solution: CG computation 2011/12

	£	£
Proceeds of sale 8.5.2011		65,000
Less Cost	15,000	
Cost of disposal	2,200	17,200
Gain		47,800
Less exempt amount		10,600
CGT assessment		37,200
CGT payable @ 37,200 @ 28%		10,416

Notes

i) The losses of Vanessa can only be used against her own future gains.

Questions without answers

1. Frank has chargeable gains of £11,500 for the year 2011/12, and capital losses of £500. His wife sells a piece of land for £10,000 on 10th May 2011 being part of a larger plot purchased in 1995 for £3,000. The remaining part had a value of £30,000 on 10th May 2011. Frank's taxable income for 2011/12 is £21,300 and his wife Florence's is £1,000.

Compute the CGT liability for 2011/12 of Frank and Florence.

2. Arnold purchased a painting in 1990 for £20,000 which he sells for £50,000 in January 2012.

Arnold's wife Patricia owned a small business which she acquired for £16,000 on the 1st January 1989. On the 1st January 2012 she sells the business for £165,000, incurring disposal costs of £344.

Both Arnold and Patricia are both higher-rate income taxpayers in 2011/12.

Compute the CGT liability of Arnold and Patricia for 2011/2012.

31 Chargeable occasions

Introduction

1. A chargeable gain or loss arises on the occasion of a disposal of a chargeable asset. For this purpose a disposal takes place in the following circumstances, each of which is examined in this chapter:

on a sale by contract

on the compulsory acquisition of assets

where capital sums are derived from assets destroyed or damaged, e.g. from insurance claims

where assets have negligible value

on the part-disposal of an asset

by value shifting

on a death

where a gift is made

Disposal by contract

2. Where an asset is disposed of by way of a contract then the date of the disposal is the time the contract is made and not, if different, the time when the asset is conveyed or transferred. For shares and securities the date of the contract note is the disposal date, and for land and buildings and house property the date of the contract to sell is the relevant date, and not the date of completion.

Compulsory acquisition

3. Where there is a compulsory acquisition of an interest in land, then the date of the disposal is the date when the amount of compensation is formally agreed.

Capital sums derived from assets

4. Compensation or insurance monies received in respect of an asset, amounts to a disposal by the owner. Thus if A has property which is damaged or destroyed by fire, then any insurance money received constitutes a disposal for CGT purposes. However, this is varied to some extent where the capital sum is used for the following purposes:

a) to restore a non-wasting asset or

b) to replace a non-wasting asset lost or destroyed.

Restoration of a non-wasting asset

5. If a capital sum is received in respect of a non-wasting asset, which is not lost or destroyed, the taxpayer can claim to have the sum deducted from the cost of acquisition, rather than treated as a part-disposal. Such a claim can only be made if:

a) the capital sum is used wholly for restoration, or the amount not restored is small relative to the capital sum or

b) the capital sum is small relative to the value of the asset.

Small is normally taken to be 5% or less.

Example

Terry purchased a picture for £35,000 in June 2009, which was damaged by fire in May 2011 Insurance proceeds of £1,000 were received in December 2011, the whole amount being spent on restoring the picture. T claims to have the sum of £1,000 not treated as a disposal. The value of the painting after the fire was estimated at £8,000.

Show the computation of the allowable expenditure carried forward.

Solution: Computation 2011/12

	£
Cost	35,000
Less insurance sum	(1,000)
	34,000
Add expenditure on restoration	1,000
Allowable expenditure c/f	35,000

Note

From a capital gains tax point of view, Terry is in exactly the same position as he was before the picture was damaged.

Example

Sam purchased a piece of antique furniture for £12,000 in May 2008. The item was damaged by water in January 2011 for which £1,500 was received by way of insurance in July 2011. The amount spent on restoration was (a) £1,500 (b) £1,430

Compute the allowable costs in each case.

Solution

a) As the whole sum was spent on restoration there is no disposal if Sam claims, and no overall adjustment to the cost of the antique.

b) In this case the whole sum was not spent, but the unused amount of £70 is less than 5% of the capital sum, i.e. £75. The £70 not spent on restoration need not be treated as a disposal, but may be deducted from the allowed cost.

Computation 2011/12

	£	£
Cost of antique		12,000
Less insurance claim:		
Spent on restoration	1,430	
Not spent	70	(1,500)
		10,500
Add expenditure on restoration		1,430
Allowable expenditure		11,930

Note: This is equivalent to the cost less the amount not spent i.e. £12,000 – £70 = £11,930.

Example

Valerie has a collection of rare books purchased in February 2001 for £70,000 which were damaged by fire in May 2011 when they were estimated to be worth £100,000. The value of the collection as damaged by the fire was £70,000. In July 2011 Valerie received £30,000 insurance compensation and the collection was restored.

Compute the CGT effects of a) claiming for restoring and b) not claiming for restoring the book collection.

Solution

a) **Restoring: CGT computation 2011/12**

	£
Original cost of collection	70,000
Less insurance claim	30,000
	40,000
Add expenditure on restoration	30,000
Allowed expenditure c/f	70,000

As the whole sum has been spent on restoration there is no disposal if Valerie so claims and no adjustment to the cost of acquisition.

b) **Not restoring: CGT computation 2011/12**

	£
Insurance proceeds	30,000
Apportioned cost $\frac{30{,}000}{30{,}000+70{,}000} \times 70{,}000$	21,000
Gain subject to CGT before annual exemption	9,000
Balance of original cost carried forward (70,000 – 21,000)	49,000
Add enhancement cost - restoration expense	30,000
Total allowable expenditure c/f, if no claim is made	79,000

Replacement of non-wasting assets

6. Where an asset is lost or destroyed and a capital sum is received by way of compensation, or under a policy of insurance, then if it is spent on a replacement asset within 12 months of the receipt of the sum (or such longer period as HMRC may allow), and the owner so claims, then:

a) the consideration for the disposal of the lost or damaged asset is taken to be such that neither a gain or loss arises.

b) the cost of the replacement asset is reduced by the excess of the capital sum over the total of the consideration used in (a) above, plus any residual or scrap value of the old asset.

Example

Quentin purchased a picture for £8,000 in 2001 which was destroyed by fire in July 2011. Insurance of £20,000 was received in December 2011 and Quentin decided to purchase another picture using the full amount of the insurance money. The scrap value of the picture was £100.

Show the computations, with and without a claim under Section 23.

Solution: CGT Computation 2011/12

a) If no claim is made

	£	£
Capital sum received December 2011	20,000	
Add residual value	100	20,100
Cost		(8,000)
Chargeable gain subject to CGT		12,100

b) If a claim is made

Deemed proceeds of sale December 2011		(8,000)
Cost		8,000
No gain or loss		–
Replacement picture at cost		20,000
Capital sum received	20,000	
Less deemed proceeds	(8,000)	
	12,000	
Add scrap value	100	
Amount deducted from original cost		(12,100)
Allowable cost carried forward		7,900

Note

Where the whole sum is not spent on a replacement asset, then some relief is available providing that the amount not spent is less than the amount of the gain.

Assets whose value becomes negligible

7. The occasion of the entire loss, destruction, or extinction of an asset (wasting or non-wasting) amounts to a disposal of that asset, whether or not any capital sum is received. Where the value of an asset has become negligible, and the inspector is satisfied that such is the case, then the owner may make a claim to the effect that the asset has been sold and immediately required for a consideration equal to the negligible value. Thus if P owns a building which is destroyed by fire, and it was not insured, then he may claim to have made a disposal and reacquisition at the scrap value. An allowable loss for capital gains tax purposes would arise, assuming that the building was not an industrial building eligible for capital allowances.

The replacement of business assets

8. Where a qualifying 'business asset' is disposed of, including the occasion of the receipt of a capital sum, then special provisions apply if the gross proceeds are either wholly or partially spent on other qualifying business assets. This "rollover relief", which only relates to certain assets used for the purposes of a trade, is covered in Chapter 32 and 33.

Value shifting

9. Under these anti-avoidance rules a disposal is deemed to occur where for example the value of a controlling interest in a company is 'watered down' in such a way that the value is passed into other shares or rights, without the occurrence of a disposal.

Hire purchase

10. Where a person enters into a hire purchase or other transactions, whereby he or she enjoys the use of an asset for a period of time, at the end of which he or she may become the owner of the asset, then the acquisition and disposal is deemed to take place at the beginning of the period of use. If the transaction is ended before the property is transferred then 'suitable adjustments' are to be made in agreement with HMRC. See Lyon v Pettigrew March 1985 STI 107.

Part-disposals

11. In general any reference to a disposal also includes a part-disposal, and where this occurs it is necessary to make some apportionment of the cost of acquisition. This is explained in Chapter 28.

Death

12. On the death of a person there is no disposal of any chargeable assets for capital gains tax purposes. The personal representative is deemed to have acquired any assets at their market value at the date of death, and any legatee also acquires the assets at the same market value, the date of acquisition being the date of death.

If a personal representative disposes of any assets other than to a legatee, e.g. in order to raise funds to pay any inheritance tax, then a chargeable occasion arises. However, in the year of death and in the two following years of assessment, the personal representative is entitled to the same annual exemptions as an individual.

Losses incurred by a personal representative cannot be set against any previous gains of the deceased. However, if the deceased had incurred any losses in the year of his or her death, then if they cannot be relieved in that year, then they can be carried back and set against gains in the previous three years.

Gifts

13. A gift of a chargeable asset does amount to a disposal, and this aspect together with the special reliefs available is examined in Chapter 32.

Student self-testing question

Jane has a collection of rare prints which cost £3,000 in May 1983. They were damaged by water in November 2010 and Jane received £17,000 by way of insurance compensation in May 2011. She spent £15,000 on restoration. The value of the prints in a damaged state was £6,000.

Compute any CGT liability arising and the amount of allowable expenditure carried forward.

Solution: CGT computation 2011/12

Capital sum received May 2011	17,000
Less spent on restoration	(15,000)
Part-disposal	2,000
Proportion of cost: $3{,}000 \times \dfrac{2{,}000}{2{,}000 + 6{,}000} =$	(750)
Gain subject to CGT	1,250
Allowable expenditure carried forward	
Cost of acquisition	3,000
Less part-disposal cost	(750)
Balance of cost carried forward	2,250

Question without answer

Zachariah had a painting which was badly damaged by fire in January 2010. The picture was originally purchased for £1,000 in July 1983. In May 2011 Zachariah received insurance compensation of £20,000 which he decides to spend on a new painting. The scrap value of the damaged painting was £50.

Show the CGT position for 2011/12 on the basis that

a) Zachariah makes a claim under Section 23 TCGA 1992

b) Zachariah makes no such claim.

32 Gifts – holdover relief

Introduction

1. This chapter is concerned with capital gains tax on gifts of chargeable assets. It begins with a list of exempt gifts and then examines the optional holdover relief for gifts of business assets.

Holdover relief can be considered here as any gain that normally arises on the gift of a business asset being deducted from the deemed acquisition cost of the person receiving the gift. Thus the person making the gift has potentially avoided a charge to capital gains tax. In the case of gifts of business assets then the relief can be valuable and provide succession for a family business or when a business asset is disposed of in a 'not at arm's length' transaction.

If the donee dies still owning the asset then as there is no CGT on death the held over gain is effectively never taxed.

Gift relief is technically a "holdover" and not a full "rollover" relief because there is one circumstance in which the held-over gain becomes chargeable without the donee disposing of the asset. That is if the donee becomes non-resident in the UK, within six tax years of the gift being made on which the holdover relief was claimed. If this happens the held-over gain is crystallised ie treated as realised by the current owner of the asset at the date of ceasing UK residence and ordinary residence. If the donee becomes non resident after more than six tax years there is currently no crystallisation of the held over gain.

2. A gift or a bargain not made at arm's length of a chargeable asset amounts to a disposal for capital gains tax purposes and is deemed to be made for a consideration equal to its market value.

Exemptions

3. The following gifts do not give rise to any chargeable gain or loss.

a) A gift to a charity or other approved institution such as the National Gallery, or the British Museum. Such a transfer is deemed to take place on a no gain or loss basis.

b) Gifts of works of art, manuscripts, historic buildings, scenic land etc., if the conditions required for inheritance tax exemption are satisfied.

c) A gift of a chattel with a market value of less than £6,000. See Chapter 28.

d) A gift of an exempt asset such as a private motor car, or the principal private residence of the taxpayer, unless otherwise taxable.

Gifts of business assets – Section 165

4. The following are the main provisions relating to gifts of business assets.

a) Holdover relief is available to an individual who makes a transfer at less than market price to a person of:

i) business assets used for the purposes of a trade, profession or vocation carried on by:

1. the transferor, or

2. his or her personal company

3. a member of a trading group of which the holding company is his or her personal company.

ii) Shares or securities of a trading company, or of the holding company of a trading company where:

1. the shares are neither quoted nor dealt in on the AIM/USM or,

2. the trading company or holding company is the transferor's personal company.

iii) agricultural property qualifying for the 100% IHT relief.

b) A personal company is one in which the individual is entitled to exercise 5% or more of the voting rights.

c) The relief must be claimed jointly by the transferee and the transferor, within six years of the date of transfer.

d) The relief is only available in respect of a business asset.

e) Holdover relief is not available:

i) if the donee is non-resident or is exempt from CGT by reason of a double tax treaty.

ii) if the recipient is a company controlled by non-residents who are connected with the donor.

f) the held over gain (in isolation) also becomes chargeable on the donee, as a CGT disposal in the year of emigration, if he/she emigrates permanently from the UK within 6 years of the transfer

Example

Beryl purchased the goodwill and freehold property of a retail business for £90,000 in 1990, which she gave to her son in May 2011 when it was worth £200,000.

Compute the chargeable gain that can be held over.

Solution: Computation 2011/12

	£
Disposal at market price	200,000
Less Cost	90,000
Chargeable gain held over	110,000

Acquisition by Beryl's son	
Market value of assets transferred	200,000
Less held over gain	110,000
Deemed cost	90,000

Example

William purchased his business premises in September 1988 for £40,000, which he gave to his son in May 2000 when it was worth £120,000. The election for hold over relief was made and accepted. On 2nd June 2011 William's son sold the premises for £200,000.

Compute the chargeable gain for 2011/12.

Solution: CGT 2000/2001

	£
Value of premises	120,000
Cost of acquisition	40,000
Held over gain	80,000
Chargeable gain	NIL
CGT 2011/12	
Proceeds of sale	200,000
Base cost (120,000 – 40,000)	80,000
Chargeable gain subject to CGT	120,000

Note

i) The gain is chargeable at 10% as the asset qualifies for entrepreneurs' relief.

ii) The annual exemption of £10,600 will also be available, unless William has other net gains in the year not qualifying for ER, which would take the annual exemption in priority to the ER gain, under FA 2010.

Gift of shares in personal company

5. If the transfer by an individual is of shares in his or her personal company then the held over gain is restricted, where there are any non-business assets in the company. The gain is restricted where either:

a) at any time within 12 months of disposal not less than 25% of the company's voting rights were exercisable by the transferor, or

b) the company is his or her personal company at any time within that period.

$$\text{Chargeable gain} \times \frac{\text{Chargeable business assets of the company at date of disposal}}{\text{Chargeable assets of the company at date of disposal}}$$

$$= \frac{\text{CBA}}{\text{CA}}$$

Example

Terry acquired all the shares of X Ltd, a trading company, for £9,000 in March 1994, and transferred them by way of a gift to Phil in May 2011 when they were worth £140,000. At the date of the gift the company's assets were valued as follows:

	£
Freehold land and buildings	30,000
Goodwill	30,000
Plant and machinery – all items > £6,000	25,000
Investment in quoted company	60,000
Inventory (stock), receivables (debtors) and cash	18,750

Solution: Computation 2011/12

	£
Proceeds of sale of shares	140,000
Less cost of acquisition	(9,000)
Chargeable gain	131,000
Held over gain: $\frac{85}{145}$ x 131,000 (see working)	(76,793)
Chargeable gain	54,207

Working

	Chargeable business assets (open market value at date of disposal)	Chargeable assets
	£	£
Freehold land	30,000	30,000
Goodwill	30,000	30,000
Investment	–	60,000
Plant and machinery	25,000	25,000
	85,000	145,000

Notes

i) The deemed cost to Phil is £140,000 – 76,793 i.e. £63,207

ii) Chargeable business assets are any assets on the disposal of which a gain would be a chargeable gain, and excludes, therefore, motor cars and items of moveable plant purchased and sold for £6,000 or less. Other plant and machinery are chargeable business assets if tangible assets (chattels) worth over £6,000 per time.

iii) Inventory (stock), receivables (debtors) and cash are exempt from capital gains tax thus these are not chargeable business assets.

iv) A business asset is an asset used for the purpose of trade.

v) Goodwill counted in the business's or company's net asset value is a chargeable business asset for an individual therefore nay amount paid for the business / the shares that exceeds the separable value of tangible assets can be deemed to relate to goodwill which is a chargeable business asset.

vi) The investment held by the company is not a chargeable business asset.

Gifts of non-business assets, works of art etc.

6. Holdover relief is also available on gifts, where both the transferor and the transferee are individuals or trusts for:

i) gifts which are immediately chargeable transfers for IHT purposes i.e. gifts to relevant property trusts (see Part V).

ii) gifts which are either exempt or conditionally exempt for IHT purposes e.g. gifts to political parties or gifts of heritage property, but not PETs.

Payment of tax by instalments

7. a) Capital gains tax on gifts not eligible for full holdover relief may be paid by ten equal annual instalments where an election is made. This only applies to the following assets:

i) Land or any interest in land.

ii) Shares or securities in a company which immediately before the disposal gave control to the person making the disposal.

iii) Shares or securities of a company (not falling in (ii)) and not quoted on a recognised stock exchange nor dealt in on the USM/AIM.

b) Where the gift is to a connected person, tax and accrued interest become payable where the donee subsequently disposes of the gift for a valuable consideration.

c) The first instalment is due on the normal due date. Instalments are not interest free unless the gifted property is agricultural land qualifying for IHT agricultural property relief.

Student self-testing questions

1. Karen purchased a business in 1990 which she gave to Mark in May 1999 when the market value was £125,000. Both Karen and Mark elected to hold over the computed gain. Mark sold the business in May 2011 for £180,000. The cost in May 1999 was £40,000. The business qualifies for entrepreneurs' relief.

Show the CGT computations.

Solution

Karen CGT Computation 1999/2000

	£
Deemed proceeds of sale (May 1999)	125,000
Cost (May 1990)	(40,000)
Gain held over	85,000

Mark CGT Computation 2011/12

	£
Proceeds of sale (May 2011)	180,000
Deemed base cost (125,000 – 40,000)	85,000
Chargeable gain before annual exemption	95,000
Eligible for entrepreneurs' rate (10%)	

Notes:

i) No CGT is payable by Karen upon the gift of the asset to Mark.

2. On 5th December 2011 Michael sold to his son Simon a freehold shop valued at £250,000 for £75,000, and claimed gift relief. Michael had originally purchased the shop from which he has run his business in July 2001 for £45,000. Simon continued to run a business from the shop premises but decided to sell the shop in May 2013 for £230,000.

Compute any chargeable gains arising. Assume the rules of CGT in 2011/12 continue to apply in May 2013.

Suggested solution

Michael's CGT position 2011/12	£
Proceeds	250,000
Less cost	(45,000)
Gain	205,000
Less gain deferred by gift relief claim	
£205,000 – (£75,000-£45,000)	(175,000)
Gain left in charge subject to ER, annual exemption	30,000

Simon's CGT position 2013/14	**£**
Proceeds	230,000
Less cost £250,000 – £175,000 gift holdover	(75,000)
Gain subject to CGT (ER is likely)	155,000

Notes:

i) In this case for Michael the excess of consideration received over the original cost (£30,000) becomes a gain immediately chargeable to CGT.

ii) Michael's disposal of the shop will only qualify for entrepreneurs' relief if he closed or disposed of his own business at the same time as he disposed of the shop to Simon.

iii) Simon is deemed to have purchased the shop for £75,000. ER will apply to Simon's gain if he disposes of his own business along with the shop, but not if he merely relocates;

iv) Simon meets the ER qualifying condition of having owned and run his business for more than twelve months before disposal.

Question without answer

1. Frank purchased a controlling interest in Nominal Ltd, a trading company, for £100,000 in 1991 which he gave to his son on 1st April 2004 when he was 48 years of age. The market value of the interest at the date of the gift was £500,000. A joint claim under Section 165 TCGA 1992 was made. Frank's son sells the shareholding for £650,000 in June 2011.

There were no non-business, chargeable assets.

Compute the chargeable gains arising in 2011/12.

2. Jack Chan, aged 45, has been in business as a sole trader since 1 May 2001. On 28 February 2012 he transferred the business to his daughter Jill, at which time the following assets were sold to her:

(1) Goodwill with a market value of £60,000. The goodwill has been built up since 1 May 2001, and has a nil cost. Jill paid Jack £50,000 for the goodwill.

(2) A freehold office building with a market value of £130,000. The office building was purchased on 1 July 2003 for £110,000, and has always been used by Jack for business purposes. Jill paid Jack £105,000 for the office building.

(3) A freehold warehouse with a market value of £140,000. The warehouse was purchased on 1 September 2003 for £95,000, and has never been used by Jack for business purposes. Jill paid Jack £135,000 for the warehouse.

(4) A motor car with a market value of £25,000. The motor car was purchased on 1 November 2005 for £23,500, and has always been used by Jack for business purposes. Jill paid Jack £20,000 for the motor car.

Where possible, Jack and Jill have elected to hold over any gains arising.

Jack has unused capital losses of £6,400 brought forward from 2010-11.

Required: Calculate Jack's Capital gains tax liability for 2011–12, and advise him by when this should be paid. (15 marks)

(ACCA December 2002 updated)

33 Business assets and businesses

Introduction

1. The disposal of a business or of any business, assets requires special consideration for chargeable gains tax purposes as there are valuable relief's available to the owners. In this chapter the following topics will be examined:

a) Replacement of business assets Sections 152 to 158.

b) Reinvestment relief for individuals.

c) Transfer of a business to a company Section 162.

d) Transfer of assets between group companies.

e) Trading stock.

f) Loans to traders.

The holdover relief in respect of a gift of business assets is outlined in the chapter on gifts, see Chapter 32.

Replacement of business assets Sections 152–158

2. Relief under these provisions enables a taxpayer to 'roll over' any gain arising on the disposal of a 'business asset', by deducting it from the cost of a replacement. The main rules are:

a) A business asset is one used for the purposes of a trade and falling within the under mentioned classes:

> land and buildings occupied by the taxpayer; fixed plant and machinery; satellites, space stations, space craft; ships, aircraft and hovercraft; goodwill; milk and potato quotas; EC agricultural quotas. Since 2002, goodwill and quotas are not chargeable assets for corporate taxpayers, and so are now excluded from this list in the case of companies only, but remain qualifying assets for individuals

b) The assets disposed of must be used throughout the period of ownership, and the latter includes assets held by a 'personal company'.

c) The new asset must be acquired within 12 months before the disposal, or within three years after, although the Inspector of Taxes has power to extend these limits.

d) Where a trader re-invests in business assets to be used in a new trade then relief is available providing the interval between the two trades is not greater than three years.

e) Partial relief is available where the whole of the proceeds of sale are not used in the replacement. In these circumstances the gain attracting an immediate charge to tax is the lower of:

   i) the chargeable gain, and

   ii) the uninvested proceeds.

   By concession HMRC regard proceeds net of disposal costs for this purpose.

f) There are special provisions where the replacement asset is a depreciating asset. See below.

g) The relief is also available to non-profit making organisations such as trade and professional associations.

h) Where a person carrying on a trade uses the proceeds from the disposal of an 'old asset' on capital expenditure to enhance the value of other assets, such expenditure is treated for the purposes of these provisions as incurred in acquiring other assets provided:

  i) the other assets are used only for the purposes of the trade, or

  ii) on completion of the work on which the expenditure was incurred the assets are immediately taken into use and used only for the purposes of the trade.

i) Where a 'new asset' is not, on acquisition, immediately taken into use for the purposes of a trade, it will nevertheless qualify for relief provided:

  i) the owner proposes to incur capital expenditure for the purpose of enhancing its value;

  ii) any work arising from such capital expenditure begins as soon as possible after acquisition, and is completed within a reasonable time;

  iii) on completion of the work the asset is taken into use for the purpose of the trade and for no other purpose; and

  iv) the asset is not let or used for any non-trading purpose in the period between acquisition and the time it is taken into use for the purposes of the trade.

j) As a general rule rollover relief should not be claimed by an individual where the gain would be covered by the annual exemption.

k) Incorporated entities use the indexation allowance in the computation of any gains to be rolled over, unincorporated entities and individuals do not use indexation.

Example

Peter purchased the goodwill of a retail business in 1989 for £15,000 and sold it on 1st December 2011 for £40,000. On 31st December 2011 Peter purchased the goodwill of a new business for £60,000.

Compute the chargeable gain.

Solution: Computation 2011/12

	£
Proceeds of sale	40,000
Less cost	(15,000)
Chargeable gain eligible for rollover	25,000
Cost of new business	60,000
Less rolled over gain on old business	(25,000)
Deemed cost	35,000

Notes:

i) The base cost on any subsequent disposal of the new business asset is £35,000.

i) There is no charge to CGT on the first disposal as all of the proceeds have been re-invested.

Example

Karen purchased a freehold factory for her business use in 1992 for £75,000. This was sold for £250,000 on 31st May 2011, and a new factory acquired for £230,000.

Compute the chargeable gain.

Solution: Computation 2011/12

		£
Proceeds of sale		250,000
Less cost		(75,000)
Chargeable gain		175,000
Less rollover relief:		
Gain	175,000	
Less amount of consideration not invested	(20,000)	(155,000)
Gain chargeable immediately		20,000

Notes

i) The base cost for subsequent disposals would be £230,000 – £155,000 i.e. £75,000.

ii) The rolled over gain is restricted by any part of the consideration not reinvested, i.e. (250,000 – 230,000) = 20,000.

Replacement with a depreciating asset

3. Where the asset is replaced with a depreciating asset then the gain is not deducted from the cost of the asset, i.e. the replacement asset, but is frozen until the earliest of the following occurs:

a) the depreciating asset is itself sold, or

b) the depreciating asset ceases to be used by the person in his or her trade, or

c) the expiry of 10 years from the date of the replacement.

A depreciating asset is one with an estimated life of 50 years or less, or one which will have such a life expectancy within 10 years from the date of acquisition, i.e. a total of 60 years at the date of acquisition.

Where a gain on a disposal is held over against a depreciating asset then provided that a non-depreciating asset is bought before the held over gain on the depreciating asset crystallises, it is possible to transfer the held over gain to a non-depreciating replacement.

Example

John sold his freehold shop property used for trade purposes for £120,000 on 1st August 2008. The property was bought for £50,000 on 1st May 2001. In December 2009 John acquired fixed plant for £130,000 which he used immediately for trade purposes until he ceased trading altogether on 31st March 2012 when the plant was scrapped. He had no other gains in the year 2011/2012.

Compute the chargeable gains when the plant was scrapped.

Solution

John's CGT computation 2009/10

	£
1.8.2009 Proceeds of sale of property	120,000
1.5.2001 Cost of acquisition	(50,000)
Chargeable gain	70,000
Less amount held over	(70,000)
Assessable gain	Nil

John's CGT computation 2011/12

	£
Held over gain crystallising	70,000
Less annual exemption	(10,600)
Gain subject to CGT	59,400
CGT at 10%	5,940

Notes

i) As the business ceased to trade the held over gain has crystallised. Entrepreneurs' relief is assumed as the trade has ceased altogether

ii) No further gain arises on the scrapping of the plant, as any proceeds of sale would be < cost. No allowable capital loss can arise on plant if the net cost is already relieved by way of capital allowances (see chapter 13).

iii) The held over gain is not deducted from the cost of the replacement depreciating asset.

Transfer of a business to a company Section 162

4. The transfer of a business to a company is a disposal of the assets of the business and can therefore give rise to a chargeable gain or loss.

A form of rollover relief exists where an individual transfers the whole of his or her business to a company in exchange for shares, wholly or partly. In effect the held over gain is deducted from the costs of the shares acquired. The gain to which this section relates is that arising on the transfer of chargeable business assets, and the amount deferred is equal to:

$$\text{The net gain} \times \frac{\text{Value of shares received}}{\text{Total value of consideration ie shares and loans}}$$

All assets of the business must be transferred although cash balances and other non-business assets may be retained as a general rule.

The taxpayer can elect for the rollover relief *not* to apply, which may be advantageous in terms of his entrepreneurs relief entitlement

Example

Andrea transfers her business to Trent Ltd on 6th April 2011 in exchange for 100,000 ordinary shares of £1 each fully paid, having a value of par, and £25,000 by way of loans. Chargeable gains on the transfer of business assets to Trent Ltd amounted to £75,000. Andrea had been in business since 1990.

Compute the chargeable gain.

Solution: Calculation of rolled over gain 2011/12

	£
$75{,}000 \times \dfrac{100{,}000}{100{,}000 + 25{,}000} =$	60,000
Chargeable gain	75,000
Less amount rolled over	(60,000)
Gain subject to CGT	15,000

Deemed cost of shares carried forward	£
Value of shares	100,000
Less rolled over gain	(60,000)
Net cost	40,000

5. Refer to Chapter 24 for more on corporate groups, in corporation tax terms. When a company disposes of a chargeable asset outside the group, then any capital gain arising will be chargeable to corporation tax. However, if the disposal is by a member of a group of companies to another group company then the disposal does not give rise to any chargeable gain or loss. This is achieved by deeming the consideration for the disposal of the asset to be such an amount that neither a gain nor a loss accrues to the company disposing of the asset. When the asset is ultimately disposed of outside the group, then a normal liability to corporation tax on any gain would arise.

The company actually disposing of the asset and any other company in the group can elect that the disposal outside the group be treated as being made by the other company. The election must be made within two years after the end of the accounting period in which the actual disposal is made.

Transfer of assets between group companies

6. a) A group comprises a principal company and all of its 75% subsidiaries.

b) A 75% subsidiary means a company whose ordinary share capital is owned by another company either directly or indirectly to the extent of at least 75%. Again ordinary share capital comprises all shares other than fixed preference shares.

c) Where the principal company is itself a 75% subsidiary of another company, then both its parent and its subsidiaries, together with the principal company, constitute a group.

d) From 1st April 2000, companies are able to transfer assets to one another on a no gain/no loss basis in a wider range of circumstances than before. In particular, it is possible to make such transfers between:

   i) two UK resident companies with a common non-resident parent company;

   ii) a UK resident company and a non-resident company within the same world-wide group, where the latter company carries on a UK trade through a branch or agency.

e) A company is not a member of a group unless the principal member of the group has itself directly or indirectly more than 50% interest in its profits and assets.

Members of a consortium are not eligible for treatment as a group for the purposes of this section, nor are close investment holding companies, unless the transfer is between close investment holding companies.

Example

Zodiac Ltd and its 75% subsidiary company Burnham Ltd had the following results for the year ended 31st March 2012.

	Z Ltd	B Ltd
Trading profits	125,000	80,000
Chargeable gains (loss)	(75,000)	100,000

Zodiac Ltd and Burnham Ltd elect that the capital loss arising from the disposal of an asset by Zodiac Ltd be treated as a disposal by Burnham Ltd.

Show the effects of the election.

Solution: Corporation tax computations AP 31.3.2012

	Z Ltd	B Ltd
Trading profits	125,000	80,000
Chargeable gains		
(100,000 – 75,000)		25,000
	125,000	105,000
Corporation tax @ 20%	25,000	21,000

Notes

i) It is not necessary for Z Ltd to transfer the asset, giving rise to the loss of £75,000, to B Ltd under section 171.

ii) The election has to be made within two years of the end of the AP in which the assets disposed of outside the group i.e. by 31.3.14.

iii) The election can be made in respect of part of an asset.

iv) Without the transfer B Ltd would be taxed on the full £180,000 of its profits chargeable to corporation tax at the marginal rate. (2 companies 300,000÷2 = 150,000)

v) Group cash savings (305,000 – 230,000) @ 20% = £15,000.

Assets appropriated from or to trading stock/inventory on a transfer between group companies

7. If the transfer is of an asset which the recipient company appropriates to its trading stock, then that company is deemed to have received a capital asset and immediately transferred that asset to its trading stock. There would thus be no capital gain or loss arising on the inter-company transfer, as it would fall within the provisions noted above.

Where the asset transferred to a group company was trading stock of the transferor company, then the latter is treated as having appropriated the asset as a capital asset immediately prior to the disposal. The value placed on the asset for trading purposes would be the transfer value giving rise to a 'no gain or loss' situation.

Miscellaneous points

8. a) When an asset is disposed of by a group company to a company outside the group, then any net capital allowances granted to any member of the group relating to the asset are taken into consideration in computing any gain or loss.

b) If a company to which an asset has been transferred, ceases to be a member of a group within six years of the date of the transfer the position is as follows.

   i) At the date of the acquisition of the asset by the company leaving the group, it is deemed to have sold and reacquired the asset at its market value.

   ii) There will therefore be a chargeable gain or loss on the difference between the market value and the original cost to the group of the asset.

This provision does not apply if a company ceases to be a member of a group by being wound up.

iii) The gain is chargeable in the A.P. the company leaves the group but it is the gain arising on intra-group transfer known as 'de-grouping charge'.

c) The provisions of rollover relief are extended to groups and enable all trades carried on by the group to be treated as one.

d) Where a company is a dual resident member of a group of companies detailed provisions exist which are designed to prevent:

i) the transfer of assets at a no gain/no loss value where the dual resident company would be exempt from CGT

ii) the granting of rollover relief for the replacement of business assets where the replacement assets are required by a dual resident company.

e) Capital losses brought into a group as a result of a company joining the group will be 'ring fenced' for disposals. In effect such capital losses will only be available for unrestricted set-off against gains on:

i) assets held by the company at the date that it joined the group or

ii) assets acquired by that company from outside the new group and used in a trade carried on by that company before joining the group.

Substantial disposals of shares – exempt from CGT

9. Sales by United Kingdom companies of 'substantial shareholdings' in other companies are tax-free, provided that certain conditions are met.

i) The relief is available for disposals by trading companies or members of a trading group (the 'investing' company).

ii) It applies to gains on the disposal of a substantial shareholding in a trading company or holding company of a trading group (the 'investee' company).

iii) A substantial shareholding means, broadly, at least a 10% interest.

iv) The substantial shareholding must have been held for a continuous period of at least 12 months in the two years immediately before the disposal.

In order to hold a substantial interest, the investing company needs to be beneficially entitled to at least 10% of the investee company's:

i) ordinary share capital; and

ii) profits available for distribution to equity holders; and

iii) assets available for distribution to equity holders in the event of a winding-up.

In determining whether a holding amounts to a substantial shareholding, shares held by other group members are aggregated over the world-wide group.

Trading stock

10. Trading stock is not a business asset for capital gains tax purposes as it is normally taken into consideration in computing taxable trading income.

Where an asset is appropriated to stock in trade then there is a deemed disposal at the date of the appropriation if a gain or loss would have arisen from a sale of the asset at its market value. An election can be made to have the gain (or loss) deducted (or added) from the value of the asset so that the ultimate profit is taxed as trading income.

If an asset is appropriated from trading stock for any purpose then it is deemed to be acquired for CGT purposes at the value taken into account in computing the taxable profit.

Example

Keith purchased an asset in October 1986 for £20,000 which he held as an investment until 31st July 2011 when it was transferred to trading stocks. Market value at 31st July was £45,000. It was sold as trading stock in December 2011 for £60,000.

Show the effects of the above both with and without an election

Solution

Without election. CGT computation 2011/12

	£	£
July 2011 market value		45,000
Less cost of acquisition		20,000
Chargeable gain subject to CGT		25,000
Trade profits		
Sale of inventory (trading stock)		60,000
Less cost		45,000
Taxable profit		15,000

With election. CGT computation 2011/12

Trade profits		
Sale of inventory (trading stock)		60,000
Market value on appropriation	45,000	
Less gain (as above)	25,000	20,000
Taxable trade profits		40,000

Notes

i) The asset must be of a kind sold in the ordinary course of trade.

ii) The appropriation must be made with a view to resale at a profit.

iii) An election is only available by a person taxable with trade profits.

Loans to traders

11. Loans made to traders may be claimed as a CGT loss in the following circumstances:

i) where a loss is incurred on a qualifying loan.

ii) where the taxpayer has to meet a guarantee made on a qualifying loan, or

iii) where a loss is incurred on a qualifying corporate bond.

The borrower must be resident in the UK and the money advanced must be used wholly for the purposes of the trade or profession carried on, or for letting qualifying holiday accommodation.

The loss arises at the time the claim is made, and not the date of the loan transaction so that indexation does not arise.

Tax efficient schemes

12. Shares that qualify for exemption from capital gains tax will not need to make use of any rollover conditions. Such shares, in addition to the ones identified in this chapter, are included in schemes such as:

i) Enterprise Investment Scheme (EIS)

ii) Venture Capital Trusts

iii) Corporate Venturing Scheme

Student self-testing questions

1. A sole trader bought a freehold factory in October 1998 and sold it for £140,000 on 18 May 2011 giving a gain of £35,900. He bought a replacement factory on 6 June 2011 for £120,000.

Requirement: Assuming a claim for rollover relief was made what is the base cost of the new factory.

Suggested solution

		£
Total gain		35,900
Amount not reinvested	(140,000 - 120,000)	(20,000)
Gain eligible for roll-over		15,900
Cost of new factory		120,000
Rolled over gain		(15,900)
Base cost of new factory		104,100
Gain chargeable immediately		20,000

2. Linda is a sole trader who bought a qualifying business asset for £341,250 on 5/11/1991 and sold it for £982,800 on 31/12/2011. A replacement business asset was acquired on 1/11/2011 at a cost of £1,092,000. This asset was sold on 3/9/2015 for £1,829,100. A rollover claim was made on the first sale only. Assume existing rules apply in 2015.

Requirement: Calculate the capital gain on the sale of the second asset.

Suggested solution

31/12/11 disposal

	£	£
Sale proceeds		982,800
Cost		(341,250)
Gain rolled over		641,550

3/9/15 disposal

	£	£
Sale proceeds		1,829,100
Cost (1/11/11)	1,092,000	
Rollover relief	(641,550)	(450,450)
Gain subject to CGT		1,378,650

3. Hadley Limited purchased a factory in November 1989 for £250,000. Not needing all the space, the company let out 15% of it. In April 2011 the company sold the factory for £600,000 and bought another in the same month for £700,000. Assume an indexation factor of 1.045 from November 1989 to April 2011.

Requirement:

Calculate:

(a) **The chargeable gain or allowable loss, if any, arising on the disposal in April 2011**

(b) **The allowable expenditure (base cost) of the new factory.**

Suggested solution

(a) Split the old factory & the new factory into qualifying and non qualifying parts and compute the gains on them separately:

	Qualifying	Non qualifying
	£	£
Disposal proceeds (85%/15%)	510,000	90,000
Less cost	(212,500)	(37,500)
Unindexed gain	297,500	52,500
Indexation allowance	(222,062)	(39,187))
212,500 and 37,500 x 1.045		
Indexed gain	75,438	13,313

The gain of £13,313 will be taxed immediately as it does not qualify for rollover relief.

b) The base cost of the new factory is reduced by the amount of the gain rolled over. It is therefore:

	£
Purchase cost	700,000
Less gain rolled over	(75,438)
	624,567

4. Harold bought a freehold shop for use in his business in June 2010 for £150,000. He sold it for £175,000 on 1st August 2011. On 8th July 2011 Harold bought some fixed plant and machinery to use in his business costing £178,000. He then sells the plant and machinery for £192,000 on 20th November 2013.

Show Harold's CGT position.

Suggested solution

Gain deferred	£
Proceeds of shop	175,000
Less cost	(150,000)
Gain	25,000

The gain is deferred in relation to the plant and machinery.

Sale of plant and machinery	£
Proceeds	192,000
Less cost	(178,000)
Gain	14,000
Total gain chargeable on sale	
(gain on plant and machinery plus deferred gain)	
£25,000 + £14,000 subject to CGT	39,000

Questions without answers

1. Tony purchased a grocery business on 1st June 1988 which he is considering selling in December 2011 for an estimated price of £400,000. The sale price is allocated between the business assets on the following basis.

	Consideration £
Freehold premises	275,000
Flat above premises (occupied by Tony since acquisition as his only residence)	40,000
Goodwill	50,000
Inventory (trading stock)	20,000
Shop fixtures	15,000
	400,000

The cost of the business at 1 June 1988 was £150,000 comprising the following:

	£
Freehold premises	60,000
Flat above premises	30,000
Goodwill	40,000
Inventory (trading stock)	15,000
Shop fixtures	5,000

Calculate the CGT liability which would arise should Tony sell the business and retire. He has no other chargeable gains arising in 2011-2012, and has taxable income of £45,000.

2. Chandra Khan disposed of the following assets during 2011/12:

a) On 15 June 2011 Chandra sold 10,000 £1 ordinary shares (a 30% shareholding) in Universal Ltd, an unquoted trading company, to her daughter for £75,000. The market value of the shares on this date was £110,000. The shareholding was purchased on 10 July 1997 for £38,000. Chandra and her daughter have elected to hold over the gain as a gift of a business asset.

b) On 8 November 2011 Chandra sold a freehold factory for £146,000. The factory was purchased on 3 January 1997 for £72,000. 75% of the factory has been used in a manufacturing business run by Chandra as a sole trader. However, the remaining 25% of the factory has never been used for business purposes. Chandra has claimed to rollover the gain on the factory against the replacement cost of a new freehold factory that was purchased on 10 November 2011 for £156,000. The new factory is used 100% for business purposes by Chandra.

c) On 8 March 2012 Chandra incorporated a wholesale business that she has run as a sole trader since 1 May 2003. The market value of the business on 8 March 2011 was £250,000. All of the business assets were transferred to a new limited company, with the consideration consisting of 200,000 £1 ordinary shares valued at £200,000 and £50,000 in cash. The only chargeable asset of the business was goodwill, and this was valued at £100,000 on 8 March 2012. The goodwill has a nil cost.

Calculate the capital gains arising from Chandra's disposals during 2011/12. You should ignore the annual exemption. ACCA

3. Astute Ltd sold a factory on 15 February 2012 for £320,000. The factory was purchased on 24 October 1997 for £164,000, and was extended at a cost of £37,000 during March 1999. During May 2000 the roof of the factory was replaced at a cost of £24,000 following a fire. Astute Ltd incurred legal fees of £3,600 in connection with the purchase of the factory, and legal fees of £6,200 in connection with the disposal.

Indexation factors are as follows:

October 1997 to February 2012	0·504 (estimated)
March 1999 to February 2012	0·438 (estimated)
May 2000 to February 2012	0·396 (estimated)

Astute Ltd is considering the following alternative ways of reinvesting the proceeds from the sale of its factory:

(1) A freehold warehouse can be purchased for £340,000.

(2) A freehold office building can be purchased for £275,000.

(3) A leasehold factory on a 40-year lease can be acquired for a premium of £350,000.

The reinvestment will take place during May 2012. All of the above buildings have been, or will be, used for business purposes.

Required:

(a) State the conditions that must be met in order that rollover relief can be claimed. You are not expected to list the categories of asset that qualify for rollover relief. (3 marks)

(b) Before taking account of any available rollover relief, calculate Astute Ltd's chargeable gain in respect of the disposal of the factory. (5 marks)

(c) Advise Astute Ltd of the rollover relief that will be available in respect of EACH of the three alternative re-investments. Your answer should include details of the base cost of the replacement asset for each alternative. (7 marks)

(15 marks)

(ACCA December 2001 updated)

End of section questions and answers

1. David Plaine resigned as a full-time working director of Plaine Sailing Ltd, an unquoted personal company, on 1st July 2011, to become non-executive chairman and president of the company. He had joined the company on 1st July 1987, acquiring 30% of the ordinary shares at a cost of £180,000.

On 1st July 2011 he sold his entire interest for £800,000.

The following is a summary of the balance sheet of Plaine Sailing Ltd as at 30th June 2011 at market values:

	£
Freehold land and buildings	800,000
Goodwill	500,000
Plant and machinery (all items > £6,000)	300,000
Inventory (stocks) and work in progress	300,183
Trade receivables (debtors)	210,146
Cash in hand	32,000
Trade payables (creditors)	100,184
Bank overdraft	164,239

Compute the chargeable gain for 2011/12 after any claim for relief Plaine could make.

Plant and machinery was sold at a loss.

Solution: David Plaine CGT computation 2011/12

	£	£
1st July 2011 Sale proceeds		800,000
Less cost		180,000
Gain subject to CGT		620,000
Annual exemption		(10,600)
Chargeable gain		609,400
CGT @ 10%		60,940

Questions without answers – Capital Gains Tax

1. Earth Ltd sold the following shareholdings during the year ended 31 March 2012:

(a) On 20 November 2011 Earth Ltd sold 25,000 £1 ordinary shares in Venus plc for £115,000. Earth Ltd had originally purchased 40,000 shares in Venus plc on 19 June 1987 for £34,000. On 11 October 2002 Venus plc made a 1 for 4 bonus issue. Retail price indices (RPIs) are as follows:

June 1987	101.90
October 2002	177.90
November 2011	236.80 (estimated)

(b) On 22 January 2012 Earth Ltd sold 30,000 £1 ordinary shares in Saturn plc for £52,500. Earth Ltd purchased 30,000 shares in Saturn plc on 9 February 2001 for £97,500. The indexed value of the 1985 pool on 3 January 2004 was £103,200. On 3 January 2004 Saturn plc made a 1 for 2 rights issue. Earth Ltd took up its allocation under the rights issue in full, paying £1·50 for each new share issued.

(c) On 28 March 2012 Earth Ltd sold its entire holding of £1 ordinary shares in Jupiter plc for £55,000. Earth Ltd had originally purchased 10,000 shares in Mercury plc on 5 May 1995 for £14,000. The indexed value of the 1985 pool on 7 March 2012 was £19,000. On 7 March 2010 Mercury plc was taken over by Jupiter plc. Earth Ltd received two £1 ordinary shares and one £1 preference share in Jupiter plc for each £1 ordinary share held in Mercury plc. Immediately after the takeover each £1 ordinary share in Jupiter plc was quoted at £2·50 and each £1 preference share was quoted at £1·25.

Required: Calculate the chargeable gain or capital loss arising from each of Earth Ltd's disposals during the year ended 31 March 2012.

Each of the three sections of this question carries 5 marks (15 marks)

(ACCA June 2003 updated)

2. Claudius had the following transactions.

(1) Sold 2,250 quoted ordinary shares of Nero plc for £23,150 in March 2012. Before making the sale he owned 6,750 shares, of which 4,500 were purchased in December 1988 for £4,599 and 2,250 were acquired in August 1992 on the occasion of the company's rights issue of 1 for 2 at 160p per share.

(2) Sold 2,550 quoted shares of Livia plc for £12,375 on 10 June 2011. His previous transactions in those shares had been as follows.

April 1988	Purchased	1,500	cost	£3,093
August 1990	Purchased	900	cost	£2,700
May 1992	Bonus issue	1 for 2		

(3) Sold 13,500 units of the Tiberius Unit Trust for £11,480 on 15 June 2011, which had cost £3,450 upon their original offer to the public in June 1987.

(4) Gave his brother 12,000 quoted shares in Augustus plc out of his holding of 30,000 shares in March 2012. He had originally purchased 22,500 shares in January 1989 at a cost of £49,500 and received a scrip issue of 1 for 3 June 1991. At the date of the gift the shares were quoted at 150p each.

Claudius's taxable income for 2011/12 is £55,000.

Requirement:

Calculate Claudius' liability to capital gains tax in respect of the year ended 5 April 2012. None of the transactions qualify for entrepreneurs' relief. (14 marks)

Part V

Inheritance tax

34 General principles

Introduction

1. In this chapter the basic features of inheritance tax are outlined under the following headings

Basic IHT rates and the nil rate band

Transfer of value – definition

Chargeable transfers

Potentially exempt transfers (PETs)

Taper relief on PETs becoming chargeable and on CLTs taxed on death

Gifts with reservation

General Scope of IHT

Excluded Property

Location of Assets

General Exemptions and Reliefs

Business and Agricultural Property Relief

Growing Timber

Quick Succession Relief

Sales within 1 or four years of death

Liabilities and Expenses

Intestacy

Post death variations

Administration and payment

Trusts and IHT (outline only)

IHT Rates and Nil Rate Bands

Chapter 35 goes on to consider inheritance tax computational examples. It should be noted that inheritance tax is a complex area and these chapters aim to provide only a basic introduction to the key concepts and principles. There are many more detailed aspects which are not covered here. The main consolidated legislation is to be found in the Inheritance Tax Act 1984 (IHTA 1984).

Note: Inheritance tax paid by trustees is beyond the scope of this basic introduction. However IHT aspects of trusts are covered below so far as relevant to the IHT affairs of individuals, namely

a) IHT implications for the individual of making a gift to a trust after 22 March 2006;

b) IHT implications for an individual of being the income beneficiary ("life tenant") under either a pre-2006 "interest in possession" (IIP) trust, a post-2006 "immediate post-death interest" (IPDI) trust, or a "disabled person's trust";

c) IHT implications for an individual of being a reversionary beneficiary under a trust (this has basically no IHT implications for the individual beneficiary, unless a gift with reservation is involved)

Basic IHT rates and the nil rate band

2. Since 1986, there are only two rates of IHT for individuals on death: 0% and 40%; and two rates on chargeable transfers during lifetime: 0% and 20%.

Headline IHT tax rates have not changed for over 20 years, but the cumulative amount of transfers charged to IHT at a zero rate (the "nil rate band") has been regularly increased, and remains the subject of frequent political debate.

At the end of this chapter is a table of the rates and the nil rate bands for tax years 2006/07 to 2011/12.

For the tax year 2011/12 the nil rate band is £325,000.

The total amount which is in principle liable to IHT on death consists of:

i) all chargeable transfers in the seven years before death, plus

ii) all the chargeable estate at death, plus

iii) any property given away before death, but subject to a "reservation" in favour of the donor or the donor's spouse at any time within seven years of the donor's death.

The significance of the nil rate band is that whenever IHT falls to be computed on a transfer of value, the nil rate band is applied to the cumulative chargeable transfers by the individual in the past seven years, in date order, to determine how much nil rate band (if any) remains to cover the next chargeable transfer (including transfers on death).

The tax due on a death transfer may be reduced by Quick Succession Relief to the extent that IHT was paid on the same property on another person's death within the past 3 years. (See paragraph 16)

Any IHT due on lifetime gifts because of the death of the donor within seven years is reduced by IHT taper relief if more than 3 years have elapsed between the relevant gift and the death, but the cumulated chargeable value of the lifetime transfer itself is not reduced by this taper relief. (See paragraph 8)

Transfer of value - definition

3. A transfer of value occurs where an individual's estate (ie property of any kind) is reduced in value as a result of a gift or disposition, and the amount of the reduction in estate value is the value transferred for IHT purposes. This may not always be the same value by which the donee's estate is increased by the gift. For example, a gift of one third of a 60% shareholding in a private company to a person who had no prior holding in the company reduces the donor's estate by the difference between a 60% and a 40% shareholding, whereas it increases the donee's estate by the market value of a 20% holding in isolation.

In the case of transfers on a death, the whole estate is a transfer of value and the value transferred is the value of the individual's whole estate immediately prior to the death.

It should be noted that investments in ISAs and PEPs, which are outside the scope of income tax and capital gains tax during life, are included in the death estate for IHT.

Chargeable transfers

4. A chargeable transfer is any transfer of value which is not an exempt transfer. A potentially exempt transfer (PET) is treated as an exempt transfer until the date on which it becomes a chargeable transfer.

Immediately chargeable transfers that do not exceed the nil rate band and thus theoretically bear IHT at the nil rate, are not the same as exempt transfers. Exempt transfers (or exempt parts of larger transfers)are ignored when comparing the cumulative total of previous chargeable transfers with the current IHT nil rate band to find whether a liability at 20% or 40% arises on the latest transfer.

Since 1986, most lifetime gifts by individuals qualify as Potentially Exempt Transfers (PETs) – see paragraph 5 for more detail on these. PETs incur no immediate liability to IHT, but are retrospectively taxed as chargeable lifetime transfers if the donor dies within seven years.

In March 2006, the rules about IHT and Trusts were substantially reformed. Since 22 March 2006, the main type of lifetime transfer which is not a PET – and is thus an immediately chargeable transfer - is a transfer of value by an individual to a Relevant Property Trust. See paragraph

The following are exempt transfers both in life and on death:

i) gifts or legacies to charities or political parties

ii) gifts or legacies to a UK-domiciled spouse or civil partner.

The chargeable value of transfers in life or on death may be reduced by business and agricultural property reliefs (see paragraph 14).

Potentially exempt transfers (PETs)

5. A potentially exempt transfer is a lifetime transfer of value made by an individual:

i) to another individual, or

ii) to a discretionary trust primarily for the benefit of a disabled person (as defined).

Although a PET is a transfer of value, no inheritance tax is due when the transfer is made.

A PET is assumed to be an exempt transfer during the whole seven years following the transfer or, if earlier, until immediately before the transferor's death.

A PET made more than seven years before death becomes a wholly exempt transfer on the seventh anniversary of the PET.

If the transferor dies within seven years, the PET becomes a chargeable lifetime transfer.

When a PET becomes chargeable on the death of the donor, it is very common for there to be no actual IHT liability on the PET itself, because the PET (being earlier in date) will rank before later transfers in taking the benefit of the donor's available nil rate band.

However the inclusion of earlier "failed PETs" in the cumulative lifetime transfers reduces the nil rate band available to the death estate and thus causes a higher tax liability on death.

In the less common situation where actual IHT (at a positive rate) becomes payable on a PET that "fails" (ie becomes chargeable on death within 7 years), the IHT liability on that PET falls by default on the PET recipient.

If the recipient cannot be traced, or the gift was declared net of IHT when made, then the tax authorities will require the IHT on the PET to be met from the estate of the donor.

If IHT on a PET is paid out of the donor's estate, it is necessary to "gross up" the value of the PET to find the IHT due on it. See the tables at the end of this chapter for the IHT grossing-up fractions applied on lifetime and death transfers made net of IHT in order to find the gross value before IHT , and chapter 37 for some examples of grossing-up calculations.

6. Other chargeable transfers made by an individual during life ("inter vivos") are not PETs. They are known as Chargeable Lifetime Transfers (CLTs). CLTs include in particular:

i) a transfer by an individual to a relevant property trust – from 22 March 2006 this term covers all trusts created by lifetime transfers, except qualifying disabled persons' trusts.

ii) a transfer by an individual to a company.

IHT liability arises on a CLT at the time the transfer is made, at 50% of the death rates. If the donor dies within seven years of a chargeable lifetime transfer then the transfer is charged additional IHT to bring the tax up to the death rates, but a) the nil rate band that applies to the further liability calculation is the one applying at date of death, and not at the time the transfer was made; and b) any further IHT is subject to IHT taper relief where the interval between the CLT and the death is three years or more.

IHT Taper relief on PETs becoming chargeable, and on CLTs taxed further on death

7. Any inheritance tax payable upon death in respect of chargeable transfers made within seven years of the death of the donor (including PETs that have become chargeable) is reduced by reference to the following table:

Years between date of % of normal	% of normal	
transfer and date of death	tax charged	tax deducted
0 – 3	100	–
3 – 4	80	20
4 – 5	60	40
5 – 6	40	60
6 – 7	20	80

Gifts with reservation

8. Where an individual makes a transfer of value, but still retains some interest in the property, then on his or her death the property is treated as part of the estate. He or she is deemed to be beneficially entitled to the whole property and it is taxed together with the rest of the estate.

Examples of gifts with a reservation are:

i) a gift of a house where the donor or their spouse /CP remains in residence – unless a "full market rent" is paid;

ii) a gift to a trust where the donor or their spouse / CP is a beneficiary (even a remote beneficiary).

9. Property is subject to a reservation if:

i) possession and enjoyment of the property is not bona fide assumed by the donee at or before the beginning of the 'relevant period', or

ii) at any time in the 'relevant period' the property is not enjoyed to the entire exclusion, or virtually so, of the donor and of any benefits to him or her by contract or otherwise.

The relevant period is the period ending on the date of the donor's death and beginning seven years before then, or the date of the gift, if later.

General scope of IHT

10. If the individual making the transfer of value is domiciled in the UK, IHT applies to all his or her property wherever it is situated. This applies even if the person is non-resident in the UK for income tax and capital gains tax..

Where the transferor is domiciled outside the UK, then only property actually situated in the UK is chargeable to IHT. This would include shares in companies whose registered office/share register is located in the UK , but not shares in an offshore company , even if that company owned property in the UK .

For IHT purposes there are special rules by which an individual who has strong or recent UK residence connections is deemed to be domiciled in the UK for IHT purposes, even if legally domiciled elsewhere.

i) a deemed UK domicile is acquired for IHT purposes once a person has been resident (for income tax purposes) in the UK for 17 of the last 20 tax years. Legal domicile is then irrelevant.

ii) when someone formerly domiciled in the UK changes their legal domicile (eg by permanent emigration), their deemed domicile for IHT purposes remains the UK for another 3 tax years after the year of change of legal domicile.

Excluded property

11. The following types of property are not liable to IHT on a lifetime transfer, and do not form part of an individual's estate on death:

a) property situated outside the UK where the owner is also domiciled (and deemed domiciled) outside the UK.

b) reversionary interests in a settlement, except those acquired for money or money's worth or those where either the settlor or his or her spouse/CP is beneficially entitled to the reversion.

c) any income entitlement /life interest in a settlement (trust) that is a Relevant Property Trust created on or after 22 March 2006.

d) any life interest in a settlement made by a non-UK domiciled person and comprising only non-UK property.

d) property of individuals killed on active service.

Location of assets

12. To qualify as excluded property owned by a non-UK domicile, the assets must be situated outside the UK. The location of assets is determined in accordance with the general principles of property and land law as follows:

Land	– Land, including leasehold property is situated where the land is physically located.
Tangible moveable property	– Assets such as furniture and paintings are situated where they are located. Coins and bank notes are situated where they are at the time of the transfer.
Shares/ securities	– These are situated where the company share register is kept.
Bearer shares	– These are situated where the certificate of title is kept.
Debts	– These are located where the debtor resides.
Business assets	– Assets of a business are located where the place of business is situated. An interest in a partnership is located where the head office is found.
Goodwill	– This is located where the business is carried on.
Trademark	– This is situated where it is registered.

General exemptions and reliefs

13. The following are the main exemptions and reliefs available in respect of lifetime and death transfers.

		OL	D
a)	Transfers between husband and wife or registered civil partners (No limit, except where the donee is not domiciled in the UK in which case the exempt amount is limited to £55,000 over seven years).	✓	✓
b)	Transfers each year up to £3,000 (the annual exemption).	✓	
c)	Small gifts to any one person not exceeding £250.	✓	
d)	Transfers by way of normal expenditure out of taxed income.	✓	
e)	Gifts in consideration of marriage £5,000 max: donor is parent to one of the parties to the marriage £2,500 max: donor is grandparent/great grandparent £1,000 max: donor is in any other relationship.	✓	
f)	Gifts to charities £ no limit: whenever made.	✓	✓
g)	Gifts to political parties £ no limit: whenever made.	✓	✓
h)	Gifts for national purposes or for public benefit.	✓	✓
i)	Gifts made during lifetime for family maintenance including the education of children.	✓	

OL = PET/other lifetime transfer

D = Death transfer

From 9th October 2007 a surviving spouse or civil partner's IHT representatives on death may claim the unused proportion of a previously deceased spouse's or civil partner's nil rate band. Effectively this means that the nil rate band is to some extent now transferable between spouses and civil partners from the first to the second death.

The new system works as follows: the executors/personal representatives handling the IHT affairs of anyone dying later than a predeceased spouse or civil partner can claim in the death IHT computation any part of a second nil rate band (measured at the time of the second death) that was unused in IHT computations applying on the death of the first spouse/CP.

The main purpose of this reform was to negate the need for complicated trust structures allowing spouses /civil partners to ensure that nil rate band was not "wasted" on the first death if (as is common) the bulk of property was left to the survivor - an exempt transfer for IHT.

For people who have had more than one predeceasing spouse or CP before their own death , all the available unused nil rate bands from all those other people's death estates may be combined, but the absolute maximum enhanced nil rate band available on the second death is double the normal nil rate band for an individual (measured at the date of the second death).

Extra unused NRB from a predeceasing partner is only available if the marriage/partnership still existed at the time of the first death. So it does not apply if the partners divorced before the first death.

In general, for all IHT purposes, "married" means legally married (even if not living together) and all spouse /civil partner treatments for IHT continue until the marriage or partnership is legally ended by divorce or dissolution regardless of living arrangements.

Business and agricultural property reliefs

14. These important reliefs are available in respect of both transfers during lifetime (both PETs and immediately chargeable transfers) and on death. They are given effect to by a reduction in the value transferred.

a) Relief for business property.

Percentage reductions available are as follows:

i)	Transfers of a business or partnership interest	100%
ii)	Transfers of business assets	50%
iii)	Transfers of shares in unquoted companies including USM, AIM	100%
iv)	Transfers of a controlling interest in a quoted company	50%

b) Relief for agricultural property

Percentage reductions available are as follows:

i)	Where the transferor has the right to vacant possession or could obtain it within 12 months after a transfer	100%
ii)	Where the transferor does not have the right to vacant possession or cannot obtain it within 12 months of the transfer.	50%

Growing timber

15. Where land in the UK, not subject to agricultural or business relief, includes growing timber then the value of the timber may be excluded from a person's estate at death. IHT becomes payable on the later sale or lifetime transfer of the timber on the value at the date of the disposal.

Quick succession relief

16. This is available in respect of property transferred on the death of a person which has borne inheritance tax within the preceding five years. The relief is given by way of a percentage reduction of the original tax paid as follows:

		Reduction
Death within	1 year	100%
Death within	2 years	80%
Death within	3 years	60%
Death within	4 years	40%
Death within	5 years	20%

Sale within 1 or 4 years of death

17. Where shares are sold at arm's length within one year of death, or land is sold within four years of death, and the proceeds of sale are less than the probate value (value for IHT purposes) at the date of death, then relief may be claimed for any reduction in the price achieved below the amount treated as originally liable to IHT, and a refund of IHT paid on the difference in value may be obtained.

Liabilities and expenses

18. In general, liabilities are taken into account in computing the value of an estate for IHT purposes insofar as they have been incurred for a consideration in money's worth or imposed by law. Liabilities forming a charge on any property, such as a mortgage on a house, are deducted from the value of that property.

Intestacy

19. Where a person dies without making a will then there are rules of intestacy which prescribe the manner in which an estate must be distributed.

Post-death variations

20. The beneficiaries under a will or intestacy can vary the terms of the Will or the standard intestacy rules regarding who gets what, so long as all of them are of full legal capacity (so minor beneficiaries cannot have their shares of the estate altered or reduced in this way).

The legal document doing this is known as a 'Post-Death Deed of Variation' and to be effective for IHT it must satisfy the following conditions.

a) The instrument in writing must be made by the persons or any of the persons who benefit or would benefit under the dispositions of the property comprised in the deceased's estate immediately before his or her death.

b) The instrument must be made within two years after the death.

c) The instrument must clearly indicate the dispositions that are the subject of it, and vary their destination as laid down by the deceased's will or under the law relating to intestate estates, or otherwise.

d) A notice of election to vary the Will for IHT and CGT purposes must be given within six months of the date of the instrument, unless the Board sees fit to accept a late election.

e) Variation will automatically apply without election if the instrument itself states that it is to have that effect.

Any liability to IHT on death will be calculated on the basis of the revised estate distribution resulting from the Deed of Variation.

Deeds of Variation have no effect for income tax until the estate is distributed under the revised terms of the Deed. Therefore income (eg rents) may accrue during an estate administration period and be taxed on the previous estate beneficiary as income, even if they have given away the capital entitlement in a Deed of variation. A Deed of Variation is not an IHT transfer of value or a CGT chargeable disposal by any person entering into it who gives away property or inheritance rights to others by means of it.

Administration and payment

21. a) The HMRC offices which deal with IHT are known as the Capital Taxes Offices.

b) Reporting lifetime transfers to the Capital Taxes Office is carried out as follows.

  i) In the case of a chargeable lifetime transfer, the transferor must report it, unless some other person such as the donee liable for the tax has already done so. The account must be delivered within 12 months of the transfer or, if later, three months from the date on which he or she first becomes liable for the tax.

  ii) In the case of a PET it is the transferee's duty to report the transfer and pay any tax within 12 months after the end of the month in which death occurs. The Executors or Personal representatives are also responsible for listing the recipients of PETs that have become chargeable, and chargeable lifetime transfers that are liable to further tax on death, on the IHT return.

c) Appeals against an IHT assessment are to the combined Tax Tribunal system.

d) For transfers on death, probate or letters of administration are not given until an IHT account (provisional, if necessary) has been rendered and any IHT due paid (subject to the provisions for paying by instalments) .

e) Where the estate is 'excepted' (small in value), then there is no duty to make an IHT return on death. This applies where:

  i) the gross value of the property at death + relevant life time-transfers $\leq$ the basic Nil rate band, and the deceased died domiciled in the UK; or

  ii) The aggregate gross value of the estate + relevant lifetime transfers $\leq$ £1.0m, and the aggregate value less any deductible liabilities and less transfers to spouse and charity) $\leq$ the basic nil rate band, and the deceased died domiciled in the UK; or

  iii) The deceased was never domiciled in the UK and the value of all UK estate $\leq$ £100,000.

f) Payments of IHT may be made by instalments for these transfers on death:

  i) land and buildings (freehold and leasehold wherever situated);

  ii) a controlling interest in a company, quoted or unquoted;

  iii) unquoted shares and securities where the value transferred exceeds £20,000 and the shares represent at least 10% of the nominal share capital;

  iv) the net value of a business, profession or vocation;

  v) timber where the proceeds of sale basis of valuation is not used.

g) Instalments are payable by 10 equal yearly amounts. Interest on IHT due on land other than land used for business or agricultural purposes is calculated on the whole amount outstanding and added to each instalment.

IHT due on other property payable by instalments only incurs interest when an instalment is in arrears.

The payment of tax by instalments is available on lifetime transfers of the appropriate property where the IHT is paid by the donee.

h) IHT is due for payment as follows:

i) On a transfer on death – six months after the end of the month in which the death takes place.

ii) On a lifetime transfer:

made from 6th April to 30th September – the following April 30th

made from 1st October to 5th April – six months after end of month of transfer.

i) IHT is paid on income that has accrued to the deceased at the date of death but was received after that date and is therefore subject to income tax on the post-death owner of the asset producing the income. Relief for this element of double taxation is given to the beneficiaries by an adjustment to their personal income tax liability on the income.

IHT and Trusts – outline

22. A trust is an arrangement whereby legal ownership of an asset or cash is vested in one or more persons (the trustee(s)) but all the benefit or income from the assets is passed on to other named person(s) (known as the trust beneficiaries). There are many choices available to the creator (known as the settlor) of a property trust or settlement. The terms on which the trust property is to be managed and held must all be set out in the Trust Deed: the settlor cannot vary them later as he or she relinquishes control of the assets when the trust is created. The Trust deed may be part of a Will if the trust is created on a death. The income benefit and capital benefit in a trust can be awarded differently. The destination of the various benefits can be laid down in ways which trustees cannot alter, or the trustees can be given discretion as to the final allocation of income and/or capital among various possible classes of beneficiary.

The trustees may also have power to accumulate income and add it to capital rather than paying it out to income beneficiaries as income.

The IHT regime for trusts was substantially changed on Budget Day 2006 from the regime which had broadly existed since 1974. Prior to 22 March 2006, all trusts were classified into three types for IHT, of which two were taxable persons in their own right (via the trustees as a body), while the third (the interest-in-possession trust) was treated as transparent with the current life tenant being treated as the owner of the underlying trusts property for all IHT purposes.

From 22 March 2006 there are still three types of trust for IHT, but an interest in possession trust created (or added to) during life time of the settlor will be a "relevant property trust" which is taxed in the same way as a fully discretionary trust.

The only exception is a disabled person's trust as defined, which retains the IHT treatment of a pre-2006 interest in possession trust, even if legally a discretionary trust (ie the disabled person has no legal right to demand payment of income from the trustees). The disabled beneficiary is treated as owning the underlying property for IHT. and all gifts into the trust are treated as PETs to that person.

Relevant Property Trusts (which now covers discretionary trusts (except for disabled person), post-2006 lifetime IIP trusts, and any pre-2006 "Accumulation and Maintenance" Trusts which were not converted into IIP trusts under transitional provisions by 6 April 2008) are separate IHT taxpayers and the trustees must keep their own IHT cumulative transfer records. IHT arises on capital transfers of value out of an RPT, and also at ten-year intervals on property within an RPT. The details of IHT for RPT trustees are not considered further here.

Inheritance tax rates and nil rate bands - individuals

Death rates

	Cumulative Chargeable transfers (gross)	IHT rate %	Grossing up rate on a net transfer
	£	%	
6.4.11 – 5.4.12 and all prior tax years since 1986/7	Up to top of Nil Rate Band	Nil	Nil
	Above nil rate band	40	2/3 (40/60)

Lifetime rates

	Chargeable transfers (gross)	IHT %	IHT on transfer (net)
6.4.11 – 5.4.12 and all prior tax years since 1986/7	Up to top of Nil Rate Band	Nil	Nil
	Above nil rate band	40	1/4 (20/80)

Nil Rate bands 6.4.07 to 5.4.12 :

	£
2007/08	300,000
2008/09	312,000
2009/10	325,000
2010/11	325,000
2011/12	325,000

35 Basic rules of computation

Introduction

1. In this chapter the basic rules of IHT computation are examined under the following headings:

Grossing up procedures

Taper relief and lifetime gifts

Chargeable lifetime transfers

Chargeable lifetime transfers – death within seven years

Potentially exempt transfers within seven years of death

Death with no chargeable transfers within seven years of death

Transfers of value made within seven years of death and earlier transfers.

Transfers of business assets

Grossing up procedures

2. Where a lifetime transfer is made and IHT is to be paid by the donor, e.g. on a transfer to a Relevant Property Trust, then it is necessary to 'gross up the net transfer' as IHT is payable on the gross amount. The donor can specify that any gift, including a PET, is to be a transfer net of IHT.

Grossing up is also necessary, at death rates, where a death estate is divided in such a way that legacies of set amounts are chargeable to IHT but the residue (the balance of the estate) is left to one or more exempt beneficiaries i.e. a charity, surviving spouse or civil partner.

Example

Amy makes a net chargeable lifetime transfer to a RPT of £340,000 on 15th May 2011. Amy has never been married, and has not made any previous lifetime chargeable transfers or PETs.

Compute the amount of the gross transfer.

Solution

		£
15.5.2011 Net gift		340,000
IHT is $\frac{20}{80} \times (340{,}000 - 325{,}000) =$		3,750
Gross transfer		343,750
Check	Gross transfer	343,750
	IHT (343,750 – 325,000) × 20%	3,750
Net transfer		340,000

The IHT of £3,750 is payable by Amy.

Taper relief and lifetime gifts

3. The inheritance tax payable in respect of transfers of value made within seven years of the death of an individual is reduced by reference to the following table.

Years between date of transfer and date of death	% of normal tax charged	% of normal tax deducted
0 – 3	100	–
3 – 4	80	20
4 – 5	60	40
5 – 6	40	60
6 – 7	20	80

4. For potentially exempt transfers no chargeable transfer is counted unless death occurs within seven years of the date of the transfer. When this arises IHT calculated at the death rates and using the nil rate band available at the date of death, but the value of the chargeable transfer at the date of the PET. The IHT on the "failed PET" is payable by the donee unless the transfer was stated to be a transfer net of IHT, in which case grossing up applies.

Other chargeable transfers (non-PETs) are taxed at half of the death rate at the time of making the transfer. If death occurs more than seven years after the date of the transfer then the position is as follows.

i) The chargeable transfer is ignored in computing the IHT payable on the value of the estate.

ii) There is no additional tax payable by the donee.

iii) IHT already paid when the transfer was made is not recoverable.

Taper relief does not affect the amount of inheritance tax payable on an estate by the executors.

The computational principles of taper relief on CLTs within 7 years before death are illustrated in paragraphs 5 and 6.

Chargeable lifetime transfers (non-PETs)

5. These transfers are chargeable at half the death rate at the time of the transfer, and where necessary must be grossed up.

Example

Mike makes a transfer of £400,000 to a relevant property trust on 1st December 2011 agreeing to pay any IHT. All exemptions had been used and Mike had made no previous transfers.

Compute any IHT payable.

Solution

	£
1.12.11 Gift to relevant property trust	400,000
IHT on net gift of £400,000	
(400,000 – 325,000) × 1/4	18,750
Gross transfer	418,750
IHT payable by Mike at lifetime rate	18,750
Check (418,750 – 325,000) at 20% =	18,750

Chargeable lifetime transfers (non-PETs) – death within seven years

6. When the transferor dies within seven years of making a chargeable transfer then the gift is retaxed at the death rates, net of any taper relief. Any IHT payable when the gift was first made is then deducted in arriving at any additional tax due by the donee.

The value of the transfer is taken at the date of the gift but any additional tax arising on the death of the donor can be calculated by reference to the lower of:

i) the market value at date of donor's death, or

ii) the proceeds of an earlier sale.

Example

Noel dies on 11th June 2011 leaving an estate valued at £100,000 to non exempt beneficiaries. On 1st June 2008 he made a gift of £350,000 gross to a relevant property trust, inheritance tax of £7,600 being paid by the trustees on the lifetime transfer. Noel had never been married.

Calculate the IHT due in respect of Noel's estate and any additional tax payable on his death relating to the chargeable lifetime transfer.

Solution

		£
11.6.2011 Value Noel's estate		100,000
Add: Gross chargeable transfers within previous 7 years		350,000
		450,000
IHT payable FA 2011 death rate		
	325,000 – Nil	–
	125,000 @ 40%	50,000
	450,000	50,000
Less notional tax at death rates on transfers of £350,000 within last 7 years.		
	325,000 – Nil	–
	25,000 @ 40% revised IHT liability on lifetime CLT	(10,000)
	350,000	
IHT payable by executors out of death estate (40% x 100,000)		40,000

Additional tax payable on lifetime gift:	£
1.6.08 Gross transfer	350,000
11.6.11 IHT (as above) due on this at death rates	10,000
Less taper relief:	
(3-4 years) 20% × 10,000	2,000
IHT liability after taper relief (borne by original donee, ie trust)	8,000
Less paid by trustees on original gift by X	(7,600)
Additional tax due by trustees on X's death	400

Notes

i) If the additional tax payable is a 'negative amount', none is recoverable by the RPT.

ii) There can be no refund of the IHT paid on the original gift into trust.

iii) Tax on the death estate is borne as the highest slice of the total assets, i.e. after allocating the nil rate band first to chargeable transfers within seven years of death.

iv) Where the cumulative chargeable lifetime transfers exceed the nil rate band on death, and there are no exempt legacies, then the estate IHT is the value of the estate at the 40% death rate. In this example £100,000 @ 40% = £40,000.

v) The lifetime gift IHT originally paid by the trustees on the gift by Mike is (350,000 – 312,000) @20% = 7,600. (£312,000 was the nil rate band for 2008/09).

v) The nil rate band for 2011/12 is £325,000.

Potentially exempt transfer within seven years of death

7. There is no inheritance tax payable when the transfer is made, since a potentially exempt transfer is assumed exempt until proved otherwise by death of the donor within seven years.Upon death within seven years of the transfer, the PET is taxable at the death rate, subject to taper relief if the interval is more than 3 years. In addition the PET (now a CLT) is added to the value of the estate to determine the rates of tax payable on the death transfer.

As with all lifetime transfers brought into charge, the estate is treated as the last transfer and the cumulative transfers in the previous seven years, as the first transfers to be allocated to the nil rate bands in date order.

8. For the purposes of calculating the tax payable by the donee (but not the estate), the market value at the date of death or the proceeds of an earlier sale by the donee may be used to compute the IHT on the lifetime gift, if this is lower than the value of the PET at the date of the transfer.

Example

Arthur dies on 10th October 2011 leaving to his daughter a net estate valued at £250,000. On 1st of December 2009 Arthur had made a gift to his son with a value of £400,000 after having used all relevant lifetime gift exemptions. Arthur had made no previous transfers of value, and had divorced his wife many years ago.

Calculate the IHT payable.

Solution

			£
10.10.2011 Value of Arthur's estate at death			250,000
Add cumulative transfers in previous 7 years			400,000
			650,000
IHT thereon (650,000 – 325,000) × 40% (2011/12 Death Rates)			130,000
Less notional tax on chargeable lifetime transfers within previous 7 years - failed PETs of £400,000:			
NRB	325,000 @ 0%	–	
balance	75,000 @ 40%	30,000	
	400,000	30,000	(30,000)
IHT payable out of death estate by executors: borne by Arthur's daughter			100,000

Tax payable by Arthur's son

1.12.2008 Value of gift	400,000
IHT thereon as above	30,000
Less taper relief: (0–3 years) 0% × 30,000	–
IHT payable	30,000

Further example – fall in value relief

Using the data in the previous example, compute the IHT payable if the PET to Arthur's son was a gift of an asset that was only worth £350,000 at the date of Arthur's death.

Solution

	£
10.10.2011 Value of Arthur's estate	250,000
Add cumulative transfers in previous 7 years	400,000
	650,000
IHT payable on estate	130,000 (as above)

IHT payable by Arthur's son on Arthur's death:

	£
1.12.09 Value of gift	400,000
Less fall in value relief (£400,000 - £350,000)	(50,000)
10.10.2010 Value of gift retrospectively	350,000
IHT on £350,000	
(350,000 – 325,000) × 40%	10,000
Less taper relief NIL (less than 3 years)	–
IHT payable by Arthur's son	10,000

Notes

i) The value of the original gift is included in calculations of IHT on the death estate. I.e. it is still 'cumulated' at the original value.

ii) The fall-in-value relief only affects the amount of any tax or additional tax due when a PET becomes a CLT on death, or a CLT becomes liable at death rates, (less taper relief if any.

iii) Additional tax due on earlier lifetime transfers because of a death is in principle a cost borne by the donee. If it is borne by the donor's estate (which could only be by specific direction of the donor) then the tax on the gift (at grossed-up rate) is an additional transfer of value under the will.

iv) In practice, the donee or the donor of a lifetime gift can often without difficulty and at fairly modest cost insure the donor's life for the next 7 years, to cover the cost of an extra IHT liability arising within 7 years of a lifetime gift. This is done using a single-premium seven-year term insurance policy, the proceeds of which would be used by the donee to pay the estimated maximum IHT. If the donor does not die within 7 years no insurance money is repayable to the donee but there is no IHT to pay either. (If the donor pays the insurance premium and writes the proceeds of the policy in trust for the donee, this is not itself a chargeable transfer of value.)

Death with no chargeable transfers or PETs within previous seven years

9. On the death of a person who has not made any chargeable transfers within the previous seven years, the death rates and nil rate band are applied to the value of the estate, subject to any exemptions and reliefs.

Example

Tony died on 14 June 2011, leaving a chargeable estate of £485,000. He had made no lifetime transfers, and was divorced from his previous spouse before she died. Compute the IHT payable.

Solution: Tony deceased IHT computation 14.6.2011

Total value of estate:		485,000
Tax payable:		
	325,000 @ 0%	–
	160,000 @ 40%	64,000
	485,000	64,000

Notes

Estate rate of IHT = $\frac{64,000}{485,000} \times 100 = 13.19\%$

The estate rate is relevant where there is any IHT payable by instalments e.g. UK land, or by different persons. It is also relevant where Double Tax Relief is claimed for overseas IHT.

Transfers of value made within seven years of death and earlier

10. Transfers of value made more than seven years before the date of death are not accumulated to arrive at the IHT rate at the date of death. However, where a transfer of value is made within the seven years before the date of death, then in determining any additional IHT payable on death by the recipient, any transfers made in the seven years before the date of that transfer must be considered.

Example

Kate made a gross chargeable transfer (after exemptions) to a discretionary trust for her adult children of £350,000 on 1st February 2003. On 1st November 2007 Kate gave her son £75,000 after annual exemptions. Kate dies on 30th August 2011, leaving an estate of £500,000 to her 3 adult children.

Calculate the IHT payable on the estate of K and on the failed PET of £75,000.

Solution			**£**
30.8.2011 Value of Kate's estate			500,000
Add transfers of value made within previous 7 years			
1.11.07 Gift to son – gross chargeable transfer			75,000
			575,000
IHT payable: (2011/12 rates)			
	325,000 Nil		–
	250,000 @ 40%		100,000
	575,000		100,000
Less notional tax on transfers within previous 7 years		£75,000	
Nil rate band covers this in full so the tax is		Nil	
IHT payable by executors out of death estate (borne by heirs)			100,000

Tax payable by Kate's son on failed PET

			Gross (FA 2011 death rates)	IHT
1.2.03	Gross transfer to discretionary trust (350,000 – 325,000 @ 40%)		350,000	10,000
1.11.07	Gift to son		75,000	30,000
	425,000		40,000	
IHT nil rate band	325,000	–		
Death rates	100,000 @ 40%	40,000		
	425,000	40,000		
Deduct transfers made more than 7 years prior to date of death			350,000	10,000
			75,000	30,000
less taper relief 3–4 years 20% × 30,000				6,000
IHT payable on failed PET				24,000

Notes

i) The IHT payable at the death rate on the failed PET is calculated by reference to the value of **all** chargeable transfers in the seven years before the date of the gift.

ii) The tax in this case actually due on the failed PET of £24,000 is not the same as the amount deducted in computing the IHT payable on the estate by the executors.

iii) The taper relief for a chargeable lifetime transfer made between three and four years before death is 20% (see chapter 35 section 7).

Business Property Relief

11. Relief is available for transfers of value during life (inter vivos) or on the death of an individual, of relevant business property.

The relief is given by way of a percentage reduction from the valuation of the property.

This section begins with a summary of the relief available, followed by a definition of relevant business property and the associated rules. Worked examples then show the computations to be made.

Summary of relief

12.

a)	Property consisting of a business or interest in a business such as a partnership or sole trader. A business includes total assets including goodwill, less liabilities.	100%
b)	Shares or securities in unquoted companies including USM/AIM.	100%
c)	Shares or securities of a quoted company which gave the transferor control of the company immediately before the transfer.	50%
d)	Business assets such as land and buildings, plant and machinery owned by the transferor as a sole trader, partner, or as a controlling director, and used in that business.	50%
e)	Business assets such as land and buildings, plant and machinery used by the transferor in a business which was settled property in which he or she had an interest in possession.	50%

Relevant business property

13. In addition to the details shown in the summary above, the following should be noted.

a) To qualify for relief, the property must have been owned by the transferor for at least two years immediately prior to the transfer. Where property replaces other property and the two years criteria cannot be met then relief is still available, provided aggregate ownership is greater than two years out of the previous five.

b) Assets not used wholly or mainly for the purposes of the business within the two year period noted in (a) above are excepted assets (e.g. investments or surplus cash) and relief is not available for those items.

c) Relief is not available for a transfer of business property which is used wholly or mainly for the following purposes:

   i) Dealing in stocks, shares or securities. (Stock market makers and discount houses are, however, eligible for relief.)

   ii) Dealing in land or buildings.

   iii) Making or holding investments.

d) The expression business includes a profession or vocation but does not include a business carried on otherwise than for gain.

e) Shares in a holding company qualify if the subsidiaries themselves qualify for relief.

f) The original property (or if sold, its replacement) must be owned by the transferee throughout the period beginning with the chargeable transfer and ending on the transferor's death to retain the full benefit of the relief.

g) Where the original property is disposed of before the transferor's death and the proceeds are used to purchase replacement property full relief is available if:

   i) the whole of the proceeds are used to purchase a replacement

   ii) both sale and purchase take place within three years of each other.

h) If only part of the original property (or its replacement) is in the transferee's possession on the death of the transferor, then only that part will be eligible for relief.

i) Relief reduces the value of the transfer before any available exemptions are given.

Where any of the relief is clawed back the additional tax payable by the transferee is calculated on the transfer before BPR. However, the net transfer i.e. after BPR included in the transferor's cumulative total remains unchanged.

Excepted assets

14. The BPR will be restricted on a transfer of shares if the company holds 'excepted assets' on its balance sheet. An 'excepted asset' is an asset that is not used for business purposes throughout the two years immediately preceding a transfer, or is not required for future use in the business. The amount of the transfer qualifying for BPR, is the value of the shares gifted multiplied by the fraction below:

$$\text{Qualifying transfer} = \text{Gift} \times \left(\frac{\text{Total assets - excepted assets}}{\text{Total assets}} \right)$$

If the company has no excepted assets, all of the value of the shares will qualify for BPR. If non-trading assets make up more than 50% of total assets, the IR may seek to deny BPR completely on the grounds that the company is not trading.

PETS and business property relief

15. If the property eligible for business property relief is transferred by a PET then tax will only become payable on the death of the transferor within seven years of the date of the transfer. BPR which has been assumed at the time of a lifetime gift (PET) to reduce the chargeable value of the PET may be lost as a result of events after the PET. BPR is not available when a PET becomes chargeable (ie on the donor's death within 7 years) unless either:

a) the property (or its identifiable replacement) is still held by the donee as relevant business property at the donor's death, or

b) the donee has died before the donor.

This rule can cause an unwelcome IHT exposure for the donee of business property. The risk of the donor's death should be covered by term life insurance if the donee does not intend to retain the gift as relevant business property.

Example

A who had made no previous transfers gave his controlling interest in Z Ltd, a private company, to his son on April 12th 2008. The interest was valued at £440,000. A's controlling interest was acquired for £50,000 in 1993. A died on the 10th August 2011 leaving an estate of £380,000. A's son has retained the controlling interest in Z Ltd.

Compute the IHT arising on A's death.

Solution

	£	£
10.8.2011 Value of A's estate		380,000
Add transfers made within previous 7 years		
12.4.08 gift to son	440,000	
Less business property relief 100% × 440,000	440,000	–
		380,000
IHT payable thereof FA 2011 rates:		
325,000 @ Nil	–	
55,000 @ 40%	22,000	22,000
380,000		22,000
Less notional IHT on gift to son of	440,000	Nil
IHT payable by executors		22,000
IHT payable on PET		Nil

Notes

i) IHT is not payable in respect of the transfer on 12th April 2008 as the transfer of value is a PET.

ii) As the business property relief of 100% applied to the gift, there is no IHT payable by A's son on the death of his father, as he has retained the gifted business as relevant business property.

iii) BP relief is given at the rate appropriate to the property at the time the gift was made.

Student self-testing questions

1. Z dies on 22nd October 2011 leaving a net estate of £250,000. During his lifetime he had made the following transfers of value, after using all available exemptions.

1st December 2005	Gift to his daughter of £130,000.
20th June 2008	Gift to an accumulation and maintenance trust of £240,000.

Compute the IHT payable on the death of Z.

Solution			£	£
22.10.2011 Z's estate				250,000
Add transfers of value made in previous 7 years				
1.12.05 Gift to daughter			130,000	
20.6.08 Gift to trust			240,000	370,000
				620,000
IHT payable (FA 2011 rates):				
	325,000		–	
	295,000 @ 40%	118,000		
	620,000	118,000	118,000	
Less notional tax on lifetime transfers of £370,000				
(370,000 – 325,000) × 40% =				18,000
IHT payable by executors				100,000
IHT payable by donees:				
1.12.05 gift to daughter within nil rate band			130,000	nil
20.6.08 Gift to accumulation and maintenance trust				240,000
Add gifts in previous 7 years				
Gift to Z's daughter (1.12.05)				130,000
				370,000
IHT payable:				
(370,000 – 325,000) × 40%				18,000
Less notional IHT on gift to Z's daughter of £130,000				–
				18,000
Less taper relief: (3-4 years) 20% × 18,000				(3,600)
Tax payable by trustees				14,400

Cumulative transfers	Gross £	Tax £
1.12.2005 Gift to daughter	130,000	
IHT payable @ FA 2011 death rates	–	–
	130,000	–
20.6.08 Gift to accumulation trust	240,000	18,000
	370,000	18,000
Taper relief		(3,600)
Less transfers made more than 7 years prior to 22.10.2011		Nil
	370,000	14,400

Notes

i) Both of the transfers during Z's lifetime are PETs.

ii) The tax due in respect of each gift is computed separately beginning first with the one furthest from the date of death, within the seven years period.

iii) IHT payable on the second gift is calculated after deducting any notional tax on the previous gift to Z's daughter which in this case is nil.

iv) Taper relief 20.6.08 –22.10.11 is three-four years.

2. B dies on 7th April 2011 leaving the following estate:

	£
20% interest in Q Ltd, an unquoted private company	125,000
Freehold land used by Q Ltd	35,000
Shares in Z plc, a quoted company (< 1% holding)	15,000
Other property (net)	312,500

Three years before his death B had transferred a 15% interest in the shares in Q Ltd to his son. B has made no other transfers but has used all his annual exemptions. B's son has retained his interest in Q Ltd which at the date of the gift was valued at £40,000, and on B's death was worth £280,000.

Calculate the IHT arising on B's death.

Solution

		£	£
7.4.2011 value of B's estate:			
20% interest in Q Ltd		125,000	
Less business property relief 100% × 125,000		(125,000)	–
Freehold land used by Q Ltd			35,000
Shares in Z plc			15,000
Other property			312,500
			362,500
Add	transfer within previous 7 years		
	Gift of shares in Q Ltd	40,000	
	Business property relief 100% × 40,000	(40,000)	–
			362,500
IHT thereon FA 2011 rates:			
	325,000 per table 2011/12	Nil	
	37,500 @ 40%	15,000	
	362,500		15,000
Less notional IT on gift within last 7 years		–	–
IT payable by executors			15,000

Notes

i) There is no inheritance tax payable in respect of the gift as it was below the threshold level of £325,000 for 2011/12.

ii) The BPR rate of 100% applies to the shares in Q Ltd and the gift to B's son.

iii) No relief is available for the freehold land used by Q Ltd as B did not have a controlling interest.

iv) The PET is valued at the date of the transfer and not the date of B's death for estate purposes. Where the death value is lower than the transfer value, that value is used to compute any IHT on the transfer at death borne by the donee.

3. Jamie, a generous uncle, makes a PET of £200,000 by a cash gift to his nephew Tom in October 2010, and suddenly dies one year later, in October 2011.

Due to previous chargeable transfers by Jamie (earlier PETs which have become chargeable on Jamie's death) only £50,000 of Jamie's nil rate band is available to cover Tom's PET. The IHT rate applicable to the rest of Tom's PET is 40% (death rates apply to lifetime transfers taxed on death).

Calculate the IHT payable on the 'failed' PET to Tom as a result of Jamie's death, if

a) Tom pays the IHT on the failed PET

b) Jamie's estate pays the IHT on the failed PET.

Solution

a) If Tom pays the IHT on the 'failed' £200,000 PET (the normal/default situation) then Tom would pay IHT of (0% x £50,000 + 40% x £150,000), i.e. £60,000.

This obligation and the tax liability would be notified to him by the Executors of Jamie's estate.

b) If the PET to Tom was stated by Jamie at the time it was made to be 'made net of IHT', or if for some other reason Jamie's estate ends up paying the IHT on the failed PET (eg Tom is now insolvent):

The value to be taxed at 40% must be **grossed up** for the tax liability taken on by Jamie.

Thus the gross transfer becomes (retrospectively)

Value taxed at nil IHT	£50,000
Value taxed at 40% (£200,000 gifted - £50,000 nil rate band) x 100/60 =	£250,000
Gross transfer value, total	£300,000
tax due on this gross value (40% of £250,000)	= £100,000

This £100,000 is payable by Jamie's estate and the grossed up amount of £300,000 is recorded in the record of chargeable PETs reported by Jamie's Executors as the gross value of the lifetime gift made to Tom.

Part VI

Value added tax

36 General principles

Introduction

1. Value added tax is a tax on the supply of goods and services made by a registered taxable person within the UK. Prior to 2008 the UK's VAT rates had been constant for many years. In response to the financial crisis of 2008, the Government announced a temporary reduction in VAT standard rate in November 2008, cutting it by 2.5% from 17.5% to 15% for a period of 13 months. From 1st January 2010 the standard VAT rate reverted to 17.5%.

Following the change of Government in May 2010, it was announced on 22 June 2010 that the UK's standard rate of VAT would be 20% from 4 January 2011.

Unlike the 2008 VAT rate change, the 2011 change is not "temporary", so may be assumed a long-term policy. Other EU countries have also recently raised their standard rates of VAT, in response to well publicised public spending deficits.

This chapter begins with a summary of the headings under which the basic rules of VAT will be described.

Summary of topic headings

2. Legislative background

VAT rates

Classification of goods and services

Zero-rated goods and services

Reduced rate goods and services

Exempt goods and services

Land and buildings

Taxable persons

Business splitting

Registration limits

Voluntary registration

Voluntary de-registration

Group registration

Companies organised into divisions

Accounts and records

Administration

Late registration

Default surcharge

Errors on VAT returns

Tax avoidance schemes

Legislative background

3. Value added tax was introduced in the UK with effect from 1st April 1973, superseding purchase tax and selective employment tax. The main provisions of VAT law are now contained in the Value Added Tax Act 1994, as amended by subsequent Finance Acts and expanded by Regulations. Many UK VAT law changes since 1973 have implemented VAT Directives issued by the European Union. Governments of all Member States are obliged to implement these Directives, as a condition of membership, with the aim of maintaining a common VAT system in the EU Fiscal Area.

The general principles of VAT are thus common to the whole EU fiscal area. VAT is levied on goods and services on a common basis of charge, but domestic VAT rates may be varied within limits by individual Member-states. The maximum rate of VAT that is currently allowed under EU law is 25% and the minimum reduced or lower rate that is allowed for social reasons is 5%. The UK's zero-rate of VAT, which still applies to certain goods and services in the UK, is a historical anomaly dating from before the UK's accession to the European Community in 1973.

VAT rates and the VAT fraction

4. VAT has to be charged on the supply of goods and services within the UK by a taxable person, unless they are exempt supplies or supplies outside the scope of VAT, at the following rates:

Standard rate	20.0%
Reduced rate	5.0%
Zero rate	0.0%

In the UK, consumer protection law requires that prices quoted directly to consumers by VAT-registered traders, such as retailers, are stated inclusive of VAT. The invoice or retail receipt should however identify the amount of VAT separately.

UK traders who sell to both consumers and businesses, or only to businesses, may quote prices net of VAT and add the VAT later on the invoice.

Since the current standard rate is 20%, it follows that the VAT element of a price stated inclusive of VAT is $^{20}/_{120}$, or $^{1}/_{6}$. This is known as "the VAT fraction", and can be applied to any VAT-inclusive price for a standard rated supply to find the VAT that is contained within it.

When the standard rate as 17.5% before January 2011, the VAT fraction was $^{17.5}/_{117.5}$ or $^{7}/_{47}$. While standard rate of VAT was temporarily 15%, the VAT fraction was $^{15}/_{115}$ or $^{3}/_{23}$.

The VAT fraction for reduced rate goods and services liable to VAT at 5% is $^{5}/_{105}$ or $^{1}/_{21}$.

Classification of goods and services

5. A taxable supply is a supply of goods or services made in the UK in the course of business by a VAT-registered trader, other than an exempt supply.

For VAT rating purposes goods and services are classified into four groups as listed below, but the last two together are for various legal definition purposes treated as one single group.

Standard-rated supplies	All goods and services not zero-rated or exempt
Exempt supplies	Goods and services which are not subject to VAT, e.g. healthcare, education, banking and insurance.

Zero-rated supplies	Goods and services which are subject to a zero rate of VAT, e.g. printed matter, public transport (see section 6).
Reduced rate supplies	Goods and services which are subject to the reduced (currently 5%) rate of VAT. These are mainly items which were formerly standard-rated (or in the case of domestic fuel and power, half-standard rated) but for social or welfare reasons have been reduced to the lowest possible rate that can now be imposed.

Definitions of zero-rated, reduced rate and exempt supplies are set out in the VAT Act, and summarised below. Standard-rated supplies are not defined in the VAT Act but this is the default classification of any good or service supplied for a consideration in the course of business, if none of the specified descriptions applies to make it exempt or zero-rated (which for this purpose includes the reduced rate).

Any reference in the VAT Acts to "zero-rated goods and services" also covers reduced-rate goods and services without this needing to be separately specified in the legislation.

Since the UK's accession to the European Community in 1973, it is not possible to introduce new categories of zero-rated supply, but the previous ones continue until amended. For example, the Conservative government in the 1990s removed the VAT zero-rating of domestic fuel and power (ie home electricity and gas bills). When Labour came to power in 1997, despite a manifesto promise to reverse this, they could not reduce the rate on domestic fuel and power any lower than 5% (where it still is).

Zero-rated (ZR) goods and services

6. Particulars of the goods and services which are zero-rated are contained in Schedule 8 to the VAT Act 1994 and there are sixteen groups each containing separate listed items, as follows.

Group 1: Food. Most food for human consumption is ZR, unless supplied as a restaurant meal or catering service, when it is SR. Cold takeaway food sold for consumption off the promises is ZR, but hot takeaway food is SR. Food and beverage products not sold as a catering service are in principle ZR but there is a long list of exceptions to this rule, meaning that certain foodstuffs and drinks are SR.

The purported basis excluding certain foods and beverages from zero-rating is that such items are 'non-essential' or 'luxuries'. Examples of items not eligible for zero rating include ice cream, sweets and chocolate, potato crisps, alcoholic drinks, fruit juices and chocolate-covered biscuits (but chocolate-covered cakes are ZR). Pet foods are also SR, but general animal feeding stuffs are ZR.

Group 2: Sewerage services and water. The supply of water and sewerage to domestic customers is ZR, but not distilled and mineral water. The supply of water and sewerage services to industry is SR.

Group 3: Books and printed matter. The supply of books and magazines, newspapers, music, maps and charts is ZR. Diaries and printed stationery (ie printed items intended to be written in or on by the purchaser) are SR. E-books supplied electronically to be printed out by the customer are SR services not ZR goods, as are online journal or newspaper subscriptions supplied for consideration, unless a printed version of the publication is included in the supply as well.

Group 4: Talking books for the blind and handicapped, and wireless sets for the blind. ZR items include magnetic tapes, tape recorders and accessories, if supplied to approved agencies such as the Royal National Institute for the Blind and similar charities.

The supply of information other than photographs to newspapers or to the public by news agencies is ZR.

Group 5: Construction of buildings. The position under this heading may be summarised as follows.

Zero-rated

i) Construction of new domestic buildings.

ii) Approved alterations to domestic listed buildings.

Standard-rated

i) Construction of new non-domestic buildings.

ii) Repair, maintenance or alteration of existing buildings.

iii) Civil engineering services or new work.

iv) Civil engineering services or repair, maintenance or alteration of existing buildings.

v) Demolition of domestic and non-domestic buildings.

vi) The construction of a building for own use in business.

Group 6: Protected buildings.

Group 7: International services.

Group 8: Transport. Zero-rating applies to the supply of passenger transport both inland and international, international freight transport, and the supply, repair and maintenance of certain ships and aircraft. Standard-rating applies to taxis (if the provider is VAT-registered), transport in cars or aeroplanes carrying fewer than six people, hire cars, car parking and luggage storage.

Group 9: Caravans and house-boats. Caravans are ZR if they exceed 7 metres in length or 2.3 metres in width, the maximum size permitted for use on public roads. Smaller towable caravans are SR, as is the supply of caravan holiday accommodation. House-boats if suitable for permanent habitation are ZR.

Group 10: Gold. The supply of gold coins which are legal tender is taxable at the standard rate. The supply of gold held in the UK, by a central bank to another central bank or a member of the London Gold Market, and reciprocal transactions, are ZR.

Group 11: Bank notes. The issue of bank notes payable to bearer is zero rated.

Group 12: Drugs, medicines, aids for the handicapped etc. The following supplies are ZR: goods dispensed by a registered pharmacist on prescription, medical and surgical appliances, electrical and mechanical appliances for a handicapped person. Other drugs and medicines dispensed without prescription are SR.

Group 13: Imports, exports etc. The transfer of goods from the UK, without a legal sale taking place, by a person carrying on a business both inside and outside the EU, to the non-EU located business is also ZR. This would cover, for example, the transfer of parts to be assembled into products from a UK VAT-registered company to its non-EU branch.

Group 14: Tax-free shops. This covers any shop situated in an airport, port or Channel Tunnel terminal approved by HMRC for the purposes of this Group, and also sales of limited amounts of goods by the providers of air or sea transport or Channel tunnel shuttle trains to passengers who have purchased transport services from them.

Group 15: Charities etc. Zero-rating applies to the supply by a charity established primarily for the relief of distress or the benefit or protection of animals, of goods donated for sale, any exports, medical or scientific equipment used solely in medical research, and appliances for the handicapped. The supply by a charity shop of goods and services purchased for resale is standard rated - there is no general exemption for charity shops (though a small charity shop may be able to keep total taxable turnover below the registration limit).

Group 16: Clothing and footwear. Children's clothing and footwear are ZR. Protective boots and helmets are SR when supplied to a person for use by his or her employees. Supplies of protective boots and helmets to any other person for industrial use remain zero rated. Also zero rated are motor cycle helmets. Other clothing is SR.

Reduced rate goods and services

7. Particulars of goods and services which are exempt supplies are contained in the 9th Schedule to the VAT Act 1994 and there are 11 groups as follows.

Group 1: Fuel and power supplied for domestic and charity use.

Group 2: Installation of energy-saving materials.

Group 3: Grant-funded installations of heating or security equipment.

Group 4: Women's sanitary products

Group 5: Children's car seats and car seat bases

Group 6: Certain residential conversions

Group 7: Certain residential renovations and alterations

Group 8: Contraceptive products (unless exempt from VAT ie NHS or private healthcare)

Group 9: Welfare advice supplied by charities/ state-regulated private welfare institutions

Group 10: Installation of mobility aids for the elderly

Group 11: Smoking cessation products.

Reduced rate supplies can in general be characterised as those on which a previously higher applicable rate of VAT has been reduced, as a deliberate policy, for social or welfare reasons.

Exempt goods and services

8. Particulars of goods and services which are exempt supplies are contained in the 9th Schedule to the VAT Act 1994 and there are 15 groups, classified as follows.

Group 1: Land. See separate heading below.

Group 2: Insurance. All forms of insurance are exempted and this includes insurance broking and agency services.

Group 3: Postal services. The conveyance of postal packets other than telegrams, by the Royal Mail is exempted up to 31 January 2011. Services rendered by persons other than the post office are taxable. However as part of EU policy to reduce distortion of competition between state and private providers, the UK Royal Mail lost its exemption in respect of parcel services and certain other postal services and from 31 January 2011 they became standard rated.

Group 4: Betting, gaming and lotteries. Examples of exempt services under this group are bookmakers, charges for bingo and profits from casino games. Admission charges to any premises where betting or the playing of games of chance takes place are however taxable at SR, as are takings from gaming or entertainment machines.

Group 5: Finance. In general, banking services relating to the borrowing or lending, receipt and transfer of money are exempt. Specific services offered by banks such as executorship and trustee work, portfolio management etc. are taxable at SR, as are the commissions from stockbroking, and management fees of unit trusts.

Group 6: Education. Non-profit educational services provided by schools, colleges, universities and youth clubs are exempt, as are the supply of goods and services to those establishments. Services provided by organisations selling training or education with a view to profit, such as correspondence courses, are taxable.

Group 7: Health and welfare. The supply of goods and services by registered healthcare providers such as doctors, dentists, opticians, occupational therapists etc. is exempted. Goods supplied under a prescription by a pharmacist are zero-rated.

Group 8: Burial and cremation. The services of undertakers in connection with a funeral or cremation are exempt, and within limits this includes charges for the supply of a coffin, shroud etc. but not flowers.

Group 9: Trade unions and professional bodies. VAT exemption is given for membership fees and other mutual services, and related goods supplied by a trade union and most non-profit making professional, learned or representational bodies.

Group 10: Sports competitions. The grant of a right to enter a competition in sport or physical recreation, where the consideration for the grant consists in money which is to be used wholly for the provision of prizes, is exempt.

Group 11: Works of art etc. The disposal of works of art in circumstances where there is no liability to capital transfer tax or capital gains tax is exempt.

Group 12: Fund raising activities by charities.

Group 13: Cultural services etc.

Group 14: Supplies of goods where input tax cannot be recovered.

Group 15: Investment gold.

Land and buildings

9. The VAT treatment of supplies of land and buildings is complex. This is a very brief summary:

Always Exempt

i) The sale of used domestic buildings

ii) Leases of used domestic buildings

iii) Leases of new domestic buildings where the lease is less than 21 years

iv) The sale of building land for domestic building

Always Zero-rated

i) Sales of new domestic buildings, provided the seller is the person constructing the building

ii) Leases of new domestic buildings where the lease is capable of exceeding 21 years.

Always Standard-rated

i) Sales of new non-domestic buildings.

ii) Sales of building land for non-domestic building.

iii) The grant of any interest, right or licence consisting of a right to take game or fish.

iv) The provision in an hotel, inn, boarding house or similar establishment of sleeping accommodation or of accommodation in rooms which are provided in conjunction with sleeping accommodation or for the purpose of a supply of catering.

v) The provision of holiday accommodation in a house, flat, caravan, house-boat or tent.

vi) The provision of seasonal pitches for caravans, and the grant of facilities at caravan parks to persons for whom such pitches are provided.

vii) The provision of pitches for tents or of camping facilities.

viii) The grant of facilities for parking a vehicle.

ix) The grant of any right to fell and remove standing timber.

x) The grant of facilities for housing, or storage of, an aircraft or for mooring or storage of, a ship, boat or other vessel.

xi) The grant of any right to occupy a box, seat or other accommodation at a sports ground, theatre, concert hall or other place of entertainment.

xii) The grant of facilities for playing any sport or participating in any physical recreation.

Either exempt or SR, depending on whether the supplier has elected to waive the exemption.

i) Sales of used non-domestic buildings

ii) Leases of used non-domestic buildings

Note that where stamp duty land tax is payable on the sale or lease of land or buildings, the consideration liable to VAT is the sale price plus stamp duty land tax.

Taxable persons

10. A taxable person is any person who is, or should be, registered for VAT. Person includes an individual, partnership, company, club, society or trust. Any person may register for VAT who is carrying on a business that involves making taxable supplies for a consideration. The business in question need not be a profit-making or profit-seeking business. VAT registration is compulsory once turnover of taxable supplies exceeds a set level (See section 13).

Business splitting

11. HMRC has indicated that the following factors will be taken into consideration in deciding whether or not an independent business exists for VAT registration purposes.

i) Appropriate premises and equipment for the business should be provided by the person carrying on the business.

ii) Day-to-day records identifying the business should be kept and where appropriate separate annual accounts.

iii) Purchase and sales invoices should be in the name of the person carrying on the trade who should be legally responsible for all trading activities.

iv) A separate bank account should be opened for the business.

v) All payroll payments should be paid by the person carrying on the business.

vi) The business should be treated as an independent business for income tax purposes.

vii) The person carrying on the business should be legally responsible for all trading activities.

Formerly, HMRC could not require separate businesses to register as a single trader for VAT purposes unless it could show that the main reason (or one of the main reasons) for keeping those businesses separate was to avoid a liability to be registered.

This limitation has been removed, and 'connected businesses which have avoided liability for VAT by artificially separating will be liable to be treated as one, whatever the purported reason for the separation'. For example, a series of limited companies running a pub, launderette or other retail outlet for only one month a year each, in order to keep the turnover of each company below the registration threshold, will be treated as one business.

Artificial separation of business activities

12. According to HMRC it is impracticable to give a complete list of all the circumstances in which a separation will be artificial, as each case will depend on its own facts. However, HMRC 'would at least make further enquiries' where:

a) Separate entities supply registered and unregistered customers.

b) The same equipment and/or premises are used by different entities on a regular basis – this may be particularly relevant where an ice cream van (for example) is used by traders in rotation.

c) A supply, which is usually a single supply, is split into separate parts – for example, a bed-and breakfast establishment where the bedroom is said to be supplied by the husband and the breakfast by the wife.

d) Where the separated parts retain the appearance of a single business: the example given being that of pub catering where 'in most cases the customer will consider the food and the drinks as bought from the pub and not from two independent businesses'. However, franchised 'shops within shops' will usually be accepted as truly independent businesses.

e) One person has a controlling influence in two or more businesses which make the same type of supply at separate locations.

Registration limits

13.

UK taxable supplies	Past turnover 1 year	Past turnover Unless turnover for next year will not exceed:	Future turnover 30 days
	£	£	£
1.4.2008	67,000	65,000	67,000
1.5.2009	68,000	66,000	68,000
1.4.2010	70,000	68,000	70,000
1.4.2011	73,000	71,000	73,000

Notes

i) Turnover of taxable supplies includes all zero and positive rated supplies.

ii) Registration is mandatory in the following circumstances:

  a) At the end of any month, if the value of the taxable supplies in the past year has exceeded the table limits.

  b) At any time, if there are reasonable grounds for believing that the value of the taxable supplies in the next 30 days will exceed the future turnover figure.

iii) For ii) a) notification to HMRC must be made within 30 days of the end of the relevant month. Registration is effective from the end of the month following the relevant month or such earlier date as may be mutually agreed.

iv) For ii) b) notification must be made before the end of the 30 day period. Registration is effective from the beginning of the 30 day period.

v) The relevant month is the month at the end of which liability to registration arises.

Voluntary registration

14. Where a person who is not liable to be registered satisfies HMRC that he or she:

i) makes taxable supplies; or

ii) is carrying on a business and intends to make such supplies in the course or furtherance of that business;

then, if the person so requests, he or she will be registered, with effect from the day on which the request is made or such earlier date as may be mutually agreed.

Voluntary de-registration

15. A registered person may apply for de-registration if his or her taxable turnover excluding VAT is not expected to exceed £71,000 (£68,000 previously) in the next year. De-registration requires the trader to account for output VAT on all stocks and taxable fixed assets on hand at deregistration as a self-supply, but subject to a de minimis of VAT due of £2,000.

Group registration

16. Under Section 43 VATA 1994, as amended, two or more companies or limited liability partnerships (collectively referred to as corporate bodies) may register as a single taxable person, known as a VAT Group, if

i) each body has a permanent establishment in the UK

ii) they are under common control, for example one or more company is a subsidiary of a common parent company, or both/ all of them are controlled by a business partnership, or by an individual.

A restriction applies where the turnover of a prospective VAT group is over £10 million per year and the group is partly owned or managed by a third party (e.g. a joint owner owning 50% of the parent company but not itself in the VAT group. This entity can only register as a group for VAT if:

i) no more than 50 per cent of benefits generated by the business go to third parties

ii) under GAAP the whole VAT group uses consolidated accounting

iii) no third party consolidates the VAT group into its accounts.

The effects of a group registration are as follows.

i) The VAT affairs are vested in one group company, known as the representative member, and only one VAT return is required.

ii) Intra-group supplies are outside the scope of (ie not subject to) VAT.

iii) All members of the group are jointly and severally liable for the VAT due from the representative member.

iv) All the limits for registration and deregistration, partial exemption, cash accounting, etc apply to the group figures.

iv) Rules exist for VAT groups with a turnover > £10m to prevent suppliers and customers being in the same VAT Group.

Companies organised into divisions – Divisional registration

17. A UK resident company carrying on business in several divisions may register its divisions separately as unincorporated traders, as follows.

i) All divisions of the company must be registered separately. It is not possible to exclude certain divisions from registration e.g. where they fall below the registration limits.

ii) Separate VAT returns are made by each division.

iii) However, the separate divisions are not separately taxed persons and the company remains liable for the whole VAT.

iv) Inter-divisional transfers are not subject to VAT.

v) Each division should be an independent unit with its own accounting and administration, carrying on business activities in separate locations.

vi) Input tax attributable to exempt supplies (exempt input tax) by the corporate body as a whole must be less than the limits referred to in Chapter 37 (Section 17).

Divisional registration is subject to the approval of HMRC.

Accounts and records

18. There are a number of detailed regulations concerning the 'book-keeping' arrangements required for VAT purposes. From 1 April 2011 almost all VAT returns must be submitted online and VAT payments made online. Paper records may still be kept supporting input VAT, etc. Electronic records are acceptable.

a) Any taxable supply of goods or services must be supported by a 'tax invoice', the details of which are described in the next chapter.

b) At regular intervals, usually quarterly, a return must be completed showing the amounts of output and input tax for the period and the net amount payable to or receivable from HMRC. The period covered by a VAT return is known as a tax period and each return must be submitted not later than one month after the end of that tax period.

c) Adequate records and accounts of all transactions involving VAT must be maintained to support both the amount of output tax chargeable, and the claims for deductible input tax – to support input tax claims the primary requirement is keep valid tax invoices received from suppliers. These records are checked on control visits by HMRC officers.

d) Books and records, including electronic records, must be kept for a period of six years. Business records include the following:

    Orders and delivery notes
    Relevant business correspondence
    Purchase and sales books
    Cash books and other account books
    Purchase invoices and copy sales invoices
    Records of daily takings e.g. till rolls
    Annual accounts – balance sheet and profit and loss accounts
    Import and export documents
    Bank statements and paying-in-slips
    Any credit/debit notes issued or received.

e) There are some optional special schemes for retailers to simplify record keeping for VAT purposes and these are covered in Chapter 37.

Administration

19. HM Revenue and Customs is the government department responsible for the administration and collection of VAT (except Import VAT, which is collected by the UK Border Agency).

Dispute and appeals procedure

In the event of a dispute between a taxable person and the VAT office, there is first an optional internal review procedure in which a Revenue Officer who has not been involved in the case before is asked to review the complaint and respond within 45 days. If this review supports the decision of the original Revenue Officer, or if there is no internal review, the taxpayer can appeal within 30 days to the Tax Chamber of the First-Tier Tribunal (this handles disputes on both direct and indirect taxes and took over all cases from the former UK VAT Tribunals on 1 April 2009). Appeals to the First-tier Tribunal might cover matters such as:

a) Registration or cancellation of registration.

b) Assessment of tax.

c) Amount of tax chargeable.

d) Amount of input tax deductible.

e) Bad debt claims.

f) Group registration matters.

g) Matters concerned with the value or categorisation of supplies.

On questions of law a further appeal can be made to the Upper Tribunal (Tax and Chancery Chamber) from which further appeal lies to the Court of Appeal (Inner House in Scotland).

As VAT is European Law, questions of the interpretation of EU Directives or Regulations, and of whether domestic VAT legislation or HMRC practice is compatible with EU law, can be referred by the judge directly from any UK Court or Tribunal to the European Court of Justice, for a definitive ruling on the relevant point of European Law. The UK courts are obliged to follow the ECJ's rulings in applying VAT law to cases before them and if anything in the UK VAT legislation is found incompatible with the EU VAT Directives then the UK Government are obliged to change the law. In deciding UK VAT cases the UK courts also take account of similar decisions on VAT matters from the courts and VAT tribunals of other EU Member States.

Late registration penalty

20. a) Failure to notify HMRC at the proper time that a business should be registered for VAT purposes may incur a tax-based penalty, subject to a minimum of £50.00.

Number of months late for registration	% of VAT due
0 – 9	5%
10 – 18	10%
19 –	15%

The amount of VAT due is the sum of VAT due from the date the registration should have been made.

The penalty is not due if the trader can satisfy HMRC that there was a reasonable excuse for the failure.

The following does not amount to reasonable excuse:

i) insufficiency of funds to pay the tax

ii) reliance on a third party to pay the tax

iii) ignorance of the law relating to registration.

b) HMRC has indicated that the following guidelines show circumstances where there might be a reasonable excuse for late registration.

i) **Compassionate circumstances** where an individual is totally responsible for running a small business and he or she, or a member of the immediate family, was seriously ill or recovering from such illness at the time notification was required.

ii) **Transfer of a business as a going concern** where such a business is taken over with little or no break in the trading activities and returns have been submitted and tax paid on time under the registration number of the previous owner.

iii) **Doubt about liabilities of supplies** where there is written evidence of an enquiry to HMRC about the liability of supplies and liability has remained in doubt.

iv) **Uncertainty about employment status** where there are genuine doubts as to whether a person is employed or self-employed or where correspondence with HMRC can be produced about these doubts.

v) **Effective date of registration earlier than required** where a person has requested registration from an earlier date than was legally required in the mistaken belief that he or she had to do so to recover input tax on stocks and assets for the business. This excuse could only apply if there was no reason to believe that taxable turnover would exceed the registration threshold from the required date.

The default surcharge – Section 59 VATA 1994

21. The following points should be noted under this heading.

a) A person will be in default if by the last day on which a return is required, HMRC have not received that return, or the tax.

b) Taxpayers can be in default for two return periods (i.e. quarters or months) in any 12 month period without incurring a monetary penalty.

c) Where the taxpayer is in default for the first time then a surcharge liability notice will be issued. The surcharge liability notice once issued remains in force for a period of 12 months during which time there must be no default.

d) While the notice is in force a default charge will arise in any quarter in which a default occurs, at the following rates, if greater than £30.00:

	% of VAT paid late
1st default	2%
2nd default	5%
3rd and subsequent defaults	10%
4th and subsequent	15%

e) A person is not liable to a surcharge if he or she satisfies the Commissioners that in the case of a default which is 'material to the surcharge':

i) the return, or as the case may be the tax shown on it, was despatched at such time and in such manner that it was reasonable to expect that it would be received within the appropriate time limit, or

ii) there is a reasonable excuse for the return or tax not having been despatched.

The following are not reasonable excuses:

i) Insufficiency of funds to pay any tax

ii) Where reliance is placed on any other person to perform any task, the fact of that reliance or any other dilatoriousness or inaccuracy on the part of the person relied upon.

f) Automatic penalties for late payment of VAT do not apply to businesses with an annual turnover of less than £150,000. HMRC will instead offer small businesses help and advice initially if they are late with VAT payments.

Errors on VAT returns

22. a) The procedures for the voluntary disclosure of errors are as noted below:

Errors amounting to £2,000 or less	Separate disclosure not required. No interest charged on underpayments whether notified or not.
Errors amounting to more than £2,000	HMRC must be notified in writing by letter or using VAT Form 652. Interest is chargeable from date when VAT was outstanding.
Default interest	This will be charged on net payments to HMRC at the prescribed rate of interest. The interest charge is not an expense of trade for income tax purposes.

b) A Serious Misdeclaration Penalty can arise if the HMRC find as a result of their enquiries that VAT has been misdeclared.

A penalty of 15% of the VAT due can be imposed but this will only apply where:

Amount misdeclared for a VAT accounting period	≥	which is the lesser of:	
		(i)	30% of the true amount of tax payable, or
		(ii)	the greater of £1.0 million and 5% of the true amount of tax for the period

c) A Serious Misdeclaration Penalty will not normally be imposed:

i) during the period from the end of an accounting period to the due date for furnishing the VAT return for the following accounting period

ii) when a VAT return is misdeclared but this has been corrected by a compensating misdeclaration in respect of the same transaction for the following accounting period, with no overall loss of VAT.

Tax avoidance schemes

23. Businesses with supplies ≥ £600,000 must disclose their use of specific VAT avoidance schemes, which HMRC publishes in a statutory list. This must be done within 30 days of the date when the first return affected by the scheme becomes due. Failure to disclose incurs a penalty of 15% of tax avoided. Businesses with taxable supplies > £10m. must disclose the use of schemes that have the hallmarks of avoidance.

Student self testing question with answer

A Ltd owns a quarry. It extracts stone from this quarry and sells the stone to B Ltd for £10,000 plus VAT. B Ltd converts all the stone into paving slabs and sells these slabs to C Ltd for £18,000 plus VAT. C Ltd owns and runs a garden centre, where the slabs are sold to the general public for a total of £32,000 plus VAT.

Requirement:

Show how VAT is charged and collected at each stage of the process. (Assume that VAT is to be accounted for at 20% throughout).

Suggested answer

	Cost price before VAT	Input tax	Selling price before VAT	Output tax	Paid to HMRC
	£	£	£	£	£
A Ltd	-	-	10,000	2,000	2,000
B Ltd	10,000	2,000	18,000	3,600	1,600
C Ltd	18,000	3,600	32,000	6,400	2,800
					6,400

37 The VAT system in more detail

Introduction

1. This chapter covers further features of the VAT system under the following main topic headings:

The VAT return	Imports – removal from warehouse
Zero rated and exempt supplies	Exports
Taxable supply of goods and services	Goods for personal use
Taxable persons	Bad debts
The supply of goods and services	Transfer of business
Place of supply	Sale of business assets
Tax point	Business assets – capital allowances
Tax invoice/credit notes	VAT on capital goods – partly exempt businesses
Value of goods and services	Rents
Mixed supplies/composite supplies	Changes in tax rates
Input tax – deductions	Cash/annual accounting schemes
Input tax – no deduction	Flat rate scheme – small firms
Fuel for private motoring	Special retail schemes
Partial exemption	Miscellaneous

The VAT return

2. A taxable person is required to charge VAT on taxable supplies to customers, called output tax, but he or she is also able to claim credit for the tax paid on business purchases and expenses, and assets known as the input tax.

At the end of an accounting period, usually a month or three months, a business has to submit a return of Value Added Tax to HMRC. This must show the total taxable supplies made and the VAT charged (output tax), together with the VAT on purchase and expense invoices received (input tax), but excluding any input VAT that is blocked from recovery. If the tax charged exceeds the amount paid then the balance is payable to HMRC. Where the output tax is less than the input tax then a repayment can be claimed.

Example

	£	£
Total taxable turnover (SR) for the quarter	100,000	
Output tax @ 20%		20,000
Total taxable inputs (SR) for the quarter	80,000	
Input tax @ 20%		16,000
Balance of VAT payable to HMRC		4,000

Zero-rated and exempt supplies

3. Goods or services which fall within the zero-rated or exempt categories do not include any VAT at all in the total invoiced price, and for this reason are often thought by students to be similar. However, there are some important differences between zero rated and exempt supplies.

a) Zero-rated goods or services are taxable outputs, but liable at a nil rate of output tax. It follows that any input tax incurred in providing those outputs can be reclaimed by the supplier, since there is no output tax collected from customers to give a normal means of setting off the supplier's input VAT.

b) Supplies of exempt goods and services are viewed as made outside the VAT system and therefore, in principle, any input tax incurred in making such supplies cannot be reclaimed by the trader. However, irrecoverable input VAT will be an allowable business cost for income or corporation tax (unless the related cost is disallowable for direct tax purposes, eg entertaining).

c) A business which makes only exempt supplies, such as an insurance company, cannot register for VAT.

d) The implications of being partially exempt (making both taxable and exempt supplies) are explained below (section 17).

Taxable supply of goods and services

4. Tax is chargeable on any supply of goods and services which are made in the UK or imported where the supply counts as being taxable. The supply must be made by a taxable person in the course of a trade, profession or vocation.

Taxable persons

5. A taxable person is any person who has registered for VAT, and this is required if the total value of his or her taxable supplies for any one year are greater than £70,000. All business activities must be aggregated in order to determine whether or not a person should register. Registration can be for an individual, partnership or limited company. The total of taxable business supplies is called taxable turnover.

The supply of goods and services

6. The supply of goods can include any of the following:

a) sale by ordinary commercial transaction

b) sale by auction or through agents

c) sale under a credit sale agreement or by hire purchase.

d) goods supplied for further processing

e) goods supplied for personal use.

The supply of services covers any which are provided for money or money's worth, and includes the hire, lease or rental of any goods. Services which are ancillary to the supply of goods such as postage and packing and delivery are normally treated as services and not as part of the goods sold, if they are shown separately on the sales invoice.

Place of supply

7. In principle only goods and services supplied in the UK are chargeable to UK VAT so that the determination of the place of supply is important.

Goods

If the goods to be supplied are physically located in the UK then they are liable to UK VAT even where they may be subsequently exported. Goods that are located wholly outside the EU fiscal area and remain so are not subject to UK VAT at any time during the course of their supply. They are said to be outside the scope of VAT. This could arise, for example, where a shipping company arranges for a consignment of goods to be sold and transferred from one country to another.

For VAT purposes the UK includes the Isle of Man, but not the Channel Isles.

Services

For VAT purposes, the place of supply of services is the place where a service is treated as being supplied. This is the place where it is liable to VAT (if any). A particular service can have only one place of supply.

Prior to 1 January 2010 the EU VAT rules about the place of supply of services were complex with many detailed exceptions, not explored here. However the basic rule was that (subject to the exceptions mentioned), services were supplied in the place "where the supplier belongs".

Belonging in this sense means where the supplier has its principal place of business or its main business establishment. So if the supplier's principal place of business was in the UK, and it was registered for UK VAT, then in general all its services would be liable to UK VAT.

Where both the supplier and the customer are in the UK then generally there is no problem about deeming the place of supply of services as this will (on basic principles) be the UK.

The problems of competing places of supply arise when the customer is not in the UK and the supplier is, or vice versa.

If the customer belongs outside the UK, and provides evidence to the UK supplier that it is in genuine business in its own country, then the supply of services is treated from 1 January 2010 as taking place where the customer belongs, not where the supplier belongs. This means that for UK VAT purposes, the supply of services to business customers outside the UK is now outside the scope of UK VAT and so no UK VAT should be charged on it.

If the Customer belongs in another EU state, and the UK supplier also has its own VAT registration in that other state (which is possible; a trader can register for VAT in any number of different EU states where it does business), then having determined the place of supply, the supplier should issue a VAT invoice showing VAT at the rate applying in that other state and include it on the VAT return in the other State.

If the Customer belongs in another EU member state but the UK supplier has no VAT registration in that other EU state, then the UK supplier treats the supply as outside the scope of VAT. However the Customer must account for VAT itself on its own purchase, using the reverse charge procedure (see section 19).

Time of supply – tax point

8. The tax point determines the period in which a supply falls, therefore when the supply should be included on the next VAT return and what rate of VAT applies if there is a change in rate. As with place of supply, the tax point rules differ depending on whether a supply is one of goods or of services.

For goods the basic tax point is the date when the goods are delivered or made available, and for services the basic tax point is the date of performance. However, there are two key exceptions.

a) If an invoice is issued within 14 days after the time when goods are delivered or made available, then the date of the invoice becomes the tax point. This practice is widely followed and enables the VAT return to be completed from invoice records. A longer period than 14 days between delivery and invoice may be agreed with HMRC if the business has a regular invoice billing cycle eg on the last day of the month,

b) If payment of consideration for the supply is made in advance of the date when goods are delivered or made available, then it is the earliest of the invoice, delivery or payment date which determines the tax point.

The same rules apply for deciding the period in which taxable inputs of goods arise, and in general if credit is taken on business purchases, then relief for input tax is often obtained before the purchase invoice is paid.

Under the standard method of accounting for VAT by retailers the actual tax point is the date on which the retailer receives payment for goods sold. See Chapter 38.

Tax invoice

9. A tax invoice is a sales invoice issued by a registered person in respect of any goods or services supplied by him or her to another taxable person. The invoice must contain:

a) supplier's name, address and VAT registration number

b) customer's name and address

c) type of supply i.e. whether a sale, sale by HP, hire or rental

d) description of goods or services supplied together with the amount payable excluding VAT

e) total amount payable without VAT

f) particulars of any cash discounts offered

g) total amount of tax chargeable.

A less detailed invoice may be used where individual supplies by a retailer amount to less than £250, including VAT.

Credit notes

10. Regulations require all registered traders to show the related VAT on credit or debit notes, whenever a price adjustment alters the amount of VAT due on a previous invoice.

Value of goods and services

11. The general rule is that the value on which VAT is chargeable is the amount of money (excluding VAT) which a customer has to pay for the goods or services supplied. This is known in VAT law as the consideration. The following should be noted.

a) Price discounts (eg for customer loyalty) must be deducted from the invoiced amount to determine the VAT value.

b) Prompt payment discounts, if offered, should be assumed to be going to be taken in full when computing the VAT on the sale price. If the prompt payment discount is not taken (i.e. the customer takes a longer credit period than the discount terms require), the difference paid by the customer is not subject to VAT.

c) If a supply is not made for money consideration then the open market value of the supply, less any VAT included in that value, should be taken as the value of the supply and VAT computed on it. This would apply for example on a part-exchange transaction.

d) The cost of the goods to the supplier may be used to determine the value of a taxable supply. This would apply to goods appropriated from trading stock for personal use, and to the trader's own built plant and machinery on which input VAT should be accounted for under the "self-supply" rules..

Mixed supplies

12. A mixed supply occurs where a single inclusive price is charged for a number of separate supplies of goods and services. Where all the supplies are taxable at the same rate then the normal rules of VAT can be easily applied to compute the VAT element. However, where different rates apply then an apportionment must be made which is 'fair and justifiable'. (See Card Protection Plan V CIR. 2001 STC)

Example

B makes a mixed supply of goods at a VAT-inclusive price of £160.00. The product costs show zero rated goods costing £30.00 and standard rated goods costing £50 (exclusive of VAT).

Solution

Computation of VAT

Proportion of total cost at SR $\dfrac{50 + \text{VAT}}{(50 + \text{VAT}) + 30} = 60/90$

VAT inclusive price of standard rated goods 60/90 × £160 = £107

VAT included = 107 × 20/120 = 18

Value of zero rated supply = 160 – 107 = 53.

Analysis of total price as apportioned

	£
Value of standard rated supply (107 – 18)	89
VAT on standard rated supply 20% × 90	18
Zero rated supply	54
Mixed supply	161

Other methods of apportionment e.g. based on market values, can be used. Apportionment must not be made where the supply is a composite supply. See below. Examples of mixed supply are:

Annual subscription to the AA (C & E v AA QB 1974 STC 192)

Fees for correspondence courses (Rapid Results College Ltd 1973 VAT TR 197) (Books are zero rated. Tuition is standard rated).

Composite supply

13. This occurs where goods and services supplied together make up a single indivisible supply, and apportionment must not be made for VAT rating purposes as the components cannot be viewed as separable. The VAT treatment of a composite supply depends on the judgment as to what is the principal supply with the other parts of a different type being classed as ancillary. If the composite supply as a whole package does not clearly qualify for exemption or zero rating then it must be standard rated.

Examples of supplies that have been held in decided cases to be composite supplies include:

Services of a launderette (supplies of water, heat, use of machinery)	Mander Laundries Ltd 1973 VAT TR 136
A course in dress design (material and guidance notes)	Betty Foster (Fashion Sewing) 1976 VAT TR 229

Input tax – Deduction

14. Input tax is the VAT charged on business purchases and expenses including imported goods, goods removed from a warehouse, and capital expenditure.

To be deductible, the input tax must be in respect of goods and services for the purposes of the business, and not of a class where the tax is specifically non-deductible.

Input tax can be reclaimed providing that it is attributable to the making of

i) standard or zero-rated supplies (which term includes reduced rate supplies)

ii) supplies made in the course of business which are outside the scope of UK VAT but would have been subject to standard or zero rate if made in the UK (eg the supplies of services deemed supplied outside the UK under the rules in section 11 above)

iii) supplies of warehoused goods.

Input tax incurred in respect of any other activity not covered by (i) to (iii) above is not reclaimable.

Input tax on business overheads or research and development expenditure can be claimed as input tax provided that the overheads or R&D are attributable to the three activities noted above. If the overhead or R&D expenditure is partially attributable to exempt supplies or to activities outside the three categories above, then only the part of the input tax that can be attributed to the three listed activities is reclaimable.

Input tax incurred in relation to exempt supplies may however be recoverable where after calculating the amount for a period, it is found to fall under specified de minimis levels. (See partial exemption, section 17 onwards)

Input tax – Blocked deduction

15. Input tax charged in respect of the following is non-deductible.

a) The purchase of private motor cars, except:

   i) Cars purchased for use exclusively for business purposes and not being capable of additional private use by the trader.

   ii) Cars used solely for business such as taxis, self drive hire cars.

   iii) Cars purchased for resale.

   VAT on the purchase of commercial vehicles is allowed as a deduction.

b) To mirror the rule that input VAT on purchased cars is usually blocked as non-reclaimable, only 50% of the input VAT applicable to the leasing of any car(s) is deductible for VAT purposes. The net rental plus 50% of VAT incurred is therefore charged in the accounts as an allowable expense for direct tax purposes. This rule does not apply to very short hires of cars eg for a few days.

c) Motor accessories. When a motor car is purchased, VAT on the accessories provided at first registration is not reclaimable, even if invoiced separately. VAT on accessories purchased and fitted later is deductible, provided that the car is still in business use.

d) Business entertainment expenses. Input tax on this kind of expenditure is only allowable where it is incurred for staff entertainment for the purposes of the business eg provision of meals and seasonal entertainment. VAT cannot be reclaimed on the entertainment of customers, suppliers or prospective customers/members of the public.

Fuel purchased by a business and used for private motoring – the scale charge

16. Input tax on all road fuel purchased by a VAT registered trader for business or private use is reclaimable providing that the business is making wholly taxable supplies to which the fuel purchases can be attributed. However, if exempt supplies are made, part of the input tax on fuel may not be recoverable.

If there is any onward supply of fuel to employees for private motoring (ie they do not fully reimburse the business for the cost of any fuel used for private mileage) , a flat rate "fuel scale charge " must be accounted for per car /employee. This charges VAT on an assumed or notional amount of fuel that is deemed to be supplied for private use to the employee(s) or the business proprietor(s) out of the VAT registered business's fuel purchases. Output tax is charged on this notional supply, and must be paid by the business, by reference to the fuel scale charge rates.

Like car income tax benefit in kind charges, VAT scale charges are based on the CO_2 emissions of the car.

VAT fuel rates 2011/12

CO_2 band	VAT fuel scale charge, 3 month period	VAT on 3 month charge 20%
	£	£
120 or below	157	26.17
125	236	39.33
130	252	42.00
135	268	44.67
140	283	47.17
145	299	49.83
150	315	52.50
155	331	55.17
160	346	57.67

CO_2 band	VAT fuel scale charge, 3 month period £	VAT on 3 month charge 20% £
165	362	60.33
170	378	63.00
175	394	65.67
180	409	68.17
185	425	70.83
190	441	73.50
195	457	76.17
200	472	78.67
205	488	81.33
210	504	84.00
215	520	86.67
220	536	89.33
225 or above	551	91.83

For monthly or annual VAT return periods, pro-rate the above charges accordingly.

Partial exemption

17. A trader who makes supplies of taxable goods and/or services, and also makes supplies of exempt goods and/or services, is referred to as a partially exempt trader. The special rules about input VAT recovery by partially exempt traders are outlined below. (Note that the term "exempt input tax" is used in the VAT legislation to refer to input tax attributed to the making of exempt supplies not taxable supplies.)

i) Where a business makes exempt supplies of financial or land-related services, and these are not incurred in the course of carrying on a business in the financial sector, then all exempt input tax can be recovered provided it has been incurred in relation to any of the following supplies:

   a) the granting of any lease or tenancy of land, or any licence to occupy land (provided that the exempt input tax related to all such supplies made by the business is less than £1,000 per tax year, and that the business does not incur any exempt input tax other than that related to those supplies listed in this paragraph)

   b) any deposit of money

   c) any services of arranging insurance

d) any services of arranging mortgages

e) any services of arranging hire-purchase, credit sale or conditional sale transactions

f) the assignment of any debt in respect of a supply of goods or services by the assignor.

If the exempt input tax is incurred in relation to supplies other than those listed above, then the tax must be taken into consideration in determining the 'de minimis limit'.

ii) A business can be treated as fully taxable (ie can recover all its input VAT) providing its exempt input tax is not more than £625 per month on average.

In addition businesses must also satisfy the additional condition that exempt input tax is no more than 50% of the VAT on all purchases.

HMRC has provided two alternative tests which may be easier for businesses to apply. If any of the three tests are satisfied the business can be treated as fully taxable:

a) If total input tax is no more than £625 per month on average and the value of its exempt supplies is no more than 50% of the value of all its supplies; or

b) If total input tax less input tax directly attributable to taxable supplies is no more than £625 per month on average and the value of its exempt supplies is no more than 50% of the value of all of its supplies.

iii) Exempt input tax must be considered where financial businesses are carried on, such as a bank, building society, money lender, credit card company etc.

iv) The standard method of calculation to be used to apportion input VAT between taxable and exempt supplies, where the business is making partially exempt and partially taxable supplies in the period, is as follows.

a) Identify the input tax that is directly attributable to taxable supplies

b) Identify the input tax that is directly attributable to exempt supplies.

c) The balance of input tax is input tax that is not attributable to any particular supplies (non-attributable input tax)

d) Calculate the percentage, rounded up to the next whole number, of such non-attributable input tax which is equal to:

$$\frac{\text{Value of taxable supplies (excl. VAT)}}{\text{Value of taxable supplies (excl. VAT)} + \text{Value of exempt supplies}}$$

e) Add the percentage obtained at (d) to the input tax already attributed to taxable supplies at (a). This input tax can be reclaimed as relating to taxable supplies.

f) Add the remainder of the non–attributable input tax [(c) less (d)] to the exempt input tax already attributed to exempt supplies, at (b)

g) If the total of exempt input tax at (f) is below the de minimis limit of £625 per month AND 50% of all input tax, then it can be reclaimed. If it exceeds the de minimis limit, it is irrecoverable.

vi) The standard method is the default method provided by the VAT Act but it is not mandatory and a trader can apply to use any other special method more suited to its business, provided advance agreement is obtained from HMRC. Commonly used special methods to allocate input tax between taxable and exempt supplies include those based on staff numbers, floorspace, purchases (whereas the standard method uses sales) or transaction counts. Any VAT partial exemption method approved by HMRC has to be 'fair and reasonable'.

vii) For convenience it is possible for a business to use last year's partial exemption fraction for the first three quarters of its VAT year and only carry out the detailed annual calculations in the final VAT quarter.

Example

A Ltd had the following transactions in the quarter to 31st December 2011:

Supplies made:	£
Standard-rated supplies (excluding VAT)	150,000
Zero-rated supplies	50,000
Exempt supplies	100,000

Input tax has been paid on input costs attributable to the following outputs and activities:

	£
Standard-rated supplies	12,000
Zero-rated supplies	–
Exempt supplies	17,000
General overheads	4,000

The general overhead input tax cannot be directly attributed to any of the listed supplies.

Compute the VAT payable for the quarter to 31st December 2011.

Solution: A Ltd VAT return: quarter to 31st December 2011

			£
Output tax 150,000 @ 20%			30,000
Input tax:	Standard-rated	12,000	
	Zero-rated	–	
	Overheads	2,680	(14,680)
VAT due			15,320

Notes

i) VAT attributable to overheads:

$$\frac{150{,}000(SR) + 50{,}000(ZR)}{150{,}000(SR) + 50{,}000(ZR) + 100{,}000(EX)} \text{ x } 4{,}000 = 67\% \text{ x } 4{,}000 = 2{,}680$$

ii) As the de minimis levels for exempt input tax have been exceeded, the business is partially exempt, and only 67% of the total input tax on overheads can be recovered. In addition, none of the £17,000 of input tax can be recovered that is attributable to making the exempt supplies.

iii) An annual computation is required to adjust any quarterly fluctuations.

Imports

18. Imports of goods

VAT is charged on most goods imported into the UK (including acquisitions from the EC) whether or not the importer is registered for VAT. In other words, private individuals also have to pay VAT on imports of goods into the UK (subject to certain personal exemptions).

Payment of VAT on imported goods is due at the time of importation or removal from a warehouse, unless deferment arrangements have been made. A registered trader approved by HMRC may defer payment of tax on goods imported in the course of business during a calendar month until the 15th of the following month (or the next working day after the 15th if that day is a holiday). The VAT is normally collected by a direct debit mandate which forms part of the application for deferment.

VAT on imported goods can be claimed as input tax subject to the normal rules. (This does not apply to imports in a private capacity, even if the importer also has a business Vat registration). The claim for the VAT as input tax must be made in the return for the accounting period during which the importation or removal from the relevant warehouse occurred.

Certain goods imported into the UK from the EC are eligible for VAT import relief.

Warehoused goods

When goods are warehoused for customs and excise purposes then payment of import VAT is usually suspended. VAT becomes payable when the goods are removed from the warehouse for use in the UK.

19. Imports of services – Reverse charge procedure

Where services are received from other EU countries outside the UK by UK businesses, and do not have any VAT applied in the state of the supplier or in the UK by the supplier, this means the supplier has classed the place of supply of the services as the UK, and not being VAT-registered in the UK they have treated the service as outside the scope of VAT on their own home-country VAT return

In this situation, the UK-registered trader (who is the customer) must operate the **reverse charge** procedure. This means it must account for both UK output VAT on the imported services (as though self-supplied) and also UK input VAT which it has in effect "charged itself" and now seeks to recover. Both figures (input VAT and output VAT) will be the same figure, and appear on the same VAT return - unless partial exemption restricts input tax recovery.

So long as the UK purchasing business is making fully taxable supplies, there is no net VAT cost to it from operating the reverse charge on imports, as the same amount is added to input VAT and output VAT in the same period. This puts it in the same cash position as if it had used a UK supplier for the services – i.e. it pays VAT on the services, but the input VAT is all recovered. However, if the UK trader is partially exempt, and the service that was supplied related wholly or partly to its making exempt supplies, then some input VAT will be irrecoverable. The same amount of UK VAT would have been irrecoverable if the same services had been purchased by the partially exempt trader from a UK supplier, and normal UK VAT had been charged. Thus the reverse charge procedure removes an unfair pricing advantage that non- UK businesses would otherwise enjoy, when selling services to UK business customers who are partially-exempt.

This example shows how the reverse charge (which works the same way across the EU fiscal area) prevents a loss of tax to the UK, by ensuring that VAT on imported services treated as supplied in the UK , and on which the VAT is recoverable in the UK, has been paid in the UK.

Exports

20. Exports of goods to an overseas customer outside the EU Fiscal area are zero rated. Where goods are sent to a final exporter in the UK then they will not be zero rated by the UK supplier, as there is a supply in the UK being made; but they can be if there is delivery to a port or a central clearance depot for shipment.

Goods for personal use

21. Where goods which belong to a business are put to private use outside the business, then a taxable supply is being made and output tax is chargeable. Thus if trading stock is withdrawn from the business for private use, or an employee uses a business asset for private purposes, in principle a taxable supply occurs.

VAT is chargeable on the cost to the business (for income tax purposes it is the market value in the case of trading stock withdrawn from a business by a sole trader) of the supply, and the tax point is the time when the goods are made available for non-business use.

The special rules for the private use of fuel for motor cars were covered at section 16 above.

Bad debts

22. Relief is available for bad debts incurred by a taxable person, and a claim for a refund of the appropriate output tax (in effect as if it were new input tax suffered) can be made where the goods or services were supplied for a monetary consideration, and VAT on the supply was paid; and one of the following applies:

a) the customer has become insolvent. This means an official determination of inability to pay debts such as bankruptcy, or the winding up of a company.

b) the trader has obtained a certificate from the 'administrator' or 'administrative receiver' of a company stating that in his or her opinion if the company went into liquidation its assets would be insufficient to pay secured and preferential creditors.

c) any debt which is more than six months old which has been written off in the trader's accounts can be claimed as a bad debt for VAT purposes. The six-month period runs from the date the payment was due under normal trade terms, not the time of supply.

d) Any business that has made a claim for input tax on a supply, but has not paid the supplier of the goods within six months, must repay the VAT.

Bad debts – Claim

23. The amount of the claim will usually be readily ascertainable by reference to the actual debt outstanding. However, where there are payments on account (not allocated by the debtor to any particular supply) then these are allocated to the earliest supplies in the account after adjusting for any mutual supplies ie contra items.

Example

R Ltd is registered for VAT. One of its customers, X Ltd, went into liquidation on 31st July 2011.

The sales ledger account for the last two months to 31st July 2011 was as follows:

R Ltd sales ledger account with X Ltd

		£			£
1.5.11	Balance b/f	12,000	30.6.11	Cheque May a/c paid	12,000
25.5.11	1. Goods (inc. VAT)	36,000	23.7.11	Cheque payment on a/c	10,000
15.6.11	2. Goods (zero rated)	9,000	31.7.11	Balance c/f	50,000
20.7.11	3. Goods (inc. VAT)	15,000			
		72,000			72,000
31.7.11	Balance b/d	50,000			

Compute the bad debt relief available to R Ltd.

Solution

Amount due from X Ltd at 31st July 2011 £50,000

		Gross	VAT
		£	£
Invoice	No. 3	15,000	2,500
	No. 2	9,000	–
	No. 1 (part)	26,000	4,333
		50,000	6,833

Notes

i) VAT on Invoice No.1 36,000 × $^{20}/_{120}$ = 6,000

Proportion $\frac{26,000}{36,000}$ × 6,000 = 4,333

ii) VAT recoverable is £6,833.

iii) Assuming VAT at 20% standard rate.

Transfer of a business as a going concern

24. a) The sale of the assets of a business as a going concern is not a supply of goods or services and is outside the scope of VAT, provided that:

i) the assets are to be used by the purchaser in carrying on the same kind of business whether as part of an existing business or not.

ii) in a case where the seller is a taxable person, the purchaser if not already registered must register for VAT immediately.

b) A sale of part of a business is not subject to VAT, provided that the part sold is capable of separate operation.

c) The purchaser cannot claim any input tax in respect of the purchase of the business, even where this has been incorrectly charged to him or her.

d) The provisions do not apply where the business is a different one after the transfer to that carried on by the seller.

e) The transfer of a sole trader's business to a limited company, or into partnership with one or more other persons falls within these transfer provisions, and is therefore outside the scope of VAT.

f) Where the business is transferred as a going concern, it is possible for the VAT Registration number of the vendor to be transferred to the purchaser, subject to certain conditions, and the approval of HMRC.

g) Where a business carried on by a taxable person is transferred to another person who is not registered at the time of the transfer, the new owner must register for VAT immediately if the treatment as outside the scope of VAT is claimed on the business sale.

Sale of business assets

25. The sale of assets used by a person in the course of business, e.g. plant and machinery, is subject to VAT as a taxable supply. This also applies where a VAT-registered person ceases to trade or deregisters for VAT (even if the assets are not immediately sold).

VAT is not chargeable on the disposal of a motor car second-hand unless input VAT was reclaimed on the purchase of the car. The circumstances when this can be done are limited to businesses where there is no possibility of private use of the car.

Other assets sold by a registered trader which have been used in the business (eg computers) are generally subject to standard rate VAT on the price charged when sold.

Business assets – cost for Capital Allowances

26. In general there is no difference between the treatment of capital goods and other inputs for VAT purposes and in most cases the input tax will be recovered and hence does not qualify as part of the cost for capital allowances. However, where a trader's supplies are exempt, or partially exempt, or the trader is not VAT registered, then they may not be able to recover all or part of the input tax on the capital goods. In such cases the VAT not reclaimable can be added to the cost of the asset for capital allowance purposes.

For motor cars the VAT is not recoverable input tax and is therefore added to the cost of the asset for capital allowance purposes.

VAT on capital goods – Partly exempt businesses

27. Input tax recovered by a trader on certain high-value capital assets when first acquired may have to be refunded to HMRC if there is a change in the business use to which they are applied eg from use in making taxable supplies to use in making exempt supplies.

The assets to which these rules apply are:

a) computers and computer equipment worth over £50,000, if their use changes within five years of acquisition.

b) land and buildings worth over £250,000, if their use changes within ten years of acquisition.

Rents

28. As noted in chapter 36 section 9, landlords can elect to charge VAT on rents from non-domestic buildings. The election must be made on a building by building basis, and once made will apply to all future transactions in the property, i.e. lettings or sales by the landlord. Businesses which are fully taxable will not be greatly affected by this change but those which are exempt or partially exempt may be affected, such as Group 2 Insurance and Group 5 Finance.

Changes in the tax rates

29. When a change in the standard rate of VAT occurs, the following rules apply.

a) Output tax is calculated under the normal rules i.e. by reference to the tax point - unless the special change of rate provisions are applied

b) Under these provisions, where the rate goes up, the tax at the old rate can be charged on goods removed or services performed before the date of change, even though a tax invoice would normally have been issued after the date of change.

c) Where a supply of services takes place which crosses the threshold date of change in rate, then the supply can be apportioned by reference to normal costing or pricing procedures. Tax at the old rate may be charged on services performed before the date of the change if the supplier apportions the total bill. However the supplier may choose not to do an apportionment.

d) It is generally the supplier's decision how to apply the tax point rules at a change in rate. The amount of input tax paid by the purchaser following a change in rate is obtained from the supplier's invoice, and only the amount actually charged can be reclaimed. For less detailed tax invoices which do not show the VAT separately, the amount of input tax can be computed at the rate appropriate at the stated tax point of the whole invoice.

Cash accounting scheme

30. The cash accounting scheme is optional for all businesses with a taxable supplies turnover of less than £1,350,000. It achieves a cash flow benefit for businesses whose customers take longer credit periods than the business takes against its own trade creditors. The main features of the scheme are;

a) VAT on inputs and outputs is included in the VAT return for the period when cash was received or paid to settle the invoice, rather than on the basis of the invoice date (or earlier tax point rule).

b) Applications for the scheme, once approved, remain in force for two years.

c) The problem of obtaining relief for VAT on bad debts does not arise since output Vat is not paid over until after the customers have paid. However, the business will not be able to reclaim input VAT until it has actually paid the relevant business cost.

Annual accounting scheme

31. This scheme is available to traders who have been VAT-registered for at least one year, and whose annual turnover is less than £1,350,000. The main features of the scheme are:

a) Businesses choosing the annual accounting make only one VAT return a year instead of the usual four. It is submitted two months after the VAT year-end

b) They make nine equal payments on account by direct debit during the year, which are each set as 10% of the total VAT paid for the previous year. A tenth, balancing, payment is made with the annual return to make up the correct amount of VAT actually due for the year.

c) Businesses already using the scheme will be able to continue until their turnover reaches £1,600,000.

Flat rate scheme – small firms

32. The flat-rate VAT scheme is available by application, and suits very small businesses.

i) Under the flat-rate scheme, traders avoid having to account internally for input VAT on all their purchases and output VAT on their supplies. Instead they calculate the net VAT liability as a flat rate percentage of their total turnover, including standard-rate, reduced-rate, zero-rate and exempt supplies.

ii) Tax invoices issued to customers do not mention the flat rate scheme and show the VAT rates applied as normal. The flat rate scheme is an alternative VAT calculation scheme that only affects the internal accounting and VAT returns of the trader.

iii) Once operating a flat-rate scheme the trader merely applies the standard quoted percentage to all business turnover, including exempt supplies, to arrive at the 'net amount of VAT' due for the period. The flat rate percentage reflects a notional average for the net output tax due after offsetting input tax on expenses (the amount actually incurred will not be relevant) and is the only calculation needed to operate the scheme. Actual input tax suffered is not reported on the VAT return.

iv) The scheme is available to traders whose annual taxable turnover, including reduced and zero rated supplies, does not exceed £150,000 in the year of entry to the scheme.

v) The flat rate percentage applied to turnover depends on the business trade classification used by HMRC. These vary between 2% for food, tobacco, and newsagent retailers to 13% for computer and IT service providers.

vi) The rates for the flat rate scheme allow for low value capital expenditure purchases. However, input VAT on VAT-inclusive capital expenditure over £2,000 can be recovered outside the flat rate scheme. Such separate treatment does not cover cars since input VAT recovery on these is generally excluded. However, where larger capital purchases have been dealt with outside the flat rate scheme, output tax on their later disposal (or deemed disposal, in the case of de-registration) is also dealt with outside the scheme.

vi) Traders using the flat-rate scheme issue invoices to their customers showing normal VAT details i.e. showing VAT at the standard , lower or zero rates, or that the sale is VAT exempt. The flat rate percentage is merely used to simplify the calculation of the net VAT payable on the trader's own VAT return. The flat-rate scheme does not affect the customers, who receive normal VAT invoices which can support their own VAT reclaims (if registered).

vii) For businesses using the VAT flat rate scheme , business accounts will be prepared using gross receipts less flat rate VAT percentage for turnover, and expenses will include irrecoverable input VAT. Limited companies are required by law to show their turnover net of VAT.

Special retail schemes

33. a) There are five standard retail schemes:

Point of sale scheme

Apportionment scheme (2 schemes)

Direct calculation scheme (2 schemes)

Details may be found at http://www.hmrc.gov.uk/vat/schemes/index.htm

b) No trader will be allowed to use any retail scheme if it is reasonably practicable for them to account for VAT in the usual way.

c) Retail schemes can only be used for retail sales. If a trader makes some retail sales and others to VAT-registered traders than the usual VAT procedures must be applied to the latter.

d) Turnover limits of £1m and £130m restrict availability of the retail schemes. Details may be found on the HMRC website.

Miscellaneous

34. i) **Pre-registration expenditure.** Input tax on pre-registration business expenditure can be included in the first VAT return after registration. In the case of input tax on goods (as distinct from services) the goods must either be still retained at the date of first registration, or have been converted into other goods still retained. For services, the expenditure must have been incurred (tax point of the invoice) within the six months prior to the date of first registration.

ii) **Business gifts**. In general traders are not required to account for VAT as a taxable supply on the value of small business gifts such as diaries and calendars. The limit on such goods is £50 per item. The treatment of a series of business gifts in any 12 month period to the same person is aligned with that of a single gift. Where the limit is exceeded, output tax is due on the value of all the gifts made up to that point.

Student self testing question with answer

Octavius Limited is a fully taxable trader and does not operate the flat rate or cash accounting VAT scheme. You are provided with the following information relating to Octavius Limited for the quarter ended 31 August 2011:

The VAT-exclusive accounts show the following

	£	£
Sales		165,000
Sales returns		(11,000)
		154,000
Purchases	96,000	
Purchases returns	(3,000)	
	93,000	
Bad debts written off	15,000	
Other expenses	24,000	
		132,000
Profit		22,000

The sales, purchases and 'other expenses' are all standard-rated for VAT.

All input VAT is reclaimable.

The sales and purchases returns are all evidenced by credit notes issued and received.

The bad debts were written off in August 2011. Payment for the original sales was due by 16 April 2011.

A sales invoice for £3,000, excluding VAT, had been omitted in error from the VAT return for the quarter to 28 February 2011.

Included in the expense figure is the cost of both business and private petrol for Managing Director's car, which had CO_2 emissions of 210g/km.

Requirement

(a) Complete the VAT account for the three month period ended 31 August 2011, showing how much VAT is payable to HM Revenue and Customs. (7 marks)

(b) When is the tax shown by (a) above payable? (1 mark)

(c) State the course of action is open to a taxpayer who disagrees with a decision by HMRC on the application of VAT. (1 mark)

(d) What are the consequences of any action taken by the taxpayer in (c) above?

(ACCA June 1995 updated)

Suggested solution

(a)

Output tax :		£
On Sales (165,000 x 20%)		33,000
On Car fuel scale charge (see table sec 16 chapter 36)		84
Less refunded on sales returns (11,000 x 20%)		(2,200)
Adjust output tax error on February VAT return (3,000x20%)		600
		31,484
Input tax:	£	
On purchases and expenses (96,000+24,000) x 20%	24,000	
Less refunded on purchase returns (3,000 x 20%)	(600)	
		(23,400)
Net VAT due to HMRC for quarter		8,084

(b) The VAT is payable within one month of the end of the quarter, i.e., by 30 September 2011.

(c) A taxpayer who disagrees with a decision by HMRC on the application of VAT may apply within 30 days to the local VAT office asking them to re-consider their decision.

(d) After re-considering their decision HMRC will either:

Confirm their original decision. The taxpayer then has 21 days to submit an appeal to the first-tier tax tribunal; or

Revise their original decision. The taxpayer then has 30 days to submit an appeal to the first-tier tax tribunal.

Questions without answers

1. You are provided with the following information relating to Portia Limited, a consultancy company, for the quarter ended 30 November 2011:

	£
Fees (standard-rated and exclusive of tax)	60,000
Rent received from sub-letting part of the company's offices	6,000
Car purchase (exclusive of VAT)	18,000
Overheads (standard-rated and exclusive of VAT)	9,000
Input VAT attributable to taxable supplies	2,000

Notes

The car was purchased on 1 September 2011 and had CO_2 emissions of 190g/km. Petrol for both private and business motoring was charged through the business and not refunded.

Bad debts of £550 (exclusive of VAT @ 20%) were written off during November 2011; the date payment was due for the services was February 2011.

Portia has not made an election to waive VAT exemption for the office rental income.

Requirement:

Calculate the VAT payable for the quarter ended 30 November 2011 and state when this will be payable to HMRC. (9 marks)

(ACCA December 1996, updated)

2. Antrobus Limited had the following transactions in the quarter to 30 June 2011:

Sales:	£
Standard-rated supplies (excluding VAT)	150,000
Zero-rated supplies	50,000
Exempt supplies	100,000

Input tax on expenses had been paid as follows:

Standard-related supplies	12,000
Zero-related supplies	5,000
Exempt supplies	9,000
General overheads	4,000

The general overhead input tax cannot be directly attributed to any of the listed supplies.

Requirement

Calculate the VAT payable by Antrobus Limited for the quarter

(5 marks)

State the records and accounts which must be kept for VAT purposes and state for how long they must be retained by the trader. (6 marks)

Total: 11 marks

(ACCA December 1995, updated)

Part VII

Tax Planning

38 Elements of tax planning

Introduction

1. This chapter is concerned with some of the basic principles of tax planning which can be applied where a taxpayer has a choice of alternative courses of action. The chapter starts by defining tax planning and outlining some of the objectives involved in this process. Some basic tax planning caveats are then considered followed by a tax planning summary table. The focus of the chapter is on the difference between income tax for the self employed and corporation tax for a small incorporated entity. This area of taxation has generated considerable interest over recent years, and as you will have seen from the sections on both income tax and corporation tax is subject to change on an annual basis.

What is tax planning?

2. Given a set of circumstances or a situation where a decision is to be made which involves the incidence of taxation, then tax planning is concerned with achieving the best result with respect to that decision from the taxation perspective. The 'best result' is usually taken to mean achieving the least amount of tax payable consistent with any cash flow advantages which are also often important.

There is no set body of knowledge called tax planning as it usually requires the application of threads of tax law and practice from across the whole spectrum of taxation and law. An exercise in tax planning therefore involves the following.

a) Identification of the specific problem to be considered.

b) Identification of the relevant parts of the tax statutes which have relevance to the problem.

c) Application of the tax rules identified to the problem.

d) Evaluation of the various options available in order to minimise the incidence of taxation.

e) Identification and examination of any other factors of a legal, commercial or financial nature which should be taken into consideration.

Objectives of tax planning

3. Tax planning objectives for individuals may be summarised as follows.

a) To reduce taxable income and/or chargeable gains falling to be assessed.

b) To lower the rate of tax which is applicable to taxable income or chargeable gains.

c) To defer the date on which tax becomes payable, thereby gaining a cash flow/interest advantage.

For companies in general, similar objectives can be applied. However, for family companies with shareholder directors/employees, tax planning for the individual must inevitably be considered together with that for the family company. This arises because in many cases most of the income of the family director/employee shareholder is in fact derived from family company sources, in the form of remuneration, benefits in kind and dividends.

Tax planning caveats

4. The following points should be borne in mind when undertaking any tax planning exercise.

a) Tax planning, sometimes called tax avoidance, should not be confused with tax evasion. The latter, which is unlawful and may lead to criminal prosecution, is associated with fraudulent or dishonest plans to avoid taxation.

b) Commercial factors should not be ignored just for the sake of a business tax planning exercise. For example, there is no point in investing in additional capital expenditure to obtain capital allowances if the capital project itself shows negative returns on investment.

c) Future financial security should not be put at risk. The making of substantial lifetime gifts to mitigate IHT on the death of the donor should be balanced against the possible shortfall in annual income which might result.

d) Possible changes in the law in the future may render current tax planning exercises less advantageous.

e) Tax plans should be flexible to accommodate, if possible, changes in circumstances. There is no permanent long-term relationship between capital and income which will meet all the requirements of all taxpayers.

f) Packaged "tax avoidance schemes" offered by any organised promoter must be disclosed to HMRC as soon as the first offer of the scheme is made to the public. HMRC maintain a register of such schemes. Taxpayers utilising any such registered scheme must disclose this fact and the scheme number in the self-assessment tax return. Advising individuals how to re-arrange their personal or business affairs with tax benefits, such as the examples below, do not count as "tax avoidance schemes" under this heading, so long as the steps involved have a main purpose and commercial effect beyond just the tax saving.

Tax planning summary

5. Individuals

I Income tax	**Employees**	**Self-employed**	**Directors**
1. Claim expenses of employment	✓	–	✓
2. Claim capital allowances for privately owned asset/Authorised mileage rates	✓	✓	✓
3. Company pension scheme: consider AVC	✓		✓
4. No company pension scheme: maximise contributions up to 100% of net relevant earnings, but subject (from 2011/12) to reduced annual maximum of £50,000.	✓	✓	✓
5. Inter-spouse transfer of assets to use PAs, lower rate tax bands, and MCAA where available	✓	✓	✓
6. Car fuel benefit/payment business mileage	✓	–	✓
7. Phase capital expenditure to save Class 4 NIC income tax	–	✓	–
8. Employ staff with earnings below NI thresholds	–	✓	–
9. Consider ISA – tax-free	✓	✓	✓
10. Consider Enterprise Investment scheme	✓	✓	✓
11. Consider Venture Capital Trust	✓	✓	✓
II Capital gains tax			
1. Consider entrepreneurs' relief on business or share disposals	-	✓	✓
2. Inter-spouse transfer of assets to minimise CGT	✓	✓	✓
3. Phase chargeable asset disposals between tax years to use Annual Exemption , and the lower CGT rate band from June 2010	✓	✓	✓
4. On a takeover, consider cash/shares split and available reliefs to minimise or defer CGT	✓	✓	✓
III Inheritance tax			
1. Maximise use of general exemptions – £250	✓	✓	✓
£3,000	✓	✓	✓
Normal expenditure – for marriage	✓	✓	✓
inter-spouse	✓	✓	✓
charitable bequests	✓	✓	✓

2.	Consider lifetime gifts/PETS – personal assets	✓	✓	✓
	business assets	–	✓	–
3.	Deeds of Variation to change distribution of a death estate to save IHT / maximise use of nil rate band	✓	✓	✓
IV	**VAT**			
1.	Consider voluntary registration to claim input tax	–	✓	–
2.	Phase capital expenditure to benefit cash flow from input tax recovery	–	✓	–
3.	Consider payment for private fuel rather than scale charge	–	✓	–
4.	Monitor turnover level as it approaches compulsory registration point	–	✓	–
5.	Consider Flat Rate, Annual Accounting and/ or Cash Accounting scheme – small firms		✓	

6. Companies

1. Extended account period: 18 months, or 2 periods of 6 and then 12 months?
2. Phasing capital expenditure to maximise Annual Investment Allowance.
3. Consider whether additional payments to shareholder directors should be made as directors' remuneration or dividends – there is a NI saving for the latter.
4. Consider dividend payments in place of normal salary.
5. Maximise pension contributions made through the company as employer.

7. Sole trader vs incorporation

This area of taxation has received a considerable amount of interest due to the number of changes that have been made in relation to the small business corporation tax rules. This section provides an example of a small business and the choice of whether to incorporate or not. It should be noted that there are many factors to consider depending on the circumstances and this section provides simply a basic comparison, based on material previously studied in the income tax and corporation tax sections.

Example

Peter is a self employed electrical engineer and makes profits of £80,000 each year. He pays £8,000 net per year into an HMRC-approved personal pension scheme. He is considering whether he should incorporate his business and pay himself a minimal salary with the balance in dividends, or continue as a sole trader.

A possible approach: Compare net disposable income (2011/12 tax rates)

Sole trader:

			£	£
Profits				80,000
Total income				80,000
PA				(7,475)
Taxable income (all non-savings)				72,525
Tax liability:	BR £35,000	@ 20%	7,000	
(pens. conts. relief) extend	BR £10,000	@ 20%	2,000	
	HR £27,525	@ 40%	11,010	
	72,525			
Total income tax				20,010
NIC:				
Class 2	2.50 p/w (paid 6-monthly)		130	
Class 4	42,475 – 7,225 @ 9%		3,173	
Excess Class 4	80,000 - 42,475 @ 2%		750	
Total national insurance contributions				4,053
Total income tax and NIC				24,063

Disposable income – sole trader	£
Profits	80,000
Less pension contributions (net cost paid)	(8,000)
less IT and NIC	(24,063)
Disposable income	**47,937**

Incorporation:

Profit before proprietor's pay (company)	80,000
Salary (cost to company)	(7,475)
employer Class 1 secondary NI (cost to company) 7,475-7,072 @ 13.8%	(56)
Pension cont'n (cost to company) (Assumed)	(10,000)
Company's taxable profit	62,469
CT @ 20%	(12,494)
After-tax profit for distribution – say distributes £49,500.	49,975

Director income:

Salary				7,475
Dividend grossed for tax purposes (£49,500 x 100/90)				55,000
Total income				62,475
PA (against non-savings income)				(7,475)
Taxable income (all dividends)				55,000
Tax liability:	BR £35,000	@ 10%	3,500	
	HR £20,000	@ 32.5%	6,500	

Total income tax	10,000
Less tax credit on dividends 10% x £55,000	(5,500)
Net income tax payable by Peter	4,500
Add Employee's class 1 NIC on salary – annual earnings period for director 7,475-7,225 @ 12%	30
Net employee income tax and primary NIC	4,530

Net disposable income - Director

Salary	7,475
Dividends (net)	49,500
less IT and NIC paid	(4,530)
less pension conts paid personally	nil
Disposable income	52,445

Total application of £80k profits:

	Incorporation £	Sole trader £
HMRC: Company tax and NI (12,494 + 56)	12,550	0
HMRC: Peter's personal tax and NI	4,530	24,063
Transfer from HMRC to pension fund to top up net pension conts received of £8,000	n/a	(2,000)
Total profits taken by HMRC	17,080	22,063
Pension savings - total cash received by pension fund of some kind (in sole trade, £8k from Peter and £2k from HMRC; under incorporation, all £10k from the company)	10,000	10,000
Peter's net disposable income	52,445	47,937
Retained earnings left in company	475	
Total pre-tax earnings	80,000	80,000
Less HMRC's 'take' (net tax and NIC)	**(17,080)**	**(22,063)**
Total value retained by Peter	**62,920**	**57,937**

Notes

i) This example produces a saving of £4,983 (22,063 – 17,080) in total taxation for the incorporation model when compared with a sole trader.

ii) This example assumes that under incorporation, Peter will make use of a non-contributory occupational director's pension scheme, with all contributions paid by the company, to save NIC. Account has been taken in the comparison of the £2000 "basic rate tax refund" benefit that is paid by HMRC into Peter's personal pension under the sole trader route, which has been set against his personal tax cost even though it is not legally deducted in that way under current tax legislation.

iii) The difference in disposable income is marked. There is a very clear NI cost saving from incorporation because of the very low salary paid (£86 of NIC costs, compared with £4,053 as a sole trader). The 2011/12 NIC threshold for employer's NIC is here assumed at £7,072; calculated as 52 x £136.

iv). There is also an income tax saving by the dividend route. The £49,500 dividend received would be grossed up at the 10% rate and accounted for in Peter's self assessment return as £55,000 of income.

On dividends, Peter's headline top rate of income tax is 32.5%. But because of the dividend tax credit and the imputation system, he actually incurs a top tax rate of only 25% and only on the top £18,000 of net dividends (£4,500 tax payable on £18,000 received).

The rest of his net dividend (£31,500) is effectively received tax-free, as the company's corporation tax covers Peter's own basic rate liability on £31,500 of dividends (£35,000 after 10/9 gross-up) .

To the £4,500 of net tax paid by Peter on net dividends must be added the company's CT payable on its pre-dividend profits, 20% of £62,469 (=20/80 x £49,975) = £12,494.

Total tax and NIC liability with incorporation is £4,983 less than for the sole trader.

The NIC and income tax savings from incorporation are slightly offset by the fact that the company gets tax relief on the pension contribution at only 20%, which therefore costs it £8,000 net, whereas Peter obtained 40% tax relief on this payment (costing him £6,000 net) when he made it personally as a sole trader. 20% of this income tax relief was given within his tax computation, by extending the basic rate band, and the other 20% by HMRC augmenting his pension contribution by £2,000, claimed by the pension provider.

v) There are many other factors to consider in choosing to incorporate a sole trade, especially in terms of personal preferences for the pension contribution, dividend and salary (or benefits) combination; and also the CGT implications of company ownership, if assets are to be held or profits retained long-term in the company. This example provides a useful basic comparison only if the choice is made not to place significant assets or retain earnings in the company.

8. Example 2 – dividend or salary: existing company

P is the 100% owner of Alpha Ltd, an unquoted trading company with a year end of 30th June 2011.

Trade profits of Alpha Ltd are £280,000 for the year ended 30th June 2011 after director's remuneration to P of £80,000. There were no dividend payments.

P would like to have available cash of about £25,000 by December 2011 and requests advice as to the tax costs of extracting this sum from the company.

Advise P.

Solution

Cash required of £25,000 – Dividend Route		**£**	**Tax cost £**
Net cash required		25,000	
Tax on a post-tax dividend of £25,000 for a HR income tax payer (see note (i)) 25,000 x 25/75		8,333	8,333
Dividend required (25,000 x 100/75)		33,333	
Grossed-up dividend liable to HR income tax 33,333 × 100/90		37,037	
HR Income tax @ 32.5% × 37,037	12,037		
Less Tax credit @ 10% × 37,037	(3,704)	(8,333)	
Net tax cost			8,333
Cash of £25,000 – Salary Route			
Net cash required		25,000	
tax and NI on net salary of £25,000 for a HR income tax payer (see note (ii)) 25,000 x 42/58		18,103	18,103
Gross salary required 25,000 x 100/58		43,103	
Marginal Income tax @ 40% × 43,103	17,241		
Marginal Class 1 NIC 2% × 43,103	862	(18,103)	18,103
Net Cash		25,000	
Employer's NIC 13.8% × 43,103	5,948		
Net Corporation Tax saving (note (iii)) (43,103 + 5,948) × 20%	(9,810)		(3,862)
Net tax cost of payment to both director & company, after company tax relief			14,241
Total profits used up in profit extraction:			£
Salary: Cash received by director			25,000
Tax and NIC received by HMRC			14,241
Total			39,241
Dividend: Cash received by director			25,000
Tax received by HMRC (no NIC)			8,333
Total			33,833

Notes

i) Higher rate dividend income tax @ (32.5 – 10)% of the grossed-up dividend is equivalent to 25% total income tax on the net dividend in the higher rate band

(100 × (32.5-10)% is equivalent to (100 – 10) × 25%).

ii) The total tax cost is £5,408 higher for the salary route than the dividend.

iii) Corporation Tax saved: extra Salary cost + Employer's NIC = £49,051 × 20% = 9,810.

9. Example 3

Mr Smith has a chain of shoe shops and expects trading profits of £200,000 for the year to 5th April 2012. He is currently operating as a sole trader and is considering whether he should incorporate his business or not. He informs you that he currently contributes £16,000 (net) each year into an approved personal pension plan. He also advises you that if he were to incorporate his business he would require a director's salary of £60,000 per year gross and that he would like the company to pay his pension for him with a non contributory arrangement.

Required:

Compute the total income tax and national insurance as a sole trader and the total income tax, corporation tax and national insurance as an incorporated entity for the year to 5th April 2012.

Solution:

Sole trader				**£**
Profits				200,000
Total income				200,000
Personal Allowance			7,475	
Restricted (200,000 – 100,000) x 1/2			(50,000)	0
Taxable income (all non-savings)				200,000
Tax liability	BR 35,000	@ 20%	7,000	
	extend BR 20,000	@ 20%	4,000	
	HR 115,000	@ 40%	46,000	
	AR 30,000	@ 50%	15,000	
	£200,000			
Total income tax				72,000
NI				
Class 2	2.50 per week		130	
Class 4	7,225-42,475	@ 9%	3,173	
excess	200,000-42,475	@ 2%	3,151	6,454
Total income tax and NI				**78,454**

Incorporation

Profit (company)				200,000
Salary cost to company				(60,000)
Employer NI (60,000-7,072 @ 13.8%)				(7,304)
Pension contribution				(20,000)
Taxable profit of company				112,696
CT @ 20%				(22,539)
Profit after tax				90,157
Director's income:				
Salary				60,000
Total income				60,000
Personal Allowance		(not restricted)		(7,475)
Taxable income (non-savings)				52,525
Tax liability	BR 35,000	@ 20%	7,000	
	HR 18,525	@ 40%	7,410	
	53,525			
Total income tax				14,410
Employee's NI 42,475-7,225 @ 12%				4,230
60,000-42,475 @ 2%				351
Total income tax and NI				18,991

Summary : Total tax costs compared

Incorporation:	
Director's tax and NI	18,991
Company's tax and NI	
(22,539 + 7,304)	29,843
Total tax and NI	**48,834**
Sole trader:	
Total tax and NI	**78,454**

Notes:

i) In this example, the owner is not extracting all the profits from the company, therefore a tax saving has arisen and incorporation results in an effective total tax saving on profits earned for the year of £29,620 (£78,454 - £48,834).

ii) Mr Smith could extract additional funds out of the business either in the form of an increase in salary or by dividends (or a combination of the two) if he required, but this would impact upon the personal tax saved by operating through a company.

iii) Mr Smith could also consider increasing his pension provision if he wished.

iv) It may be more efficient for Mr Smith to draw out a dividend payment instead of part of the salary of £60,000, as shown in example 2 above.

Question without answer

1. Mr Chapman, a single man, is about to start a business which will be engaged in the repair of domestic appliances. His starting date is 1 April 2011 and he will make up accounts to 31 March each year.

His business plan shows that he is likely to make a taxable profit in the first few years, before any salary for himself, of approximately £80,000 per annum.

He is uncertain whether he should set up the business as a sole trader or as a limited company and seeks your advice. He has advised you that, if the business is run as a company, he will require a gross salary of £50,000 per annum.

Mr Chapman has no other sources of taxable income.

Required:

Draft a report for Mr Chapman, indicating the important differences from a tax and NIC point of view, of the two alternative methods of running the business. Your answer should contain, as an appendix, computations showing the overall tax and NIC burden which will arise in each case. Assume 2011/12 tax rules and rates apply throughout.

(15 marks)

(CIMA November 1997, updated)

39 Additional questions without answers

Exam–type Questions on Corporate Taxation and VAT

Question 1

MJL Ltd is a small manufacturing company and has prepared the following income statement (profit and loss account) for the 18 month period to 31 March 2012.

		£
Sales		481,045
Cost of Sales	(note 1)	(199,655)
Gross profit		281,390
Distribution costs	(note 2)	(13,124)
Administrative expenses	(note 3)	(154,800)
Operating profit		113,466
Profit on sale of car park land	(note 7)	45,800
Interest payable on business overdraft		(2,800)
Dividends from unconnected UK companies	(note 8)	18,000
Rent receivable on car park land	(note 7)	3,500
Profit before taxation		177,966

(1) Cost of Sales includes

- Depreciation of £7,800
- Cost of refurbishment of a machine which was purchased for £1,200 (second-hand) from a bankrupt competitor in January 2011, but which turned out to be completely unusable in MJL Ltd's trade until it had been adapted at a cost of £3,750

(2) Distribution costs include

- A car leasing payment of £3,467 incurred on a 3 year operating lease, taken out in July 2011, of a car emitting 175g CO_2/km

(3) Administrative expenses include:

- Depreciation of £4,000
- A Gift Aid charitable payment to Oxfam of £750 paid on 1 March 2012
- A closing provision of £10,750 for employer pension contributions to top up the staff retirement pension scheme, which had not yet been paid to the pension provider by 31 March 2012
- Legal fees related to sale of land in May 2011, £800

(4) At 1 October 2010 MJL Ltd has unrelieved trading losses of £27,500 and a capital loss of £4,500 agreed and brought forward from prior periods.

(5) MJL Ltd has a capital allowances general pool written down value brought forward of £25,620 at 1 October 2010.

(6) There were no fixed asset additions in the period other than the second hand machine bought in January 2011 (see Note 1) and no disposals of fixed assets other than the land sold in May 2011 (see Note 7).

(7) The profit on sale of land recognised in the accounts related to a car park area that the company had originally used for its own business but had ceased to need, so it was rented out to a public car park operator at £500 per month from 1 October 2010 to 30 April 2011.

This car park land was sold outright to the car park operator (the former tenant) in May 2011 for £65,000, realising a chargeable gain of £18,600 for corporation tax purposes.

(8) Dividends were received as follows:

November 2011	£13,500
February 2012	£ 4,500

Required:

(a) Compute the tax-adjusted trading profits of MJL Ltd, before capital allowances, for the 18 month period of account to 31 March 2012. **(9 marks)**

(b) Compute maximum capital allowances claimable by MJL Ltd for the corporation tax accounting periods covered by this 18 month period of account. **(6 marks)**

(c) Compute MJL Ltd's profits chargeable to corporation tax for the relevant corporation tax accounting periods, assuming that maximum capital allowances and loss reliefs are claimed. **(7 marks)**

(d) Compute MJL Ltd's corporation tax liability for the relevant accounting periods, if it has three associated companies. **(8 marks)**

(Total 30 marks)

Question 2

Cardigan Cars Limited has 3 activities: new cars, children's car seats and finance. The VAT records for the quarter to 30 September 2011 show the following information:

Activity	New cars	Children's car seats	Finance	Head office
	£	£	£	£
Sales turnover, net of any VAT	675,000	195,000	90,000	
Rate of VAT	20%	5%	Exempt	
VAT on divisional purchase and expense invoices	97,500	8,250	11,750	
VAT on general overhead expense invoices				5,000

On 30 September 2011 Cardigan Cars Limited wrote off a bad debt due from Idle Interiors Limited of £12,000 inclusive of VAT at the standard rate of 20%. The debt was in respect of one £5,000 invoice for a car dated 1 February 2011 and a second invoice of £7,000 for another car dated 2 July 2011.

(a) Required: Calculate the VAT payable or refundable for the quarter ended 30 September 2011. **(9 marks)**

Archway Garages, the first land and buildings used by Cardigan Cars Limited, were bought in January 1995 for a price of £390,000, with a further £2,500 of professional fees as expenses of the acquisition.

The land and buildings were sold in February 2001, when the company moved to new premises. The sales proceeds of the old Archway land and buildings in February 2001 were £575,000. The proceeds were used to buy the new land and buildings at Bath Buildings in February 2001 for £550,000 and to pay for a magazine advertisement costing £25,000.

The company claimed rollover relief for the replacement of business assets on the change of business premises.
In May 2011 the new land and buildings at Bath Buildings were sold for gross proceeds of £638,000, incurring selling commission of £3,000.

(b) Required: Calculate the Corporation Tax payable as a result of the disposal of the new land and buildings, assuming Cardigan Cars Limited pays Corporation Tax at the full rate.(Assume the RPI in May 2011 was 234.5 (estimated)). **(12 marks)**

Note: For the purposes of this question you should assume the directors of Dixon Ltd do not intend to make an irrevocable election to exclude a foreign branch from UK (election proposed in Finance Bill 2011, at time of writing).

(c) Evaluate the extent to which Value Added Tax (VAT) contributes to desirable characteristics of the UK tax system (such as certainty, equity, convenience, and efficiency). **(9 marks)**

(Total 30 marks)

Question 3

(a) Splash Ltd is a UK resident company that manufactures hot tubs. It prepares financial statements to 31 March each year.

On 1 April 2011 the tax written down values of Splash Ltd's plant and machinery were as follows:

	£
General pool	149,280
Single short-life asset (2 years old)	13,440

During the year to 31 March 2012, Splash Ltd made the following purchases and sales of plant, equipment and motor vehicles.

		Cost/ (proceeds) £
14 April 2011	Purchased energy-saving plant	64,500
15 April 2011	Sold a lorry	(14,160)
5 May 2011	Purchased new machinery	50,000
15 May 2011	Purchased Toyota car CO_2 140 g/km	10,800
12 June 2011	Sold the short-life asset	(5,520)
22 Sept 2011	Purchased Fiat car CO_2 180 g/km	23,760

The plant purchased in April 2011 was certified energy-saving plant.

The lorry sold on 15 April 2011 had originally cost £21,600.

Required (a):

Calculate the maximum plant and machinery capital allowances available to Splash Ltd for the year ended 31 March 2012. (10 marks)

(b) Dixon Limited is a successful UK trading company selling office equipment.

Its directors are considering expansion overseas to carry on the same trade in a non-UK country where the managing director has good business contacts.

They propose to do this either by setting up either a branch operation (a non-UK branch of the existing company) or a wholly-owned subsidiary company (a separate company, incorporated and resident in the non-UK country).

They have tested the overseas market, and consider there is a good chance that the overseas operation would be profitable from the start. However there is also a possibility that it will incur losses in at least the first two years of operation.

The overseas country in question charges a direct tax of 10% on the profits of all businesses located there and has a double taxation treaty with the UK.

Required (b):

Advise Dixon Limited's directors, in connection with the choice between setting up the overseas operation as a branch or as a subsidiary:

(i) How UK tax is charged on the profits of an overseas branch of a UK company and how the UK tax position differs if the same net profits are made in a non-UK subsidiary company, which later pays a dividend to its UK parent company. (4 marks)

(ii) Whether net trading losses of an overseas branch can be set against UK profits for tax purposes and how this situation differs if the overseas operation is a wholly-owned subsidiary company. (3 marks)

(iii) In what circumstances the UK tax authorities can seek to adjust the transfer prices charged for goods sold from a UK company to an overseas subsidiary company and why they might choose to use this power. (3 marks)

(Total 20 marks)

Question 4

On 1 October 2011 the tax written down values of plant and machinery of Zebra Limited were as follows:

	£
General pool	10,600
Special rate pool	16,400
Short-life asset	2,900

The following transactions took place during the year ended 30 September 2012:

		Cost/(Proceeds) £
1 November 2011	Sold office equipment	(12,800)
15 December 2011	Sold the short-life asset	(800)
8 January 2012	Purchased packaging equipment	29,200
14 January 2012	Sold the Subaru car CO_2 emissions 180g/km	(9,700)
26 February 2012	Purchased Renault car CO_2 emissions 145g/km	15,800
19 May 2012	Purchased Honda low emissions car CO_2 emissions 105g/km	19,700
15 June 2012	Purchased air cooling system features integral to a building	30,000

None of the assets disposed of were sold for more than their original cost.

(a) Required: Calculate the maximum capital allowances available to Zebra Limited for the year ended 30 September 2012. (9 marks)

Avocado plc was formed on 1 October 2011 and on that date it bought 100% of Banana Limited, 80% of Citrus Limited and 60% of Damson Ltd, which are all subsidiaries of Avocado plc. The results for the relevant periods of account are:

	Avocado plc Year to 30 September 2012	Banana Ltd Year to 30 September 2012	Citrus Ltd Year to 30 September 2012	Damson Ltd Year to 30 September 2012
Trade profit (loss)	Loss (320,000)	1,200,000	250,000	325,000
Interest income	80,000	-	-	-
Loss on property rentals	Loss (12,000)	-	-	-
Capital loss	Loss (4,000)	-	-	-
Gift Aid donations	(9,000)	-	-	-

Required:

(b) Demonstrate how the losses of Avocado plc can be relieved using the single company loss reliefs and clearly showing the amount of any unrelieved losses and Gift Aid donations at 30 September 2012. (6 marks)

(c) Advise the directors of Avocado plc how group loss relief may be beneficial to the Avocado plc group. (5 marks)

(Total 20 marks)

Question 5

Shelby Limited acquired 15,000 shares in Tobacco Exploitation plc in January 1995 at a cost of £29,000. In October 2000 Tobacco Exploitation plc made a bonus issue of 1 new share for every 2 held. In May 2004 Shelby Ltd bought its share of a 1 for 4 rights issue at a price of £1.60 per Tobacco Exploitation plc share. In May 2011 Shelby Limited sold one third of its shareholding in Tobacco Exploitation plc for a price of £13,000.

(a) Required: Calculate the chargeable gain or allowable loss on disposal of Tobacco Exploitation plc shares in May 2011. (Assume the RPI in May 2011 was 234.5 (estimated)) (9 marks)

(b) The managing director of Shelby Ltd also requires advice on the tax treatment of certain proposed payments that will be made by the company in the next accounting period.

These payments are:

A) A political donation to the UK Liberal Democratic Party of £5,000.

B) The cost of taking 10 key sales staff and directors to an important sales conference in Morocco (cost per head, £2,000 including flights, hotel, conference fee and meals).

C) A fine of £3,500 for exceeding the axle weight permitted for the company's delivery lorries.

(b) Required: Advise the managing director whether or not each of the proposed payments A to C can be treated for tax purposes as a trading expense of the next corporation tax accounting period by Shelby Ltd. Give reasons for all your answers, either from specific rules of tax law or from general principles of the UK tax system. (6 marks)

(c) Required: Using examples from the UK tax system, evaluate the extent to which the government is attempting to affect taxpayers' behaviour with respect to cars. (5 marks)

(Total 20 marks)

Exam–type Questions on Personal Taxation, excluding IHT

Question 6

Assad is aged 35, and was employed as a mechanic until April 2011. His last salary payment, received on 30 April 2011, was £2,000 gross, from which PAYE tax was deducted of £320. Assad then decided to become a self - employed taxi driver, commencing business on 1 May 2011.

For the first 3 months he leased a car (Car 1) for business use. He made no private journeys in Car 1, which had a CO_2 emissions rating of 180g/km. In return for the monthly lease charge of £600 the lease company met all the car 1 running expenses except insurance and fuel.

On 1 August 2011 Assad terminated the Car 1 lease, having purchased a new car (Car 2) for £20,000, which had a CO_2 emissions rating of 172g/km. From the time of purchase, Car 2 was used in the business, and also 20% privately by Assad.

Assad used his business mobile phone 40% for private purposes.

Assad has drawn up his first accounts to 30 April 2012, showing the following results for the twelve month period:

	£	£
Taxi fares collected		46,200
Tips received		4,100
		50,300
Expenses:		
Commissions paid to taxi booking company	2,850	
Car expenses (see analysis below)	6,900	
Taxi operating licence (12 months)	1,980	
Traffic Speeding fine (incurred while working)	80	
Mobile phone contract (£40 a month)	480	
Meals /drinks while working at night	750	
Depreciation of Car 2	6,000	
Training course in computing	250	
		(19,290)
Net trading profit		31,010

The analysis of the Car expenses account is as follows:

	Car 1£	Car 2 £
Petrol	750	2,500
Leasing cost of car 1 (3 months)	1,800	
Running costs for car 2 (9 months) (servicing, car tax etc)		850
Car insurance – Car 1 (May to August)	250	
- Car 2 (September to April)		750
	2,800	4,100
Total		6,900

From 6 June 2011, Assad rented out a bedroom in his house for £300 per month. Assad has calculated that the fair share of house bills (heating, electricity, etc) relating to the let bedroom is £25 a month.

Assad also received dividend income of £6,300 in January 2012 (cash amount received).

Required:

(a) Calculate Assad's adjusted trading profit, after claiming any available capital allowances, for the period of account to 30 April 2012.

(11 marks)

(b) Write brief notes explaining to Assad your treatment of the following expenses as allowable/ disallowable against his business income in the tax-adjusted profits computation:

(i) Car 2 running expenses and depreciation

(ii) Speeding fine incurred

(iii) Car 1 leasing costs

(iv) Computer training course (6 marks)

(c) Calculate Assad's taxable income and income tax liability for the tax year 2011/12, and the amount of tax still due. (9 marks)

(d) Calculate Assad's Class 4 national insurance liability for 2011/12. (2 marks)

(e) Either calculate the amount, or if preferred, describe how you would calculate it if you had the necessary information, that should be paid by Assad as the first payment on account of income tax and class 4 NIC due for the tax year 2012/13. (2 mark)

(Total 30 marks)

Question 7

Simon, aged 45, is employed as a Public Relations consultant by Bogota Ltd. For the year ended 5 April 2012, he has provided the following information:

1. His basic annual salary was £38,000.
2. He received a performance bonus of £2,934 on 31 October 2011. This related to the six months ended 30 September 2011. On 1 April 2012 he was notified that he was entitled to a bonus of £1,250 for the six months to 31 March 2012, and this was paid to him on 30 April 2012.
3. He had the use of a diesel-engined company car from Bogota Ltd from 6 May 2011 (date of first registration) until after 5 April 2012. The car's list price was £22,500 but the company negotiated a 15% discount from a dealer. All business and personal fuel was paid for by the company and

Simon uses the car privately every week. The car has a CO_2 emission rating of 163g/km. Simon did not have a company car for the first month of tax year 2011/12.

4. Simon had a company mobile phone, on which he was allowed to make private calls. The phone cost the employer rent and charges of £360.

5. He was reimbursed £275 by Bogota Ltd during the year for expenses incurred entertaining clients.

6. Simon received an interest-free loan of £15,000 from Bogota Ltd on 6 June 2011, which he repaid on 6 December 2011.

7. Simon paid £200 per month into the Bogota Ltd occupational pension scheme, by direct deduction from his salary. This pension scheme is not contracted out of the state second pension.

Simon had no other income in the year 2011/12, but he sold a painting in November 2011 for £18,000. He had purchased the painting in 1998 for £2,500. He had no personal capital losses brought forward at 6 April 2011.

Simon tells you in July 2012 that he plans to leave his employment and become a self- employed PR consultant . He plans to advertise his services widely, and has already identified potential new clients.

He also hopes to sell some of his self-employed services to Bogota Ltd after he leaves their full-time employment. His current manager is willing to offer him some short-term tasks on a "freelance" basis, working with teams he knows.

Required:

a) Calculate Simon's assessable employment income for 2011/12.
(12 marks)

b) Calculate Simon's Class 1 NIC liability, and his employer's total NIC liability, in respect of earnings and benefits in 2011/12. (3 marks)

c) Calculate Simon's capital gains tax liability for 2011/12, and state when he must pay the capital gains tax. (5 marks)

d) Advise Simon how he would be wise to carry out his self-employed activities, including any services provided for a fee to Bogota Ltd, if he wishes to resist any suggestion from the tax authority that he is still an employee of Bogota Ltd. (7 marks)

e) Explain how it would alter Simon's UK tax position if occasional work that he does for Bogota Ltd after he leaves employment there were viewed as a return to employment, not as self-employment. (3 marks)
(Total 30 marks)

Question 8

(a) Lydia Smith has an established trading business and also lets 2 properties. Her income and losses for the four years to 31 March 2012, and expected results for the year to 31 March 2013, are as follows:

Year ending	31/03/09	31/03/10	31/03/11	31/03/12	Expected 31/03/13
Trading profit	28,000	25,000	10,000	Loss (65,000)	43,000
Bank deposit interest, net cash received	240	320	400	NIL	NIL
Property letting:					
16 Park Row	-	Loss (4,000)	10,500	Loss (5,000)	NIL
12 Highfield Grove	-	7,600	Loss (3,000)	11,000	6,500

Lydia always claims relief for losses as early as possible.

Required: Calculate Lydia's taxable income for each of the four years to 31 March 2012, and the expected taxable income for the year to 31 March 2013, showing appropriate claims for loss relief. (10 marks)

b) Ron is a higher rate income taxpayer and has the following disposals of assets during 2011/12, which were his only transactions relevant to Capital Gains Tax:

i) Sold a fish and chip shop for £250,000 in October 2011, from which £12,500 selling commission was deducted. The fish and chip shop cost £160,000 in August 1997. Ron claims entrepreneurs' relief on the disposal.

ii) Sold part of a plot of land in February 2012 for £40,000. The whole piece of land had cost £25,000 in November 1997. The value of the part retained was £30,000 in February 2012.

iii) Sold a sculpture for £10,000 in March 2012. The sculpture cost £18,500 in January 1991, with an additional £1,500 of acquisition costs.

Required: Calculate Ron's Capital Gains Tax liability for 2011/12.

(10 marks)

(Total 20 marks)

Question 9

(a) Gareth commenced business as a landscape architect on 1 November 2010 and prepared his first accounts to 30 April 2012. He purchased office equipment assets costing £11,500 on 1 November 2010, on which he claimed an Annual Investment Allowance equal to the full cost of the assets.

His tax-adjusted trading profit for the period ended 30 April 2012, before deducting the above capital allowances claim, was £67,500.

Required:

(i) Calculate the trading profits assessable for income tax purposes on Gareth for the tax years 2010/11, 2011/12 and 2012/13. (7 marks)

(ii) State the amount of Gareth's overlap profits and show how you have calculated this figure. (2 marks)

(iii) Is there anything which Gareth could have done to avoid having overlap profits arising in his business? (2 marks)

(b) Mary-Anne is 77 years old and is registered blind. She has the following income in 2011/12:

State pension (no tax deducted at source)	£5,200
Private pension (before £650 tax deducted at source under PAYE)	£7,440
Income from dividends (amount received)	£2,160
Income from Cash ISAs (amount received)	£1,780
Interest income from bank deposit accounts (amount received)	£8,000

Required:

Calculate Mary-Anne's income tax liability for tax year 2011/12, showing how much tax is still payable or repayable after the end of that year. (9 marks)

(Total 20 marks)

Question 10

(a) Sam Street commenced trading on 1 May 2010 and prepares business accounts to each 31 December thereafter.

In May 2010 she bought the following assets:

Plant and machinery for her rented workshop	78,334
Office furniture	4,500
3 Computers (3 year maximum useful life)	2,300
Photocopier/printer	500
A car which she uses privately for 25% of its annual mileage (CO2 emissions, 156 g/km)	15,000

In the year to 31 December 2011 the following fixed asset transactions took place:

Sold an item of machinery for £3,500 which had originally cost £2,600.

Bought a van costing £11,500 to use for business deliveries.

Sold the 3 computers when they were 18 months old in November 2011, for £150 in total.

Required: Calculate the capital allowances available to Sam for her first two periods of account, assuming that she always claims the maximum allowances and makes elections to get quicker relief wherever possible. (12 marks)

(b) Roberta has been a sole trader since 1990. On 31 March 2012 she transferred her business to her daughter Jill, at which time the following assets were sold to Jill :

- A shop with a market value of £150,000. It had been purchased on 1 August 2004 for £80,000 and has always been used for Roberta's business. Jill paid Roberta £50,000 for the shop.
- A warehouse with a market value of £120,000. It had been purchased in 1995 for £45,000 and has never been used for business purposes by Roberta but rented out. Jill paid Roberta £40,000 for the warehouse.

Wherever possible, Roberta and Jill have elected to hold over the gift element of the capital gains arising to Roberta on these sales.

Required: Assuming that gift holdover claims are made where possible, calculate Roberta's capital gains, before annual exemption, for 2011/12. Ignore entrepreneur's relief. (8 marks)

(Total 20 marks)

Index

The index numbers refer to chapters or to chapter.sections.

Tax rates 2011/12

Income tax

Starting rate 10%	Savings income £0 – £2,560 band	
Basic rate	Savings/Non savings 20%	Dividends 10%
Higher rate	Savings/Non savings 40%	Dividends 32.5%
Additional rate	Savings/Non savings 50%	Dividends 42.5%

Taxable income	Band	Rate	Tax payable on band
£	£	%	£
0 – 35,000	35,000	20	7,000
35,001 – 150,000	115,000	40	46,000
150,000 +		50	

Personal reliefs 2011/12

	£
Personal allowance	7,475
Abatement income level	100,000
Allowances: Aged 65–74	
Personal allowance	9,940
Abatement income level	24,000
Allowances: aged 75+	
Personal allowance	10,090
Married couple's allowance (65 before 6.4.2000) min £2,800*	7,295
Abatement income level for both above – PA abates before MCA	24,000
Blind person's allowance	1,980

Relief only at 10%*

National Insurance 2011/12

Retirement pension – single person – based on adequate contributions from a 30 year working life £5,312

Self employed

Class 2 contributions		£2.50 per week
Class 4 contributions	9.0% of profits between	7,225 – 42,475
	2.0% above	42,475

Class 1 Employed earners from 6th April 2011

£ per week earnings	Not contracted-out	Contracted-out COSR	Contracted-out COMP
Employee			
Earnings up to £139 a week – ET	Nil	Nil	Nil
Earnings between £139 and £817 a week	12.0%	10.4%	10.4%
Earnings over £817 a week	2.0%	2.0%	2.0%

Employer			
Earnings up to £136 a week	Nil	Nil	Nil
Earnings between £136 and £817 a week	13.8%	10.1%	12.4%
Earnings over £817 a week	13.8%	13.8%	13.8%
Class 1A Benefits in Kind	13.8%	13.8%	13.8%

Corporation tax

	Years to 31st March	
	2012	**2011**
Financial year	**FY11**	**FY10**
Full rate	26%	28%
Small profits rate	20%	21%
Small profits rate fraction	3/200	7/400
Small profit levels:		
Lower relevant amount	£300,000	£300,000
Higher relevant amount	£1,500,000	£1,500,000

Small profits rate marginal relief formula: (U-A) x N/A x (the fraction)

Employees' Car Benefit	Employees' Car Fuel Benefit
List price × CO_2 emission% 15% for a car with up to 125g/km CO_2 emissions, increasing by 1% for every 5g/km to a maximum of 35% 3% supplement for diesels 10% rate for cars with 80 - 120g/km emissions 5% rate for cars with up to 75g emissions	£18,800 × CO_2 emission % for the car (as determined at left)

Capital allowances

Plant and machinery

Annual investment allowance 100% on £100,000 of expenditure per 12 months

Enhanced capital allowances	FYA	100%
Low Emission Cars	FYA	100%

Writing down allowance (WDA)

General pool of plant and machinery and cars with CO_2 emissions of 160 g/km or less	20% per year
Special rate pool features integral to a building, long life assets and cars with CO_2 emissions of more than 160 g/km	10% per year

Business Premises Renovation Allowance 100%

Capital gains tax

	Rate	Exempt Amount for year
Individuals	18% within income tax basic rate band 2011/12, otherwise 28%	10,600

Lease premium
Capital element of a premium received on a lease of less than 50 years

P x 2% x (n – 1)

where

P = premium
n = length of lease in years

Value added tax

Standard rate	20.0% (1/6 x gross)
Lower/ Reduced rate	5%
Zero rate	0%
Registration threshold	£73,000 taxable turnover in cumulative 12 month period
(From 1 April 2011)	£73,000 taxable turnover in next 30 days

Inheritance tax

IHT on transfers on death on or after 6th April 2011

Chargeable transfer bands	Rate of IT
£	%
0 – 325,000	Nil
325,001 +	40